C0-DKL-079

Study Guide

Volume 1: To 1815

A HISTORY OF WORLD SOCIETIES

Second Edition

James A. Schmiechen
Central Michigan University, Mt. Pleasant

John P. McKay
University of Illinois at Urbana-Champaign

HOUGHTON MIFFLIN COMPANY • BOSTON

Dallas   Geneva, Illinois   Palo Alto   Princeton

Copyright © 1988 by Houghton Mifflin Company. All rights reserved.

No part of this work may be reproduced or transmitted in any form or by any means, electronic or mechanical, including photocopying and recording, or by any information storage or retrieval system without the prior written permission of Houghton Mifflin Company unless such copying is expressly permitted by federal copyright law. Address inquiries to Permissions, Houghton Mifflin Company, One Beacon Street, Boston, MA 02108.

Printed in the U.S.A.

Library of Congress Catalog Card Number: 87-81264

ISBN: 0-395-46502-8

ABCDEFGHIJ-H-8987654321

CONTENTS

TO THE STUDENT

HOW TO STUDY HISTORY AND PREPARE FOR EXAMS

The study of history can be rewarding but also perplexing. Most history courses require you to read and understand large bodies of detailed information. The history student is expected to perform many tasks—memorize information, study the reasons for change, analyze the accomplishments and failures of various societies, understand new ideas, identify historical periods, pick out broad themes and generalizations in history, and so forth. These jobs often present difficulties. This guide will make your study easier and increase your efficiency. It has been developed to help you read, study, and review *A History of World Societies*, and regular and systematic use of it will improve your grade in this course. You may use the guide in a variety of ways, but for best results you might choose the following approach:

1. *Preview the entire chapter* by reading the chapter objectives and synopsis; then quickly read through the study outline, noting the reading with understanding exercises. All of this will take only a few minutes but is an important first step in reading. It is called *previewing*. By pointing out what the chapter is about and what to look for, previewing will make your reading easier and improve your reading comprehension.

2. *Now read your assignment in the textbook*. Pay attention to features that reveal the scope and major emphasis of a chapter or section, such as the chapter title, chapter and section introductions, questions, headings, conclusions, and illustrative material (e.g., maps and photographs). Note study hint 3 on page ix about underlining.

3. After reading, *review what you have read* and check your comprehension by going over the chapter outline once again—but this time make sure that you understand

all the points and subpoints. If you do not fully understand a particular point or sub-point, then you need to return to the text and reread. It is not at all uncommon to need to read the text at least twice.

4. Continue your review. *Answer the review questions* that follow the study outline. It is best to write out or outline your answer on a sheet of paper or a note card. Be sure to include the supporting facts. Reread your answers periodically. This process will help you build a storehouse of information and understanding to use at the time of the exam.

5. Now work on the definitions, identifications, and explanations in the study-review exercises provided in each chapter of the *Study Guide*. This will help you to under-stand and recall both concepts and specific facts. Know not just who or what, but also why the term is significant. Does it illustrate or represent some fundamental change or process? Note that if a particular term appears in the text *and* in your lec-ture notes, it is of special importance. Do the geography exercises found in all appro-priate chapters. This is important because they will enable you to visualize the sub-ject matter and thus remember it better. It will take a few minutes, but the payoff is considerable.

6. Last, *complete the multiple-choice and fill-in exercises* for each *Study Guide* chapter. Some of these questions look for basic facts, while others test your under-standing and ability to synthesize material. *The answers are at the end of the Guide.* If you miss more than two or three, you need to restudy the text or spend more time working on the *Guide*.

ADDITIONAL STUDY HINTS*

1. *Organize your study time effectively*. Many students fail to do well in courses be-cause they do not organize their time effectively. In college, students are expected to read the material before class, review, and do the homework on their own. Many history teachers give only two or three tests during the semester; therefore, assuming personal responsibility for learning the material is vital. Mark up a semester calendar to show scheduled test dates, when term projects are due, and blocks of time to be set aside for exam study and paper writing. Then, at the beginning of each week, check the calendar and your course outlines and notes to see what specific preparation is

---

*For a complete text and workbook written to meet the needs of students who want to do their best in college, see James F. Shepherd, *RSVP, The Houghton Mifflin Reading, Study, and Vocabu-lary Program*, Third Edition (1988).

necessary for the coming week, and plan your time accordingly. Look at all the reading with understanding exercises in this *Study Guide* and try to estimate how much time you will need to master study skills. Set aside a block of time each day or once every several days for reading your text or studying your lecture notes and working in the *Study Guide*. Despite what one observes on college campuses, studying is not done most effectively late at night or with background music. Find a quiet place to study alone, one where you can tune out the world and tune into the past.

2. *Take good lecture notes.* Good notes are readable, clear, and above all reviewable. Write down as much of the lecture as you can without letting your pen get too far behind the lecturer. Use abbreviations and jot down key words. Leave spaces where appropriate and then go back and add to your notes as soon after the lecture as possible. You may find it helpful to leave a wide margin on the left side for writing in subject headings, important points, and questions, as well as for adding information and cross-references to the text and other readings. One way to use your notes effectively is by *reciting*. Reciting is the act of asking a question and then repeating the answer silently or aloud until you can recall it easily. Above all, do not wait until the night before an exam to use lecture notes you have not looked at for weeks or months. Review your lecture notes often and see how they complement and help you interpret your reading.

3. *Underline.* Too often students mark almost everything they read and end up with little else than an entire book highlighted in yellow. Underlining can be extremely helpful or simply a waste of time in preparing for exams; the key is to be selective in what you underline. Here are some suggestions:

a. Underline major concepts, ideas, and conclusions. You will be expected to interpret and analyze the material you have read. In many cases the textbook authors themselves have done this, so you need to pinpoint their comments as you read. Is the author making a point of interpretation or coming to a conclusion? If so, underline the key part. Remember, learning to generalize is very important, for it is the process of making history make sense. The author does it and you must learn to identify his or her interpretation as well as conflicting interpretations; then to make your own. Here is where your study of history can pay big rewards. The historian, like a good detective, not only gathers facts but also analyzes, synthesizes, and generalizes from that basic information. This is the process of *historical interpretation*, which you must seek to master.

b. Underline basic facts. You will be expected to know basic facts (names, events, dates, places) so that you can reconstruct the larger picture and back up your analysis and interpretations. Each chapter of this guide includes several lists of important items. Look over these lists before you begin to read, and then underline these words as you read.

c. Look at the review questions in the *Study Guide*—they will point to the major themes and questions to be answered. Then, as you read, underline the material that answers these questions. Making marginal notations can often complement your underlining.

4. *Work on your vocabulary*. The course lectures and each chapter in the text will probably include words that you do not know. Some of these will be historical terms or special concepts, such as *polis*, *feudalism*, or *bourgeoisie*—words that are not often used in ordinary American speech. Others are simply new to you but important for understanding readings and discussion. If you cannot determine the meaning of the word from the context in which it appears or from its word structure, then you will need to use a dictionary. *Keep a list of words* in your lecture notebook or use the pages in the back of this guide. Improving your historical and general vocabulary is an important part of reading history as well as furthering your college career. Most graduate-school entrance exams and many job applications, for instance, have sections to test vocabulary and reading comprehension.

5. *Benefit from taking essay exams*. Here is your chance to practice your skills in historical interpretation and synthesis. Essay exams demand that you express yourself through ideas, concepts, and generalizations as well as by reciting the bare facts. The key to taking an essay exam is preparation. Follow these suggestions:

a. *Try to anticipate the questions on the exam*. As you read the text, your notes, and this guide, jot down what seem to be logical essay questions. This will become easier as the course continues, partly because you will be familiar with the type of question your instructor asks. Some questions are fairly broad, such as the chapter-objective questions at the beginning of each chapter in this guide; others have a more specific focus, such as the review questions. Take a good look at your lecture notes. Most professors organize their daily lectures around a particular theme or stage in history. You should be able to invent a question or two from each lecture. Then answer the question. Do the same with the textbook, using the *Study Guide* for direction. Remember, professors are often impressed when students include in their essay textbook material not covered in class.

b. *Aim for good content and organization*. Be prepared to answer questions that require historical interpretation and analysis of a particular event, series of events, movement, process, person's life, and so forth. You must also be prepared to provide specific information to back up and support your analysis. In some cases you will be expected to give either a chronological narrative of events or a topical narrative (for example, explaining a historical movement in terms of its social, political, and economic features). Historians often approach problems in terms of cause and effect, so spend some time thinking about events in these terms. Remember,

not all causes are of equal importance, so you must be ready to make distinctions—
and to back up these distinctions with evidence. This is all part of showing your
skill at historical interpretation.

When organizing your essay, you will usually want to sketch out your general
thesis (argument) or point of interpretation first, in an introductory sentence or
two. Next move to the substance. Here you will illustrate and develop your argument by weighing the evidence and marshaling reasons and factual data. After you
have completed this stage (writing the body of your essay), go on to your conclusion, which most likely will be a restatement of your original thesis. It is often
helpful to outline your major points before you begin to write. Be sure you answer
all parts of the question. Write clearly and directly. All of this is hard to do, but you
will get better at it as the course moves along.

6. *Enhance your understanding* of important historical questions by undertaking additional reading and/or a research project as suggested in the "Understanding History
Through Reading and the Arts" and "Problems for Further Investigation" sections
in the *Study Guide*. Note also that each textbook chapter has an excellent bibliography. Many of the books suggested are available in paperback editions, and all of
the music suggested is available in most record-lending libraries and record stores.

7. *Know why you are studying history*. Nothing is worse than having to study a subject that appears to have no practical value. And indeed, it is unlikely that by itself
this history course will land you a job. What, then, is its value, and how can it enrich
your life? Although many students like history simply because it is interesting, there
are a number of solid, old-fashioned reasons for studying it. It is often said that we
need to understand our past in order to live in the present and build the future. This
is true on a number of levels. On the psychological level, identification with the past
gives us a badly needed sense of continuity and order in the face of ever more rapid
change. We see how change has occurred in the past and are therefore better prepared
to deal with it in our own lives. On another level, it is important for us to know how
differing political, economic, and social systems work and what benefits and disadvantages accrue from them. As the good craftsperson uses a lifetime of experience
to make a masterpiece, so an understanding of the accumulated experiences of the
past enables us to construct a better society. Further, we need to understand how
the historical experiences of peoples and nations have differed, and how these differences have shaped their respective visions. Only then can we come to understand
how others view the world differently from the ways in which we do. Thus, history
breaks down the barriers erected by provincialism and ignorance.

The strongest argument for the study of history, though, is that it re-creates the
big picture at a time when it is fashionable and seemingly prudent to be highly spe-
cialized and narrowly focused. We live in the Age of Specialization. Even our universities often appear as giant trade schools, where we are asked to learn a lot about a

little. As a result, it is easy to miss what is happening to the forest because we have become obsessed with a few of the trees. While specialization has undeniable benefits, both societies and individuals also need the generalist perspective and the ability to see how the entire system works. History is the queen of the generalist disciplines. Looking at change over time, history shows us how to take all the parts of the puzzle—politics, war, science, economics, architecture, sex, demography, music, philosophy, and much more—and put them together so that we can understand the whole. It is through a study of the interrelationships of the parts over a long expanse of time that we can develop a vision of society. By promoting the generalist perspective, history plays an important part on today's college campus.

Finally, the study of history has a more personal and surprisingly practical application. It is becoming increasingly apparent to many employers and educators that neglect of the liberal arts and humanities by well-meaning students has left them unable to think and reason analytically and to write and speak effectively. Overspecialized, narrowly focused education has left these students seriously deficient in basic verbal skills, placing them at a serious disadvantage in the job market. Here is where this course can help. It is universally recognized that studying history is an excellent way to develop the ability to reason and write. And the moving pageant of centuries of human experience you are about to witness will surely spark your interest and develop your aptitude if you give it the chance.

ACKNOWLEDGMENTS

The authors are indebted to Professors Gabriel Chin, Patricia Ramft, John Robertson, Nina Robertson, and James Dealing, all of Central Michigan University, for their suggestions in the preparation of the "Understanding History Through Reading and the Arts" and "Problems for Further Investigation" sections of this guide; to Annette Davis and Ardith Jones for their help in the preparation of the manuscript; and to Chris Uganski for his assistance in the preparation of the test sections.

CHAPTER 1

ORIGINS

CHAPTER OBJECTIVES

After reading and studying this chapter you should be able to answer the following questions:

Q-1.   How did wild hunters become urban dwellers?
Q-2.   What caused Mesopotamian culture to take root and become predominant in the ancient Near East?
Q-3.   What contributions to Western culture did the Egyptians make?
Q-4.   How did the Hittites affect Near Eastern culture?

CHAPTER SYNOPSIS

This first chapter of the book explores how civilization in the western world began in the Near East in the area that became modern-day Israel, Iraq, Iran, and Egypt. It was here that agriculture and cities first emerged in the West. Here is where writing was invented, where law, science, and mathematics developed, and where the religious standards of the modern West evolved. The chapter begins by describing two prehistoric periods, the Paleolithic, or Old Stone, Age, and the Neolithic, or New Stone, Age, which set the stage for early civilization. Although the invention of tools, the control of fire, and the discovery of the uses of language and art by the Paleolithic people were remarkable achievements, it was the Neolithic people's use of systematic agriculture and settled life that was one of the most important events in world history.

Systematic agriculture was encouraged, indeed sustained, by the four great river valleys in which the earliest civilizations arose. These rivers — the Nile, Tigris-Euphrates, Indus, and Yellow — allowed cultivation of land and hence increased population in the areas known as, respectively, Egypt, Mesopotamia, India, and China.

As these early people gave up the nomadic life for the settled life of towns and agriculture, civilization, which meant law, government, economic growth, and religion, became possible. By around 3000 B.C., the first urban-agricultural societies had emerged in Mesopotamia — the fertile land between the Tigris and Euphrates rivers. The most important of these early communities of farmers and city builders were the southern Mesopotamians, called the Sumerians. Sumerian society was a mixture of religious ritual, war, slavery, and individual freedom. The Sumerians' greatest achievement was their system of writing, a system called cuneiform. The conquerors of Sumer, people called Semites from the northern part of Mesopotamia, spread Sumerian-Mesopotamian culture throughout the Near East. They were followed by the more important Babylonians, a people whose city, Babylon, dominated the trade of the Tigris and Euphrates. The Babylonians united Mesopotamia and gave the world one of its most important law codes, the code of Hammurabi. This code tells us how Mesopotamian people lived: how husbands treated their wives, how society dealt with crime, how consumer protection evolved, and so forth.

Egyptian society grew alongside the Nile River, which sheltered and isolated its people more effectively than the rivers of Mesopotamia. Egypt was first united into a single kingdom in about 3100 B.C. The focal point of all life in ancient Egypt was the pharaoh. His tomb, the pyramid, provided him with everything that he would need in the afterlife. Egyptian society was a curious mixture of freedom and constraint. Slavery existed, and life was void of modern Western concepts of freedom and human rights.

Between 2000 and 1200 B.C., Egypt and the entire Near East were greatly influenced by two migrations of Indo-Europeans that disturbed and remolded existing states. While all of Mesopotamia became unified under the Hittites, Egypt was first influenced by the Hyksos and then by the introduction of monotheism by the pharaoh Akhenaten. During one of the resulting periods of political disintegration a number of petty kingdoms grew up, although the old culture of the Near East — especially that of Mesopotamia — lived on in the kingdoms of the newcomers.

STUDY OUTLINE
(See pp. vii–xii in this guide for suggestion on studying and preparing for exams.)

  I. The Paleolithic and Neolithic ages
      A. The Paleolithic, or Old Stone, Age (ca 400,000 B.C.–7000 B.C.)
          1. Human survival depended on the hunt; people did not farm
          2. Paleolithic people learned to control fire and make tools from stone and clothes from animal skins
              a. Social organization allowed them to overpower animals

   b. They had some knowledge of plants and agriculture

   c. Kinship and tribe ties were crucial

  3. The greatest accomplishments of Paleolithic peoples were intellectual: thought and language

  4. The first art — cave paintings and small clay statues — dates from this time

 B. The Neolithic, or New Stone, Age (7000–3000 B.C.)

  1. The planting of crops and the domestication of animals — the "Agricultural Revolution" — was the age's greatest achievement

   a. Systematic agriculture ended people's dependence on hunting and allowed people to settle in towns and eventually cities

   b. Agriculture began in four areas (the Near East, western Africa, northeastern China, and Central and South America) at roughly the same time

  2. Systematic agriculture led to population increase, trade, and the division of labor

  3. The settled lifestyle allowed time to develop new tools and techniques

  4. Systematic agriculture gave rise to towns and, eventually, urban life

  5. In arid regions, irrigation was undertaken — resulting in the need for a central government

II. Rivers and civilizations

 A. Neolithic farming and the evolution of urban civilization

  1. *Civilization* means shared beliefs, social and political organization, and art

  2. Four different river valley civilizations emerged — but they all had some things in common

   a. All developed in great river valleys — the Nile, the Tigris-Euphrates, the Indus, and the Yellow river valleys

   b. These rivers allowed for easy communication and provided fertile land

   c. The river valleys were different in terms of climate and soil, leading to different crops and methods of agriculture

   d. The Nile is gentle, while the Tigris and Yellow rivers brought unpredictable floods

   e. Irrigation practices varied as well, but all rivers demanded and brought about human cooperation

 B. The results of river civilizations

  1. More farmable land was made available, and hence population grew in numbers and wealth

  2. More complex forms of government were needed, greater specialization of labor took place, and some people began to search for divine knowledge

        3.   Writing was invented

III. Mesopotamian civilization

    A.   The first cities were built in Mesopotamia (ca 3500–1700 B.C.)

        1.   The Sumerians and the Semites turned to an agricultural-urban way of life

        2.   The Sumerians made Mesopotamia the "cradle of civilization"

    B.   Environment and Mesopotamian culture

        1.   Geography greatly affected the political life and mental outlook of people in Mesopotamia

            a.   The land is desert: Only irrigation made farming possible

            b.   Rivers isolated cities from one another, making them independent and willing to fight to remain so

            c.   Floods and droughts made life difficult and people pessimistic

IV. Sumerian society

    A.   Religion-centered life

        1.   The Sumerians tried to please the gods, especially the patron deity of the city

        2.   Monumental architecture — the ziggurat, or temple — evolved from religion

        3.   Recent discoveries indicate that a king (*lugal*) ruled and that most property was held privately

    B.   Varieties of freedom and dependence

        1.   The temple priests were wealthy and powerful but did not govern the city

        2.   The nobility — the king and his family, the chief priests, and the high palace officials — controlled most of the wealth and held most of the power

        3.   The commoners were free and had a political voice

        4.   Individual citizens owned much of the city's land

        5.   Slavery existed in Sumerian society

V. The spread of Mesopotamian culture

    A.   The short-lived empire of Sargon

        1.   In 2331 B.C., Sargon, a Semitic chieftain, conquered Sumer and spread Mesopotamian culture throughout and beyond the Fertile Crescent

        2.   The Ebla tablets reveal much about Sargon's work and the Mesopotamian influence, but they have added very little to biblical scholarship

    B.   The triumph of Babylon

        1.   Babylon's economic potential helped Hammurabi unify Mesopotamia

        2.   War and Hammurabi's genius enabled Babylon to become the cultural center of Mesopotamia

C. The invention of writing and the first schools
  1. Pictograph writing — the forerunner of cuneiform writing — existed long before Sumerian society
  2. Sumerian cuneiform evolved from a pictographic system to a phonetic system
  3. The Sumerian educational system was widely copied
D. Mesopotamian thought and religion
  1. Mathematics
    a. The Mesopotamian numerical system was based on units of sixty
    b. Mesopotamians developed the concept of *place value*
    c. They emphasized practical uses — for example, construction — rather than theorizing
  2. Medicine
    a. Demons and evil spirits were believed to cause sickness
    b. Treatment was by magic, prescription, and surgery
  3. Theology, religion, and mythology
    a. The Mesopotamians believed in a hierarchy of anthropomorphic, all-powerful gods
    b. The aim of worship was to appease the gods
    c. The Mesopotamians created myths and an epic poem — the *Epic of Gilgamesh* — to learn of life and immortality
    d. Their myths about the creation of the universe and of human beings later influenced Jewish, Christian, and Muslim thought
E. Daily life in Mesopotamia
  1. Hammurabi's code was based on several principles
    a. Equality before the law did not exist: there were milder penalties for members of the nobility than for commoners and slaves
    b. When criminal and victim were social equals, punishment fit the crime
    c. Individuals represented themselves, fair trials were guaranteed, and officials who failed to protect the innocent were penalized
  2. Hammurabi's law code reflects what life was like
    a. The law provided for consumer protection and for preventing crime
    b. The code contains many laws about farming, irrigation, crops, and animals
    c. Marriage was a business arrangement between the groom-to-be and his future father-in-law
    d. Women had little power within the family while husbands had absolute power
VI. Egypt, the land of the pharaohs (3100–1800 B.C.)
A. Geography

1. Egypt was known as the gift of the Nile
2. The Nile unified Egypt
3. Egypt was nearly self-sufficient in raw materials
4. Geography shielded Egypt from invasion and immigration

B. The god-king of Egypt
1. Egypt was politically unified under a pharaoh, or king, who was considered to be a god in human form
2. The greatness of the pharaohs is reflected in their tombs, the pyramids
    a. The pyramid was believed to help preserve the pharaoh's body so that his *ka* would live on
    b. Tomb paintings, originally designed for the *ka*, give a vivid picture of everyday life

C. The pharaoh's people
1. Social mobility existed, but most people were tied to the land and subject to forced labor
2. Peasants could be forced to work on pyramids and canals and to serve in the pharaoh's army
3. The pharaoh existed to prevent internal chaos, which could lead to war and invasion

VII. Hyksos in Egypt (1640–1570 B.C.)
A. About 1800 B.C., Semites (Hyksos) began to push into Egypt, Mesopotamia, and Syria from the Arabian peninsula
B. Their "invasion" of Egypt was probably gradual and peaceful
C. The Hyksos brought new ideas and techniques to Egyptian life

VIII. The New Kingdom in Egypt (1570–1200 B.C.)
A. A period of wealth, imperialism, and slavery
1. The eighteenth-dynasty warrior-pharaohs Ahmose, Tutmose I, and Tutmose III created the first Egyptian empire and inaugurated the New Kingdom
2. Warrior-pharaohs built huge granite monuments and created an empire

B. Akhenaten and monotheism
1. The pharaoh Akhenaten was interested in religion, not conquests
    a. His monotheistic religion was unpopular
    b. Akhenaten and his wife, Nefertiti, attempted to impose monotheism on Egypt
2. Akhenaten's attack on the traditional gods was seen by some as dangerous
3. Akhenaten built a new capital and used art to convey his ideas
4. In the end monotheism did not take hold

IX. The Hittite empire
A. Migration of new groups

1. Hittites were a part of the Indo-European migrations at the time the Hyksos entered Egypt
    a. The term *Indo-European* refers to a large family of languages, spoken throughout most of Europe and much of the Near East
    b. The original home of the Indo-Europeans may have been Central Europe
- B. The rise of the Hittites and Hittite society
    1. Hattusilis I led the Hittites to conquer Anatolia and then moved eastward as far as Babylon
    2. The Hittites adopted the Mesopotamian culture
- C. The era of Hittite greatness (ca 1475–1200 B.C.)
    1. Through wise diplomacy and war, the Hittites came to control much of the Near East
        a. The Hittites defeated the Egyptians at the battle of Kadesh
        b. The Hittites often ruled through vassal-kingdoms and protectorates
        c. Along with Egyptians, the Hittites provided the Near East with an interlude of peace
- D. The fall of empires
    1. The fall of Egypt and the Hittites in the thirteenth century B.C. allowed for the growth of small kingdoms
        a. Both Egypt and the Hittite Empire were destroyed by invaders
        b. The old cultures of Mesopotamia, however, lived on through a dark age

REVIEW QUESTIONS

Q-1. What were the major accomplishments of the Paleolithic peoples? Why were their lives so precarious?

Q-2. Why are the artistic creations of Paleolithic and Neolithic people important to the historian?

Q-3. Explain how systematic agriculture affected the lives of these early peoples. Why did farming and the domestication of animals constitute a revolution in human life?

Q-4. What effect did the geography of Mesopotamia have on the lives of the people who lived between the Tigris and Euphrates rivers?

Q-5. What importance did the Nile River have in the economic and political development of Egypt?

Q-6. What was the role of the pharaoh in Egyptian society?

Q-7. Why were artistic works placed in the pharaoh's tomb?

Q-8. How much freedom existed in Egyptian society? Was Egypt an oriental slave state?

Q-9.   Who unified Mesopotamia and how was it accomplished? Was it inevitable that Mesopotamia become unified?

Q-10.   Describe the evolution of Sumerian writing.

Q-11.   Describe the Mesopotamian religion. How did the Mesopotamians explain life and the universe?

Q-12.   What role has myth played in Western culture? Does society live by myths today?

Q-13.   What does the code of Hammurabi tell us about social and business relationships in Mesopotamia?

Q-14.   Describe Mesopotamian family and marriage practices. How were women treated in Mesopotamian society? How do you account for their powerlessness?

Q-15.   What were the religious beliefs of Akhenaten and his wife, Nefertiti? Why were their ideas seen as a threat by some Egyptians?

Q-16.   Who were the Indo-Europeans, and how did they affect the history of the Near East?

Q-17.   Who were the Hyksos, and what changes did they bring to Egypt? What was the Egyptian response?

Q-18.   What were the contributions of the Hittites to Near Eastern history?

Q-19.   What was the cause of the coming of the "dark age" in the thirteenth century B.C.?

Q-20.   What were the differences and similarities among the civilizations of the Nile, Tigris-Euphrates, Indus, and Yellow river valleys?

STUDY-REVIEW EXERCISES

Define the following key concepts and terms.

pankus assembly - voting members

anthropomorphic gods human form; powerful; immortal

monotheism worship of one god

cuneiform form of writing developed by Sumerians

systematic agriculture caused change from stone age to modern civilization

ziggurat massive stepped tower that dominated Mesopotamia first monumental architecture of mesopotamia

Battle of Kadesh

place value

pharaoh A King; "Great House".

Identify each of the following and give its significance

Mursilis I

Amon-Re King of the Gods

ka invisible counterpart of body

Ebla tablets

Epic of Gilgamesh Poem produced by Sumerians
Hero searches for eternal life

Akhenaten a pharaoh concerned with religion not conquest

Nefertiti wife of Akhenaten

Neanderthal Man Found in Neander Valley, Germany; could
think, use tools, and cope w/environment

Homo sapiens Thinking man

Sumer

Indo-European large family of languages

code of Hammurabi Code of law that differed with
social status of offender and punishment fit the
crime

Hattusilis I

eighteenth-dynasty pharaohs Created first Egyptian Empire

Explain who the following groups of people were and why they were important

Sumerians Farmers; city builders - Settled in southern
mesopotamia; Built shrines to gods in center of city
and built their houses around them

Semites Responsible for spreading Sumerian
culture

Amorites

Hittites

Hyksos *Rulers of the Uplands*

Explain and describe how (a) agriculture and (b) writing evolved

Test your understanding of the chapter by answering the following questions.

1. The author of *On the Origin of Species* (1859). ___Charles Darwin___
2. His law code demanded that the punishment fit the crime.
    ___Hammurabi___

3. A term meaning "king" or "great house." ___pharaoh___
4. The people whom the Egyptians called the "Rulers of the Uplands" were the
    ___Hykos___

5. The pharaoh who advocated monotheism was ___Akhenaten___
6. The two empires that fell in the thirteenth century B.C. were
    ___Egyptian___ and ___Hittite___

7. The capital city of Mesopotamia under Hammurabi was ___Babylon___
8. Most ordinary people in ancient Egypt *were*/*were not* tied to the land and subject to forced labor.
9. Under Hammurabi's code, the husband *could*/*could not* sell his wife and children into slavery.
10. The agricultural revolution is the chief event of the *Paleolithic*/*Neolithic* Age.

11. Mesopotamia was the land between the ___Tigris___
    and ___Euphrates___ rivers.
12. The code of Hammurabi indicates that burglary *was*/*was not* a serious problem in Babylon.
13. Egyptian agricultural self-sufficiency and productivity were due to the yearly
    flooding of the ___Nile___ River.

Number the following events in correct chronological order.

1. __6__ Rise of the Hittite Empire

2. __3__ Unification of Mesopotamia under Babylon

3. __5__ Reign of Akhenaten

4. __2__ Establishment of Sumer

5. __4__ Hyksos invasion of Egypt

6. __1__ Establishment of systematic agriculture

MULTIPLE-CHOICE QUESTIONS

1. Which of the following were characteristics of Paleolithic society?
   a. Written language, extensive law codes, and irrigation technology
   b. Highly structured sociopolitical groups, pacifism, and great amounts of leisure time
   c. Hunting technology, primitive art, and violence
   d. A powerful merchant class, widespread currency, and *laissez-faire* capitalism

2. The most influential ancient Near Eastern culture was the
   a. Egyptian culture.
   b. Mesopotamian culture.
   c. Assyrian culture.
   d. Hittite culture.

3. Amon-Re was the Egyptian god (king) of
   a. the dead.
   b. fertility.
   c. the gods.
   d. agriculture.

4. The ziggurat, the world's first monumental architecture, was a monument to the
   a. pharaoh.
   b. Sumerian gods.
   c. Battle of Nineveh.
   d. Great Flood.

5. According to the code of Hammurabi, tavern keepers who watered down drinks were
   a. sent to jail.
   b. sold into slavery.
   c. drowned.
   d. dragged through a field.

6. The Ebla tablets, discovered in 1976, prove
   a. the close connection between Mesopotamia and Syria, plus the presence of a written language.
   b. that there was no Mesopotamian influence on the Bible.
   c. that Mesopotamian culture remained *only* in Mesopotamia.
   d. that no link existed between Mesopotamian literature and religion and Old Testament theology.

7. Charles Darwin's theory of human evolution was unpopular among many people in his day because it
   a. was based on faith.
   b. lacked any scientific evidence.
   c. seemed to contradict the Bible.
   d. was condemned by British politicians.

8. Egyptians obeyed the pharaoh because the pharaoh was considered to be
   a. semidivine.
   b. divine.
   c. on the level of ordinary mortals, who could thus identify with him.
   d. so cruel that he had to be obeyed.

9. The law code of King Hammurabi in Mesopotamia
   a. included a great deal of legislation on agriculture and irrigation canals.
   b. handed down mild punishments for almost all crimes.
   c. treated all social classes equally.
   d. did not protect the consumer.

10. Irrigation is a special feature of
    a. Sumer.
    b. Anatolia.
    c. Syria.
    d. Assyria.

11. Geography influenced Sumerian society by
    a. making communications within the region easy.

b. making communications within the region difficult.
c. providing the inhabitants with everything they needed.
d. providing an abundance of precious metals.

12. Rivers in Mesopotamia were important because they
a. were a unifying factor.
b. drained off excess water.
c. kept out invaders.
d. made irrigation possible.

13. The Sumerians responded to their environment by
a. achieving rapid political unification.
b. developing a pessimistic view of life.
c. appreciating the value of floods.
d. developing an appreciation of nature.

14. The ziggurat was
a. an agricultural community.
b. a temple to the gods.
c. the king's palace.
d. a military camp.

15. The *lugal* in Mesopotamia was the
a. secular war-leader and administrator.
b. chief priest of the temple.
c. council of elders.
d. legal owner of a slave.

16. Marduk was the chief god of the
a. Sumerians.
b. Egyptians.
c. Amorites.
d. Hittites.

17. The greatest achievement of Neolithic peoples was the
a. exploration of world masses.
b. invention of art.
c. custom of burial of the dead.
d. development of agriculture and settled life.

18. The surplus of food in Neolithic communities led to the following development:
a. increase of population.

b. shorter life spans.

c. increase of disease.

d. increase in warfare.

19. Neolithic people changed their environment by
a. following the wild herds.
b. domesticating animals.
c. settling in permanent villages.
d. indulging in cannibalism.

20. The geographical location of Egypt meant that the country was
a. divided into many isolated areas.
b. a crossroads of commerce.
c. subject to external invasion.
d. nearly self-sufficient.

21. The common people of Egypt were
a. completely without legal rights.
b. at the bottom of the social scale.
c. divided on the basis of color.
d. related to the Mesopotamians.

22. The most influential ancient Near Eastern culture was the
a. Hittite.
b. Mesopotamian.
c. Egyptian.
d. Assyrian.

23. The Hittites were
a. Persians.
b. Semites.
c. Akkadians.
d. Indo-Europeans.

24. The Egyptian god Osiris was closely associated with
a. Isis.
b. Aton.
c. Amon-Re.
d. Serapis.

25. Akhenaten was interested in fostering
a. military expansion.

b. worship of Aton.
c. agricultural improvements.
d. a return to traditional values.

26. Which of the following was a goal of King Hammurabi of Babylon?
    a. To treat all classes of citizens equally
    b. To live at peace with his neighbors, regardless of the cost
    c. To make Sumer the religious capital of all Mesopotamia
    d. To unify Mesopotamia

27. Ancient Mesopotamian religion is characterized by
    a. Monotheism.
    b. deification of natural elements.
    c. a highly personal chief god.
    d. a commitment to Allah.

28. The Kassites
    a. invented writing.
    b. defeated the Babylonians.
    c. expelled the Hyksos.
    d. founded Ebla.

GEOGRAPHY

1. Referring to Map 1.1, use the following space to describe the geographical features that affected Egypt's economic and political development.

2. Referring to Map 1.1, use the space below to describe the geographical features that account for Mesopotamia's economic and political development.

3. Referring to Map 1.2 and the section on Rivers and Civilizations in Chapter 1, what were the differences and the similarities among the four great river valleys?

UNDERSTANDING HISTORY THROUGH READING AND THE ARTS

The life and times of the great pharaohs make interesting reading. Two excellent books are L. Cottrell, *Life Under the Pharaohs* (1964), and C. Desroches-Noblecourt, *Tutankhamen* (1965). Desroches-Noblecourt has also written an account of Egyptian art entitled *Egyptian Wall Paintings from Tombs and Temples* (1962) that is richly illustrated and informative, while C. Aldred's *Egyptian Art in the Days of the Pharaohs** (1985) examines nearly 3,000 years of Egyptian art in terms of the religious, historical, and environmental forces of Egypt. The early cave paintings, pottery, and gold ornaments of the Neolithic and Bronze Age artists and the metalwork of the Iron Age artists and others are examined in T. Powell, *Prehistoric Art** (1985).

The importance of the Sumerians in the origins of civilization is the subject of S. N. Kramer's excellent survey, *The Sumerians: Their History, Culture and Character** (1984), and among the best introductions to Egyptian civilization is C. Aldred's *The Egyptians* (1984). Everyday life in the Egyptian village during the New Kingdom is interestingly evoked by J. Romer in *Ancient Lives: Daily Life in Egypt of the Pharaohs* (1984).

PROBLEMS FOR FURTHER INVESTIGATION

Precisely who were the Sumerians, and what were their contributions to the origins of civilization in Mesopotamia? The history of the discovery and study of the Sumerians is described in Tom B. Jones, ed., *The Sumerian Problem** (1969).

The origins and early development of agriculture, urban life, trade, and writing in the Near East have raised questions still hotly debated among historians and archaeologists. Excellent introductions to these issues can be found in a volume of readings from *Scientific American* titled *Hunters, Farmers, and Civilizations: Old World Archeology** (1979).

*Available in paperback.

READING WITH UNDERSTANDING
EXERCISE 1

LEARNING HOW TO UNDERLINE OR HIGHLIGHT THE MAJOR POINTS

Underlining (or highlighting with a felt-tipped pen, as many students prefer) plays an important part in the learning process in college courses. Underlining provides you with a permanent record of what you want to learn. It helps you in your efforts to master the material and prepare for exams.

The introductory essay (pp. vii-xii) provides some good guidelines for learning how to underline effectively, and you should review it carefully before continuing.

Further Suggestions

1. In addition to underlining selectively, *consider numbering the main points* to help you remember them. Numbering helps make the main points stand out clearly, which is a major purpose of all underlining or highlighting.

2. *Read an entire section through before you underline or highlight it.* Then, as you read it a second time, you will be better able to pick out and underline key facts, main points, and sentences or paragraphs that summarize and interpret the information.

3. *Avoid false economies.* Some students do not mark their books because they are afraid that the bookstores will not buy them back. This is a foolish way to try to save money for two reasons. First, students must of necessity invest a great deal of time and money in their college education. By refusing to mark their books, they are reducing their chances of doing their best and thus endangering their whole college investment. Probably the only alternative to marking your books is making detailed written notes, which is more difficult and much more time consuming.

Second, carefully underlined books are *a permanent yet personal record of what you study and learn.* Such books become valuable reference works, helping you recall important learning experiences and forming the core of your library in future years.

Exercise

Read the following passage once as a whole. Read it a second time to underline or highlight it. Consider numbering the points. On completion, compare your underlining with the model on the next page, which is an example of reasonable and useful underlining. Finally, compare the underlined section with the chapter outline in the *Study Guide.* You will see how the outline summary is an aid in learning how to underline major points.

EGYPT, THE LAND OF THE PHARAOHS
(3100-1200 B.C.)

The Greek historian and traveler Herodotus in the fifth century
B.C. called Egypt the "gift of the Nile." No other single geographical factor had such a fundamental and profound impact on
the shaping of Egyptian life, society, and history as the Nile. Unlike the rivers of Mesopotamia it rarely brought death and destruction. The river was primarily a creative force. The Egyptians
never feared the relatively calm Nile in the way the Mesopotamians feared their rivers. Instead they sang its praises:

> Hail to thee, O Nile, that issues from the earth and comes to
>   keep Egypt alive! . . .
> He that waters the meadows which Re created,
> He that makes to drink the desert . . .
> He who makes barley and brings emmer [wheat] into being . . .
> He who brings grass into being for the cattle.
> He who makes every beloved tree to grow . . .
> O Nile, verdant art thou, who makest man and cattle to live.[15]

In the minds of the Egyptians, the Nile was the supreme fertilizer
and renewer of the land. Each September the Nile floods its valley, transforming it into a huge area of marsh or lagoon. By the
end of November the water retreats, leaving behind a thin covering of fertile mud ready to be planted with crops.

The annual flood made the growing of abundant crops almost
effortless, especially in southern Egypt. Herodotus, used to the
rigors of Greek agriculture, was amazed by the ease with which
the Egyptians raised their crops:

> For indeed without trouble they obtain crops from the land
> more easily than all other men. . . . They do not labor to dig
> furrows with the plough or hoe or do the work which other
> men do to raise grain. But when the river by itself inundates
> the fields and the water recedes, then each man, having sown
> his field, sends pigs into it. When the pigs trample down the

seed, he waits for the harvest. Then when the pigs thresh the grain, he gets his crop.[16]

As late as 1822, John Burckhardt, an English traveler, watched nomads sowing grain by digging large holes in the mud and throwing in seeds. The extraordinary fertility of the Nile valley made it easy to produce an annual agricultural surplus, which in turn sustained a growing and prosperous population.

Whereas the Tigris and Euphrates and their many tributaries carved up Mesopotamia into isolated areas, the Nile served to unify Egypt. The river was the principal highway and promoted easy communication throughout the valley. As individual bands of settlers moved into the Nile valley, they created stable agricultural communities. By about 3100 B.C. there were some forty of these communities in constant contact with one another. This contact, encouraged and facilitated by the Nile, virtually ensured the early political unification of the country.

Egypt was fortunate in that it was nearly self-sufficient. Besides the fertility of its soil, Egypt possessed enormous quantities of stone, which served as the raw material of architecture and sculpture. Abundant clay was available for pottery, as was gold for jewelry and ornaments. The raw materials that Egypt lacked were close at hand. The Egyptians could obtain copper from Sinai and timber from Lebanon. They had little cause to look to the outside world for their essential needs, which helps to explain the insular quality of Egyptian life.

Geography further encouraged isolation by closing Egypt off from the outside world. To the east and west of the Nile valley stretch grim deserts. The Nubian Desert and the cataracts of the Nile discourage penetration from the south. Only in the north did the Mediterranean Sea leave Egypt exposed. Thus, geography shielded Egypt from invasion and from extensive immigration. Unlike the Mesopotamians, the Egyptians enjoyed centuries of peace and tranquillity, during which they could devote most of their resources to peaceful development of their distinctive civilization.

Yet Egypt was not completely sealed off. As early as 3250 B.C. Mesopotamian influences, notably architectural techniques and materials and perhaps even writing, made themselves felt in Egyptian life. Still later, from 1680 to 1580 B.C., northern Egypt was ruled by foreign invaders, the Hyksos. Infrequent though they were, such periods of foreign influence fertilized Egyptian culture without changing it in any fundamental way.

The God-King of Egypt

The geographic unity of Egypt quickly gave rise to political unification of the country under the authority of a king whom the Egyptians called "pharaoh." The details of this process have been lost. The Egyptians themselves told of a great king, Menes, who united Egypt into a single kingdom around 3100 B.C. Thereafter the Egyptians divided their history into *dynasties*, or families of kings. For modern historical purposes, however, it is more useful to divide Egyptian history into periods. The political unification of Egypt ushered in the period known as the Old Kingdom, an era remarkable for its prosperity and artistic flowering, and for the evolution of religious beliefs.

EGYPT, THE LAND OF THE PHARAOHS
(3100-1200 B.C.)

Geography

1

The Greek historian and traveler Herodotus in the fifth century B.C. called Egypt the "gift of the Nile." No other single geographical factor had such a fundamental and profound impact on the shaping of Egyptian life, society, and history as the Nile. Unlike the rivers of Mesopotamia it rarely brought death and destruction. The river was primarily a creative force. The Egyptians never feared the relatively calm Nile in the way the Mesopotamians feared their rivers. Instead they sang its praises:

> Hail to thee, O Nile, that issues from the earth and comes to
> keep Egypt alive! . . .
> He that waters the meadows which Re created,
> He that makes to drink the desert . . .
> He who makes barley and brings emmer [wheat] into being . . .
> He who brings grass into being for the cattle.
> He who makes every beloved tree to grow . . .
> O Nile, verdant art thou, who makest man and cattle to live.[15]

In the minds of the Egyptians, the Nile was the supreme fertilizer and renewer of the land. Each September the Nile floods its valley, transforming it into a huge area of marsh or lagoon. By the end of November the water retreats, leaving behind a thin covering of fertile mud ready to be planted with crops.

1a

The annual flood made the growing of abundant crops almost effortless, especially in southern Egypt. Herodotus, used to the rigors of Greek agriculture, was amazed by the ease with which the Egyptians raised their crops:

> For indeed without trouble they obtain crops from the land more easily than all other men. . . . They do not labor to dig furrows with the plough or hoe or do the work which other men do to raise grain. But when the river by itself inundates the fields and the water recedes, then each man, having sown his field, sends pigs into it. When the pigs trample down the

seed, he waits for the harvest. Then when the pigs thresh the grain, he gets his crop.[16]

As late as 1822, John Burckhardt, an English traveler, watched nomads sowing grain by digging large holes in the mud and throwing in seeds. The extraordinary fertility of the Nile valley made it easy to produce an annual agricultural surplus, which in turn sustained a growing and prosperous population.

2   Whereas the Tigris and Euphrates and their many tributaries carved up Mesopotamia into isolated areas, the Nile served to unify Egypt. The river was the principal highway and promoted easy communication throughout the valley. As individual bands of settlers moved into the Nile valley, they created stable agricultural communities. By about 3100 B.C. there were some forty of these communities in constant contact with one another. This contact, encouraged and facilitated by the Nile, virtually ensured the early political unification of the country.

3   Egypt was fortunate in that it was nearly self-sufficient. Besides the fertility of its soil, Egypt possessed enormous quantities of stone, which served as the raw material of architecture and sculpture. Abundant clay was available for pottery, as was gold for jewelry and ornaments. The raw materials that Egypt lacked were close at hand. The Egyptians could obtain copper from Sinai and timber from Lebanon. They had little cause to look to the outside world for their essential needs, which helps to explain the insular quality of Egyptian life.

4   Geography further encouraged isolation by closing Egypt off from the outside world. To the east and west of the Nile valley stretch grim deserts. The Nubian Desert and the cataracts of the Nile discourage penetration from the south. Only in the north did the Mediterranean Sea leave Egypt exposed. Thus, geography shielded Egypt from invasion and from extensive immigration. Unlike the Mesopotamians, the Egyptians enjoyed centuries of peace and tranquillity, during which they could devote most of their resources to peaceful development of their distinctive civilization.

5   Yet Egypt was not completely sealed off. As early as 3250 B.C. Mesopotamian influences, notably architectural techniques and materials and perhaps even writing, made themselves felt in Egyptian life. Still later, from 1680 to 1580 B.C., northern Egypt was ruled by foreign invaders, the Hyksos. Infrequent though
6   they were, such periods of foreign influence fertilized Egyptian culture without changing it in any fundamental way.

The God-King of Egypt

The geographic unity of Egypt quickly gave rise to political unification of the country under the authority of a king whom the Egyptians called "pharaoh." The details of this process have been lost. The Egyptians themselves told of a great king, Menes, who united Egypt into a single kingdom around 3100 B.C. Thereafter the Egyptians divided their history into *dynasties*, or families of kings. For modern historical purposes, however, it is more useful to divide Egyptian history into periods. The political unification of Egypt ushered in the period known as the Old Kingdom, an era remarkable for its prosperity and artistic flowering, and for the evolution of religious beliefs.

CHAPTER 2

SMALL KINGDOMS AND MIGHTY
EMPIRES IN THE NEAR EAST

CHAPTER OBJECTIVES

After reading and studying this chapter you should be able to answer the following questions:

Q-1. How did the Hebrew state evolve, and what are the distinguishing features of Hebrew life and religious thought?
Q-2. What enabled the Assyrians to overrun their neighbors, and how did their cruelty finally cause their undoing?
Q-3. How did Iranian nomads create the Persian Empire?

CHAPTER SYNOPSIS

The power vacuum that followed the fall of the great empires was significant because it allowed less powerful peoples to settle and prosper independently and, as a result, make particularly important contributions to Western society. Foremost among these peoples were the Phoenicians, who used their freedom to sail in the Mediterranean Sea and build a prosperous commercial network, and the even smaller kingdom of the Hebrews. Modern archaeology tends to confirm the Old Testament account of the Hebrews' movement from Mesopotamia into Canaan, enslavement in Egypt, and subsequent liberation and establishment of a homeland in Palestine. Important in this process was the Hebrews' vision of their god, Yahweh. A covenant with Yahweh — centering on the Ten Commandments — formed the basis of Hebrew life and law and provided the energy with which the kings Saul, David, and Solomon, along with the great prophets, unified the Hebrews into a prosperous society based on high standards of mercy and justice. Their unique monotheism, combined with settled agriculture and urban life, provided the framework for the Hebrews' daily

17

life. A chief feature of this life was its ability to change, best seen in the evolution of the family from a strong patriarchy based on the extended family to a more liberated urban nuclear family.

The power vacuum in the Near East evaporated in the ninth century with the rise of the Assyrians, the most warlike people the Near East had yet known. For two hundred years the Assyrians ruled an empire that stretched from the Persian Gulf across the Fertile Crescent and westward through northern Egypt. Despite their brutality, the Assyrians owed their success less to calculated terrorism than to efficient military organization. The Assyrian Empire fell swiftly in 612 B.C., and had it not been for modern archaeological work may have continued to be unknown.

The Persian Empire, which grew out of the unique geographic position of what is now Iran, was the most tolerant and humane empire to date. The empire began in 550 B.C. with the first conquests of Cyrus the Great. The next two hundred years of Persian rule in the Near East were marked by efficient administration and respect for the diverse cultures of conquered states. Out of this benevolent rule came an important new religion, Zoroastrianism, which gave to Western society the idea of individual choice in the struggle between goodness and evil. All in all, these seven hundred years were marked by chaos, order, diversity, and unity, as the Near East forged some of its most important achievements.

STUDY OUTLINE

I. The children of Israel
    A. The power vacuum created by the fall of the Hittite and Egyptian states allowed lesser states to thrive
        1. The Phoenicians were outstanding seafarers, merchants, and explorers
        2. Among their achievements were the building of Carthage and the development of a new alphabet that related one letter to one sound
    B. The collapse of Egypt and the Hittites and the growth of small kingdoms
        1. According to the Old Testament, the Hebrews followed Abraham out of Mesopotamia into Canaan, and from there migrated into the Nile delta, where eventually they were enslaved
        2. Moses then led the Hebrews out of Egypt and into Canaan, where they built a political confederation
        3. Under Saul and David, the Hebrews built the Kingdom of Judah, with its capital at Jerusalem
        4. King Solomon built a great temple and extended Hebrew power
            a. The temple was the symbol of Hebrew unity
            b. At his death the kingdom was divided in two (see Map 2.1)
            c. The northern half became Israel while the southern half was Judah (see Map 2.1)

        d. Judah, the home of Judaism, survived for several centuries

C. The evolution of Hebrew religion
1. The Hebrew religion was monotheistic, centered on the covenant with the god Yahweh
2. Yahweh which means "he causes to be," was a personal god
3. Jewish law and ethics, with their stress on justice and mercy, evolved from the Ten Commandments of Yahweh and the words of the prophets

D. Daily life in Israel
1. The end of nomadic life and coming of urban life changed family and marriage customs
    a. Communal land ownership gave way to family ownership
    b. The extended tribal family gave way to the *nuclear* family, although urbanization weakened family ties and the power of the father
    c. The end of nomadic life led to monogamous marriages
    d. Most marriages were legal contracts arranged by the parents
    e. Divorce was available only to the husband
2. Hebrew society placed strong emphasis on rearing children
    a. Children, particularly sons, were important for economic reasons
    b. Both parents played a role in the child's education
3. Family farming was at the center of Hebrew life
    a. Children worked in agriculture with their parents
    b. However, peace and prosperity brought about a decline of the small family farm and a rise of large estates and slave labor
    c. The rise of urban life brought new job opportunities and increased trade
    d. Craft and trade specialization thrived
    e. At first commerce was dominated by the king and/or foreigners

II. Assyria, the military monarchy
A. Growth of militarism and political cohesion among the Assyrians
1. Assyrian attacks on Near Eastern states continued for 200 years
2. Assyrians created an empire that extended from Mesopotamia to central Egypt
3. Conquest bred revolt, which in turn led to brutal Assyrian retaliation

B. Assyrian success was due to effective military organization, and new military techniques and equipment were developed

C. Assyrian rule
1. The Assyrians organized an empire with provinces and dependent states
2. A good communication system was established, and calculated terrorism was practiced
3. The Babylonians and the Medes destroyed Assyria in 612 B.C.

III. The empire of the Persian kings
A. The Persians were Indo-European Iranians who unified many cultures into a tolerant and humane empire

B. Iran's chief geographical features — mountains and a great central plateau between the Tigris-Euphrates valley and the Indus valley

C. The first Iranians — the coming of the Medes and Persians
1. The first Iranians were nomadic Medes and Persians with great horsemanship skills
2. They established a patchwork of small kingdoms centered on agricultural towns
3. These towns became centers for agriculture, mineral extraction, and horse-breeding
4. The Iranians of the north, the Medes, grew strong enough to help overthrow the Assyrian Empire

D. The creation of the Persian Empire
1. The founder of the Persian Empire, Cyrus the Creat (559–530 B.C.) held enlightened views
    a. He made the land of the Medes into his first *satrapy*
    b. He viewed Persia and Medea as the state of Iran
    c. His empire gave respect, toleration, and protection to its conquered people
    d. His Persian empire was multicultural
2. Next Cyrus won control of the west as far as the Greek coast of Anatolia — where he first conquered the lands of Croesus
3. Then Cyrus marched to eastern Iran (Parthia, Bactria) to strengthen Iran from warring nomads
4. He conquered Babylonia and gave protection to the Jews

E. Thus Spake Zarathustra, the religion of Iran
1. At first Iranian religion was polytheistic, simple, and primitive
2. Zoroaster gave Iranian religion new ideas
    a. Most information about this unique new religion comes from the hymns and poems called *Zend Avesta*
3. b. Life is a battleground between good and evil, and each individual can decide between the two
    c. Eternal fate (the Last Judgment) will be decided on the basis of one's deeds in life
    d. The conversion of King Darius to Zoroastrianism led to its spread throughout the empire

F. The Persian Empire
1. Cyrus's successors rounded out the empire to India in the east and Anatolia, Egypt, and Libya in the west
    a. The empire was divided into twenty satrapies
    b. Roads were built so that royal couriers could enable the king to rule effectively

    c. The conquered people, left free to enjoy their traditional ways of life, were grateful for Persian rule

    d. For over two hundred years the Persians gave the Near East a period of peace that allowed people to enjoy their native traditions

REVIEW QUESTIONS

Q-1. Why is the Old Testament such an important source for historians in reconstructing Hebrew society?

Q-2. What are the main features of the Hebrew religion? How important was religion in the daily life of the people?

Q-3. What effect did the end of nomadic life have on Hebrew property and marriage practices?

Q-4. Describe Hebrew attitudes toward children. What was childhood like for Hebrew sons and daughters?

Q-5. What changes did prosperity and urbanization bring to Hebrew life?

Q-6. What impact did Assyria have on the Near Eastern world? Was its influence longlasting?

Q-7. Describe the extent of the Assyrian Empire. What were the secrets of Assyrian success?

Q-8. Iran has been described as the "highway between East and West." Explain.

Q-9. Describe the accomplishments of Cyrus the Great. Why was this conqueror regarded by many non-Persians as a liberator and benefactor?

Q-10. Zoroaster gave the Near East some novel ideas about divinity and human life. What were these ideas?

Q-11. Describe the Persian system of imperial rule. In what ways was it different from or similar to that of the Assyrians?

STUDY-REVIEW EXERCISES

Define the following key concepts and terms.

nuclear family

monotheism

polygamy

monogamy

Yahweh

Hebrew Covenant

Zoroastrianism

satrapy

Torah

Identify and give the significance of the following.

Sargon II

Nubians

Solomon's Jerusalem temple

Libyans

Phoenicians

Ten Commandments

Moses

Zend Avesta

kingdom of Kush

Jeremiah

Ark of the Covenant

Old Testament

Nineveh

Cyrus the Great

Siyalk

Ahura

Medes

Persians

Explain each of the following and give its significance by noting the basic ideas of each and the ways in which they were unique: (a) the Hebrew religion and (b) Zoroastrianism.

Test your understanding of the chapter by answering the following questions.

1. With the coming of peace and prosperity, the tendency in Hebrew society was toward (a) greater concentration of landholding, (b) more small family

    farms, (c) a decline in slavery. _____
2. As opposed to the early Hebrew law, the Torah, later legal tradition in Hebrew society tended to be *more/less* humanitarian.
3. The Hebrew religion was based on a personal covenant with one god,

    _____ Yahweh _____.
4. The two groups of Iranian peoples united by Cyrus the Great were the

    _____ Medes _____ and the _____ Persians _____.
5. With the rise of the Persian Empire, the balance of power in the Near East shifted to the *east/west* of Mesopotamia.
6. For administrative purposes, the Persians divided their empire into twenty

    _____ Satrapies _____, or provinces.
7. In early Hebrew society, the existence of concubines and polygamy *was/was not* uncommon.

8. The most important of the Iranian peoples were the _____ Persians _____.
9. The Jews *did/did not* consider it their duty to spread the belief in their one god.

MULTIPLE-CHOICE QUESTIONS

1. The power vacuum that followed the fall of the empires of the Hittites and the Egyptians from about the thirteenth century was important because it
    a. resulted in the end of Egypt as an influential culture in the Near East and Africa.
    b. led to the unification of the Near East under Hebrew rule.
    c. allowed less powerful peoples, such as the Phoenicians and the Hebrews, to settle and prosper independently.
    d. led to four centuries of backwardness and cultural regression.

2. The Hebrew family pattern evolved from a(an)
    a. extended family to an urban nuclear family.
    b. nuclear family to an extended family.
    c. strong emphasis on monogamy to an emphasis on polygamy.
    d. matriarchy to a patriarchy.

3. Which of the following was a result of Moses' covenant with Yahweh?
    a. The end of monotheism for the Hebrews
    b. The concept of the Jews as God's chosen people
    c. The rejection of all strict moral codes of behavior
    d. The worship of statues and "graven images"

4. Which of the following is true in regard to marriage in early Hebrew society?
    a. Divorce was available only to the husband.
    b. Mixed marriages were always encouraged.
    c. Marriages were usually undertaken as a result of affection and physical attraction of the partners.
    d. The bride's father was expected to provide her with a dowry.

5. According to the Old Testament, the Hebrews were guided out of Mesopotamia and into Canaan by
    a. King David.
    b. King Solomon.
    c. Moses.
    d. Abraham.

6. Peace and prosperity in Israel brought about
    a. increased landholding for small farmers.
    b. a breakup of the large estates.
    c. an end to slave labor.
    d. the decline of the small family farm.

7. The outside threat that most pushed the Hebrew tribes into a centralized political organization was
   a. Egypt.
   b. the Philistines.
   c. Assyria.
   d. the Persians.

8. The symbol of Hebrew unity, center of the priesthood, and great accomplishment of Solomon was the
   a. temple in Jerusalem.
   b. Old Testament.
   c. Hebrew family.
   d. great palace of the Hebrew kings.

9. In ancient Hebrew society, the early education of children was in the hands of
   a. a private tutor.
   b. the child's mother.
   c. the child's father.
   d. the temple priests.

10. The prophets of later Hebrew religious tradition pushed the emphasis in Hebrew religion
    a. toward mercy and justice.
    b. toward Yahweh's punishment of mankind.
    c. toward monotheism.
    d. all of the above.

11. Which other major religions were fundamentally influenced by Judaism?
    a. Christianity and Hinduism.
    b. Buddhism and Islam.
    c. Buddhism and Hinduism.
    d. Christianity and Islam.

12. The first king to reign over the Hebrews was
    a. David.
    b. Solomon.
    c. Saul.
    d. Darius.

13. Yahweh was originally the
    a. universal god.
    b. god of the Jews.

    c. god of fertility.
    d. god of battles.

14. The Assyrians are known for their
    a. assumption of Egyptian culture.
    b. exploration of the Mediterranean Sea.
    c. grim imperialism.
    d. advances in agricultural technology.

15. The founder of the Persian empire was
    a. King Darius.
    b. Zoroaster.
    c. Cyrus the Great.
    d. Siyalk.

16. The Persians acquired many of their military and political practices and organizational genius from the
    a. Hebrews.
    b. Sumerians.
    c. Assyrians.
    d. Philistines.

17. The most brutal and militaristic of the Near Eastern peoples were the
    a. Medes.
    b. Persians.
    c. Phoenicians.
    d. Assyrians.

18. The Phoenicians are best known as
    a. great militarists.
    b. prosperous urban merchants and sea traders.
    c. religious innovators.
    d. rulers of the entire Near East after the fall of Persia.

19. The Phoenicians
    a. overthrew the Egyptian kingdom.
    b. developed a thriving agricultural community.
    c. waged large-scale wars against the Hebrews.
    d. became merchants and explorers.

20. One means by which the Assyrians maintained control over conquered peoples was

    a. benevolent tolerance.
    b. passive resistance.
    c. bilateral disarmament.
    d. calculated terrorism.

21. Assyrians made noteworthy advancements in
    a. social reform.
    b. military technology.
    c. constitutional government.
    d. economics.

22. Iran's chief geographical feature is
    a. a great central plateau between the Tigris-Euphrates and the Indus valleys.
    b. a thick mountainous region.
    c. a dense tropical coastal area as its western edge.
    d. the eastern portion of the Fertile Crescent.

23. The goal of Cyrus the Great, after he successfully united Iran, was to
    a. conquer and destroy the existing states in the Near East.
    b. win control of the West and eliminate the threats from the nomadic invaders.
    c. wipe out Zoroastrianism.
    d. force the Hebrews to give up the worship of their god.

24. The Persian king Cyrus the Great carried out a foreign policy based on
    a. torture and submission to Persian traditions.
    b. tolerance of other cultures.
    c. universal acceptance of the Zoroastrian religion.
    d. the law code of Hammurabi.

25. The successors of Cyrus the Great divided his empire into
    a. three separate kingdoms.
    b. twenty satrapies.
    c. an east and a west province.
    d. six military districts.

26. Which of the following ideas was stressed by Zoroaster?
    a. Individual choice is predetermined
    b. Only good exists in the universe
    c. Each individual will face a last judgment
    d. Life ends with death

27. The Persian king who converted to Zoroastrianism was
     a. Darius.
     b. Xerxes.
     c. Cambyses.
     d. Cyrus.

28. The Persians achieved good communications through
     a. a network of roads.
     b. expert navigation of waterways.
     c. effective use of smoke signals.
     d. messenger pigeons.

GEOGRAPHY

1. Describe the geographic features of Iran and explain how they have influenced the course of Near Eastern history. How does the economic development of early Iran reflect its geography?

2. Referring to Maps 2.2 and 2.3 in the text, describe the extent of the Assyrian and Persian empires. How did the two differ in terms of its attitude toward other peoples and cultures?

PROBLEMS FOR FURTHER INVESTIGATION

Students interested in ancient Near Eastern religion and the idea of one god should start with R. J. Christen and H. E. Hazelton, eds., *Monotheism and Moses** (1969), or the more general work, *A History of Religious Ideas,** 3 vols. (1978–1985), by M. Eliade. Problems of interpretation and investigation in the history of the ancient Near East are set forth, along with an excellent bibliography, in M. Covensky, *The Ancient Near Eastern Tradition** (1966). The effect of infectious diseases on ancient civilization is considered in W. McNeill, *Plagues and Peoples* (1976).

There are many interesting research topics related to archaeological study and the Old Testament. For instance, the biblical flood story did not originate with the Hebrews, and Hammurabi's law code is not the oldest. The sources of the story and the code and other lively subjects relating to the ancient Near East are considered in S. N. Kramer, *History Begins at Sumer, Twenty-seven "Firsts" in Man's Recorded History** (1959). Hebrew law and morality are dealt with in G. Mendenhall, *Law and Covenant in Israel and the Ancient Near East* (1955), and J. Goldwin, *The Living Talmud: The Wisdom of the Fathers and Its Classical Commentaries** (1954), is an interesting essay on Jewish life and religion.

How are the Old Testament's accounts of the early history of the Hebrews corroborated by the findings of archaeologists who have excavated in the Middle East? In fact, archaeological data do not always agree with the Biblical accounts. For a good introduction, read K. Kenyon, *Archaeology in the Holy Land** (1979). Also informative is D. J. Wiseman, ed., *Peoples of Old Testament Times* (1973).

UNDERSTANDING HISTORY THROUGH READING AND THE ARTS

Reading the Old Testament is one of the best sources for learning the history and culture of the Near East. See especially the major history books of the Old Testament: Joshua, Judges, Ruth, I and II Samuel, I and II Kings, Nehemiah, and Esther.

Michael Grant, *The History of Ancient Israel* (1984), provides an eminently readable discussion of early Hebrew society and the rise of the Hebrew monarchy. A briefer summary is Harry M. Orlinsky, *Ancient Israel** (1960). Hebrew law and morality are described in G. Mendenhall, *Law and Covenant in Israel and the Ancient Near East* (1955); and J. Goldwin, *The Living Talmud: The Wisdom of the Fathers and Its Classical Commentaries** (1954), offers an interesting essay on Jewish life and religion.

*Available in paperback.

CHAPTER 3

ANCIENT INDIA TO CA A.D. 200

CHAPTER OBJECTIVES

After reading and studying this chapter you should be able to answer the following questions:

Q-1. How did the ancient Indians respond to many of the same problems that the peoples of the ancient Near East were confronting?
Q-2. How did they meet the challenge of the land itself?
Q-3. What kinds of social organization developed in India and what religious and intellectual values did these civilizations generate?

CHAPTER SYNOPSIS

This chapter explores the important cultural developments in early India. The author begins with a discussion of how geography helped dictate India's history. As in Mesopotamia, it was in the areas of settled agriculture — the Indus and Ganges river valleys — that the story of Indian civilization began to unfold. Geography, particularly the Himalayan mountain range, also provided a certain amount of isolation and protection from the outside world, although for India contact with the lands to the west speeded up political and agricultural development. Most important, plains, southern mountains, plateaus, and river valleys have divided India into many subregions.

　　　In 1921 archaeologists discovered that a thriving urban society had existed in India as early as the year 2500 B.C. Therefore, our picture of India begins with the great but mysterious cities of Mohenjo-daro and Harappa and their Indus peoples. These cities were great because they were sophisticatedly engineered cities with highly centralized governments, and mysterious because the archaeologist and historian are still unwrapping their essence. Here a form of writing developed, great planned cities arose, a central grain storage system was formed, markets and monumental buildings were erected, and a great bath was built. All of this depended on the cultivation of the Indus valley and the domestication of animals. It is not known why these Indus cities disappeared, but there are many theories.

The arrival of the Aryan peoples on this scene was a turning point in Indian history, and this chapter points to the importance of the old and sacred Hindu scriptures, the Rigveda, as our source of knowledge on the Aryan peoples. These warlike wanderers from the north transformed the Ganges river valley from a jungle into tightly organized kingdoms based on village agriculture. The three most salient aspects of this entirely new Indian society were its concept of kingship, its caste system of priest, warrior, peasant, serf, and outcaste, and its religion based on the concept of the wheel of life and Vedic literature. Along with its system of slavery, these influences played lasting roles in Indian society. Out of the Vedic tradition evolved Jainism (based on the ideas of a life of asceticism, nonviolence, and an all-encompassing *karma*) and Hinduism (rooted in the idea of reaching *brahman* through *dharma*).

In India, the great king Ashoka extended the Mauryan empire and not only embraced Buddhism but also became one of its greatest patrons. He was a tough militarist and centralizer but also a man of compassion and nonviolence who taught his people the civic virtue of *dharma.* Above all, Ashoka represents the impact that Buddhism had on Asian life. The original Buddhist philosophy, based on the Eight-fold Path to *nirvana*, or true happiness, provided an ordered and human way in which all people, despite their caste, could deal with life's difficulties and find ultimate fulfillment. Between 250 B.C. and A.D. 200 Ashoka's empire gave way to foreign invaders. It was during this time that Indian culture spread to its neighbors — including the Chinese adoption of Buddhism.

STUDY OUTLINE

  I. India, the land and its first tamers (ca 2500–1500 B.C.)
      A. India's geography
          1. India is a geographically protected and self-contained land mass as large as western Europe
          2. It is made up of three significant areas
              a. A ring of mountains — the Himalayas — in the north
              b. The great valleys of the Indus and Ganges rivers, which provide India with most of its fertile land
              c. A southern peninsula of coastal plains and the dry and hilly Deccan plateau
          3. Geography has protected India from its neighbors as well as dividing the country into subregions

      a.   The Himalayas have protected India from wandering people and
             sheltered it from the northern cold
      b.   The Himalayas and the southern monsoons provide India with
             most of its water
      c.   The Punjab and the valley of the Indus river are the best areas
             for agriculture

B. The Indus civilization, ca 2500–1500 B.C.

   1. About 2500 B.C., settlers entered the Indus valley
      a.   They created an urban culture based on large-scale agriculture
      b.   Cultural exchange and trade was carried on with the peoples
             of Mesopotamia
      c.   The best-known cities were Mohenjo-daro and Harappa
      d.   It is now believed that other settlers filtered in from western
             Asia
   2. Mohenjo-daro and Harappa tell us much about Indus civilization
      a.   These cities were well-planned, were defended by citadels, and
             had tall brick houses with open central courtyards
      b.   A sophisticated system of municipal drainage attests to a strong
             central urban government
      c.   Among the public buildings was a state granary, a marketplace,
             a palace, and a huge bath called the Great Bath
   3. Prosperity depended on intensive cultivation of the valley and control
      of flood waters with embankments
   4. Although little is known of their religion, these early people were con-
      cerned about fertility
      a.   They worshipped a mother-goddess
      b.   They showed a concern for animals and the need for an equilibrium
             with nature
   5. This Mohenjo-daro and Harappa civilization perished mysteriously

II. The ascendancy of the Aryans, ca 1500–500 B.C.

A. The arrival of the Aryans was a turning point in Indian history

   1. The Aryans were Nordic wanderers who were a part of the great
      Indo-European movement
   2. The ancient Hindu *Rigveda* hymnbook tells us about the Aryans
      and native Indians
   3. The Aryans were warlike and lived in tribes headed by a *raja*, or chief
   4. Tribes were made up of warriors, priests, commoners, and slaves
   5. For 600 years, the Aryans pushed into the jungles of the Ganges
      valley, founded Delhi, and blended their culture with that of others

B. The shaping of Indian society

   1. The push into the jungle resulted in the establishment of kingdoms
      under strong absolute rulers

        a.   The priests, or *brahmins*, became powerful allies of the king
        b.   The organized village evolved as a way to care for the land
        c.   The villages were closely knit and based on mutual cooperation
    2.   Sustained agriculture promoted prosperity, population growth, and the rise of cities
    3.   Frequent warfare led to the absorption of weak and small states by larger ones
    4.   A caste system emerged first in order to separate Aryan from non-Aryan
        a.   A *caste* is a hereditary class of social equals
        b.   By about 500 B.C. the four main groups were the priests, warriors, peasants and serfs, and outcastes
        c.   The outcastes, or untouchables, were those who entered society later or those who had been expelled from their caste
        d.   Slavery became an economic and social institution
  C. Early Indian Religion
    1.   The Aryan gods represented natural phenomena such as fire, war, and dawn
        a.   The *brahmins* presided over ritual and sacrifice
        b.   This religion became sterile and unsatisfying to many
    2.   Through asceticism, religion was reformed, ritual sacrifice was seen as symbolic gesture, and the idea of a "wheel of life" evolved
        a.   *Samsara* is the doctrine of transmigration of souls through rebirth
        b.   *Karma* is the belief that deeds determine the status of one's next life
        c.   Hence, righteous living could bring improvement in the next life
        d.   Escape from the wheel of life was through *atman* and *Brahman*
        e.   This brought high status to the *brahmins*
III. India's spiritual flowering
  A. Hinduism, Jainism, and Buddhism evolved in the fifth and sixth centuries B.C.
    1.   All three descend from the old Vedic religion, although Jainism and Buddhism were rejections of it and Hinduism
        a.   Buddhism and Jainism began as schools of moral philosophy preoccupied with ethical conduct
        b.   Both originally rejected the existence of gods, but later they recognized gods
  B. Hinduism
    1.   Hinduism is rooted in the caste system and in the idea that the *Vedas* are sacred
    2.   It is a diverse religion that is tolerant and welcomes new doctrines and beliefs
    3.   Hinduism is a guide to life, the goal of which is to reach *Brahman* through four steps

4. *Dharma* is the moral law all Hindus must observe
5. Eventually Hinduism began to emphasize that certain gods were a manifestation of Brahman
6. The beloved hymn the *Bhagavad Gita* is a guide to how to live in the world and honor *dharma*
7. In it Arjuna, the human hero, meets Krishna, the god, who teaches Arjuna the relationship between human reality and the eternal spirit

C. Jainism
1. Its founder, Mahavira, taught that the doctrine of *karma* extended to all animate and inanimate objects
2. Eternal happiness is achieved when the soul rids itself of all matter
3. Thus it was necessary for one to adopt a life of aceticism and to avoid evil
4. Nonviolence became a cardinal principle of Jainism

D. Siddhartha Gautama and Buddhism
1. Siddhartha Gautama — the Buddha — found universal enlightenment through meditation
   a. He abandoned Hinduism
   b. He advocated the Four Noble Truths — that pain, suffering, frustration, and anxiety are inescapable parts of human life
   c. They are caused by human weakness — over which people can triumph by adopting the Eightfold Path
2. The Eightfold Path
   a. First one needs to clearly understand the pain and misery of one's life
   b. Next, freedom from pain can come through right conduct and speech, and through love and compassion
   c. A "right livelihood" is also necessary, as is "right endeavor"
   d. "Right awareness" and "right contemplation" complete the path
   e. With the eighth step, one achieves *nirvana* — a state of happiness and release from effects of *karma*
3. Buddhism taught that everything changes with time
   a. It rejected the Hindu doctrine of transmigration
   b. It redefined the Hindu idea of rebirth
   c. It placed little emphasis on gods, although it stressed the idea of an infinite and immortal divine power
   d. The success of Buddhism was due to its popular appeal
   e. The Sangha was an order of Buddhist monks
4. After Buddha's death, Buddhism split into two branches
   a. The Theraveda branch claimed to be pure and more strict and was popular in southeastern Asia
   b. The Mahayana branch, which stressed that other Buddhas may yet come, dominated in China, Japan, Korea, and Vietnam

      c. Mahayana Buddhism created a pantheon of Buddhas and *bodhisattvas*

IV. India and the West, ca 513–298 B.C.
- A. Western India (the Indus valley) was conquered by Persia in the sixth century B.C.
  1. This conquest by Darius I did not extend far beyond the Indus river
  2. It introduced India to the ways of other cultures
     - a. The use of coined money was adopted
     - b. The Aramaic language was adapted to fit Indian needs
     - c. India participated in trade with the West
     - d. Rough stone architecture was begun, as in Taxila
- B. Alexander the Great invaded the Indus valley in 326 B.C.
  1. He found Taxila to be a great city
  2. The invaders left behind many Greek settlements as well as a political power vacuum — to be filled by Chandragupta

V. The Mauryan Empire (ca 322–232 B.C.)
- A. Chandragupta united much of India into the great Mauryan empire
  1. Taking advantage of the vacuum left by Alexander, he defeated his enemies
  2. The Seleucid monarchy surrendered its eastern provinces to Chandragupta
  3. He divided India into provinces
     - a. Each province was assigned a governor, and agents would inspect the province periodically
     - b. A complex bureaucracy was established, as was an army
     - c. He took elaborate precautions against intrigue

VI. The reign of Ashoka (ca 269–232 B.C.)
- A. The prince Ashoka became king of India and extended the borders of this Mauryan empire
  1. In the early years of his reign, he was an efficient and content king
  2. After the savage campaign in Kalinga, he looked for a new meaning in life and turned to Buddhism
- B. He adopted a highly paternalistic policy and view toward his people — as seen in his building of shrines, roads, and resting places
- C. Under Ashoka India enjoyed peace, prosperity, and humane rule

VII. India and its invaders, 250 B.C. to A.D. 200
- A. After Ashoka's reign India was repeatedly invaded and became highly fragmented — although Indian civilization eventually triumphed
- B. The most important development during this era was the spread of Buddhism to China

REVIEW QUESTIONS

Q-1.   Describe India's geography by discussing its three geographical areas.

Q-2.   What have archaeologists been able to tell us about the economic, civil, and religious arrangements of the Indus valley cities of Mohenjo-daro and Harappa?

Q-3.   Describe the political and social organization of Aryan-Indian society.

Q-4.   Describe the evolution of Aryan-Indian religion from its rigid ritualist beginnings to the idea of the "wheel of life."

Q-5.   Strictly speaking, the Jains could adhere to their beliefs only by starving to death. Explain.

Q-6.   What are the principal beliefs of Hinduism? Is it an ethical philosophy or a religion?

Q-7.   What effects did contact with Persia and Alexander the Great have on India?

Q-8.   How and why was Chandragupta able to unite much of India? Describe the political scene he stepped into and the tactics he employed in his successful reign.

Q-9.   What are the principal beliefs within Buddhism? Describe the evolution and spread of Buddhism after Siddhartha Gautama's death.

Q-10.   Describe the accomplishments of King Ashoka of India.

Q-11.   What contributions did the Kushans make to Indian and world history? In what way were they similar to the Parthians of Iran?

STUDY-REVIEW EXERCISES

Define the following key concepts and terms.

the wheel of life

dharma

the *caste* system

Aryan/non-Aryan

Mauryan empire

Eightfold Path

Nirvana

Identify each of the following and give its significance.

Deccan plateau

Mohenjo-daro and Harappa

Khyber Pass

raja chief - head of Aryan tribe

Aryans Entered India from NW - Indo/Europeans

brahmins priests

outcastes those who didn't have social place

atman Brahman eternal truth and and reality

Vedas

Bhagavad Gita

Mahavira

Taxila

Chandragupta

Upanishads

Moksha release from wheel of life

Great Bath

Explain each of the following by describing its origins and citing its principal ideas.

Jainism animals, plants, objects, humans have living
souls - founded by Vardhamana Mahavira

Hinduism _____

Test *your understanding of the chapter by answering the following questions.*

1. The Indo-European people who entered from the northwest and settled in India at about the time the Indus civilization fell are known as the

   __Aryans__

2. The disappearance of the Indus cities Mohenjo-daro and Harappa can be attributed to (a) mass starvation, (b) murder by the invading Aryan peoples,

   (c) climate changes, (d) unknown causes. _____

3. The socially impure people in Indian society — those who had lost their status or entered society after its divisions had been set — were known as

   __outcastes__.

4. The man who stepped into the power vacuum left by Alexander's exit from India, and who united much of India into the Mauryan empire, was

   __Chandragupta__

5. In Buddhist teachings, *nirvana* means __true happiness__.

6. Ancient India included not only the modern nation of India but also, in whole

   or in part, the nations of __Pakistan   Afghanistan__.

7. India's two great river valleys are the __Ganges__

   and the__Indus__.

8. The founder of the religious philosophy of Buddhism was

   __Siddartha Gautma__.

9. The Buddhist program designed to move one from pain and misery to *nirvana*

   is known as the __Eightfold__ Path.

10. Buddhism had its origins in (a) India, (b) China. _____

11. The Indian king who extended the Mauryan empire while paying great attention

    to the welfare of his people was __Ashoka__.

MULTIPLE-CHOICE QUESTIONS

1. The ancient Indus civilization developed writing
    a. similar to hieroglyphics.
    b. related to Chinese pictographs.
    c. that remains undeciphered today.
    d. that was phonetic in character.

2. The Indus civilization declined because of
    a. disease epidemics.
    b. changes in climate.
    c. violent civil unrest.
    d. reasons that are still unknown.

3. The *Rigveda* is
    a. an epic poem of early India.
    b. the oldest of the Hindu scriptures.
    c. one of the Aryan gods.
    d. both a and b.

4. The brahmins were the
    a. wealthy class.
    b. priest class.
    c. warrior elite.
    d. slaves.

5. In India, the untouchables were
    a. foreigners.
    b. heretics.
    c. the lowest caste.
    d. a blanket term for lepers, criminals, and other pariahs.

6. The ancient Indus civilization extended over an area
    a. in modern Bangladesh.
    b. larger than present-day Pakistan.
    c. covering all of India.
    d. that is now the Punjab.

7. Throughout history, the most important unit of Indian society has been the
    a. clan.
    b. city.
    c. village.
    d. kingdom.

8. Aryan religion became unsatisfying to many because it
   a. was sterile and ritualistic.
   b. emphasized sin and punishment.
   c. had no personal god.
   d. promised no afterlife.

9. The Khyber Pass is important to Indian history because
   a. Buddhism entered India through it.
   b. India's first civilization grew up around it.
   c. numerous peoples have entered India through it.
   d. most Indian trade has passed through it.

10. The houses built by the Indus civilization were strikingly modern in respect to
    a. architecture.
    b. lighting.
    c. plumbing.
    d. ventilation.

11. The Eightfold Path is
    a. the place caravan routes converged in Mesopotamia.
    b. Buddha's code of conduct.
    c. the Hindu version of the Ten Commandments.
    d. a series of garden paths in Emperor Ch'in's palace.

12. Siddhartha Gautama was called *Buddha*, which
    a. was his surname.
    b. means "Enlightened One."
    c. means "Noble Soul."
    d. both b and c.

13. Buddha's Four Noble Truths teach that
    a. pain and suffering in human life stem from greed and selfishness.
    b. it is possible to understand human frailties and to triumph over them.
    c. both a and b.
    d. none of the above.

14. Ashoka took up Buddhism as a result of his
    a. grief over the death of his wife.
    b. friendship with a Buddhist monk.
    c. remorse over the carnage of a military campaign.
    d. dissatisfaction with Hindu teachings.

15. Ashoka's government could best be described as
    a. authoritarian.
    b. paternalistic.
    c. bureaucratic.
    d. centralized.

16. In the Hindu religion, *karma* is the
    a. state of moral perfection.
    b. sum of one's good and bad deeds.
    c. concept of reincarnation.
    d. path to moral perfection.

17. In Hindu religion, *dharma* is
    a. belief in reincarnation.
    b. a complex moral law.
    c. the basis for the caste system.
    d. the state of spiritual perfection.

18. Hinduism readily accepts new sects, doctrines, and beliefs because it
    a. holds that passing judgment is immoral.
    b. acknowledges varied ways to worship the same principle.
    c. considers tolerance a high virtue.
    d. both a and c.

19. The Persian conquest affected India in that it
    a. depressed economic growth.
    b. brought a large Persian population into India.
    c. isolated India from world affairs.
    d. introduced many new ideas into India.

20. The Indians adopted the use of coined money from the
    a. Aryans.
    b. Persians.
    c. Chinese.
    d. Greeks.

21. The Indian hymnbooks that not only contain historical information but also provide much of the basis for Hinduism and Jainism are the
    a. guidebooks.
    b. *atman* texts.
    c. *Vedas.*
    d. *pater familias.*

22. Which of the following ideas is part of the beliefs of Jainism?
    a. Karma is limited to only *brahmins*.
    b. The soul must strive to include all matter.
    c. A life of nonviolence is advocated.
    d. The doctrine of rebirth is totally rejected.

23. The founder of Jainism was
    a. Vardhamana Mahavira.
    b. Bhagavad Gita.
    c. Siddhartha Gautama.
    d. Brahman.

24. In Hinduism, Brahman is the
    a. city of pilgrimmage.
    b. sacred text.
    c. moral law.
    d. supreme principle of life.

25. What city in the northern Indus valley became important during the period of Persian control?
    a. Taxila
    b. Harappa
    c. Mohenjo-daro
    d. Calcutta

26. The Indian ruler who embraced and tried to spread Buddhism was
    a. Chandragupta.
    b. Gautama.
    c. Ashoka.
    d. Kautilya.

27. Slavery in ancient Indian society can best be described as
    a. nonexistent.
    b. similar to slavery in ancient Mesopotamia.
    c. limited to household tasks.
    d. flourishing but never mentioned in Indian law.

28. The urban culture of the Indus civilization was centered around
    a. vast armies.
    b. vital trade routes.
    c. large-scale agriculture.
    d. the great Himalayan mountains.

GEOGRAPHY

1. On the outline map of India, mark the (a) early Indus valley civilization, including Harappa and Mohenjo-daro, and (b) Himalayan mountains, Deccan plateau, Vindhya mountains, and Ganges River.
2. In the space below, explain how each of the following affected early Indian life:

Himalayas

Indian Ocean

Khyber Pass

Ganges River

Indus River

3. On the outline map show the area covered by the Mauryan empire under Ashoka. Why was Ashoka important for the development of local travel within India? What was the result of contact between India and China?

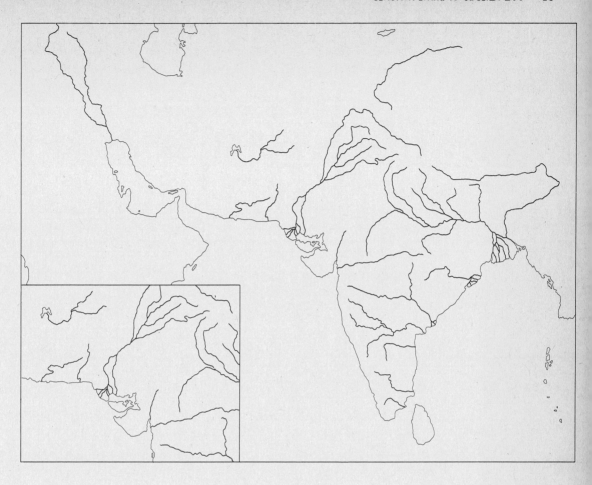

UNDERSTANDING HISTORY THROUGH READING AND THE ARTS

India's history began with the Indus civilization, but it was with the Aryan invasion that the dominant Hinduism evolved. Also, it was here that a functional stratification of Aryan tribal society led to the classic Indian caste system. For the major documents on these developments see W. T. de Bary, ed., *Sources of Indian Tradition* (1958), and D. C. Kosambi, *Ancient India: A History of Its Culture and Civilization* (1965).

PROBLEMS FOR FURTHER INVESTIGATION

Indian thought tends to be more religious than worldly, whereas the reverse is true for China. How can this difference be explained? Begin your investigation with several basic books on Eastern thought and religion, such as *Buddhism, Its History and Literature* (1923) by T. W. Davids, and *Hinduism and Buddhism* (1922) by H. M. Eliot.

CHAPTER 4

THE RISE AND GROWTH OF CHINA TO A.D. 200

CHAPTER OBJECTIVES

After reading and studying this chapter you should be able to answer the following questions:

Q-1.   How did the early Chinese people interact with the geographical features of climate, soil, and land?
Q-2.   How were their responses both similar to and different from those of ancient Near Eastern and Indian peoples?
Q-3.   How did the Chinese shape their society?

CHAPTER SYNOPSIS

China's history is rooted in the fertile land of the Yangtze and Yellow river valleys, which made China's oldest ruling dynasty, the Shang, rich and powerful. During this era important steps were taken in architecture and bronze work, and the written Chinese language began. When the Chou overturned the Shang dynasty, it built on established Shang culture. Its discovery of iron manufacture changed warfare and agriculture, and its low military camps became great walled cities. On the basis of the new concept of the "Mandate of Heaven," the Chou kings instituted a system of political dependencies — first a centralized form with the Chou kings in control, and then a decentralized form as new border states successfully challenged the interior. This was important for China's history because, out of the movement of the Chou aristocracy from the interior to the border states, came China's civil service.

The Chou period was China's most important intellectual age. Interestingly, this intellectual exploration focused not on religious mysticism or aceticism but

47

largely on the discovery of universal rules for human conduct. Confucianism, an attempt to follow the universal laws of conduct and order, stressed family loyalty and gentlemanly virtue and has been important in the evolution of the Chinese concept of civil service. Taoism is a philosophy based on the Way of Nature, whereas Legalism stressed the authoritarian state.

When the Ch'in leader deposed the last Chou king in China in 256 B.C. he ushered in a new age of empire during which China flourished economically, culturally, and socially. The Ch'in rulers not only extended the borders of China as far south as northern Vietnam, but they also embarked on a rigorous and sometimes ruthless program of centralization that touched the lives of nearly all Chinese. The big losers were the old feudal landlords who were torn from their states, while the peasants were given greater land rights — although they suffered under heavy taxation. Discontent, particularly among the peasants, led to the overthrow of the disliked Ch'in. The new Han dynasty followed along the Ch'in path, but it practiced less oppression. The Hun threat from the north was met with the building of the Great Wall; and trade followed conquest in the southeast and south. Confucianism made a comeback — but this time as an important political theory based on the concept of the "Mandate of Heaven." Scholarship flourished in other areas as well, particularly in history, which came to reflect the Chinese belief in civilization as cyclical. Daily life in the Han era reflects the important and honorable place agriculture occupied in Chinese life. Here important advances were made in agricultural technology. The chapter points to the variety of urban life: The rich were able to live in great style, while the poor often suffered outrage and violence with no hope of justice or retribution. It is in this Han era that we see important economic change — all the way from the invention of paper to the building of canals. As a result, China stood as a major emporium of luxury goods for the rest of the world for many centuries to come.

CHAPTER OUTLINE

   I.   China, the land and its challenge
      A. The geography of China
         1. Geography has isolated China from the west and north
            a. To the west, between India and China, were the Himalayas and Pamirs
            b. To the north were the Gobi desert and the Monogolian plateau, and to the south was vast jungle
            c. Its link to the civilization of the West was through the northwest corridor through Central Asia and past India
         2. Chinese society developed along two immense river basins: the Yellow and Yangtze

     a.   In the north, the Yellow River provides loess — fertile land — but it can also bring great flooding

     b.   The Yellow River had to be tamed with dikes in order to provide land for wheat and millet farming

     c.   The Yangtze valley in the south is used for rice farming

     d.   Making up the southern border of China is the Hsi River

II.   The Shang dynasty, ca 1523–1027 B.C.

   A. The Shang dynasty rose to power in northern China

     1. The king, with the aristocrats and bureaucrats, directed the work and life of the people

     2. Warfare was a constant feature of Shang life

     3. Most common people worked as serfs or slaves in agriculture

     4. Common homes were similar to Neolithic pit homes

     5. Other commoners worked as craftsmen and some did important work in bronze

   B. The king and nobility lived in great style

     1. Their houses built on huge platforms of pounded earth set a pattern for Chinese architecture

     2. They enjoyed magnificent bronze work

     3. After death, people of royal blood were expected to intercede with the gods — a custom that is the forerunner of ancestor worship

   C. Origins of Chinese writing

     1. Writing emerged out of the Shang religion

     2. Thousands of signs — with phonetic values — were created

     3. A simplified and standardized script was important in unifying the Chinese

     4. The Koreans and the Japanese built their written language on Chinese writing

III. The triumph of the Chou dynasty (ca 1027–221 B.C.)

   A. The rule of the Chou

     1. The Chou, an agricultural people of the Wei basin, overturned the Shang dynasty in the eleventh century B.C.

       a.   They made no break with Shang culture

       b.   They originated the political concept of the "Mandate of Heaven"

       c.   To effectively rule all China, a second capital was built at Loyang on the northern plain

     2. The Chou kings delegated power by way of a Chinese form of feudalism

       a.   At first the kings dominated their political dependencies

       b.   Then new border states emerged and became independent kingdoms and defeated the king in 771 B.C.

      c.   This caused a decline in the power of the Chou kings, who retreated to their eastern capital of Loyang

      d.   During the Era of the Warring States the Chou dynasty fell and in 221 B.C. the ruler of Ch'in conquered all other states

B. Social change and cultural advancement in the Chou period

    1.   Impoverished aristocrats of the interior states gravitated to the provinces, where they served as officials; this was the beginning of China's civil service

    2.   Armed camps grew into great walled cities

    3.   The discovery of the use of iron, metalworking, and the invention of the horse harness changed agriculture and warfare

    4.   Metal technology resulted in improvement in agricultural technology

IV. The birth of Chinese philosophy

A. Confucianism

    1.   Confucius, a teacher from a poor but aristocratic family, did not write anything or achieve a high political position

       a.   He was largely interested in how to achieve orderly and stable human relationships

       b.   His sayings were collected in a book called the *Analects*

       c.   He believed that there is a universal law that all humans should follow

    2.   Confucius was interested in human conduct

       a.   The family, with male and aged members superior, was considered the basic unit of society

       b.   A Confucian gentleman was a man of integrity, education, and culture — all to be reached through education and self-discipline

    3.   Confucianism was a vital ingredient in the evolution of an effective civil service

       a.   It offered advice on how to create a well-ordered, sound, and powerful state

       b.   It emphasized nonviolence

B. Taoism

    1.   The Taoists attribute their ideas to the work of Lao-tzu and to the book *Tao Te Ching (Book of the Way and Its Power)*

    2.   Taoism argues that peace and order can come only from following Tao, the "Way of Nature"

    3.   This means that happiness comes only when one abandons the world and reverts to nature

    4.   Taoism held that the best government is one that does little and establishes few laws

    5.   The people should be treated well but left uneducated

    6.   Taoism became a philosophy of consolation for a chosen few

C. Legalism
    1. Legalism was actually a number of distinct but related schools of practical thought
    2. Among its founders were the Han Fei-tzu and Li Ssu, both of whom were influenced by Confucianism and Taoism
    3. They believed that human nature is evil and that the ideal state was an authoritarian state in which the people are well treated but uneducated and barred from dissent
    4. Legalism was too narrow to compete with Confucianism and Taoism
V. China, the age of empire
    A. The Ch'in dynasty unified China
        1. The first emperor brought political unity to China
            a. The emperor and his adviser worked to build a highly centralized state
            b. The nobility were forced to move to the capital and attend court
            c. Their estates were reorganized into large provinces
        2. Other Ch'in innovations contributed to making China highly centralized
            a. The emperor controlled the provinces through governors and other officials
            b. A population census led to great government planning and control
            c. Under the first emperor the Chinese written script was standardized, as were weights, measures, and coinage
            d. Standardization of the axle length of carts allowed for improved transportation
        3. Improvements were made in agriculture and industry
            a. Peasant land rights were expanded
            b. Irrigation and tools increased agricultural production
            c. The textile industry was promoted
            d. Increased trade led to the growth of cities
    B. Foreign danger and internal unrest
        1. The first emperor ordered the building of the Great Wall
            a. It was to protect China from the Huns in the north
            b. The older, smaller walls were joined to stretch 3,000 miles from the sea inland
        2. The Ch'ins were unpopular rulers
            a. They attacked Confucianism and its scholars
            b. They imposed heavy taxes and forced labor on the peasants
            c. Massive revolts occurred when the first emperor died
            d. A new dynasty, the Han, was established in 202 B.C. by Liu Pang
    C. The glory of the Han dynasty, 206 B.C.–A.D. 220
        1. Liu Pang retained the main features of Ch'in rule, although political centralization was relaxed
            a. Emperor Han Wu Ti drove the Huns farther north and opened relations with India

    b.   Western Korea was added to the empire as was Canton, the south-eastern coast, and northern Vietnam

  2. Han conquests brought closer contact with distant peoples

    a.   In the south, China and Vietnam exchanged culture and goods

    b.   Further south, in Funan, Indian culture prevailed, while new trade routes were opened between China, Vietnam, and Burma

    c.   Under the Han rule China enjoyed unparalleled peace and prosperity

D. Han Confucianism and intellectual revolt

  1. During the Han era, a revived Confucianism applied the "Mandate of Heaven" theory to dynasties

    a.   The emperor needed to watch for signs of heavenly displeasure

    b.   He was to protect China, maintain order, and not overly interfere in the lives of the people

    c.   Violation of these duties would bring a withdrawal of the Mandate

    d.   Confucianism saw history as cyclical, not progressive

  2. Chinese history, then, became the study of dynasties

    a.   Ssu-ma-ch'ien was a path-breaking historian who wrote *Records of the Grand Historian*

    b.   His work was carried on by the Pan family

  3. Great advances were made in medicine by Ching Chi and in astronomy by Chang Heng

E. Daily life during the Han dynasty

  1. The peasant farmer was the backbone of Chinese society

    a.   Peasant households were small, and all members worked in the fields

    b.   Peasants were often beset with plague, famine, flood, drought, and harsh governments

    c.   In the north the primary crops were millet, barley, and wheat; in the south the primary crop was rice.

    d.   Hemp, bamboo, and fruit and mulberry trees supplemented peasant income

    e.   Tea and sugar were luxury items grown in the south

  2. The Han minister Chao Kuo introduced a new planting system

  3. Because farming was "intensive," few work animals existed

  4. A new plow, a hammer system for milling, and irrigation pumping are examples of China's new agricultural tools

  5. The agricultural year was well ordered — with February as the beginning of the New Year

  6. City life varied greatly

    a.   The rich lived in splendid houses, had costly clothing, and ate well

b. The rich enjoyed concerts while commoners flocked to puppet and acrobatic shows

c. Gambling was popular; crime was common

7. Silk and lacquered goods were in demand

8. Paper was invented during the Han period

9. Han workmen excelled in iron metalworking, and bronze remained popular for a host of goods

10. Merchants were considered lowly and dishonorable and, with the marketplace, came to be regulated by the state

11. Canals were built to provide north-south transport of goods

F. The fall of Han China

1. The Han empire was weakened by war and the emperor's spending

    a. The peasants suffered as landlords shifted the tax burden to them

2. The emperor Wang Mang tried to reform society, but he failed

3. Later, the Han emperors found themselves facing the same problems

4. This, along with peasant uprisings, caused revolts and victory for the great landlords

5. During the following era of the Three Kingdoms (A.D. 221–280) further disorder and barbarism occurred

6. China was left open to invasion by Mongolian nomads

    a. In the fifth century, the Toba assumed control of northern China

    b. They quickly adopted the Chinese political system, culture, religion, and outlook

REVIEW QUESTIONS

Q-1.   What sort of political and social structure was created by the Shang rulers?

Q-2.   "Writing emerged out of Shang religion." Explain.

Q-3.   What is the basic political principle behind the idea of the "Mandate of Heaven"?

Q-4.   Describe the Chou feudal system. Explain how it evolved over time to become highly decentralized.

Q-5.   What were the major features of social change and cultural advancement in the Chou period?

Q-6.   What is the basis of Confucianism? Is it a "religion" in the sense of devoting attention to an afterlife and god?

Q-7.   Compare and contrast Taoism and Legalism. What are the central ideas of each?

Q-8.   What were the innovations and tactics used by the Ch'in dynasty to unify China?

Q-9.   How did the Ch'in emperors treat the nobility of China? Why?

Q-10.   Did the Ch'ins bring benefits or hardship to the Chinese people?

Q-11.   What was the purpose behind the construction of China's Great Wall? Did the wall fulfill its intended purpose?

Q-12.   What were the economic and intellectual accomplishments of the Han dynasty?

Q-13.   Describe Chinese peasant life during the Han dynasty in terms of family and work.

Q-14.   Discuss the economy of Han China. What were its essential features in terms of resources, agricultural and industrial products, and trade?

Q-15.   Was the fall of Han China due to internal or external factors? Explain.

Q-16.   How did Chou political events shape and influence Chinese society in the border states?

STUDY-REVIEW EXERCISES

Define the following concepts and terms.

Mandate of Heaven

Legalism

Confucianism

Taoism

Identify each of the following and give its significance.

Emperor Han Wu Ti

Ssu-ma-ch'ien

Three Kingdoms era

Mahayana Buddhism

Mithridates

General Crassus

Pan Chao

Explain who the following people were and give their significance.

Toba

Ch'in

Han

Describe each of the following and give its <u>economic</u> significance.

Stone Tower

Wu Ti's conquest of northern Vietnam

Chao Kuo innovations

Ts'ai Lun

Chinese horse-collar

China's east-west canal system

Test your understanding of the chapter by answering the following questions.

1. Most scholars agree that ancient Chinese culture *was/was not* largely a product of massive foreign invasion.
2. The origins of writing in China appear to be deeply rooted in the religion of

   the ___Shang_____ dynasty.
3. As opposed to the major developments in Indian religion, the Chinese thinkers were most interested in (a) a mystical religion based on divorce from the

   material world or (b) philosophies to deal with human problems. _____
4. The ___Yellow_____ River has been called "China's sorrow" because of the disastrous floods it has caused.
5. The dynasty that gave China its name and marked the beginning of its imperial

   age was the_____Han_____ dynasty.

6. The Confucian idea that irresponsibility on the part of the emperor brings about the withdrawal of heavenly support is known as the

   _____ Mandate of Heaven _____.

7. The author-historian of the path-breaking *Records of the Grand Historian* was

   _____ Ssuma chaien _____.

8. China's first emperor stripped the _____ noble _____ class of its power.

9. Ts'ai Lun worked the fiber of rags, hemp, and bark into _paper_.

10. The first emperor of China ordered construction of what is probably mankind's

    most immense construction project, the _Great wall_.

MULTIPLE-CHOICE QUESTIONS

1. The writing used in Shang China
   a. was wholly pictographic.
   b. was based on an alphabet.
   c. contained about 100 symbols.
   d. none of the above.

2. Legalist philosophy taught that
   a. humans are basically good.
   b. humans are basically evil.
   c. human behavior follows unchanging laws.
   d. the rule of law must be respected.

3. Confucius believed
   a. in social equality.
   b. in an exclusive, hereditary aristocracy.
   c. that gentlemen could be self-made.
   d. none of the above.

4. The selection of the Chinese civil service was based on
   a. wealth.
   b. social class.
   c. merit.
   d. both a and b

5. Hundreds of years before the Europeans did, Chou metalsmiths used
    a. bronze.
    b. steel.
    c. cast iron.
    d. tin.

6. It may be generally said of the Chinese philosophies that they
    a. were obsessed with life after death.
    b. emphasized reincarnation.
    c. were based on mysticism.
    d. shared a secular outlook.

7. Taoist philosophy was embraced by the
    a. priesthood.
    b. masses.
    c. ruling class.
    d. merchant class.

8. The Ch'in rulers were unpopular because they
    a. imposed an alien culture on the Chinese.
    b. took over the feudal estates.
    c. imposed heavy taxes and forced labor on the Chinese.
    d. claimed a large share of each rice crop.

9. Confucian thought survived Ch'in efforts to eradicate it because
    a. scholars fled to India.
    b. it was taught under other names.
    c. devoted scholars had hidden or memorized their books.
    d. it was taught to "illiterates."

10. More is known about the ancient Chinese elite than the common people
    because
    a. only the elite were buried in elaborate tombs.
    b. travelers from Europe wrote only of the wealthy.
    c. books written by the commoners were burned by the Ch'in.
    d. Chinese writers wrote primarily about the elite.

11. On Chinese farms, most brute labor such as plowing was performed by
    a. cattle.
    b. horses.
    c. farmers.
    d. slaves.

12. The Confucian "Mandate of Heaven" theory views history as
    a. a progressive movement forward.
    b. a repetition of similar events.
    c. a "roller coaster" of progression and regression.
    d. predetermined by heaven.

13. As a result of the Toba barbarians' conquest of China,
    a. Toba culture was forced on the defeated Chinese.
    b. the Toba adopted many Chinese customs.
    c. ancient Chinese culture was largely lost.
    d. none of the above.

14. Which of the following was a religious practice in Shang China?
    a. Polygamy
    b. Human sacrifice
    c. Meditation
    d. Fasting

15. In Chou times, the Chinese state was
    a. highly centralized.
    b. feudal in nature.
    c. an absolute monarchy.
    d. a loose confederation.

16. A novel use of writing in Chou China was in
    a. maintaining tax records.
    b. keeping census data.
    c. recording history.
    d. recording rights and obligations of feudal lords.

17. As a result of the decline of the Chou dynasty, many of the impoverished aristocrats of interior China
    a. took over the dynasty.
    b. disappeared.
    c. became peasant farmers.
    d. moved to the border states.

18. The prevailing attitude toward the merchant class in Han China was that
    a. they were necessary but lowly.
    b. state regulation was unnecessary.
    c. they were cast out of society.
    d. they were held in high esteem, especially by the upper classes.

19. The Yangtze River differs from the Yellow River in that
    a. irrigated rice agriculture predominates along its shores.
    b. it is impossible to navigate.
    c. the Chinese were unable to tame it.
    d. its climate is dry and cold.

20. What is the correct chronological order of the following dynasties?
    a. Shang, Chou, Ch'in, Han
    b. Han, Ch'in, Shang, Chou
    c. Chou, Shang, Han, Ch'in
    d. Ch'in, Han, Chou, Shang

21. The greatest advancement in agriculture during the Chou Dynasty was the
    a. use of Neolithic farming methods.
    b. use of metal technology.
    c. discovery of crop rotation systems.
    d. improvement of irrigation systems.

22. Which school of thought has had the most profound impact on China?
    a. Buddhism
    b. Taoism
    c. Confucianism
    d. Legalism

23. According to Confucius, the basic unit of society is the
    a. individual.
    b. family.
    c. village.
    d. state.

24. Which of the following statements about Legalism is true?
    a. It encouraged the study of history and philosophy.
    b. It embraced the political ideas of Confucius.
    c. It was ruthless in its approach to government.
    d. It believed that man's nature is good.

25. During the Ch'in dynasty, communication was improved by the
    a. construction of inland canals.
    b. employment of swift messengers.
    c. standardization of writing, coinage, weight, and measures.
    d. paving of roads.

26. The backbone of Han society was the
    a. urban nobility.
    b. bureaucracy.
    c. emperor.
    d. peasant farmer.

27. The favored metal of the nobility in the Shang era was
    a. bronze.
    b. iron.
    c. tin.
    d. manganese.

28. An unparalleled time of peace and prosperity occurred during
    a. Shang rule.
    b. Chin rule.
    c. Han rule.
    d. Chou rule.

GEOGRAPHY

1. On the outline map of China, sketch in (a) the geographical features that make up China's western, northern, and southern boundaries and (b) the two great river basins — the Yellow and the Yangtze.
2. What effect might these geographical features have had on Chinese politics and economic life?

3. Explain how and why power in China flowed from the interior to the border regions during the Chou dynasty.

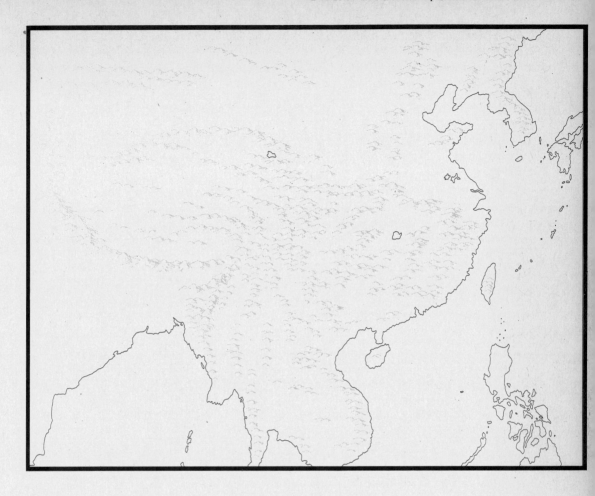

UNDERSTANDING HISTORY THROUGH READING AND THE ARTS

China's geographical isolation and the lineage-based policy (the Chou feudalism) set the foundations for the development of the unique Chinese culture. To read further on this subject of China's geography and culture, begin with two books by K. C. Chang, *The Archaeology of Ancient China* (1986) and *Art, Myth and Political Authority in Ancient China* (1983).

What did the Han artists produce, what technical factors influenced them, and what does their work tell us about life in Han China? These and other questions are answered in a book by Wilma Fairbank, *Adventures in Retrieval: Han Murals and Shang Bronze Medals* (1972). The book centers on Han art-relief work on huge stone slabs. A wider look at Han cities, architecture, agriculture, and crafts is *Han Civilization* (1982) by Wang Zhongshu.

PROBLEMS FOR FURTHER INVESTIGATION

In our times different beliefs often divide the peoples of the world. It is interesting and challenging to find out how and why these differences emerged and how people became parochial under cultural tradition. With regard to belief, we should read Eastern and Western religions simultaneously and comparatively. For China the following are recommended: Max Weber, *The Religion of China: Confucianism and Taoism*, trans. by H. Gerth (1951); D. Howard Smith, *Chinese Religions* (1968); and Benjamin Schwartz, *The World of Thought in Ancient China* (1985).

One way to gain fuller insight into the civilization of ancient China is to study its historians. *History of the Former Times* (A.D. 32–92), by Pan Ku, is one of the most renowned and influential of all Chinese historical works. A number of Pan Ku's 100 chapters have been reprinted as biographical sketches of a variety of people from Han society in *Courtier and Commoner in Ancient China* (1974), edited and translated by T. B. Watson. Further insight into the way the Chinese wrote their history can be found in W. G. Beasley and G. Pulleyblauh, *Historians of China and Japan* (1961).

CHAPTER 5

THE LEGACY OF GREECE

CHAPTER OBJECTIVES

After reading and studying this chapter you should be able to answer the following questions:

Q-1.   What geographical factors helped to mold the Greek city-state?
Q-2.   How and why did the Greeks develop different political forms, such as tyranny and democracy?
Q-3.   What did the Greek intellectual triumph entail?
Q-4.   How and why did the Greek experiment fail?

CHAPTER SYNOPSIS

Ancient Greece made an invaluable contribution to human progress and the development of Western civilization. Greek society explored a remarkable range of the problems that beset men and women of all ages: the nature of God and the universe, the dimensions of human sexuality, the challenges of war and imperialism, the proper relationship between the individual and the state. The Greeks were also great thinkers and actors. They have become an example of both human excellence and human frailty, for the Greeks eventually destroyed themselves through war and imperialism. An important question this chapter seeks to answer is why the Greek experiment failed.

The chapter stresses the importance of geographical isolation and proximity to the sea in the political and economic development of the city-state, or polis. It also describes how Greek (Hellenic) religion, art, and life were intimately interwoven. Although believed to be immortal, the Greek gods were attributed human qualities. In honoring their gods the Greeks honored the human spirit and sought human excellence.

For the Greeks, the search for truth and meaning in life was pursued not only through mythology and religious experience but through rational philosophy — by great thinkers such as Socrates, Plato, and Aristotle — and the arts as well. The plays of the great dramatists Aeschylus, Sophocles, and Euripides have led generations of people to examine life's basic conflicts. The Greeks saw drama, comedy, sculpture, and philosophy as ways to relate to their gods and discover the truth about life. Bisexuality and homosexuality were taken for granted in Greek society.

The reasons for Greek aggression in the Aegean world are explored, as are the reasons for the war between the two Greek superpowers, Sparta and Athens. These two states represented opposing political systems and different philosophies of life. Daily life in Athens included sophisticated art and great literature, but the economic system was simple and based on slavery to a large extent. Although it was war that saved Greece (and the West) from the oriental monarchy of the Persians, it was also war *within* Greece — especially among Sparta, Athens, and Thebes — that destroyed the freedom of the Greeks and brought on their conquest by the ambitious Philip II of Macedonia.

STUDY OUTLINE

I. Hellas: the land
    A. The mountains both inspired the Greeks and isolated them from one another, hindering unity
    B. Good harbors encouraged interest in Asia Minor and Egypt
II. The Minoans and Mycenaeans (ca 1650–1100 B.C.)
    A. The Greeks had established themselves in Greece by ca 1650 B.C.
        1. The first and most important Greek-speaking culture was probably at the city of Mycenae
            a. Modern archaeologists Schliemann and Evans began the process of discovering the lost cultures of Mycenae and Crete
        2. In addition, an early Greek culture, called Minoan, grew up on the island of Crete
            a. The head of Crete was a king; its political-economic centers were a series of palaces
            b. The Minoan culture was wealthy and had bronze implements
        3. From their main palace at Cnossus, Mycenaeans built cities at Thebes, Athens, Tiryns, and Pylos
            a. The king and his warrior-aristocracy exercised political and economic control
            b. Scribes kept records, but little is known of the ordinary people except that an extensive division of labor existed
        4. Minoan-Mycenaean contacts turned from peace to war ca 1450 B.C.

        a. The Minoan capital of Cnossus was destroyed for unknown reasons

        b. Thereafter the Mycenaeans grew rich but eventually were destroyed, probably because of internecine war

    5. The fall of the Mycenaean kingdoms ushered in a "Dark Age" of Greece from 1100–800 B.C., but migrations took Greek-speaking people to the Aegean area and Asia Minor

  B. Homer and the heroic past (1100–800 B.C.)

    1. Bronze Age and Dark Age epic poems idealized the past

    2. The *Iliad* and the *Odyssey* contributed to the rebirth of literacy — but these poems are not accurate history

        a. The *Iliad* by Homer points to the flaws in the human character and the whims of the gods

        b. The *Odyssey* is also about human nature and unpredictable gods

III. The polis

  A. The polis, or city-state

    1. Athens, Sparta, and Thebes were the chief city-states

    2. The acropolis was the religious center of the polis, and the agora was its marketplace and political center

    3. The polis was both an agricultural and an urban center

    4. The polis was an intimate community of citizens that tended to exclude outsiders and maintain its independence jealously

    5. There were four types of polis government: monarchy, aristocracy, oligarchy, and democracy

  B. The exclusiveness and individualism of each polis led to constant war and the eventual decline of Greece

IV. The Lyric Age (800–500 B.C.)

  A. Overseas expansion following the breakdown of the Mycenaean world

    1. The expansion of Greeks throughout the Mediterranean was due to land shortage and the desire for adventure

    2. Greek communities extended from the Black Sea to North Africa and into Spain

  B. The growth of Sparta into a powerful polis

    1. Sparta's victory in the Messenian wars extended its boundaries and enslaved the Messenians

    2. The warriors, or *hoplites*, demanded and received political rights

    3. The Lycurgan regime brought about military tyranny in Sparta

    4. The Spartans disdained wealth and luxury and glorified war

  C. Evolution of Athens

    1. Athens moved from an oppressive aristocracy to democracy

        a. Poor peasants demanded legal reforms

        b. Draco's code — Athens' first law — established the fact that the law belonged to all citizens

       c.   Peasants looked to *tyrants* for land reform
    2.   Solon, poet and aristocrat, was elected *archon*
    3.   Solon's reforms benefited the common man
    4.   Pisistratus reduced the power of the aristocracy
    5.   The rule by tyrants was followed by Cleisthenes' reorganization of the state and the creation of democracy
        a.   *Demes* — a local political unit — were the basis of political citizenship
        b.   *Ostracism* was a way to get rid of dangerous politicians
    6.   Athenian democracy proved that a large number of people could run the affairs of state and enjoy equal rights

V.   The Classical Period (500–338 B.C.)
   A. The deadly conflicts — war between the Greeks and the Persians (499–404 B.C.)
     1.   Xerxes invaded Greece in 480 B.C., but the Persian forces were eventually defeated at Salamis and Plataea
     2.   The defeat of the Persians ensured that Greek, not oriental, culture would prevail in the West
     3.   The Athenians established the Delian League to continue the fight against Persia and then turned it into their own empire
     4.   They imposed their will on others — which led to war between Athens and Sparta in 459 B.C.
     5.   The Peloponnesian War between Sparta and her allies and Athens brought about the destruction of Greek civilization
   B. Athenian arts in the age of Pericles
     1.   Pericles turned Athens into the showplace of Greece
     2.   The Athenian acropolis became the center of Greek religion and art
     3.   The art and architecture of the acropolis served to praise both the gods and human life
     4.   To the Greeks, drama aided in the understanding of basic truths about life and society
     5.   Aeschylus, Sophocles, and Euripides were the three greatest dramatists of Athens
   C. Daily life in Periclean Athens
     1.   Material life was simple, and home production of goods was common
     2.   Slavery was common
     3.   Agriculture and small crafts were the major types of labor
     4.   Women were protected by law but did not have equal rights with men
        a.   The *ideal* woman led a secluded life, but courtesans, such as Aspasia, led open and free lives
        b.   Women raised families, engaged in domestic work, and (for poor women) worked much the same as men

     5. Both family life and homosexuality were important parts of Greek life

     6. Religion was important — but the Greeks had no central creed or church

  D. The flowering of philosophy

     1. The Greeks of the Classical Period viewed the universe in terms of natural law, not mythology

     2. Thales, Anaximander, and Heraclitus made important contributions to the sciences

     3. Hippocrates was the founder of modern medicine

     4. The Sophists taught excellence and believed that nothing is absolute

     5. Socrates attempted to discover truth by continuous questioning

     6. Plato's philosophy is based on the idea that reality exists only in the immaterial world

     7. Plato sought to define the perfect society

     8. Aristotle's ideas about the universe lasted for thousands of years

  F. The final act (403–338 B.C.)

     1. With Athens defeated in the Peloponnesian War, Sparta strove for empire

     2. Thebes then destroyed Spartan power

     3. Finally, conquest by Philip of Macedonia meant an end to Greek freedom

REVIEW QUESTIONS

Q-1. Describe the early Greek Minoan and Mycenaean cultures. What caused their eventual destruction?

Q-2. Describe the function of the acropolis and the agora in the Greek polis.

Q-3. How did climate and population affect polis life?

Q-4. Define and explain the function of (a) *monarchy*, (b) *aristocracy*, (c) *oligarchy*, and (d) *democracy*.

Q-5. Describe the relationship between religion and civic duty in the polis.

Q-6. Discuss the nature of Mycenaean culture. What were the repercussions of the fall of the Mycenaean kingdoms?

Q-7. Why is Homer an important source for us in attempting to understand ancient Greek society?

Q-8. Describe the causes of Greek expansion from ca 750 to 550 B.C.

Q-9. How did the Spartans settle the problems of overpopulation and land hunger?

Q-10. Discuss life in Sparta in terms of (a) the military, (b) the family, and (c) economic needs.

Q-11. In what ways did Athenian democracy differ from modern democracy?

Q-12. Describe the accomplishments of Draco, Solon, Pisistratus, and Cleisthenes.

Q-13. What were the causes of the conflict between Athens and Sparta? The outcome? Are there any parallels to the world of today?

Q-14. What was the purpose of the acropolis? What role did architecture and building play in the age of Pericles?

Q-15. What role did drama and comedy play in the life of the polis and the people?

Q-16. What was the position of women in Greek society? Were women completely powerless?

Q-17. What is meant by *Pre-Socratic* thought? Describe the thought of Thales, Anaximander, and Heraclitus.

Q-18. How widespread and important was homosexuality in Greek society? Did the Greeks regard homosexuality as deviant behavior?

Q-19. How would you judge Hippocrates' ideas? What were the strengths and deficiencies of his views on illness?

Q-20. What were the causes and the outcome of the Theban-Spartan conflict?

STUDY-REVIEW EXERCISES

Define the following key concepts and terms.

polis

rationalism in art and architecture

natural laws versus mythological explanation of the universe

deme

Pre-Socratic thought

Sophist relativism

Hippocrates' theory of four humors

empirical knowledge

Identify each of the following and give its significance.

Mycenaeans

Minoans

Cnossus

Messenian wars

helot

Parthenon

Draco's law code

Marathon

Delian League

Peloponnesian War

ostracism

hoplites

Identify the following people and explain their importance.

Homer

Hippocrates

Socrates

Solon

Lysander

Plato

Zeus

Aristotle

Cimon

Sophocles

Xerxes

Pericles

Odysseus

courtesans

Aspasia

Explain the following forms of government.

monarchy

aristocracy

tyranny

Fill in the following blank lines with the letter of the correct answer.

__F__   1. He thought that the basic element of the universe is water.

__D__   2. This Pre-Socratic thinker was the first to use general concepts.

__B__   3. He theorized that the earth is made of invisible, indestructible atoms.

__A__   4. He is known as the father of medicine.

__C__   5. He thought that excellence and happiness could be learned through continuous questioning.

__E__   6. He believed that visible things are merely copies of ideas.

__H__   7. He claimed that the universe revolves and is spherical.

a. Hippocrates
b. Democritus
c. Socrates
d. Anaximander
e. Plato
f. Thales
g. Pericles
h. Aristotle

Test your understanding of the chapter by answering the following questions.

1. The three major Greek city-states were __Athens__,
    _____ __Sparta__ , and __Thebes__ .

2. The Olympian gods (were)/were not seen as having human qualities.

3. The democratic Athenians *did*/*did not* conquer other people and force them to submit to their rule.
4. He defeated a Theban-Athenian army in 338 B.C. to win control of Greece.

   Phillip of Macedonia

5. Sophocles' character Antigone supports the idea of the presence of *divine law*/*the state* in human conduct.
6. The hoplites of Sparta *were*/*were not* successful in gaining political rights.
7. In general, the peasants of Athens *supported*/*opposed* rule by the tyrants.

MULTIPLE-CHOICE QUESTIONS

1. The Delian League was transformed into a means of imperialistic expansion by which of the following city-states?
   a. Sparta
   b. Thebes
   c. Athens
   d. Corinth

2. The polis can be best described as a
   a. community of citizens.
   b. religious community.
   c. community of merchants.
   d. community of warriors.

3. Mycenaean Greece was destroyed by
   a. internecine warfare.
   b. social unrest.
   c. foreign invaders.
   d. famine and plague.

4. The *Iliad* and *Odyssey* were
   a. sacred writings.
   b. collections of laws.
   c. historical records.
   d. epic poems.

5. Solon was an Athenian
   a. tyrant.
   b. reformer.
   c. king.
   d. priest.

6. Greeks at first used the word *tyrant* to denote a
    a. leader who ruled without legal right.
    b. cruel leader who oppressed the poor.
    c. champion of the commercial classes.
    d. dictator who suppressed democracy.

7. Cleisthenes was famous because he
    a. made Athens a major commercial center.
    b. suppressed popular unrest.
    c. was the most successful Athenian tyrant.
    d. created the Athenian democracy.

8. Athens used the Delian League to
    a. colonize the Mediterranean.
    b. fight the Persians.
    c. promote Mediterranean trade.
    d. spread Greek culture.

9. Aristophanes was popular because
    a. the government tried to censure his plays.
    b. he was the most religious Athenian poet.
    c. he justified Athenian imperialism.
    d. he was a critic of political and social life.

10. Most Greeks supported themselves by
    a. fishing.
    b. trading.
    c. warfare.
    d. farming.

11. Athenian women had
    a. the status of slaves.
    b. full citizens' rights.
    c. protection under the law.
    d. greater rights than men.

12. Greek homosexuality was considered
    a. the curse of the lower classes.
    b. a threat to family life.
    c. an insult to religion.
    d. for many a normal practice.

13. From 750 to 550 B.C., the Greeks settled in many parts of the Mediterranean basin, from the Black Sea to Spain. Which of the following was the *most* important reason for the movement?
    a. The increase in population
    b. The desire for a new start
    c. The love of excitement and adventure
    d. Natural curiosity about what lay beyond the horizon

14. Which of the following statements *best* describes Athenian democracy?
    a. Every citizen, both male and female, enjoyed all political rights.
    b. All male citizens performed the duties of government, but citizenship was withheld from many people.
    c. Athenian democracy was a sham and espoused no real democratic principles.
    d. Athenian democracy had no limitations.

15. Hallmarks of Greek geography are
    a. broad plains and abundant rainfall.
    b. mountains and a mild climate.
    c. swamps and a humid climate.
    d. hills and rough winters.

16. While the government of the polis could take many different forms, it was *least* likely to be a(n)
    a. monarchy.
    b. theocracy.
    c. oligarchy.
    d. democracy.

17. Greek-speaking peoples
    a. were indigenous to Greece.
    b. arrived during the Heroic Age.
    c. arrived during the Bronze Age.
    d. arrived during the age of colonization.

18. The most important result of Greek colonization was that it
    a. opened up the Near East.
    b. brought the Greeks into contact with Northern Europe.
    c. established Greek culture in the Mediterrean.
    d. put a stop to barbarian invasions.

19. Archilochos was a pioneer because he
    a. portrayed the great deeds of the Heroic Age.

b.   was one of the first lawgivers.
c.   was a lyric poet who described his own experiences.
d.   described the nature and functions of the gods.

20. The Spartan polis aimed at producing
a.   successful merchants.
b.   skillful sailors.
c.   wise lawgivers.
d.   brave soldiers.

21. Draco was famous because he
a.   reformed the Spartan polis.
b.   created democracy.
c.   gave Athens its first law code.
d.   was the last king of Mycenae.

22. Solon sought to
a.   champion the landed aristocracy.
b.   give relief to the poor.
c.   promote the rise of tyranny.
d.   support the priesthood.

23. Athenian art in the age of Pericles was marked by
a.   religious sentiment.
b.   humanistic values.
c.   romantic exuberance.
d.   unrestrained sentimentalism.

24. The average Athenian house was a
a.   simple structure with a courtyard.
b.   huge, rambling building.
c.   multiple-family dwelling.
d.   modest hut.

25. The hallmark of Pre-Socratic philosophy was its
a.   dependence on mythology.
b.   emphasis on reason and observation.
c.   desire to explain religion.
d.   reliance on magic.

26. Aristotle is important because he
a.   preserved the writings of Plato.

b. disproved the theories of the Pre-Socratics.
c. explored many areas of philosophy and science.
d. defended religion against science.

27. Choose the sequence that places historical developments in the correct chronological order.
a. Lyric Age, Classical Age, Dark Age, Bronze Age
b. Bronze Age, Dark Age, Lyric Age, Classical Age
c. Classical Age, Dark Age, Bronze Age, Lyric Age
d. Dark Age, Bronze Age, Classical Age, Lyric Age

28. The war between Athens and Sparta was called the
a. Greek Civil War.
b. Persian War.
c. Peloponnesian War.
d. Trojan War.

GEOGRAPHY

1. Show on the outline map of the Aegean basin the approximate location of the following places.

Athens	Crete	Asia Minor	Mount Olympus
Sparta	Mediterranean Sea	Lesbos	Marathon
Thebes	Aegean Sea	Peloponnesus	Mycenae
Troy	Ionian Sea	Ionia	

2. The geography of Greece encouraged political fragmentation. Explain.

3. Using Map 5.2 as a reference, describe the area that came under Greek control as a result of its overseas expansion. What were the causes of this expansion?

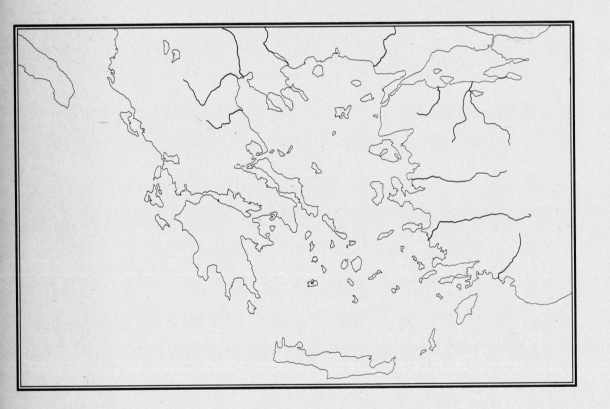

UNDERSTANDING HISTORY THROUGH READING AND THE ARTS

The best short introduction to Greek society — including the polis, religion, war, and the Greek mind — is H. D. F. Kitto, *The Greeks** (1951). Students interested in the development of Greek thought and the Greek way of thinking should read W. K. C. Guthrie, *The Greek Philosophers** (1950, 1960). The two best books on Greek sexuality are H. Licht, *Sexual Life in Ancient Greece* (trans., J. H. Freese, 1932), and K. Dover, *Greek Homosexuality* (1978). The "Suggested Reading" section of the text lists additional books on gender and sexuality in Greek life.

Nothing can be of more value in understanding the Greeks than to go directly to their great literature. The two dialogues of Plato, *Protagoras* and *Meno,** W. K. C. Guthrie (trans., 1956), are among the best of Greek prose. *Protagoras*, his dramatic masterpiece, deals with the problem of teaching the art of successful living, while *Meno* considers the immortality of the soul and the idea that learning is knowledge acquired before birth.

The elegance and excellence of Greek sculpture and architecture are explored in Chapter 5, "Greek Art," in H. W. Janson, *History of Art* (1962), and Greek mythology is interestingly told in E. Hamilton, *Mythology* (1942).

Gore Vidal's historical novel, *Creation** (1981) — much of which is based on the accounts of Herodotus — imparts a lively, well-informed impression of the size and cultural complexity of the Persian empire (and the intrigues in the Persian royal court) during the days of Darius, Xerxes, and the Persian invasions of Greece.

PROBLEMS FOR FURTHER INVESTIGATION

Why did the Greek democracy eventually fail? Was Greek society truly democratic? Students interested in pursuing the subject of Greek politics and political theory should begin with J. N. Claster, ed., *Athenian Democracy** (1967), which is a collection of interpretations by various historians, and B. Tierney et al., *Periclean Athens — Was It a Democracy?** (1967).

Did the Trojan War actually take place? If so, when? What did Heinrich Schliemann actually find at Troy? All these problems are taken up in an engaging work by Michael Wood, *In Search of the Trojan War* (1985), a well-illustrated companion volume to a six-part BBC television series with the same title.

*Available in paperback.

CHAPTER 6

HELLENISTIC DIFFUSION

CHAPTER OBJECTIVES

After reading and studying this chapter you should be able to answer the following questions:

Q-1. How was the development of philosophy, religion, science, medicine, and economics affected by the meeting of East and West?
Q-2. What did the spread of Hellenism mean to the Greeks and the people of the Near East?
Q-3. Did the spread of the Greek spirit by Philip and Alexander lay the groundwork for later cultures?

CHAPTER SYNOPSIS

This chapter shows how the ancient Near Eastern cultures such as Egypt and Persia and the Greek, or Hellenic, culture came together to form a new, Hellenistic culture during the time of Alexander the Great. The Hellenistic age created throughout the Near Eastern and Mediterranean world both the political confusion and cultural unity that prepared the way for the triumph of Roman imperialism.

Alexander the Great organized the Greek states, defeated and conquered Persia, and then marched on to India, part of which was incorporated into his Macedonian state. Along the way he founded new cities and military colonies, all of which became agencies by which Greek (Hellenistic) culture spread throughout most of the Mediterranean and Near Eastern world. When he died, his empire became a frontier of opportunity for large numbers of Greeks in search of jobs, wealth, and power. Thus, Greek men and women settled throughout the East, forming an elite class of professionals and administrators. These Greek settlers also carried

Greek literature, law, engineering, architecture, and philosophy into every corner of the Near East and the Mediterranean.

Important new discoveries in science and medicine were made in the Hellenistic period. Philosophy flourished, led by the competing doctrines of the Cynics, the Epicureans, and the Stoics, and for the first time became popular among common people. There were also important advances in food production, trade, and mining. Thus, although the Hellenistic age is often regarded as a period of stagnation, it was actually a time of change and accomplishment.

STUDY OUTLINE

I. Alexander the Great and the crusade to conquer Asia Minor
    A. Alexander's invasion of Persia
        1. Alexander became king in 336 B.C. and invaded Asia in 334 B.C.
        2. By 324 B.C., he had defeated the Persians to avenge the Persian invasion of Greece and had pushed into India
        3. He built a huge Macedonian-Greek monarchy in place of the Persian Empire
    B. He therefore opened the East to Hellenism
II. The spread of Hellenism
    A. Cities and kingdoms of the Hellenistic age
        1. The new polis was not politically free but rather a part of a kingdom
            a. The polis was not self-governing but subject to interference from the king
            b. Legal and social inequality existed in the Hellenistic polis; Greeks had greater rights
        2. The Hellenistic kingdoms were frequently at war as they attempted to solidify their kingdoms and gain the loyalty of subjects
        3. These Hellenistic cities formed the cultural foundation on which Roman and Christian cultures were to spread and flourish
    B. The Greeks open the East
        1. The Hellenistic kingdoms in Asia and Egypt provided Greeks with lucrative jobs
        2. Greeks dominated the administrative and military branches of the kingdoms
        3. But the Hellenistic kings could not gain the complete loyalty of their soldiers and professionals, and thus their kingdoms were weakened
    C. Greeks and Easterners: the spread of Hellenism
        1. Greek culture spread unevenly
            a. A Greco-Egyptian culture evolved slowly in Egypt

   b. Under the Seleucid kings, Greek and Eastern culture merged in Asia Minor

   c. For most Easterners only the externals, such as the common Greek dialect called *koine*, were Greek

III. Economic scope of Hellenism

  A. The commercial link between East and West was the most important Hellenistic development

   1. Alexander's conquests brought the East and West together for trade

   2. Overland trade to India and a sea route to Italy were established

   3. Eastern grain was essential to Greece and the Aegean Sea area; in return Greece exported oil, wine, and fish

   4. The slave trade flourished because slavery was important to the Hellenistic economy

  B. Industry

   1. Cheap labor left no incentive to invest in machinery

   2. Important changes in pottery style took place, but production methods remained unchanged

  C. Agriculture

   1. Advances were made in seed and in improving and writing handbooks on farming

   2. The Ptolemies of Egypt made great strides in irrigating the land, partly because of their strong central government

IV. Religion and philosophy in the Hellenistic world

  A. Religion in the Hellenistic world

   1. The Greek religious cults centered on the Olympian gods

   2. The cults, consisting mainly of rituals, did not fill the religious needs of the people

   3. While some turned to philosophy, many others turned to a belief in *Tyche*, which meant fate or chance

   4. There was a growth in mystery religions (such as the Serapis and Isis cults) to fill emotional and ethical needs

   5. Isis, who promised life after death, was the most important goddess of the new mystery cults

   6. The most important development was a growing belief in one god who ruled over all people

  B. Philosophy and the common man

   1. During the Hellenic period common people became interested in philosophy

   2. The Cynics believed that the rejection of the material life brings freedom

   3. Diogenes, the greatest of the Cynics, stressed living according to nature and without allegiance to a particular city or monarchy

4. The Epicureans taught that pleasure through self-discipline was the chief good
5. The Stoics stressed the unity of man and universe and resignation to one's duty
   a. Zeno, the Stoic, made Stoicism the most popular Hellenistic philosophy
   b. Participation in worldly affairs was encouraged, but leading a virtuous life was most important
   c. Their idea of *natural law* was of great significance

V. Hellenistic women
   A. The Hellenistic period brought royal women back into politics
   B. Women became important in art, literature, and medicine
   C. Although the Stoics regarded women as inferior, the Cynics treated them as equals
   D. Women became economically more important and as a result had more opportunities than in Hellenic times

VI. Hellenistic science and medicine
   A. Aristarchus developed the heliocentric theory; Euclid of Alexandria compiled a text on geometry
   B. Archimedes, an inventor and theoretician, sketched out basic principles of mechanics and hydrostatics
   C. Eratosthenes, under the patronage of King Ptolemy, made advances in mathematics and geography
   D. Theophrastos founded the study of botany
   E. The Dogmatic school of medicine, under Herophilus and Erasistratus, used vivisection and dissection to gain knowledge of the body — including the nervous system
   F. The Empiric school rejected magic and stressed observation and use of medicine and drugs, including opium
   G. Many quacks did untold harm but were popular

VII. Conclusion: The Hellenistic age was a golden age in terms of the spread of Greek culture and new developments in science, medicine, and popular philosophy

REVIEW QUESTIONS

Q-1. What were the major achievements of Alexander? Does he deserve to be called "the Great"?

Q-2. Trace the expansion of the Macedonian kingdom into Asia. What were the reasons for this movement?

Q-3.   How did the Hellenistic polis differ from the earlier Greek polis? Why?
Q-4.   What did the new Hellenistic kingdoms offer the Greeks? Why couldn't these kingdoms gain the loyalty of the Greek immigrants?
Q-5.   How successful was Greek culture in penetrating the cultures of Egypt and the East?
Q-6.   Trace the developments in agriculture and industry in Hellenistic society. Why was there so little invention of machinery?
Q-7.   Explain the interregional trade patterns of the Hellenistic world. What products did the various parts of the Hellenistic world specialize in?
Q-8.   What kinds of commodities would one find in the cargo of the eastern caravans?
Q-9.   Did the position and power of women in Hellenistic society change from those of earlier periods? Explain.
Q-10.   Discuss the religious and philosophical trends in the Hellenistic world. Why did the common person become interested in philosophy?
Q-11.   Compare and contrast Cynicism, Epicureanism, and Stoicism.
Q-12.   Define *natural law*. Why is this an important idea?
Q-13.   Trace the development of medical science in the Hellenistic era. What advances were made over the Hellenistic period?
Q-14.   Some have regarded the Hellenistic period as stagnant and degenerate. Do you agree? What evidence exists to support your view?

STUDY-REVIEW EXERCISES

Define the following key concepts and terms.

Hellenism Greek culture, language, thought, way of life

philhellenic independent state run by its citizens free of outside power

sovereign

Tyche

natural law

heliocentric theory

empirical tradition

Explain the major ideas and accomplishments of the following Hellenistic people.

Aristarchus of Samos

Euclid

Archimedes

Eratosthenes

Theophrastos

Herophilus

King Ptolemy

Explain the ideas and beliefs of three new Hellenistic schools of philosophy.

Philosophical School	*Founder*	*Principal Ideas and Beliefs*
Cynics		
Epicureans		
Stoics		

Identify the following and give its significance.

Hellenistic period

Aetolian League

koine

Alexander the Great

Zeno

Isis

dogmatic school of medicine

empiric school of medicine

Test your understanding of the chapter by answering the following questions.

1. Epicurus taught that the gods had *no*/*great* effect on human life.
2. The most popular philosophy of the Hellenistic world was
   _____ Stoicism _____.
3. The Cynics advised men and women to *accept*/*discard* the traditional customs and conventions.
4. The founder of the Cynics was _____ Anisthenes _____,
   who believed that nothing natural was dirty or shameful.
5. The Hellenistic world *did*/*did not* see much trade in manufactured goods.
6. Alexander the Great's conquest of Persia was completed by about the year
   _____ 324 BC _____.
7. The Greek immigrants in the Hellenistic kingdoms generally *did*/*did not* develop a strong loyalty to the state.
8. Philip of Macedonia's son was _____ Alexander the Great _____.
9. The name for Greek language, culture, thought, and lifestyle is
   _____ Hellenism _____.
10. Alexander led a campaign of revenge against the
    _____ Persian _____ Empire in 334 B.C.
11. The most important goddess of the Hellenistic world was
    _____ Isis _____.
12. The political and economic power of women tended to *increase*/*decrease* during the Hellenistic period.
13. *Tyche* was the common Hellenistic belief in _____ fate, chance or doom _____.

14. Generally, the Greeks tended to be *tolerant/intolerant* toward other religions.

15. _____ *Isis* _____ was the goddess of marriage, conception, and childbirth.

MULTIPLE-CHOICE QUESTIONS

1. The Epicureans believed that one could find happiness by
    a. becoming involved in politics.
    b. experiencing pain.
    c. retiring within oneself.
    d. pleasing the gods.

2. The most important achievement of the Stoics was the
    a. idea of rejecting the state.
    b. cult of Isis.
    c. education of Alexander.
    d. concept of natural law.

3. Which of the following statements about Hellenized Easterners is true?
    a. They rejected everything except Greek religion.
    b. They adopted much but retained the essentials of their own culture.
    c. They became thoroughly assimilated into Greek culture.
    d. They had no culture of their own.

4. Within the Hellenistic world Greeks formed the
    a. middle class of merchants.
    b. favored class.
    c. slave class.
    d. priest class.

5. Alexander's troops refused to proceed farther after they reached
    a. Persia.
    b. India.
    c. Bactria.
    d. China.

6. Alexander made his greatest contribution toward understanding between West and East when he

a. forced Greeks to marry barbarians.
b. established the Greek church in India.
c. established colonies for Greek emigration.
d. encouraged the adoption of barbarian food and dress.

7. Women's position improved during the Hellenistic age because of
   a. the Greeks' belief that women were equal.
   b. full citizenship rights conferred by law.
   c. their increased activity in economic affairs.
   d. their noble and self-sacrificing deeds.

8. Of all the post-Alexander empires, the greatest strides in agriculture were made by the
   a. Ptolemies in Egypt.
   b. Macedonians.
   c. Seleucids.
   d. Athenians.

9. The Greek word *Tyche* means
   a. revelation.
   b. honor.
   c. to be strong.
   d. fate.

10. The author of the still-influential book *The Elements of Geometry* was
    a. Euclid.
    b. Archimedes.
    c. Aristarchus of Samos.
    d. Eratosthenes.

11. In the Hellenistic period philosophy was
    a. the pastime of the wealthy.
    b. the profession of specialists.
    c. a propaganda tool of kings.
    d. an outlet for common people.

12. The Cynics thought that people should
    a. avoid pain.
    b. live according to nature.
    c. uphold the norms of society.
    d. enjoy luxury in moderation.

13. Epicurean philosophy taught the
    a. overthrow of monarchies.
    b. virtue of self-discipline.
    c. value of religion.
    d. value of pleasure.

14. The Stoics evolved the idea of
    a. might makes right.
    b. pain against pleasure.
    c. the unity of mankind and the universe.
    d. the unity of mankind and the state.

15. Aristarchus of Samos is important because he thought that the
    a. sun revolved around the earth.
    b. moon revolved around the earth.
    c. earth revolved around the sun.
    d. sun and moon were fixed bodies.

16. Which of the following sciences got its start in the Hellenistic period?
    a. Economics
    b. Physics
    c. Botany
    d. Geology

17. The discoverer of the nervous sytem was
    a. Herophilus.
    b. Erasistratus.
    c. Heraclides.
    d. Serapion.

18. The Empiric school of medicine emphasized the
    a. study of anatomy.
    b. study of physiology.
    c. use of vivisection and dissection.
    d. cure of sickness through observation and drugs.

19. Hellenistic industry relied chiefly on
    a. labor-saving machines.
    b. new techniques of production.
    c. increased use of animal power.
    d. use of manual labor.

20. Hellenistic kings gave Greek immigrants
    a. enormous economic and social opportunities.
    b. a new sense of identity.
    c. a stronger sense of personal security.
    d. the opportunity to wield political power.

21. All but which of the following was characteristic of Egypt under the Ptolemies in the third century B.C.?
    a. Many great cities were built.
    b. The Ptolemies made no great effort to spread Greek culture.
    c. Native Egyptians had little chance for advancement to high office.
    d. Greek immigrants formed an elite upper class.

22. In the Hellenistic period women began to
    a. hold more religious positions.
    b. participate in politics.
    c. be more secluded.
    d. receive equality under the law.

23. The most important Cynic philosopher was
    a. Diogenes.
    b. Antisthenes.
    c. Socrates.
    d. Ptolemy.

24. Hellenistic culture made its greatest strides in
    a. literature.
    b. art.
    c. politics.
    d. science.

25. The greatest thinker of the Hellenistic period was
    a. Archimedes.
    b. Eratosthenes.
    c. Plutarch.
    d. Euclid.

26. One aspect of Hellenistic economics was an increase in
    a. material demands.
    b. the volume of trade.
    c. trade with the West.
    d. labor-saving machines.

27. Cynicism, Stocism, and Epicureanism were
    a. religious beliefs.
    b. philosophies.
    c. nations.
    d. Egyptian dynasties.

GEOGRAPHY

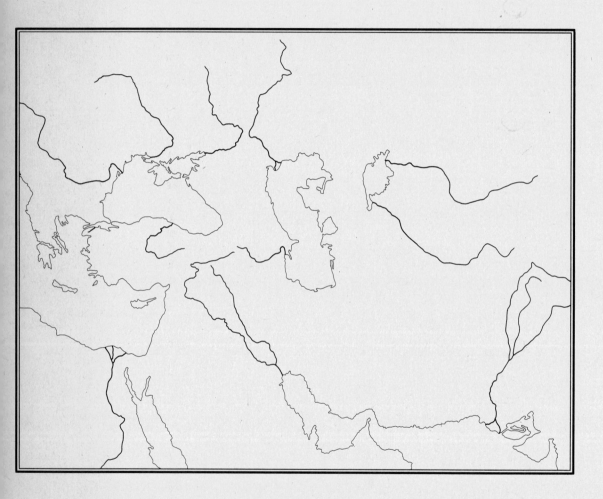

1. Using the text Map 6.2 as a guide, show on the outline map the location of the following places of importance in the Hellenistic world.

Ptolemais	Indus River	Tigris River	Euphrates River
India	Mesopotamia	Mediterranean Sea	Asia Minor
Persia	Nile River	Black Sea	Alexandria
Red Sea	Persian Gulf	Caspian Sea	Arabian Sea
Macedonia	Persepolis	Egypt	Arabian Desert

2. Shade in the area conquered by Alexander the Great.
3. Show with a dotted line a route by which goods might have moved between Greece, Asia Minor, Egypt, and the Far East.

UNDERSTANDING HISTORY THROUGH READING AND THE ARTS

Alexander the Great is the subject of two fairly recent biographies: R. L. Fox, *Alexander the Great* (1974), and P. Green, *Alexander of Macedon, 356–323 B.C.* * (1973). A fascinating historical novel about life, love, and adventure with Alexander is M. Renault, *The Persian Boy* * (1972). The Jewish war of liberation against their Hellenistic Syrian overlords is one of a number of subjects dealt with in V. Tcherikover, *Hellenistic Civilization and the Jews* (trans., S. Applebaum, 1959). Many of the remarkable personages of the Hellenistic Age — including Cleopatra and Ptolemy of Egypt — are featured in N. Davis and C. Kraay, *The Hellenistic Kingdoms: Portrait Coins and History* (1973). This fascinating book is also of value for anyone interested in the use of ancient coins in understanding the past.

For developments in architecture see T. Fyfe, *Hellenistic Architecture* (1963), and for painting and sculpture see C. Havelock, *Hellenistic Art* (1970). The traditions of Hellenistic literature and culture are explored in T. Webster, *Hellenistic Poetry and Art* (1964).

PROBLEMS FOR FURTHER INVESTIGATION

Did the Hellenists make any significant contributions to science and medicine? To pursue this question begin with E. Hamilton, *The Greek Way to Western Civilization* * (1943).

What were the reasons for Alexander the Great's conquest of the Near Eastern world? Begin your research with A. R. Burn, *Alexander the Great and the Hellenistic*

*Available in paperback.

*World** (1964). And to answer the question of Hellenistic contributions in science, begin your study with G. E. Lloyd, *Greek Science After Aristotle* (1963).

How did Greek philosophy change in this period? What are Stoicism and Cynicism? Those interested in Greek thought should see a book of essays, interpretations, and source material entitled *The Greek Mind** (1957) by W. R. Agard and *Hellenistic Philosophy* (1974) by A. Long.

*Available in paperback.

READING WITH UNDERSTANDING
EXERCISE 2

LEARNING TO IMPROVE YOUR UNDERLINING SKILLS

Read the following paragraphs, in which some words are printed in italic type to help you find the major points. Read the passage a second time and underline or highlight one or two sentences in each paragraph that best summarize the paragraph's major point. Now study and review these points. Finally, close the book and on a piece of notepaper summarize the major points *with a few words* under the heading "The Success of Benedictine Monasticism." Compare your summary with that found at the end of the exercise.

The Success of Benedictine Monasticism

Why was the Benedictine form of monasticism so successful? Why did it eventually replace other forms of Western monasticism? The answer lies partly in its *spirit of flexibility and moderation*, and partly in the *balanced life* it provided. Early Benedictine monks and nuns spent part of the day in prayer, part in study or some other form of intellectual activity, and part in manual labor. The monastic life as conceived by Saint Benedict did not lean too heavily in any one direction; it struck a balance between asceticism and idleness. It thus provided opportunities for persons of entirely different abilities and talents—from mechanics to gardeners to literary scholars. Benedict's *Rule* contrasts sharply with Cassiodorus's narrow concept of the monastery as a place for aristocratic scholars and bibliophiles.

Benedictine monasticism also *suited the social circumstances of early medieval society*. The German invasions had fragmented European life: the self-sufficient rural estate replaced the city as the basic unit of civilization. A monastery too had to be *economically self-sufficient*. It was supposed to produce from its lands and properties all that was needed for food, clothing, buildings, and the liturgical service of the altar. The monastery fit in—indeed, represented—the trend toward localism.

Benedictine monasticism also succeeded partly because it was so *materially successful.* In the seventh and eighth centuries, monasteries pushed back forest and wasteland, drained swamps, and experimented with crop rotation. For example, the abbey of Saint Wandrille, founded in 645 near Rouen in northwestern Gaul, sent squads of monks to clear the forests that surrounded it. Within seventy-five years, the abbey was immensely wealthy. The abbey of Jumièges, also in the diocese of Rouen, followed much the same pattern. Such Benedictine houses made *a significant contribution to the agricultural development* of Europe. The socialistic nature of their organization, whereby property was held in common and profits pooled and reinvested, made this contribution possible.

Finally, *monasteries conducted schools* for local young people. Some learned about prescriptions and herbal remedies and went on to provide medical treatment for their localities. A few copied manuscripts and wrote books. This training did not go unappreciated in a society desperately in need of it. Local and royal governments drew on the services of *the literate men and able administrators* the monasteries produced. This was not what Saint Benedict had intended, but the effectiveness of the institution he designed made it perhaps inevitable.

ANSWER

The Success of Benedictine Monasticism

1. A flexible and balanced life

2. Economically self-sufficient

3. Economically successful, especially in agriculture

4. Provided education for young and able administrators for governments

CHAPTER 7

THE RISE OF ROME

CHAPTER OBJECTIVES

After reading and studying this chapter you should be able to answer the following questions:

Q-1. How did Rome rise to greatness?
Q-2. What effects did the conquest of the Mediterranean have on the Romans?
Q-3. Why did the Roman Republic collapse?

CHAPTER SYNOPSIS

Whereas the Greeks gave the Mediterranean world cultural unity, Rome gave it political unity and a political heritage. The *pax Romana*, or peace of Rome, allowed the spread of Roman law, justice, and administration as well as the further diffusion of Greek culture — especially into the European world. This chapter traces the origins of that legacy from the Etruscans in the eighth century B.C. through the troubled but dynamic days of the republic in the first century B.C. Between these two periods the Romans built an enormous empire, gave the world important lessons in politics, and established some new concepts in law.

There are three major themes in this chapter. The first is assimilation and creativity. The Romans, like the Macedonians before them, readily adopted the culture of Hellenic Greece. Earlier, the Romans had copied many of the customs of the ancient Etruscans. Just as important, the Romans created new institutions and founded new ideas — such as in the areas of law and politics. Conquest and imperialism are the second theme. The Romans became empire builders almost by accident. A conflict in southern Italy led to foreign involvement, first in Sicily and then in North Africa during the Punic wars between Rome and Carthage. The third theme is the effect of imperialism on Rome. Did imperialism bring more harm than blessings? The chapter evaluates the economic and political changes that military victory brought, noting how the coming of empire meant a change in lifestyle and, according to some Romans, such as Cato, a general moral deterioration. Certainly, foreign conquests created large standing armies and veterans who played a growing role in Roman politics. Once this happened, government by constitution was doomed.

STUDY OUTLINE

I. The land and the sea: the geography and early settlement of Rome
    A. The land and the sea
        1. Italy's small and shallow rivers did not encourage trade, but the land was fertile and productive and the mountains not as divisive as those of Greece
        2. The two great fertile plains of Italy are Latium and Campania
        3. The Romans established their city on seven hills along the Tiber River in Latium
    B. The Etruscans and Rome (750-500 B.C.)
        1. Between 1200 and 750 B.C., many peoples moved into Italy from the north
        2. Etruscan urban life came to dominate much of Italy
        3. According to legend, Romulus and Remus founded Rome in 753 B.C.
        4. The Etruscans passed many customs and practices on to the Romans
        5. The Etruscans turned Rome into an important city and brought it into contact with the Mediterranean world
    C. The Roman conquest of Italy (509-290 B.C.)
        1. Much of early Roman history is based on legends and tales, eventually brought together by Livy
        2. According to tradition, the Romans founded a republic in 509 B.C. and thereafter worked to expel the Etruscans
        3. In 390 B.C., invading Gauls sacked Rome
        4. Between 390 and 290 B.C., the Romans conquered much of Italy, including Etruria, Campania, and southern Italy
        5. Rome's success was due, in part, to her policy of sharing power with conquered peoples and extending citizenship to them
    D. The Roman state
        1. In the early republic power resided in the hands of the members of the aristocracy, called the *patricians*; commoners were called *plebeians*
        2. Rome was ruled by people's assemblies, elected magistrates, and — most important — the senate

        a. The senate advised the consuls and magistrates, and its advice had the force of law

        b. The senate provided stability and continuity to the republic

        c. The assembly *comitia centuriata* was dominated by the patricians

        d. In 471 B.C. the plebeians gained their own assembly, the *concilium plebis*

        e. In effect the two consuls and the senate ran the state

    3. Rome's greatest achievement was its development of the concept of law — *ius civile*, *ius gentium*, and *ius naturale*

        a. Civil law developed to protect people and property

        b. Gradually, the concept of universal law applicable to all societies developed

  E. Social conflict in Rome

    1. The plebeians' desire for equality and justice led to a struggle with the patricians, called the Struggle of the Orders

    2. A general strike led to concessions being granted to the plebeians — partly because of patrician fears of hostile neighbors

    3. The plebeians won legal and land reforms

        a. The *lex canuleia* allowed for intermarriage

        b. The Law of the Twelve Tables — a codification of previously unpublished laws — was the result of plebeian legal reform

        c. Later, the patricians were forced to publish legal procedures, too, so plebeians could enjoy full protection under the law

    4. Licinius and Sextus brought about further reform for the plebeians, but the struggle did not end until the passage of *lex Hortensia* in 287 B.C.

II. The age of overseas conquest, 282–146 B.C.

  A. Roman imperialism developed gradually

    1. The Romans did not have a preexisting strategy for world conquest

    2. Roman imperialism took two forms: aggression in the West and patronage in the East

  B. Rome's need to control southern Italy and then Sicily meant it needed to control the sea

    1. This led to the First Punic War, fought over Sicily and won by Rome

    2. The Second Punic War found Carthage attacking Rome by way of Spain, then over the Alps with a major victory at Cannae by Hannibal in 216 B.C.

    3. But Rome's commander Scipio invaded Spain and then a Roman victory at Zama in 202 B.C. meant that the western Mediterranean would be Roman

    4. But a Third Punic War meant further conflict with Carthage

    5. Rome conquered the eastern Mediterranean — including the Greek states, Pergamum, and Egypt

III. Old values and Greek culture
   A. Consequences of empire
      1. The building of empire brought about the end of traditional values and encouraged a new materialism and urban life
   B. The "traditional ideal" of a simple and virtuous life, represented by Marcus Cato
      1. In traditional Rome the paterfamilias held immense power within the family
      2. Women spun and wove cloth at home, supervised slaves, and nursed their children
      3. Their main meal was at midday
      4. The Romans developed an agricultural system to adjust to the seasons and the soil — multiple plowings and a variety of plows were used
      5. Slavery was common; relations between master and slave were often good
      6. Religion played an important role in Roman life; Romans believed that the gods could give divine favor to them
   C. The new spirit of wealth and leisure, represented by Scipio Aemilianus
      1. For the new Romans, victory in war meant materialism and the pursuit of pleasure
      2. Greek culture — Hellenism — came to dominate Roman life
      3. Greek works were translated into Latin
      4. Hellenism stimulated the growth of Roman art, literature, and leisure activities such as bathing and dinner parties
      5. Despite this hedonism, Rome prospered for six more centuries
IV. The late republic (133–27 B.C.)
   A. War and the demands of the new empire created serious political problems
      1. The republican constitution no longer suited Rome's needs
      2. The army became a threat
      3. Rome's Italian allies agitated for the rights of citizenship
   B. War and the new empire also caused economic problems
      1. Many veterans sold their war-ruined farms to the big landowners and migrated to the cities
      2. A large number of urban poor emerged
      3. The Gracchus brothers sought a solution to the problem of the veterans and the urban poor
         a. Tiberius Gracchus angered aristocrats and the senate by proposing land reform
         b. The murder of Tiberius Gracchus by the senators initiated an era of political violence — although the land reform was begun
         c. Gaius Gracchus demanded further land reform and citizenship for all Italians
         d. Gaius was killed by the senate while new foreign threats emerged

4. Marius reformed the army by promising land to recruits — hence changing the relationship between the army and the state
5. Social war in Italy and factional chaos in Rome continued
6. Sulla became dictator of Rome, and civil war followed
7. Cicero urged a balance of political interests — or "concord of the orders"
8. The First Triumvirate (Pompey, Caesar, and Crassus) controlled Rome after Sulla, but Caesar dominated
9. Conflict between Caesar and Pompey resulted in more civil war
10. The Second Triumvirate (Augustus, Antony, and Lepidus) followed Caesar's rule
11. In 31 B.C., Augustus put an end to civil war by defeating Antony at the battle of Actium

REVIEW QUESTIONS

Q-1. Who were the Etruscans and of what importance were they to the early Romans?

Q-2. What do the early Roman legends reveal about Roman values and ideas? Are legends valid sources for the historian?

Q-3. How did Rome differ from Greece with regard to ideas about the state, citizenship, and participation in the state?

Q-4. Define *ius civile*, *ius gentium*, *ius naturale*. Where did political power lie in republican Rome?

Q-5. What were the causes and the outcome of the Struggle of the Orders?

Q-6. What were the motives and events that caused Rome to become an expansionist state?

Q-7. What were the causes and results of the Punic wars?

Q-8. Why did Sicily and Spain become battlegrounds for the Punic wars? What was Hannibal's military strategy?

Q-9. Trace the territorial expansion of Rome that came about as a result of war. By what year could the Romans declare the Mediterranean to be *mare nostrum*?

Q-10. Describe the role of the *paterfamilias* in Roman life.

Q-11. How were women and children treated in Roman society? How does the status of Roman women compare to that of women of the Hellenistic period?

Q-12. Discuss the institution of slavery in Roman society. Is slavery ever a humane institution?

Q-13. How did the Romans regard their gods? Was religion important to the Romans? Did Christianity completely replace Roman religion? Explain.

Q-14. Contrast the interests and lifestyles of Marcus Cato and his family and Scipio Aemilianus. Do you believe that Greek culture corrupted the Romans? What causes certain elements within society to break with their past?

Q-15.   What impact did the imperial expansion of Rome have on the economic and political condition of the republic? Who were the winners and the losers?

Q-16.   What did the Gracchus brothers intend to do for Rome? Why was there so much opposition? What were the results?

Q-17.   What were the reasons for instability in Rome from about the time of Gaius Marius in 107 B.C. to Augustus in 31 B.C.? Was dictatorship the only answer?

STUDY-REVIEW EXERCISES

Define the following key concepts and terms.

lex Canuleia

Pyrrhic victory

ius naturale

mare nostrum

paterfamilias

pax Romana

latifundia

senatus populusque Romanus

imperialism

Identify each of the following and give its significance.

Punic wars

First Triumvirate

comitia centuriata

Ennius

Terence

concilium plebis

Law of the Twelve Tables

lex Hortensia

plebeians

Roman senate

Hannibal

Cincinnatus

Marcus Cato

Scipio Aemilianus

Gauls

Etruscans

Roman baths

<u>*Explain*</u> *who the following people were and the role each played in the troubled years of the late republic.*

Gracchus brothers

Cicero

Sulla

Pompey

Julius Caesar

<u>*Test*</u> *your understanding of the chapter by answering the following questions.*

1. The Punic wars were between Rome and ____Carthage____.

2. The general strike of the plebeians in 494 B.C. *did/did not* gain them rights.
3. Once the Romans had conquered southern Italy, they found themselves in

   need of controlling ___Sicily_____

   and then ___Carthage_____
4. The Romans *did/did not* hold racist attitudes toward their slaves.
5. After the wars of conquest the Romans began to express *more/less* interest in Hellenism.
6. The Roman sky god ___Jupiter_____ became the equivalent of the Greek Zeus.
7. Roman art tended to be more *idealistic/realistic* than Greek art.
8. Prior to 90 B.C., all Italians *did/did not* hold Roman citizenship.
9. The wealthy landowning aristocracy in Rome was known as the

   _____patricians_____ class.

Number the following events in correct chronological order.

1. __3__ End of the First Punic War

2. __6__ Roman conquest of Spain

3. __1__ Invasion of Italy by the Gauls

4. __4__ Defeat of Hannibal at Zama

5. __5__ Completion of the Roman conquest of the eastern Mediterranean

6. __2__ Invasion of Italy by Pyrrhus

MULTIPLE-CHOICE QUESTIONS

1. As a result of the wars of conquest, the small, independent Roman farmers
   a. gained vast new markets for their grain.
   b. found their farms in ruins.
   c. became an important political power.
   d. got rich.

2. Overall, the Romans' greatest achievements were in the field of
    a. empire building.
    b. agriculture and trade.
    c. the arts.
    d. literature.

3. Rome's greatest achievement was to
    a. conquer peoples and let them govern themselves.
    b. always live peacefully with its neighbors.
    c. always peacefully incorporate peoples into the Roman system.
    d. conquer peoples and incorporate them into the Roman system.

4. The goal of the Gracchi was to
    a. exploit the urban poor and the peasant farmers.
    b. join the patricians.
    c. aid the urban poor and the peasant farmers.
    d. deny citizenship to certain Romans.

5. According to Roman legend, the founders of Rome were
    a. the Greeks.
    b. the tribe of Autun.
    c. Livy and his family.
    d. Romulus and Remus.

6. The Roman citizen who returned to his farming after defeating his country's enemy was
    a. Augustus of Spoleto.
    b. Cincinnatus.
    c. Lycurgus.
    d. Sulla.

7. The chief magistrates of republican Rome — the officials who administered the state and commanded the army — were known as
    a. consuls.
    b. quaestors.
    c. praetors.
    d. senators.

8. During the Second Punic War the Carthaginian leader who attempted to conquer Rome was
    a. Philip of Carthage.
    b. Hannibal.

    c.   Alexander.

    d.   Meneius Agrippa.

9. Most ordinary Roman women

    a.   had little influence in family affairs.

    b.   spent most of their time performing religious rituals.

    c.   had considerable influence and responsibility in the family economy.

    d.   exercised total control of the children's upbringing.

10. Which of the following best represents the status of Roman slaves?

    a.   The Romans thought slaves were inferior human beings.

    b.   The Romans thought of slavery in racial terms.

    c.   The Romans thought of slavery primarily as a byproduct of Rome's military victories.

    d.   Freedom was often granted to slaves by their masters.

11. The First Triumvirate was composed of

    a.   Marius, Pompey, and Crassus.

    b.   Sulla, Caesar, and Cicero.

    c.   Pompey, Caesar, and Cicero.

    d.   Pompey, Caesar, and Crassus.

12. All but one of the following are principal geographical characteristics of Italy.

    a.   Few good harbors except in the south

    b.   The Appenine mountain range running east/west and cutting the peninsula in half

    c.   Few navigable rivers

    d.   Two large fertile plains

13. The reformers Licinius and Sextus were

    a.   patricians.

    b.   Etruscans.

    c.   ex-slaves.

    d.   plebeians.

14. Typical of the Roman population, the great Roman Cato and his family had their main meal

    a.   in the evening.

    b.   at no particular time of the day.

    c.   at midday.

    d.   only when entertaining guests.

15. The father of Latin poetry was
    a. Eilliam.
    b. Ennius.
    c. Scipio Aemilianus.
    d. Cato.

16. The conservative and traditionalist elements of Rome regarded the public baths as
    a. the only way to encourage reform in public health.
    b. a good way of using Greek culture for the benefit of Rome.
    c. a waste of time and an encouragement to idleness.
    d. important as places for political discussion.

17. The wars during the time of republican Rome
    a. left Rome a strong and prosperous agriculture.
    b. left Roman farms in a state of decay.
    c. caused Rome to look elsewhere for its food supply.
    d. caused a decentralization of land ownership.

18. The Roman leader who was murdered because he proposed that public land be given to the poor in small lots was
    a. Sulla.
    b. Tiberius Gracchus.
    c. Cato.
    d. Caesar.

19. The consul who reorganized the Roman army and introduced the use of the sword and javelin as standard weapons of the legionaries was
    a. Cincinnatus.
    b. Tiberius.
    c. Sulla.
    d. Marius.

20. By the time of the late republican period in Rome, most industry and small manufacturing was in the hands of
    a. plebeians.
    b. slaves.
    c. Christians.
    d. the army.

21. The Etruscans
    a. were a historically mysterious people who greatly influenced Roman cultural and governmental development.

  b. conquered the Greeks.
  c. were conquered by the Persians.
  d. are an easily identifiable group that had no real influence on Rome.

22. In early Rome, the ideal of individual behavior was a
   a. bold, brash manner, putting Rome first.
   b. dignified, simple manner, putting Rome first.
   c. dignified, simple manner, putting the family first.
   d. bold, brash manner, putting the family first.

23. Which sequence of events is in chronological order?
   a. The conquest of Spain, Pyrrhus's victory, Hannibal's trip over the Alps
   b. Hannibal's trip over the Alps, the conquest of Spain, Pyrrhus's victory
   c. Pyrrhus's victory, Hannibal's trip over the Alps, the conquest of Spain
   d. The conquest of Spain, Hannibal's trip over the Alps, Pyrrhus's victory

24. The Struggle of the Orders was a power struggle between
   a. Augustus and Marc Antony.
   b. the patricians and the plebeians.
   c. Caesar and Pompey.
   d. the praetors and consuls.

25. Much of early Roman history is embellished by
   a. Romulus's personal diaries.
   b. Rome's innovative artistic genre.
   c. irrefutable facts.
   d. legend and myth.

26. The common people of Rome were the
   a. plebeians.
   b. Etruscans.
   c. consuls.
   d. patricians.

27. The Second Triumvirate was composed of
   a. Pompey, Crassus, and Caesar.
   b. Sulla, Marius, and Cicero.
   c. Octavian, Marc Antony, and Lepidus.
   d. Licinius, Sextus, and Tiberius.

28. The consul who defeated Jugurtha by instituting innovative army reforms
   was

a. Julius Caesar.
b. Tiberius Gracchus.
c. Scipio Africanus.
d. Caius Marius.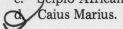

GEOGRAPHY

1. Using the text Map 7.1 as your guide, mark the location of each of the following on the outline map provided below and then in the space below state how each area or city was conquered by the Romans.

   Latium

   Etruria

   Campania

   Tarentum

2. On the outline map mark the location of the following geographic features and then indicate in the space below the significance of each. In what manner did each influence the history of Rome?

   Apennine Mountains

   the Po River Valley

   the Latium and Campania plains

   the Tiber River

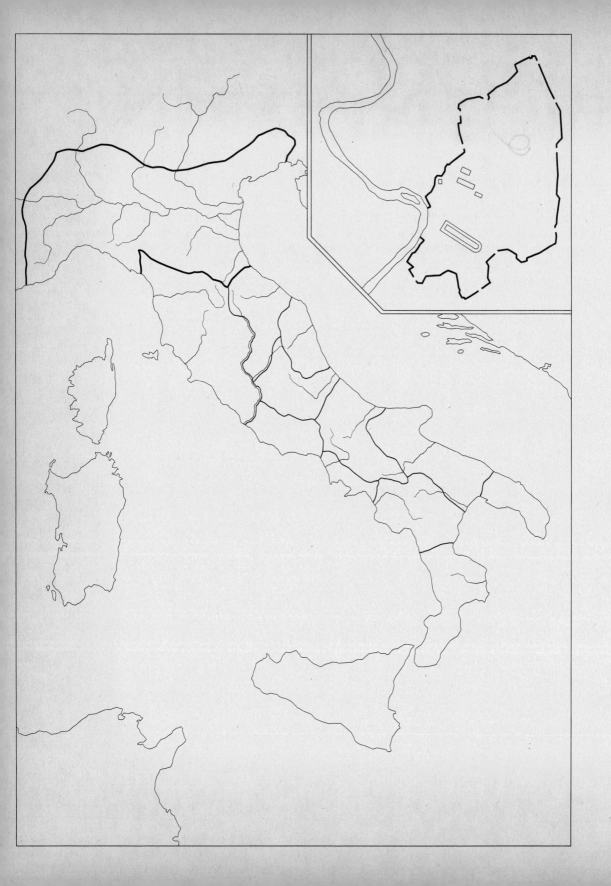

UNDERSTANDING HISTORY THROUGH READING AND THE ARTS

Much of the culture and beliefs of the peoples of the Italian peninsula can be understood through a study of Etruscan and Roman art. For an interestingly written and illustrated beginning source see Chapters 6 and 7 of H. W. Janson, *History of Art* (1962). The best of Roman literature includes Cicero's essay *On Moral Obligation* (trans., J. Higgenbotham, 1967). Other works by Cicero can be found in J. and A. Raubitschek, trans., *Selected Works of Cicero* (1948). A revised and modernized version of Caesar's own story of his conquest of Gaul is found in S. Brady, *Caesar's Gallic Campaigns* (1967). If you are interested in Roman mythology see J. Lindsay, *Men and Gods on the Roman Nile* (1968), and M. Grant, *Myths of the Greeks and Romans* (1965), and for Roman accomplishments in sculpture, town planning, painting, and the like see M. Wheeler, *Roman Art and Architecture** (1985).

PROBLEMS FOR FURTHER INVESTIGATION

Students interested in doing research or writing a report on the origins of the Roman Empire may get some ideas from D. Hood, ed., *The Rise of Rome** (1970).

Two books for students wanting to pursue the subject of religion in ancient Rome are M. Grant, *The Jews in the Ancient World* (1973), and T. R. Glover, *The Conflict of Religions in the Early Roman Empire* (1960).

*Available in paperback.

CHAPTER 8

THE PAX ROMANA

CHAPTER OBJECTIVES

After reading and studying this chapter you should be able to answer the following questions:

Q-1. How did the Roman emperors govern the empire and spread Roman influence into northern Europe?

Q-2. What was the effect of the *pax Romana* on the Mediterranean and European world?

Q-3. How did the empire meet the grim challenges of barbarian invasion and economic decline?

Q-4. Why did Christianity sweep across the Roman world to change it fundamentally?

CHAPTER SYNOPSIS

When Julius Caesar's nephew Augustus became "the First Citizen of the State" in 31 B.C., Rome began a new era called the Augustan Age. This was the "golden age" of Rome in terms of economy, literature, and imperial expansion. Under the Roman Empire the Mediterranean and European peoples enjoyed a long tradition of firmly established personal freedom. The *pax Romana*, or peace of Rome, encouraged the spread of Roman law, justice, and administration as well as the further diffusion of Greek culture, especially into the European world. This era of peace occurred in part because of the constitutional monarchy Augustus established, which lasted until the third decade, when once again Rome became wracked by civil war. The emperor's power, however, rested mainly with the army, which he controlled. Indeed, control of the army became a growing problem for Augustus and his successors, many of whom owed their power to some military rebellion in the provinces. Thus, in the long run, Augustus's settlement was not successful. Nevertheless, his contributions were many.

Augustus's treatment of the imperial subjects in the conquered provinces was just, and his expansion of the empire north and east into Europe was of enormous importance for subsequent European history. His reign also ushered in a great age of Latin literature. And it is through reading the works of Virgil, Livy, and Horace, all of whom are discussed in this chapter, that we are able to gain a sense of what Roman people were like and what they expected of life.

The development and spread of Christianity also occurred during this era. Paul of Tarsus turned the Jewish cult of Jesus into a universal religion based on the ethics of love and forgiveness. Many Romans misunderstood the early Christians and regarded them as atheists because they refused to worship Roman gods. Finally, in the fourth century A.D., Christianity was made the official religion of Rome. Oddly, what had begun as a Judaean hope for salvation from Rome became Rome's state religion.

In the third century A.D., the breakdown of government and order ushered in an age of civil war and barbaric invasion from which Rome never fully recovered. The reforming emperors Diocletian and Constantine were able to restore the old system only partially. They were not able to turn around the depression and decline in trade and agriculture.

Why did Rome "fall"? Certainly, economic and political explanations are important, but they do not tell the entire story. In a real sense there is no answer because the Roman Empire did not actually fall at all but instead slowly merged into a new medieval world. It was Rome and Christianity that provided Europe with the framework for a new age.

STUDY OUTLINE

I. Augustus's settlement (31 B.C.–A.D. 14)
   A. Augustus's goal was to reestablish the republic after years of civil war, to demobilize the army, and to meet the danger of barbarians
   B. The principate and the restored republic
      1. Augustus reestablished the republic but did not give the senate power equal to his own
      2. Augustus became *princeps civitatis*, "the first Citizen of the State," and held other political, religious, and military titles
      3. His control of the army was the main source of his power
         a. New colonies were founded by the soldiers, thus spreading Roman culture further
         b. The colonies were important in unifying the Mediterranean world

4. Overall, the system was a new "constitutional monarchy"
5. Augustus eventually established the practice of dynastic inheritance of the principate

C. Augustus's administration of the provinces
   1. He saw no reason to interfere with the colonies' traditions
   2. The cult of Roma et Augustus gave the empire unity

D. Roman expansion into northern and western Europe
   1. Augustus continued Caesar's push into Europe
   2. In Gaul he founded towns and built roads
   3. He pushed into Spain, Germany, and eastern Europe

E. Literary flowering
   1. The Augustan Age was a productive age of Latin literature
   2. Virgil wrote about the greatness and virtue of Rome in his masterpiece the *Aeneid*, thus spreading Roman culture
   3. Livy's history was one of Rome's gifts to the modern world
   4. Horace praised the simple life and Rome's greatness

II. The coming of Christianity
   A. The colony of Judaea suffered during the Roman civil wars, and hence Jewish resentment of Rome arose
   B. Hatred of King Herod and the Romans led to civil war in Judaea
   C. Two anti-Roman movements existed
      1. The Zealot extremists fought Rome
      2. The militants believed that the coming of the Messiah would end Roman rule
   D. Pagan religious cults were numerous, but it was the new mystery cults that met the needs of the people for security and emotional release
   E. Jesus was a teacher who claimed to be the Messiah of a spiritual kingdom
      1. His teachings were in the orthodox Jewish tradition
      2. He taught his followers not to revolt against Rome
   F. Pontius Pilate, the Roman prefect, was worried about maintaining civil order, so he condemned Jesus to death
   G. Peter continued the Jesus cult in accord with Jewish law
   H. Paul of Tarsus transformed the Jesus cult and made it applicable to all people — particularly those who were attracted to the mystery religions
   I. Christianity was attractive for many reasons
      1. It was open to all, including non-Jews, women, the poor, and common people
      2. It held out the promise of salvation and forgiveness
      3. It gave each person a role and a sense of community

III. The Julio-Claudians and the Flavians (27 B.C.–A.D. 96)

    A.   The Julio-Claudians
        1.   Augustus's dynasty was known as the Julio-Claudians
        2.   Claudius created a system of imperial bureaucracy and extended Roman frontiers, including the conquest of Britain in A.D. 43
        3.   The army began to interfere in politics
        4.   Civil war proved the Augustan settlement a failure
    B.   The Flavian dynasty
        1.   Vespasian created a monarchy
        2.   Domitian defeated barbarian tribes at the frontiers to extend the empire, but his cruelty brought on his assassination
IV. The Age of the "Five Good Emperors" (A.D. 96–180)
    A.   The age of Five Antonines was one of prosperity
    B.   The Antonine monarchy
        1.   The principate became an emperorship
        2.   The emperors were the source of all authority
        3.   Hadrian reformed the bureaucracy
    C.   Changes in the army
        1.   Under the Flavians the boundaries of the empire became fixed
        2.   The army was a source of economic stability and a Romanizing agent
  V. Life in the "golden age"
    A.   Imperial Rome
        1.   The government provided the citizens of Rome with free grain, oil, and wine
        2.   Free, often brutal, entertainment was provided
            a.   Gladiatorial fighting was popular
            b.   The most popular was chariot racing
        3.   Most Romans worked hard and lived average lives
    B.   The provinces prospered under the Antonines
        1.   From Augustus onward, free farming and immigration thrived
        2.   The army brought farming and towns to new areas
        3.   Under the Romans, eastern Mediterranean trade expanded, and grain production in northern Europe increased as the provinces became linked in a vast economic network
        4.   Manufacturing, such as glass and pottery making, tended to move from Italy to the provinces, especially to northern Europe
        5.   Northern and Western European cities enjoyed growth and peace under Roman rule
VI. Civil wars and invasion in the third century
    A.   Commodus's reign led to civil war; over twenty emperors ascended the throne between 235 and 284
    B.   Civil war left the empire open to invasion

    C.   Barbarians on the frontiers found gaps in the Roman defenses
        1.   In A.D. 258, the Goths burst into Europe
        2.   The Alamanni, Franks, Saxons, and other tribes invaded the empire
    D.   Invasion brought turmoil and impoverishment to farm and village life
        1.   The breakdown of the system led to crime and disorder
        2.   Much of the damage was done by officials and soldiers

VII. Reconstruction under Diocletian and Constantine (A.D. 284–337)
    A.   The end of political turmoil under Diocletian's reign
        1.   Diocletian claimed the gods had chosen him to rule as *dominus*; his power became absolute
        2.   Because the empire was too big for one person to govern well, Diocletian reorganized it
            a.   Imperial authority was split between two emperors — Diocletian in the east and an *augustus* in the west
            b.   Each emperor was assisted by a *caesar*, and each half was split into two prefectures
            c.   The power of the provincial governors was reduced
            d.   Diocletian's division between east and west became permanent
    B.   Inflation and taxes
        1.   The monetary system was in ruins and highly inflated
        2.   Diocletian attempted to curb inflation through wage and price controls
        3.   The new imperial taxation system led to a loss of freedom as people became locked into their jobs
    C.   The legalization of Christianity
        1.   Constantine realized that Christianity could serve his empire
        2.   Many Romans misunderstood Christianity
            a.   The pagans accused the Christians of atheism
            b.   Overall, persecutions were minor and limited even during the third-century turmoil
            c.   Christianity was legalized by Constantine, and in 380 it was made Rome's official religion
    E.   The construction of Constantinople
        1.   Constantine built a new capital for the empire at the site of Byzantium
        2.   The focus of the empire shifted to the east

VIII. Rome and the East
    A.   Romans versus Iranians
        1.   The Parthians, heirs of the Persian empire, were defeated by the Romans
        2.   The Parthians' place was taken by the Sassanids, who fought a long struggle against the Romans in Asia

3. Not until Diocletian and Constantine did Rome firmly establish its rule in western Asia

B. Trade and contact

1. The Parthians were the middlemen in the trade between China and the Roman Empire
   a. A network of roads linked Parthia to China, India, and the West
   b. The most famous road was the "Silk Road"
   c. The Parthians exported exotic goods to China in exchange for iron and luxury goods
   d. Parthian traders carried Chinese goods overland from the Stone Tower to points in the West
   e. Ideas and art also passed along these roads
2. The Parthians also presided over maritime trade between the West and the East
3. China's growth under the Han brought closer contact between China and the Roman world
4. Han emperor Wu Ti opened the Silk Road for new exchanges of goods and ideas

REVIEW QUESTIONS

Q-1.   What were the sources of Augustus's power? Was Augustus a "dictator" in the modern sense?

Q-2.   What were Augustus's accomplishments with regard to the administration and expansion of the empire?

Q-3.   What does the work of the writers during Rome's Augustan Age of literature tell us about Roman life and what the Romans thought important?

Q-4.   Why was the relationship between Rome and its colony Judaea so strained in the age of Augustus? What were the motives and responses of both Jews and Romans?

Q-5.   Did Jesus intend to found a new religion? Explain by evaluating the work of this teacher.

Q-6.   What role did Paul of Tarsus play in the evolution of Christianity, and what might have happened if Peter of Jerusalem had kept control over the cult?

Q-7.   Why was Christianity attractive? How was this religion unlike that of the Greeks and Romans?

Q-8.   What was the system of picking the *princeps civitatis* after the death of Augustus? Did the system work?

Q-9.   Under what circumstances did the Flavian dynasty come about, and what were its contributions?

Q-10.   What features of the Roman army made it a source of both strength and weakness for the empire?

Q-11. What is meant by the term *barracks emperors*?

Q-12. What was the pattern of immigration, and what were the reasons for the increase in free farming after the time of Augustus?

Q-13. What were the causes and the results of the civil wars between A.D. 235 and 284?

Q-14. Discuss the impact the barbarians had on the empire. Were the invasions the cause or the result of a political breakdown?

Q-15. Explain the changes in the concept and power of the emperor under Diocletian and Constantine. Why did these changes occur?

Q-16. Why did the number of small farmers and the amount of personal freedom decrease during and after the period of civil war?

Q-17. What did Diocletian and Constantine do to restore and strengthen the empire?

Q-18. Describe the political climate in Judaea within which Jesus of Nazareth emerged. Did this influence the course of "religious" history?

Q-19. Why were many Romans distrustful of Christianity?

STUDY-REVIEW EXERCISES

Define the following key concepts and terms.

Messiah

princeps civitatis

pax Romana

imperator

the Julio-Claudian dynasty

apocalypse

villa

Identify each of the following and give its significance.

Goths

Jesus

Paul of Tarsus

Antonines

King Herod of Judaea

Parthians

Silk Road

Zealots

gladiatorial fighting

Five Good Emperors

Mithraism

Commodus

barracks emperors

Constantine

Virgil

Ferdinand Lot

Explain *the contributions of each of the following to Rome and the Roman Empire.*

Augustus

Claudius

Hadrian

Vespasian

Diocletian

Constantine

Explain the subject matter and the central theme of each of the following books.

Virgil, *Georgics*

Virgil, *Aeneid*

Livy, *Ab Urbe Condita*

Test your understanding of the chapter by answering the following questions.

1. Augustus (did)/did not believe that the colonies should be self-governing and culturally independent.
2. The capital of the Roman Empire was eventually moved to the new eastern

    city of _____Constantinople_____.
3. From the time of Augustus, the power of the principate tended to (increase)/decrease.

4. Christianity was made the official religion of Rome in the year __380__.
5. The Roman government (did)/did not provide free food and entertainment for the citizens of Rome.
6. With the reign of Augustus, free farming tended to (increase)/decrease.
7. For the most part, the Roman persecutions of Christians were (minor)/widespread.
8. Under the Five Good Emperors the areas of northern and western Europe underwent a period of economic (expansion)/decline.

Number the following events in correct chronological order.

1. __5__ The first barbarian invasion

2. __3__ The "Year of the Four Emperors"

3. __2__ The execution of Jesus of Nazareth

4. __1__ The ending of the republican civil wars by Augustus

5. __4__ The golden age of Rome under the "Five Good Emperors"

6. __6__ The building of Constantinople

MULTIPLE-CHOICE QUESTIONS

1. The man most responsible for the spread of Christianity to non-Jews was
   a. emperor Diocletian.
   b. St. Peter.
   c. Livy.
   d. Paul of Tarsus.

2. In 31 B.C., Augustus established a new government for Rome that was a
   a. republic.
   b. constitutional monarchy.
   c. democracy.
   d. dictatorship.

3. Augustus's attitude toward the provinces was one of
   a. neglect.
   b. oppression.
   c. prejudice toward minorities.
   d. respect for local customs.

4. Which of the following was an anti-Roman group in Judaea?
   a. Zealots
   b. Baruchs
   c. Essenes
   d. Hittites

5. The backbone of Roman agriculture in the Augustan Age was
   a. slave labor.
   b. imported foods from the empire.
   c. captured barbarian labor.
   d. small free farmers.

6. Before Constantine legalized Christianity, the Romans demanded that the Christians
   a. worship the Roman gods.
   b. observe the ritual of sacrifice to the gods.
   c. deny Christ as a god.
   d. go back to their Jewish beliefs.

7. The city that Constantine made the capital of the eastern Roman Empire was
   a. Kiev.
   b. Constantinople.

c. Alexandria.
d. Athens.

8. During the reign of Augustus, the direction of Roman conquest was toward
    a. Judaea.
    b. northern Europe.
    c. Britain.
    d. the Black Sea.

9. Above all, Virgil's *Aeneid* is a(n)
    a. plea for Christianity.
    b. argument against Roman imperialism and war.
    c. vision of Rome as the protector of good in the world.
    d. history of the fall of Athens.

10. The Roman-appointed king of Judaea was
    a. Herod.
    b. Jesus.
    c. Philip Augustus.
    d. Cato.

11. In order to avert starvation and unrest, the government of Rome provided free grain, oil, and wine to
    a. the military only.
    b. the poor only.
    c. all citizens.
    d. no one.

12. The Flavian period came about largely because of
    a. military interference in the selection of the emperor.
    b. the Flavian control of the banking system.
    c. military defeat of Rome by the Goths.
    d. revolution in Judaea.

13. The "golden age" of the Roman Empire was in which period?
    a. Severi
    b. Flavian
    c. Julio-Claudian
    d. Antonine

14. Roman colonies differed from the Greek colonies of Archilochus's time in that they

   a.   were strictly agricultural.
   b.   remained part of the home country.
   c.   provided valuable cultural links with the home country.
   d.   were only military.

15. The Roman poets were primarily concerned with, and their core works dealt
     with,
     a.   mythology.
     b.   the great battles of history.
     c.   divinity.
     d.   humanity.

16. After Augustus's death, the Roman army
     a.   became more mobile.
     b.   engaged in more conquest.
     c.   became a garrison force.
     d.   was limited to Roman-born soldiers.

17. A military problem that confronted Augustus was the fact that
     a.   the army was under the command of the senate.
     b.   the army was much too large.
     c.   the army had no contact with Roman culture.
     d.   all of the above.

18. The Roman colonial empire was largely a result of
     a.   commercial contacts between Rome and the Mediterranean.
     b.   the Roman takeover of the empire of Alexander.
     c.   the spread of Christianity.
     d.   the need to find space for the army and its veterans.

19. In general, Augustus's treatment of the Jews was
     a.   brutal.
     b.   complete neglect.
     c.   tolerant and respectful.
     d.   none of the above.

20. Roman literature of the "golden age"
     a.   was "otherworldly" in its themes.
     b.   rejected the legendary traditions of Rome.
     c.   stressed human rather than divine themes.
     d.   tended to be simple and emotional rather than intellectual in conception.

21. The Apocalypse of Baruch was the idea, held by some Jews, of
    a. the coming destruction of the Roman Empire.
    b. the coming of a Messiah to save Israel.
    c. a great period of misery and suffering to be followed by peace.
    d. all of the above.

22. Many Romans were distrustful of Christianity because
    a. it denied the existence of Roman gods.
    b. it appeared to believe in cannibalism.
    c. it was highly ritualistic.
    d. all of the above.

23. *Georgics*, by Virgil, is a poetic work about
    a. Roman expansion.
    b. gladiatorial fighting.
    c. agriculture.
    d. seafaring.

24. After the fall of the Parthians in 226, the adversary of Rome at its western borders was the
    a. Sassanids.
    b. Lydians.
    c. Chinese.
    d. Indians.

25. The Parthians were profit-taking trade intermediaries between
    a. England and continental Europe.
    b. the Goths and the Huns.
    c. Rome and China.
    d. Spain and Gaul.

26. A major overland trade route between ancient Iran and ancient China was called the
    a. Wu Ti Trail.
    b. Silk Road.
    c. Imperial Pass.
    d. Asian Connection.

27. The historian who appreciated Augustus's republican virtues was
    a. Horace.
    b. Virgil.
    c. Herodotus.
    d. Livy.

28. The first Roman emperor to fix prices and wages in a failed attempt to curb inflation was
    a. Augustus.
    b. Diocletian.
    c. Hadrian.
    d. Constantine.

GEOGRAPHY

1. Using Map 8.1 in the text as a guide, show on the outline map on page 123 the boundaries of the Roman Empire under Augustus; then use Map 8.2 to show the empire's division under Diocletian.
2. Locate and label on the outline map the following places.

Rome	Sicily	Britain	Rhine River
Byzantium	Crete	Danube River	Carthage
Jerusalem	Teutoburger forest		

3. Describe the Roman penetration into northern and western Europe. What kinds of problems did the Romans face, and what techniques did they use in their successful conquests?

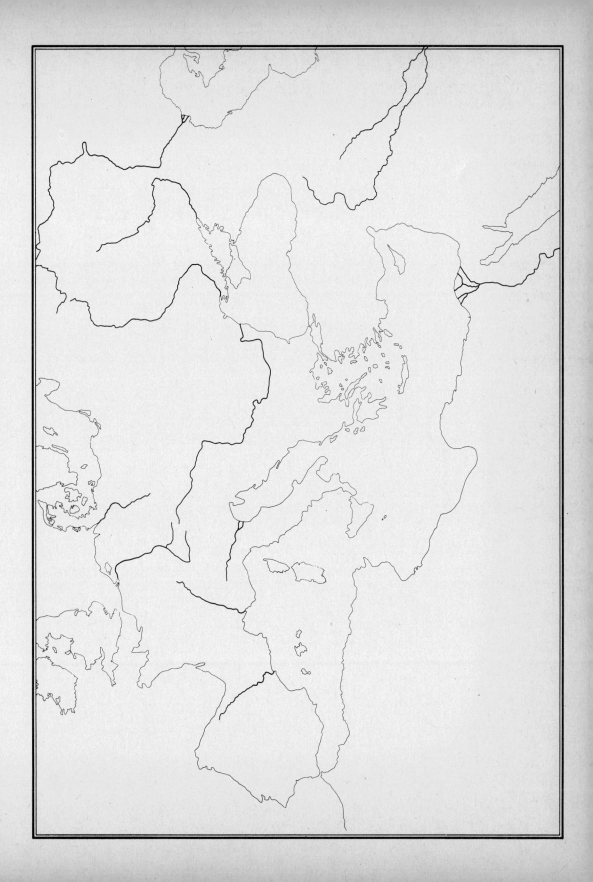

UNDERSTANDING HISTORY THROUGH READING AND THE ARTS

Reading biography can be an interesting and rewarding way of discovering the past. A. Schweitzer's *The Quest of the Historical Jesus* (1948) is a superb work, and A. D. Nock's *St. Paul* (1938) is an interesting study of one of the most important men in world history. *Rome in the Augustan Age* (1962) by H. Rowell is about Augustus, the man whose imprint on the empire was immense. Also recommended is R. Warner, *The Young Caesar* (1958). R. Graves's *I, Claudius** (1934) is an exciting account of the families, the work, and the loves of the emperors from Augustus to Claudius.

Because the source of most Roman art was Greece, there is hardly such a thing as a "Roman" style. Only in architecture were the Romans truly original. The arch and vault and construction projects such as sewers, bridges, roads, and aqueducts were among Rome's great enterprises. Chapter 7, "Roman Art," in H. W. Janson's *History of Art* (1962) is an excellent review. A more detailed account is G. Rivoira, *Roman Architecture* (1930).

The Romans produced some of the world's greatest literature. Virgil's *The Aeneid* is twelve books of some of mankind's most-read poetry. For an insight into the working of this poetic genius see W. Knight, *Roman Virgil** (1966). Of interest to students in science and philosophy would be the essay *On the Nature of the Universe** (trans., R. Latham, 1967) by the Roman Lucretius, a poet and Epicurean, and Ovid's *The Love Poems of Ovid** (trans., H. Gregory, 1964) can be enjoyed by all.

PROBLEMS FOR FURTHER INVESTIGATION

The reasons for the decline of Roman civilization have interested scholars for hundreds of years. Even the people of Rome were obsessed with the feeling of deterioration. Many prophecies, including the biblical Book of Revelation, foretold the end of the empire. The problems of decline and identification of its causes are the subjects of a scholarly book, *The Awful Revolution* (1969) by F. W. Walbank. The subject is also dealt with in the Problems in European Civilization series' *Decline and Fall of the Roman Empire** (1962) by D. Kagan. These can be supplemented by G. Milner, *The Problem of Decadence* (1931).

*Available in paperback.

CHAPTER 9

THE MAKING OF EUROPE

CHAPTER OBJECTIVES

After reading and studying this chapter you should be able to answer the following questions:

Q-1.   How did the Greco-Roman heritage, the Germanic traditions, and Christianity act on one another and contribute to the making of a new Europe?
Q-2.   What influence did the Byzantine culture have on the making of European civilization?

CHAPTER SYNOPSIS

Between 400 and 900 a distinctly European society evolved. The basic ingredients of this new European civilization were the Greco-Roman culture, the customs and traditions of the Germanic peoples, and Christianity.

Diocletian had divided the Roman Empire into two major parts. The capital of the western half was Rome; the capital of the eastern half was Constantinople. The eastern (Byzantine) empire lasted for nearly a thousand years after the disintegration of the western empire in the fifth century. Imperial administration in the West had, by 476, given way to massive Germanic invasions. Within Europe the strongest power and the only stabilizing force was the Roman church, which, largely by default, came to be the major political as well as spiritual power. In the eastern empire the emperor held supreme authority over the church. In Rome, however, the bishops formulated the theory of the church's ultimate power over the state. The church in the West assimilated much of the Greco-Roman culture and used its intellectual passion and administrative talent to tame and transform the Germanic tribes. Of equal importance in the making of Europe were the monastic orders, which after about 529 were unified under the *Rule* set forth by Saint Benedict.

While Germans were being baptized and were consolidating themselves into great kingdoms, the new threat of Islam pushed into Europe. Founded by Mohammed in the early seventh century, the religion of Islam united the Arabs and in a short period produced one of the most expansionist cultures the world has ever witnessed. By the early eighth century, Muslims had conquered Spain and were pushing into France.

Both the Byzantine and the Islamic empires were important for European development. Both preserved much Greco-Roman knowledge, a great deal of which was not rediscovered in the West until much later, and they made important contributions to law, science, and medicine. Germanic tradition and custom were also important in that development. But above all, it was Christianity that gave Europe its strength and unity.

STUDY OUTLINE

I.   The growth of the Christian church
    A.   The word *church* can mean several things, but at this time it was often applied to the officials — or *papa* — who presided over all Christians
    B.   The church and the Roman emperors
        1.   Constantine supported and legalized Christianity in 312
        2.   Theodosius increased the power of the church and made Christianity the official religion of the Roman Empire
        3.   The emperors were important in enforcing theological uniformity in the church
            a.   Constantine summoned the Council of Nicaea in 325 to combat Arianism
            b.   The council supported the doctrine (the Nicene Creed) that Christ was of the same substance as God, and this became the orthodox position, supported by the state
        4.   Bishop Ambrose formulated the theory that the church was supreme over the state
    C.   Inspired leadership in the early church
        1.   Many talented Romans, such as Ambrose, became administrators and workers in the church
            a.   The church adopted the Empire's system of dioceses
            b.   Bishops came to preside over dioceses
        2.   The bishop of Rome eventually became the supreme head (the pope) of the church in Europe
        3.   Because the position of emperor disappeared in the West, the Roman bishop became the chief civil authority in Italy

         a. It was said that Pope Leo I saved Rome from Attila
         b. Pope Gregory acted as civil authority

D. The missionary activity of the early Christians
1. The Roman soldier Martin of Tours brought Christianity to Gaul while Saint Patrick brought Christianity and Roman culture to Ireland
    a. Under Saint Columba, Iona in Scotland became an important Christian center
2. Augustine and other missionaries carried Christianity to the Germans
3. Two forms of Christianity — Roman and Celtic — clashed, but the Roman form won out at the Synod of Whitby in 664
4. Because of the Germans' warlike customs and different culture their assimilation into Christianity was slow
    a. The Christian emphasis on poverty, universal brotherhood, and love of enemies was difficult for German warriors to accept
    b. The Christian concepts of sin and repentance were also hard for them to understand

E. Conversion and assimilation
1. The missionaries pursued a policy of assimilating pagan customs and beliefs into Christianity
2. Penitentials — manuals used to examine one's conscience — were used by priests to teach people Christian virtue, as was preaching

II. Christian attitudes toward classical culture
A. The early Christians were hostile toward pagan Roman culture
1. Early Christians believed that Roman culture was useless and immoral
2. They hated the Romans because they had crucified Christ and persecuted his followers

B. Christianity's compromise and adjustments to Roman culture
1. Most early Christians had pagan backgrounds
2. Early Christians had no objections to homosexuality
3. Saint Paul and Saint Jerome incorporated pagan thought into Christianity

C. Saint Augustine and the synthesis of pagan and Christian thought
1. Augustine is the most important Christian thinker of his time
    a. His book, *The Confessions*, is one of the most influential in Europe
    b. Contrary to Donatism, Augustine believed that Christians should change society
    c. He believed that human beings are basically weak and evil
    d. He believed that the state is a necessary evil to protect people and that ultimate authority in society lies with the church
2. Augustine assimilated Roman-pagan history and culture into Christianity

III. Monasticism and the *Rule* of Saint Benedict
    A. Early eremitical life was at first viewed as dangerous by the church
        1. There were many experiments in communal monasticism in the fifth and sixth centuries
    B. Benedict of Nursia's *Rule* became the guide fo all Christian monastic life
        1. The Benedictine *Rule* was a flexible and simple code and encouraged all kinds of labor and participants
            a. Monks took part in regular prayer and study
            b. Three vows were taken — stability, conversion of manners, and obedience
            c. The *Rule* illustrated the assimilation of Roman logic and law into monasticism
            d. The *Rule* encouraged newcomers and people of all classes toward religious life
        2. Benedictine monasticism played an important role — including agricultural development and government training — in European life

IV. The migration of the Germanic peoples
    A. The migrations or *volkerwanderungen*
        1. Germanic tribes had been pushing against the Roman Empire's frontiers since 250 (see Map 9.3)
            a. The Huns, who moved westward from China to the east, drove the Goths into the empire
            b. In 378, the Visigoths defeated the Romans, and full-scale Germanic invasions began
        2. The Germans migrated into Europe possibly because they were overpopulated, had food shortages, and were attracted to Roman wealth
        3. Except for the Lombards, their conquests on the continent ended around 600
            a. The Visigoths in Gaul; the Vandals in North Africa
        4. They replaced Rome as rulers of Europe and established a number of kingdoms, the most important being the Frankish kingdom under the chieftain Clovis, who founded the Merovingian dynasty

V. Germanic society
    A. Germanic kinship, custom, and class
        1. The basic social and political unit was the tribe
            a. The tribe, or *Volk*, was united by kinship
            b. Every tribe had its own customs, and these customs were its law
        2. The tribes were led by a king, or chieftain
        3. The *comitatus*, or warband, was the beginning of a warrior nobility
    B. Germanic law
        1. Under Salic Law each person had a *wergeld*, or monetary value, and each offense had a fine

      2. German law — as shown by the Salic Law — aimed not at justice but at the reduction of violence

  C. German life was greatly influenced by the forests

      1. The pagan Germans believed that gods inhabited the forests, so they would not cut down trees or clear the land for farming

      2. Germanic peoples lived in cooperative agricultural villages

      3. The end of their animistic beliefs encouraged them to exercise greater control over their environment

      4. They often lived in wattle huts

      5. They adopted Roman taste and practices

  D. Anglo-Saxon England

      1. The exit of the Romans in 407 led to the establishment of seven Germanic kingdoms in England

      2. Britons fled to the west, and the Germans destroyed Roman culture

      3. Celts, Picts, and Britons remained strong in Wales and Scotland

      4. Alfred, king of Wessex, unified England in the ninth century

VI. The Byzantine East

  A. The Roman Empire divided

      1. The western part was controlled by the Germans

      2. The eastern part continued the traditions and institutions of the old empire

  B. Differences between the Byzantine East and the Germanic West

      1. Because imperial protection of the western empire disappeared in the fifth century, the Roman church assumed much civil authority

      2. In the eastern part of the empire, Roman culture was preserved

      3. In the West there were conflicts between church and state leaders, while in the East the state was supreme over the church

         a. In the West the spiritual ideals of confessor, martyr, and virgin were seen to exist in "saints" who were socially prominent persons

         b. In the East the saints were seen to avoid society

  C. External threats and internal conflicts

      1. Justinian's wars left the Byzantine empire weak

      2. Then the Slavs took the Balkans while the Arabs took the eastern provinces — the result of a long series of wars

      3. Despite these losses, the empire was left with greater cultural unity and was forced to undertake internal reorganization

         a. The empire was divided into *themes* (military districts) governed by *strategoi* (generals) — all supported by a new native peasant army

         b. Therefore, the empire was now dependent on native soldiers, not foreign mercenaries

    4. Military losses also resulted in an increase in popular piety and icon worship

        a. Iconoclasts (those who opposed icon worship) argued that people should not worship the image itself

        b. This resulted in a great theological split; Leo III ordered the destruction of all icons in 710, but they were officially restored in 843

        c. This raised the issue of the right of the emperor to interfere into the affairs of the church

        d. It also led to a great split (or *schism*) between the eastern and the western Christian churches

  D. The Law Code of Justinian

    1. The law codes of the emperors Theodosius and Justinian are among the most important contributions of the Byzantine Empire

    2. The *corpus juris civilis* — the civil law — is the foundation of European law

        a. This is made up of the Code, the Digest, and the Institutes

  E. Byzantine intellectual life

    1. The Byzantines kept scholarship alive, especially history

    2. They passed Greco-Roman culture on to the Arabs

    3. They were not creative in science or mathematics

    4. They made advances in the art of war and in medicine

VII. Private Life

  A. Tenth-century Constantinople was the greatest city in the Christian world

    1. It was the seat of the imperial court, the church, and the locus of international trade

    2. Byzantine politics was complicated, entangled, and full of intrigue, assassination, and military revolt; the Nicephorus murder of 969 is a good example

    3. Foreign trade was controlled by Jewish, Muslim, and Italian (largely Venetian) merchants

    4. Byzantine Greeks avoided commerce, and Byzantine society was attached to rural ideals and a landed aristocracy

    5. Monasticism played an important part in society, and the monasteries were rich

  B. Private life centered on the Byzantine *oikos*, or household

    1. The *oikos* included family and servants

    2. The artisans lived in their shops, the middle class in apartments, and the aristocrats in mansions

    3. To protect women, upper-class houses were designed to segregate women, keeping them in a *gynaikonitis*, or women's apartment

    4. Arranged marriage was a means of social advancement; little is known of Byzantine sexual practices

REVIEW QUESTIONS

Q-1.   Describe the role of the Roman emperors and the empire in the growth of Christianity from an outlawed movement to the most important power in Rome.

Q-2.   Why did Rome become the capital of the Christian church in the West?

Q-3.   Using the kingdom of Kent as an example, explain how the Christian missionaries converted the pagans. What devices and techniques did they use in the assimilation of Germanic people into Christianity?

Q-4.   Why and how did the Christian rejection of paganism turn to compromise?

Q-5.   What ideas did Saint Augustine contribute to Christian thought?

Q-6.   What was happening to Rome at the time Saint Augustine wrote *The City of God*? How could this have influenced his philosophy that the City of God is more important than the city of man?

Q-7.   What was the purpose of monasticism? Why is Benedict of Nursia one of the most important figures in the history of Christian monasticism?

Q-8.   Describe the Benedictine *Rule*. Why was it the most successful monastic rule?

Q-9.   The monasteries were completely isolated from European life and played no role in European society. Agree or disagree with the preceding statement. Explain the reasons for your decision.

Q-10.   In 378, a Visigothic army defeated the Roman army. Why was this a turning point in European history? Who were the Germans and what were their motives and interests?

Q-11.   What patterns of social and political life existed in German society and what was the economy like?

Q-12.   How and why did Germanic law evolve and how did it work?

Q-13.   Why did Christianity dramatically change the way Germans viewed and used their environment?

Q-14.   Name the kingdoms of the English Heptarchy. What were their origins and what role did King Alfred of Wessex play in this development?

Q-15.   Compare and contrast the Byzantine and western European societies in terms of (a) political development and (b) religion.

Q-16.   Describe and give examples of the church-state conflict in the West. Why was this conflict not a problem in the eastern part of the empire?

Q-17.   The Byzantine civilization is often pictured as decadent and unproductive. Is this a correct evaluation? Explain.

Q-18.   Explain: "Byzantium served the West as both a protector from the East and a preserver of ancient culture."

Q-19.   Who were the iconoclasts, and what was the result of their struggle?

Q-20.   What were the main features of Byzantine private life? Why were women segregated in the household?

STUDY-REVIEW EXERCISES

<u>Define</u> *the following key concepts and terms.*

ekklesia meaning church - St. Paul meant the local community of Christian believers

Justinian's Code set out to bring order to Roman science/philosophy
of law   backbone of juris civilis (body of civil law)

catholic comes from Greek word meaning general, universal worldwide
Christians sought to make faith catholic - believed everywhere

penitentials manuals for examination of conscience written by
Irish poets - Penance usually meant fasting to mend soul

Salic Law

The City of God

Rule of Saint Benedict Purpose - to draw people away from being attached
to real world and love oneself and to love god. Simple code for
oikos ordinary men. Outlined monastic life. Ex. of how
Greco-Roman heritage and Roman patterns are preserved

gynaikonitis

Byzantine

strategoi

Arianism denies that Christ is devine and that he had
always existed with God the Father

wergeld

heresy the denial of a doctrine of faith. Orthodox
Christians branded Arianism heresy

dioceses

schism - the split (continuous) between the Roman Catholic
and greek orthodox churches resulting from theological
themes disagreements between the bishop of Rome and the patriarch
of Constantinople

<u>Identify</u> *each of the following and give its significance.*

Dooms of Ethelbert

Theodosius

Byzantine Empire

King Alfred of Wessex

Augustine the missionary

Bishop Ambrose

Pope Leo I

Saint Martin of Tours/Saint Patrick

Saint Augustine's *Confessions*

Saint Jerome

Clovis *Defeated Gallo-Roman general Syagrius and took over Loire. Converted to Orthodox christianity*

Saint Benedict

Justinian

Explain the following events and tell why they are important.

Synod of Whitby, 664

Battle of Tours, 733

Hegira, 622

Council of Nicaea, 325

Theodosius-Ambrose dispute

Test your understanding of the chapter by answering the following questions.

1. Overall, the Benedictine monastic movement *did*/*did not* result in economic and material benefits to Europe.

2. This emperor legalized Christianity in the year 312. _Constantine_
3. In Germanic society each person's monetary value to the tribe was called the

    wergeld   .
4. Of the two parts of the old Roman empire — east and west — it was the

    East   that was politically and culturally more stable
    and progressive.
5. The early church fathers believed that the church (was)/*was not* ultimately
    superior to the state.
6. This important Christian philosopher was the author of *The Confessions*.

    St. Augustine
7. After the year 476 it was _the Pope_   ,
    not emperors, who held power in the western Roman world.
8. The Germanic peoples' pre-Christian view of their environment *aided*/(retarded)
    their material standard of living.
9. This book, written at the time of Rome's destruction, argues that humanity is
    divided between those who live the earthly life of selfishness and those who
    life according to the spirit of God.

    City of God
10. The head of the Byzantine Church was the *emperor/pope.* patriarch

MULTIPLE-CHOICE QUESTIONS

1. At the Council of Nicaea in 325 it was decided that
    a. the Arians were correct.
    b. emperors should not participate in theological disputes.
    (c.) Christ was of the same substance as God.
    d. God and Christ were of different substances.

2. Writers of penitentials tended to be most concerned about the people's
    a. faith in God.
    b. rejection of Roman authority.
    c. baptism and the end of fighting.
    (d.) sexual behavior.

3. The major accomplishment of Alfred the Great was
    (a.) the unification of the Anglo-Saxon kingdoms.

b. the conversion of Britain to Christianity.
c. the defeat of Rome's last emperor.
d. a new law code.

4. Saint Augustine is important in European history because he
    a. worked out the theory of papal supremacy.
    b. compiled the writings of Jesus into a New Testament.
    c. assimilated Greco-Roman thought into Christianity.
    d. was the first bishop of Rome.

5. The Benedictine *Rule* was primarily designed to
    a. spread Christianity to the Germans.
    b. draw the individual away from love of self.
    c. encourage new economic ventures.
    d. train officials for government.

6. Collections of early Germanic laws dealt primarily with
    a. sex.
    b. civil rights.
    c. property rights.
    d. fines for criminal offenses, such as theft, murder, rape, and so forth.

7. The Germanic peoples held animistic beliefs. This means that
    a. the meat of animals should not be eaten.
    b. gods or spiritual forces live in natural objects such as rivers.
    c. bulls or cattle are sacred.
    d. animals, like human beings, have souls.

8. The most important ecclesiastical statement about church-state relations was formulated by
    a. Arius of Alexandria.
    b. the emperor Theodosius.
    c. the emperor Diocletian.
    d. Ambrose of Milan.

9. Religious conversion means
    a. baptism.
    b. a turning of the heart and mind to God.
    c. confession.
    d. confirmation.

10. Missionaries got pagan peoples to accept Christianity through which of the following?
    a. Preaching and teaching
    b. Living exemplary lives
    c. The adaptation of pagan places and practices to Christian use
    d. All of the above

11. Unlike elsewhere, church organization was closely associated with local monastic life in
    a. Germany.
    b. Scotland.
    c. Ireland.
    d. Italy.

12. Cassiodorus identified monasticism entirely with
    a. prayer and mortification.
    b. study and learning.
    c. manual labor.
    d. all of the above.

13. The monastic vows in the *Rule* of St. Benedict were
    a. poverty, chastity, and obedience.
    b. the Work of God.
    c. stability, conversion of manners, and obedience.
    d. none of the above.

14. Benedictine monasticism replaced other forms of early Christian monasticism largely because
    a. of its moderation, flexibility, and balanced life.
    b. the emperors encouraged it.
    c. Benedictine monks were cleverer.
    d. Europeans were especially suited to the eremitical life.

15. The Byzantine emperor Justinian secured a permanent place in European history for his
    a. defeat of the Slavs and Turks.
    b. production of the *corpus juris civilis*.
    c. marriage to Theodora.
    d. invention of the cyrillic alphabet.

16. The *corpus juris civilis* was
    a. snippets of the works of Herodotus, Procopius, and Aristotle.

b. Russian, Roman, and Greek laws.
c. Roman law and Greek practices.
d. the body of civil law of Justinian.

17. The Western intellectual debt to Islam is primarily in the area of
    a. law.
    b. mathematics and medicine.
    c. a code of ethical behavior.
    d. literature.

18. Historians' knowledge of the early Germanic tribes comes from
    a. collections of laws.
    b. archaeological evidence.
    c. mosaic art.
    d. all of the above.

19. Christian manuals called penitentials were used by priests and missionaries to
    a. instruct newly baptized peoples in Christian attitudes and ideals.
    b. teach that sex was evil.
    c. provide information on abortion.
    d. urge Christians to avoid pagans.

20. The best-known scientific discovery of Byzantium was
    a. Greek fire.
    b. artillery.
    c. the army medical corps.
    d. the theory that the sun revolved around the earth.

21. Which of the following statements about the Benedictine *Rule* is true?
    a. It applied to men only.
    b. It was strictly inflexible.
    c. It emphasized love of self.
    d. It encouraged nonintellectual labor.

22. Under siege in the seventh and eighth centuries, Constantinople was saved by
    a. Byzantine naval superiority.
    b. Arab mercenaries.
    c. the leadership of Constantine.
    d. adept diplomacy.

23. Byzantium eventually lost the Balkans to the
    a. Arabs

    b. Slavs.
    c. Sassanids.
    d. Egyptians.

24. Heraclitus divided Byzantium into military districts governed by
    a. *satraps.*
    b. *themes.*
    c. *strategoi.*
    d. iconoclasts.

25. A permanent schism between the Roman Catholic and Greek Orthodox churches occurred in
    a. 626.
    b. 730.
    c. 843.
    d. 1054.

26. Which of the following characterizes Byzantine monasteries?
    a. Monks were held in little esteem.
    b. Monasteries were influential and wealthy.
    c. Bishops seldom came from monasteries.
    d. The spread of monasteries was slow within Byzantium.

27. The destruction of all icons was ordered by
    a. Heraclitus.
    b. Justinian.
    c. Leo III.
    d. Romanus III.

28. Which is true of the iconoclast controversy?
    a. It was merely a theological dispute.
    b. It strengthened Byzantine influence in Italy.
    c. It was encouraged by the Pope.
    d. It raised questions concerning the separation of church and state.

GEOGRAPHY

1. Using Map 8.1 in the text as a guide, show on the outline map the boundaries of the Roman Empire at the time of Hadrian.
2. Using Map 9.1 in the text as a guide, draw in the invasion routes of the seven invasion groups.

3. Locate and label the battle site of Tours. Why was this battle significant?

4. Locate and label the following places.

Constantinople	Mecca	Red Sea	Paris
Rome	Jerusalem	Black Sea	Egypt
Arabian Desert			

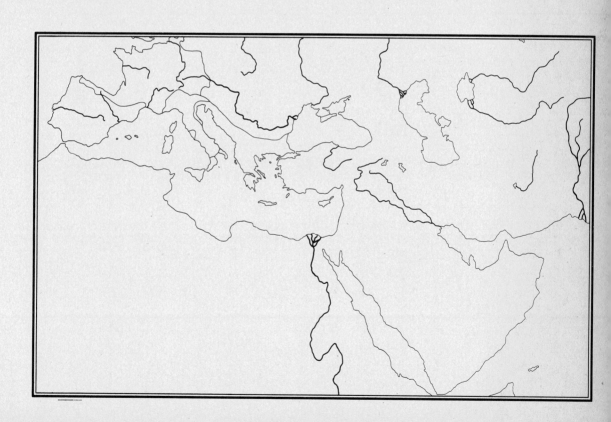

5.   Who were the Anglo-Saxons, and how did they affect the peoples of Britain?

UNDERSTANDING HISTORY THROUGH READING AND THE ARTS

The best architectural statement of the Byzantine age is the Hagia Sophia (Church of Holy Wisdom), built between 532 and 637 in Constantinople in the age of Justinian. After the Turkish conquest it became a mosque and the minarets were added. See E. H. Swift, *Hagia Sophia* (1940), and N. Pevsner, *An Outline of European Architecture** (7th ed., 1963), Chapters 1 and 2.

PROBLEMS FOR FURTHER INVESTIGATION

How did monastic life and organization affect the making of Europe? Begin your investigation with the general survey by David Knowles, *Christian Monasticism* (1969).

Reading biographies is an excellent way to further your understanding of this period of expansion and change. P. Brown, *Augustine of Hippo* (1967), and T. Andrae, *Mohammed: The Man and His Faith** (1970), are biographies of two important men of the post-Roman world. A. Bridge, *Theodora: Portrait in a Byzantine Landscape* (1977), and R. Browning, *Justinian and Theodora* (1971), are a good way to look into Byzantine court life.

Scholarship on women in the Middle Ages is just underway. Highly acclaimed by undergraduates is a collection of essays by R. Reuther and E. McLaughlin, eds., *Women of Spirit: Female Leadership in the Jewish and Christian Tradition* (1979). It includes women from the first century to modern times. See also M. Rose, ed., *Women in the Middle Ages and the Renaissance: Literary and Historical Perspectives* (1986).

Challenging but rewarding for undergraduates, especially those interested in psychology or interdisciplinary history, is C. Redding, *A World Made by Men: Cognition and Society, 400–1200* (1985). It applies Piaget's theories to the Middle Ages.

*Available in paperback.

CHAPTER 10

THE ISLAMIC WORLD, CA 750–1400

CHAPTER OBJECTIVES

After reading and studying this chapter you should be able to answer the following questions:

Q-1. Who were the Arabs, and what were the main tenets of the Muslim faith?
Q-2. What factors contributed to their remarkable expansion, and how did they govern their vast territories?
Q-3. What position did women hold in Muslim society?
Q-4. What were the main features of the great Muslim cities of Baghdad and Cordoba?
Q-5. How did the Muslims view Western society and culture?

CHAPTER SYNOPSIS

This chapter explains how the religion of Islam that emerged from the teachings of Muhammad brought unity, power, cultural and economic growth, and intellectual creativity to much of the world. With the monotheistic creed of Islam the old pre-Islamic world of tribal localism, family ties, and agriculture was converted into a cosmopolitan world that emphasized urban culture, trade, and social status based on wealth and merit. Little is known of Muhammad's life, but his messages from Allah formed the ideas central to Islam — the ideas of a last judgment, predestination, and the *jihad*, or the war of conversion. By 751 the Muslims had expanded eastward as far as China and to the west as far as Spain.

When Muhammad died in 632, the Muslim *umma*, or community, was in danger of disintegration. With Abu Bakr and his successors, however, the office

141

of caliph evolved. Although originally an elective office, it became a dynastic (hereditary) office based on ceremony and military might. The caliph became the center of a highly centralized state that was administrated by a central administrative bureau (the *diwan al-kharai*) a legal council called the *ulema*, and a sophisticated communication system called the *barid*. Almost immediately following Muhammad's death, the Muslim world was split into two factions with differing theological and political views: Shi'ites, who claimed to have been given divine authority from Muhammad, and Sunnis, who looked to the Qur'an for authority and who were generally more worldly. The Shi'ites were the followers of Ali, one of the first caliphs, who was assassinated when the opposition Umayyad (Sunni) dynasty was founded.

Under the Abbasid dynasty (750–1258) the caliphate began its fall and the Islamic state moved toward decentralization. The chief adviser to the caliph, called the *vizier*, assumed much power, and by the mid-tenth century the caliphs had become largely symbolic. When the Seljuk Turks took over the eastern Muslim world, the caliph became largely a puppet of the Turkish sultan. This Turkish invasion was part of a general breakdown of Muslim unity — as independent Muslim states were established in Spain, North Africa, and elsewhere. By the thirteenth century the invading Mongols, first under Jenghiz Khan, disrupted that unity even further.

A basic Muslim doctrine was that of social equality. Islamic teaching opposed the pre-Islamic tribal emphasis on family membership and birth as the criterion for social status. Although society was divided into four classes, it was wealth and talent and not birth that became the sign of social distinction. The Qur'an and Islamic law intended to reverse pre-Islamic tribal custom and treat women as spiritual and sexual equals of men. By the early years of the Umayyad dynasty (the seventh century) women had achieved significant equality in religious, economic, and political life. Nevertheless, by the later Umayyad years the situation had reversed, and women were regarded as incapable and unfit for public affairs. Polygamy (which weakens the position of women within society) was practiced, and the harem had become a symbol of male dominance.

Islamic society was geared toward mercantile rather than agricultural interests. Its economic world was held together by a vast commercial network — carried out on a great number of commercial seaways (the Black and Caspian seas, the Arabian Gulf, and the Mediterranean Sea being the most important) and land routes (from North Africa to China). Through this network moved all kinds of goods, from silk and peacocks to slaves and white lead, that brought fabulous wealth to some merchants and provided the basis for a gracious and sophisticated urban culture. Both Baghdad and Cordoba are examples of the remarkable material and intellectual wealth found in Muslim urban centers.

Equally important, the wealth of Baghdad, Cordoba, and the Muslim world in general gave rise to a great intellectual flowering, much of which was international as Muslim scholars drew on Greek, Hebrew, Persian, and other sources. In the centuries that correspond to the Western medieval era the Muslim world far surpassed the Christian Western world in its intellectual achievements.

STUDY OUTLINE

I. The Arabs and Islam
  A. In Muhammad's time (the early sixth century) Arabia was inhabited by Semitic (largely Bedouin) tribes in the interior and an agricultural-urban people, the Hejazi, in the southern valleys and towns
  B. The Hejazi were wealthy, had wide commercial contacts with their neighbors, and were polytheistic in religious belief
  C. Pre-Islamic Bedouin and Hejazi societies were regulated by *local* tribal custom and ritual, although they held certain religious rules in common
II. Muhammad and the faith of Islam
  A. Little is known of Muhammad's life; he was a merchant who married a rich widow and at age forty had a profound religious experience
  B. According to Muhammad, God (Allah) sent him messages through the angel Gabriel
    1. These messages were the basis of Muhammad's preaching to the people of Mecca
    2. After his death they became the Qur'an, the sacred book of Islam
  C. The central beliefs in Islam were submission to God (Allah), the revelations as given by Muhammad, and the last judgment and afterlife
    1. In the last judgment God separated the saved from the damned
    2. Heaven could be entered only through adherence to a strict behavioral code — including regular praying, fasting, avoiding alcohol and usury, practicing an austere sexual morality, and eating a regulated diet
    3. Believers who died for the faith, in the act of *jihad*, were guaranteed salvation
  D. Islam united the peoples of Arabia
  E. The faith has similarities to Judaism and Christianity: it follows the Hebrew scriptures and, like Christianity, believes in a Last Judgment
III. The Expansion of Islam
  A. Muslim expansion to the west
    1. Because Muhammad was unpopular in Mecca, he fled (the *Hegira*) to Medina, where he was highly successful
    2. By 632 he had brought all of Arabia under Islam
    3. Between 632 and 733 Syria, Egypt, North Africa, and Persia came under Muslim domination; the capital was moved from Medina to Damascus

4. In 711 the Muslims took Spain and held it until the *reconquista* in the twelfth century; in 733, however, Muslim expansion into France was halted at the Battle of Tours

B. Muslim expansion to the east
   1. By 751 the Muslims had driven eastward into Afghanistan and central Asia, and had met a Chinese army at the Talas River
   2. From Persia they entered the Indus Valley and founded a colony; in the eleventh century more of India came under Islam

C. Reasons for the spread of Islam
   1. The Muslims believed in the Holy War, or *jihad*, through which the world would be converted to Islam
   2. In reality, Muslims distinguished between Christians and Jews, who were required to submit to Muslim rule, and atheists or polytheists, who were required to convert or face execution
   3. Muslim success was also due to economic motives, theological and political quarrels among enemies, and dissatisfaction among Byzantine subjects
   4. Muslim military organization was superior because of the material benefits it offered to its soldiers, its tight administration, and its practice of establishing military towns

IV. The Consolidation of the Islamic state
   A. The caliphate
      1. When Muhammad died in 632, the Muslim *umma* (community) was in danger of disintegrating into separate tribal groups
      2. The *umma* was maintained by establishing, first under Abu Bakr, the office of *khalifa*, or caliph — meaning leader and successor to Muhammad
         a. Muslim teaching held that political and social authority exists only as an agent of the laws of God
         b. Abu Bakr governed on the basis of his personal prestige within the *umma*
      3. Under Abu Bakr's successors, the caliphate emerged as an institution, and the caliphs were elected by their peers — although this caused civil war
         a. Beginning with caliph Mu'awiya the caliphal office became dynastic
         b. Under Mu'awiya, the tribal chieftains became increasingly subject to the caliph, while the caliph increased his control over the army
         c. All of this allowed Mu'awiya to select his son Yazid as his successor
         d. A court based on ceremony was promoted, and new office of *hajib* or chamberlain was established
      4. The assassination of caliph Ali in 661 gave rise to a theological division of Muslim society into the *Shi'ites* and *Sunnis*

      a. The Shi'ites, supporters of Ali and the Abbasid faction, claimed that Muhammed had given divine knowledge to the descendants of Ali

      b. The Sunnis, who supported the Umayyad faction, looked to the Qur'an for ultimate authority, regarded the Shi'ites as heretics, and were accused of being worldly

      c. During the Umayyad period the Shi'ites caused dissension, and in 744 the Abbasids set up a new dynasty with its capital at Baghdad

      d. The main difference between the Abbasids and the Umayyads is that the Umayyads were Arabian in outlook and the Abbasids were Persian in outlook: While the Abbasids allowed disintegration of the caliphate, the Umayyads held to one-man rule

  B. Administration of the Islamic state

    1. The Muslims appointed *emirs*, or governors, to administer the various parts of the empire; this was supplemented by other administrative innovations

      a. The *diwan* (financial bureau) became the core of the Muslim administration

      b. Sacred law was interpreted by a group of scholars called the *ulema* — which led to the establishment of a body of law, the *shari'a*

      c. The central administrative agency, the *diwan al-kharai*, collected the tax on land (*kharaj*) and the *jizya*, a poll tax, and used these funds to carry out public works

      d. For communication within the empire a system of communication called *barid* was established

    2. During the Abbasid period the office of vizier, the chief assistant to the caliph, was established, and some viziers gained great wealth and power

    3. In theory the empire was governed by the caliph, but in practice merchants and property owners had broad local autonomy

V. Decentralization of the Islamic state

  A. With the Abbasid dynasty independent local dynasties were set up in Spain (at Cordoba, North Africa, Khorasan, and elsewhere)

  B. The decline of the Abbasids and the office of caliph

    1. In the mid-ninth century a Turkish guard reduced the caliph to virtual insignificance

    2. Rebellions, agricultural decline, hostile commercial interests, and an extravagant court life contributed to the decline of the caliph

      a. The creation of the military office of *amir al-umarra* reduced the caliph to a symbolic role

      b. The Shi'ite Buyids' custom of "blinding" the caliphs marks the complete collapse of the Abbasid caliphate

  C. The assault of the Turks and Mongols

1. In the tenth century the Seljuk Turks took Baghdad and made the caliph a puppet of the Turkish *sultan* (meaning "he with authority")
2. The Shi'ite Fatimids set up a Muslim state (with its capital at Cairo) that covered the area from Morocco to Sicily and Egypt — henceforth there were three centers of Islam: Cordoba, Cairo, and Baghdad
3. In the thirteenth century the Mongols under Jenghiz Khan and his grandsons established a large empire that stretched from northern China to Europe and swept away the Abbasid caliph in Baghdad
   a. Egypt, North Africa, and Spain remained free from Mongol rule
   b. The Turks eventually converted to Islam and thereby injected new vigor into the faith

VI. The Life of the people
   A. Pre-Islamic tribal customs
      1. Muhammad's teachings opposed the pre-Islamic tribal ideals of family membership and birth as the center of tribal life
      2. A basic Muslim doctrine was that of social equality
   B. The four classes of society
      1. The caliph's household and the military and aristocracy
      2. Converts or neo-Muslims — largely professionals and merchants
      3. A class of *dhimmis*, or "protected people," who were largely Jews and Christians living under Muslim rule
      4. The slaves, both in the army and in household service
   C. Women in classical Islamic society
      1. The Qur'an intended to relieve women from the harsh treatment they had been subject to under Arabian tribal law
      2. The Islamic sacred book gave women spiritual and sexual equality as well as considerable economic rights, and in the early Umayyad period women enjoyed economic, religious, and political rights
      3. In the later Umayyad period the status of women declined: Society came to regard women as subordinate to men, polygamy was advocated, and a distrust of women's sexual instincts was held by men
         a. A woman's body was considered shameful and thus should not be seen in public
         b. All of this led to the practice of secluding women in harems
   D. Trade and commerce
      1. Muslims held a cultural and religious belief that trade and commerce were more worthwhile than agriculture
      2. The most important mercantile waterways for the Muslims were the Black Sea, the Caspian Sea, the Volga River, the Aral Sea, the Gulf of Aden, the Arabian Sea, and the Indian Ocean
      3. By land the Muslims traded across North Africa, south to the Sahara Desert, and east into China

      a. Between the eighth and twelfth centuries the Islamic world func-
tioned as a free-trade area

      b. The Muslims developed new business techniques — including the
joint stock company and the *sakk*, or check

    4. Muslim trade brought benefits to consumers, scientific advances, and,
for many merchants, great wealth

E. Urban centers

    1. Baghdad was the center of the Muslim world

    2. The court of Harun al-Rashid was a brilliant spectacle of harems,
ceremony, and entertainment — as told in *The Thousand and One
Nights*

    3. Cordoba in Spain was equally cosmopolitan and wealthy and an im-
portant educational and manufacturing center

F. Intellectual life

    1. The unity of the Muslim world fostered a period of great intellectual
activity, during which scholars drew on Semitic, Hellenic, and Persian
civilizations

    2. Advances were made in mathematics (algebra), medicine, and philosophy

    3. Western Europe acquired much of its knowledge of the ancient Greek
philosophers through Muslim translations

G. The Muslim view of the West

    1. The Muslim assault on the West left much bitterness and a fierce
European intolerance toward Muslims — including a strong anti-Muslim
position taken by the Christian Church

      a. The knightly class in Europe believed that its obligation was to
fight the Muslims

      b. Western literature, such as the *Inferno*, portrayed the Muslims as
agents of the devil

    2. Muslims, in turn, rejected European culture and viewed Christianity
as a flawed religion

    3. Because Muslims considered it backward and ignorant, the medieval
West had no influence on the Islamic world

STUDY-REVIEW QUESTIONS

Q-1. What were the main tenets of Islamic religion, and in what way could these
be seen as a challenge to pre-Islamic Arabian society?

Q-2. Discuss the Islamic belief in the last judgment. How does this relate to the
concept of *jihad*?

Q-3. What were the reasons for the success of the spread of Islam?

Q-4. What was the caliphate? How do you account for its rise and its fall?

Q-5. It is said that the Islamic state underwent a process of decentralization, which began in the ninth century. What was this process, and why did it occur?

Q-6. Compare and contrast the interests and beliefs of the Sunni and the Shi'ite factions within Islam.

Q-7. Who were the Seljuk Turks, and what role did they play in Islamic society?

Q-8. It is said that Islamic society was based on wealth and not birth. Explain this. In what sense was this a change from pre-Islamic society?

Q-9. Describe the four classes within Muslim society. Who were the *dhimmis*? What was the position of slaves in Muslim society?

Q-10. What was the basis of the Muslim economy? Describe and give examples.

Q-11. Describe life in the Baghdad court. What does Arabian fiction tell us about court life?

Q-12. Muslim intellectual life was international in nature. Explain. What were the major intellectual achievements of the Muslims?

Q-13. Discuss the changing role of women in Muslim society. Were women better or worse off under the Islamic religion than they had been under tribal customs?

Q-14. Describe the Muslim view of the West. What were the reasons for this view?

STUDY-REVIEW EXERCISES

Define and give the significance of the following key concepts and terms.

jihad holy war - suggests God sent Prophet to establish justice on earth - believers were ensured happiness deity is carrying out the war of conversion

vizier caliphs chief adviser on matters of gen. policy, supervising bureaucratic administration, superintending the army, governers and foreign policy

caliphate or caliph

ulema group of scholars excel in learning and prety - interpreted law of Qur'an and Sunna

umma a muslim community

sultan

polygamy having more than one spouse

harem secluding women behind a curtain or screen

Shi'ites supporters of Ali

Sunnis
Muslims that kept to the practice and beliefs of the Islamic community

Allah

last judgment

emir

barid

diwan financial bureau established by Umar

shari'a body of law covering social, criminal, political, commercial and ~~cul~~ ritualistic matters

dhimmis protected people – Jews, Christians, Zorastrians living under muslim rule

reconquista The Christian reconquest of Spain

Identify the following people and give their importance.

Bedouins resided in Arabia

Hejazi

Muhammad – prophet of Allah – God of Muslims

Fatimids

Umayyads

Abbasids

Jenghiz Khan Leader of Mongols – Empire from China to Korea

Mongols

Mu'awiya

Abu Bakr

Harun al-Rashid

Explain the importance of the following cities.

Cordoba

Baghdad

Mecca Muslims must make pilgrimage once in lifetime to Meca

Medina Muhammad and believers forced to Medina. Area of his teachings began to rise

Damascus

Cairo

Test your understanding of the chapter by answering the following questions.

1. The messages received by Muhammad from an angelic being form the

   _____ Qur'an _____, the sacred text of Islam.

2. In the seventh and eighth centuries Muslim women had (more/less) property rights than Western women.

3. Jews and Christians formed a third class in Islamic society called the

   _____ dhimmis _____, or "protected people."

4. The religious fervor with which the Muslim military fought can in part be attri-

   buted to the necessity of _____ jihad _____, or Holy War of conversion.

5. The administrative and commercial capital of the Muslim world and the city where the caliph Harun al-Rashid presided over his glamorous court was

   _____ Bhagdad _____.

6. The book that contains the tales of Aladdin and his lamp, Sinbad the sailor, and Ali Baba and the forty thieves is entitled

   _____ Arabian Nights _____.

MULTIPLE-CHOICE QUESTIONS

1. *Islam* literally means
    a.   the day of judgment is at hand.
    b.   submission to God.
    c.   the Qur'an is sacred.
    d.   Muhammad is the prophet of Allah.

2. The Hejazi differed from the Bedouins in that they
    a.   were not Arabs.
    b.   were monotheistic.
    c.   were urbanized.
    d.   rejected tribal customs.

3. Women in pre-Islamic Arab society
    a.   had no legal status.
    b.   were allowed a great deal of independence.
    c.   had the same property rights as men.
    d.   lived only in villages.

4. Concerning law, a Muslim believes that
    a.   government must make law and enforce it.
    b.   there is a clear distinction between temporal and spiritual domains.
    c.   God is its sole source.
    d.   it must depend on the ruler.

5. Abu Bakr was the first
    a.   *hajib.*
    b.   Shi'ite.
    c.   Abbasid.
    d.   caliph.

6. Muslim imperial administration was patterned after the
    a.   Greeks.
    b.   Egyptians.
    c.   Romans.
    d.   Sassanids.

7. The sacred law, or *shari'a*, was revealed through the Qur'an and the *sunna* and interpreted by the
    a.   *ulema.*
    b.   *qudis.*

c.   *diwan.*
d.   *barid.*

8.   Which of the following is true of the early Abbasid period?
a.   Population declined.
b.   The office of vizier emerged.
c.   The economy shrunk.
d.   The caliphs reduced the size of the bureaucracy.

9.   Which of the following is true of the Buyids?
a.   They were a fanatical Sunni clan.
b.   They were replaced as masters of the Abbasid caliphate by the Mongols.
c.   They ended the political control of caliphate over the Muslim empire.
d.   They put an end to the Abbasid caliphate.

10.   The Mongols
a.   killed the last Umayyad caliph.
b.   eventually embraced Islam.
c.   sacked and conquered Egypt.
d.   were Confucian scholars.

11.   The second class in Islamic society consisted of
a.   slaves.
b.   *dhimmis.*
c.   the aristocracy.
d.   converts.

12.   In the early Umayyad state, women
a.   played an active role in the community.
b.   could not own property.
c.   had no freedom of movement.
d.   could not participate in politics.

13.   Compared to Christian Europe, Muslim civilization during the Middle Ages
can best be described as
a.   vastly inferior.
b.   inferior in most areas but superior in others.
c.   equally advanced.
d.   greatly superior.

14.   The Umayyad dynasty was centered at
a.   Cordoba.

   b. Damascus.
   c. Baghdad.
   d. Mecca.

15. Muslim conquest of western Europe reached as far as
    a. the Straits of Gibraltar.
    b. the Pyrenees Mountains.
    c. southern France.
    d. the mouth of the Rhine River.

16. Muslim society tended to view trade and commerce as
    a. very respectable and highly esteemed.
    b. second only to agriculture as a way of life.
    c. necessary but held in low esteem.
    d. prohibited by the Qur'an.

17. Islam, Judaism, and Christianity are similar in that all three
    a. worship on Sunday.
    b. originated at the same time.
    c. are monotheistic.
    d. have always been humane toward infidels.

18. The Abbasid dynasty differed from the Umayyad dynasty
    a. by moving their capital to Damascus.
    b. because they were Shi'ites.
    c. because their administration and culture was Persian.
    d. by always maintaining strict one-man rule.

19. The Muslim attitude toward medieval Europe was one of
    a. admiration.
    b. envy.
    c. indifference.
    d. aversion.

20. Slaves in the classical Islamic world were
    a. employed mostly in the army or as household servants.
    b. treated as outcasts.
    c. used mostly for heavy agriculture labor.
    d. of little value and subsequently quite rare.

21. Which of the following statements about Shi'ites is true?
    a. They based their beliefs on the Qur'an and the *Sunna*.

b.   They supported the Umayyads but opposed the Abbasids.

c.   They were most often in the majority.

d.   They claimed a special religious knowledge derived from Ali.

22. Which Muslim city in southern Spain was noted as a great educational center?

a.   Cordoba

b.   Damascus

c.   Cairo

d.   Baghdad

23. Muslim expansion into central Asia in the eighth century reached as far as

a.   the province of Khorasan.

b.   the Talas River.

c.   northern Persia.

d.   Tashkent.

24. Muhammad prescribed a strict code of moral behavior that included

a.   payment of the *jizya* to the caliph.

b.   maintenance of large harems.

c.   a pilgrimage to Mecca during the lifetime of each Muslim.

d.   the necessity of prayer five times a week.

25. The Muslim concept of female sexuality believed that women

a.   have no sex drive.

b.   are sexually insatiable.

c.   should have no more than four husbands.

d.   should remain chaste.

26. Muslim women wear veils in public.

a.   to distinguish which harem they come from.

b.   because women are all considered ugly.

c.   to protect themselves from the harmful sun.

d.   because all parts of their bodies are considered capable of arousing sexual desire.

27. The Muslim scholar al-Khwarizmi was a pioneer in

a.   music.

b.   philosophy.

c.   mathematics.

d.   engineering.

28. Muslim scholarship far surpassed that of the West in the field of
  a. medicine.
  b. warfare.
  c. religion.
  d. music.

UNDERSTANDING HISTORY THROUGH READING AND THE ARTS

The glamour of the Baghdad court is the background for one of the great classics of Arabian literature, *The Thousand and One Nights*, also known as *The Arabian Nights*. This fictional account offers the student an excellent way to view an important aspect of Baghdad life.

PROBLEMS FOR FURTHER INVESTIGATION

The changing status of women in Muslim society is discussed in two books, L. Beck and N. Keddie, eds., *Women in the Muslim World* (1982), and F. Hussain, ed., *Muslim Women* (1984).

  To pursue the subject of the religion of Islam begin with Bernard Lewis, ed. and trans., *Islam: From the Prophet Muhammad to the Capture of Constantinople* (1974), and for a further look at the relationship between religion and social structure see R. Levy, *The Social Structure of Islam* (1957).

CHAPTER 11

TRADITION AND CHANGE IN ASIA, CA 320-1400

CHAPTER OBJECTIVES

After reading and studying this chapter you should be able to answer the following questions:

Q-1. What effect did the movement of new peoples, such as Arabs, Turks, and Mongols, into Asia have on the traditional societies already established in Asia?

Q-2. How were new religious and cultural ideas received by the long-established cultures of Asia?

Q-3. What political and economic effects did these changes have on both the newcomers and the native Asians?

CHAPTER SYNOPSIS

This chapter examines the buildup and breakdown of centralized authority in India, China, and Japan from about 320 to 1400. The central theme in this story is how political and cultural unification emerged alongside both invasion by the Muslim Turks and the Mongols and the sweep of Islam and Buddhism across Asia.

Under the Gupta kings India enjoyed a long period of peace, much political unity, and cultural flowering — in short, a golden age. Advances were made in literature, drama, and the sciences. Village life became regularized, the caste system proliferated and hardened, and distinct marriage and family customs evolved. Equally important, Indian civilization spread to Southeast Asia.

China also experienced a golden age of cultural creativity and national unification. At the same time it drew much from the outside world and labored under internal disruption. Under the Sui, T'ang, and Sung dynasties, China was reunited and Buddhism won a place for itself because it offered a variety of solutions to

157

social and political chaos and was able to accommodate itself to local thought, beliefs, and conditions. In the political sphere, the Chinese developed an effective civil service system — a system that had its roots in Confucianism and the idea of governing through a highly educated and cultured central bureaucracy. This bureaucracy, or civil service, is one of the most important features of Chinese history and is largely a product of the T'ang dynasty — the dynasty that is probably China's greatest.

The three-hundred-year Sung dynasty was similar to that of the T'ang in several ways. Economic and cultural vitality accompanied a number of important technological innovations, including the invention of paper money and printing. However, the political unity that the Sung provided was broken in the thirteenth century when the Mongolian tribes of the north burst upon China. By 1271 all of China was ruled by foreigners. After one hundred years of rule, the Mongols were driven out and a new dynasty, that of the Ming, was established.

Political unity in Japan emerged in the third century when the Yamato clan subordinated other clans and created the emperorship. Out of this the Shinto religion evolved, Chinese culture was absorbed, and Buddhism was introduced. The pro-Chinese party in Japan, particularly under Prince Shotoku, went far in introducing Buddhist ethical and Confucian political thought — thereby making Japan a model of the Chinese bureaucratic state but at the same time helping it remain distinctly Japanese. As it was in China, Buddhism proved responsive to popular needs. Politically, the Heian era was important because of the victory of the aristocracy over the central government of the emperor and shogun, thereby ushering in the samurai-shoen system, which was based on a twofold bond between the lord and samurai. Above all, Japan (like China and India during this period) illustrates the movement toward a distinct native culture that owed much to the movement of ideas back and forth between East and West.

STUDY OUTLINE

I. India, from triumph to invasion, ca 320–1400
  A. The Gupta empire, ca 320–480
    1. The founder of the new empire was Chandragupta
    2. His son, Samudragupta, put an end to India's weakness and fragmentation
      a. He defeated rulers of the southern states and made alliances with frontier states
      b. He adhered to the idea of a just king ruling according to *dharma*
    3. Chandragupta II (ca 375–415) brought the Gupta empire to its height
      a. He overthrew the Shakas in western India
      b. This enabled India to come into direct contact with Middle Eastern trade and culture

    4. The Hun invasion ended the Gupta dynasty
    5. Nevertheless, the Gupta Age was a golden age
        a. Literature and drama reached new heights
        b. Advances were made in mathematics and science
B. Daily life in India
    1. A major feature of Indian society is the Indian stress on stability and tradition
    2. Agricultural life dominated Indian society
        a. The average farmer and his extended family worked a plot near the village
        b. A water supply and irrigation systems were crucial to the poor farmers
        c. Many kinds of crops were planted — rice, beans, cereals — and livestock was raised
    3. Indian merchants held a respected position in society and had access to great wealth
    4. Craftsmen and tradesmen congregated in certain districts of the village
        a. A variety of trades existed
        b. Leatherworkers were outcasts, whereas masons, carpenters, brickmakers, and blacksmiths were respected
        c. Indian potters restricted themselves to purely functional pottery
    5. The layout of the village was usually regular and simple
        a. The typical village was divided into quarters, with two main streets intersecting at the center
        b. The streets were unpaved and the houses were shared by people and animals
        c. This square or rectangular village was surrounded by walls and a moat
        d. A pond outside the walls served as the only water source
        e. Villages of some size had a marketplace, parks, and gardens as well as slums
    6. The old caste system of four groups proliferated during the Gupta period
        a. Subdivisions based on work or tribal affiliation increased the number of castes to about 3,000
        b. Each caste had its own rules and a governing body
        c. Marriage and the extended family were the focus of life
        d. Multiple wives and honoring the dead were common features
        e. Sons were given special attention, but all children were pampered
    7. Education of boys of the upper castes was based on religious initiation
        a. A period of studying the *veda* was in the hands of the *gurus*
        b. After education, marriage was arranged

        c. A daughter was betrothed before her first menstrual period, and
            her husband was usually three times her age
        d. The newly married couple lived in the house of the bridegroom's
            father
    8. An Indian wife had two main duties, household management and
        producing children — preferably sons
        a. By custom and law, her husband was her master
        b. Women rarely left the house
        c. Among high-caste Hindus, wives were expected to perform *sati*
        d. In reality, many wives "ruled the roost"
        e. Wives were treated with great respect and care during pregnancy
  C. India under siege (650–1400)
    1. The foreign invaders (Arabs, Turks, Mongols) swept into India
        a. Muslim Arabs attacked the Sind and the Indus valley
        b. They took Afghanistan, the Punjab, and then the valley of the
            Ganges
    2. The Islamic conquest of northern India was by the Turks and by way
        of the northwest corridor
        a. Sabuktigin and Mahmud led the Turks, eventually taking the Punjab
            and the valley of the Ganges
        b. After Mahmud's death, Turks from Afghanistan renewed the
            Muslim attack on India
        c. Muhammed of Ghur conquered most of northern India and rooted
            out the Hindu and Buddhist religions
        d. Qutb-ud-din established the sultanate of Delhi and ruled northern
            India from the Indus to Bengal
        e. The Muslim rulers brought Iranians and Iranian culture, including
            architecture, to India
    3. The most lasting influence of the Muslim attack was religious
        a. Islam replaced Hinduism and Buddhism in the Indus valley and
            in Bengal
        b. Elsewhere a devotional Hinduism called *bhakti* evolved
        c. By 1336 the south had pushed back the Muslims, and in 1398
            the Turk Timur destroyed the Muslim order in the Punjab
        d. Buddhism, however, was driven out of India while Hinduism
            flourished
II. China's Golden Age, 580–ca 1400
  A. Buddhism reaches China
    1. Merchants, travelers, and sailors brought it from India and the Kushan
        Empire during the period 220 to 589
    2. Buddhism appealed to many segments of Chinese society
        a. Chinese scholars were interested in Buddhist concepts

       b.   Chinese rulers saw it as a source of power, whereas others liked its egalitarianism

       c.   For many, particularly the lower classes, Buddhism's promise of eternal bliss was comforting

   3.   China changed Buddhism to meet specific Chinese needs

       a.   The T'ien-t'ai sect was favored by intellectuals

       b.   The Pure Land sect was the most popular with the masses and was very lenient

       c.   The True Word sect was ritualistic, whereas the Ch'an sect stressed naturalism and individual responsibility

       d.   The Buddhist monasteries and their monks often assumed secular economic functions

       e.   Buddhism was incorporated into Chinese art

B. The T'ang Dynasty, 618–907

   1.   The Sui Dynasty restored economic prosperity, partly because of the new Grand Canal

   2.   Its successor, the T'ang Dynasty, was probably the greatest in Chinese history

       a.   Its founder was T'ai-tsung, who continued Sui reforms

       b.   His land reforms benefited the peasants and boosted agricultural productivity

       c.   His division of China into departments and his bureaucracy gave China the world's most sophisticated political system

       d.   The Han method of training the bureaucracy was revived

       e.   This became the mandarin system of professional public service

       f.   The mandarin system encouraged education and resulted in cultural unity

   3.   The T'ang conquered Turkestan, allied Tibet with China, and spread Chinese culture throughout East Asia

C. The Sung Dynasty, 960–1279

   1.   With the fall of the T'ang Dynasty in 755, China was fragmented into weak and independent states

   2.   Chao Kuang-yin, founder of the Sung Dynasty, unified China by annexing the south to his northern holdings early in his reign

   3.   The early Sung period was a period of economic growth and prosperity

       a.   The population had increased to 100 million, and urbanization accompanied an expanded agricultural economy

       b.   Coal and iron production increased because of technological advances

       c.   Improvements in communications, particularly water transport, encouraged trade in tea and porcelain

   4.   Cultural and technological innovations emerged under Sung rule

       a. Printing was invented and encouraged scholarship

       b. Gunpowder was invented, as were the abacus, water wheel, and bellows

  5. Urbanization sped up

       a. Rich urbanites indulged in luxury products

       b. Women suffered a decline in social status

  6. In 1126 the Jurchen pushed the Sung out of northern China

       a. The Sung dynasty remained in the south, with its capital at Hangchow

       b. This southern Sung empire flourished, particularly in maritime trade

       c. Paper money and a banking system were developed and further encouraged economic growth

D. Cultural blossoming of the T'ang and Sung

  1. The T'ang and Sung eras nourished Chinese culture

       a. The art of porcelain production flourished

       b. Royal monuments and tombs illustrate the realistic and graceful painting and sculpture of the period

       c. Poetry became a medium of expression for the mandarins and Buddhist scholars

       d. T'ang poetry was formal in composition but humorous and emotional in subject

       e. Li Po and Po Chü-i illustrate the simple naturalism of the Chinese poets

       f. The invention of printing encouraged all scholarly activity, including the literary innovation of the encyclopedia

  2. Schools of Neo-Confucian thought emerged

       a. Wang An-shih advocated land and economic reform to help the poor farmers

       b. The Ch'eng-Chu school added metaphysics to Confucianism

       c. The historian and philosopher Chu Hsi explained how evil develops and how it can be corrected

  3. Sung painters sought both exact realism and mystical romanticism

E. The Mongol conquest, 1215–1368

  1. Jenghiz Khan conquered northern China

       a. From this base he captured Peking and northern China

       b. Kublai Khan annexed southern China by 1279 and founded the Yuan Dynasty

       c. North and south China were united commercially, and the mandarin system was altered only in its composition

       d. The Mongols' repressive laws included dividing society into four classes

       2.   Marco Polo's writings familiarized Europeans with the East

       3.   Secret societies of Chinese, such as the Red Turban, organized against the Mongols

          a.   By 1368 Hung-wu, a Buddhist ex-monk, and his rebels had pushed the Mongols out of China

          b.   He established the Ming Dynasty and became its first emperor

III. Japan, dawn of the Rising Sun

    A. The Japanese islands

       1.   The heart of Japan is its four major islands

          a.   They are mountainous and rugged, with numerous small valleys

          b.   Japan's climate ranges from subtropical to a region of cold winters

          c.   Rainfall is abundant, and earthquakes, typhoons, and tidal waves common

       2.   The sea has dictated much of Japan's life and history

          a.   An inland sea provides an avenue of communication and acts as a political and cultural unifier

          b.   The sea has protected the Japanese from outsiders

    B. Early Japan and the Yamato state

       1.   Early Japan was an agricultural society dominated by a warrior aristocracy

          a.   Peasants and slaves served the warrior-nobles

          b.   Clans exerted authority over local areas

       2.   The Yamato clan came to dominate much of Japan

          a.   The Yamato chieftain proclaimed himself emperor

          b.   They brought other clans and their chiefs into their political and religious organization

          c.   The *Shinto* religion emerged out of the Yamato hierarchy of gods at Honshu

          d.   Shinto was a happy religion that stressed ancestor worship and the beauty of nature

          e.   By controlling parts of Korea, the Yamato opened Japan to Chinese influence

       3.   Buddhism came to Japan in 538

          a.   It was appealing because it served Japan's needs, brought Chinese culture, and had political appeal

          b.   The pro-Buddhist faction reformed the state by introducing Chinese practices

       4.   Prince Shotoku led the way in this political reform

          a.   He wrote the "Seventeen Article Constitution," based on Buddhist and Confucian thought

          b.   He began a professional civil service by studying Chinese methods and arts

      5. The Taika reformers and the Nara era represent the continuation of a Japanese effort to emulate China and adopt Buddhism

C. The Heian era, 794–1185
    1. Beginning in 770, a reaction against Buddhism and Chinese culture ended Japan's intellectual-cultural childhood
      a. However, Buddhism thrived under the new Tendai and Shingon sects
      b. Furthermore, the simplicity and egalitarianism of the Pure Land and the Lotus sects made Buddhism even more popular
      c. Japanese architects and artists developed unique Japanese styles
      d. Chinese writing was modified with the adoption of phonetic syllables
      e. This led to a literary flowering, including the writing of history and the birth of the novel
    2. The Heian era gave rise to political struggle
      a. The aristocrats — such as the Fujiwaras — won out over the emperors
      b. The emperor's land reform laws actually strengthened the opposing aristocracy
      c. Using the *samurai*, the Taira and Minamoto clans defeated the emperor
      d. The Minamotos established the Kamakura shogunate in 1192

D. The land and the samurai
    1. A new Japanese society evolved out of a system of *shoen* and *samurai* authority
      a. This is a way of organizing society through and by powerful local figures and landholding
      b. The economic base of the warrior class (the *samurai*) was the village and its land — called a *shoen*
      c. The shoen grew out of the ninth century practice of tax evasion
      d. The shoen land was cultivated by peasant farmers, some of whom were independent (the *mvoshu*)
      e. The *samurai* gave the lord loyalty and service in return for a fief
      f. Unlike European feudalism, early Japanese feudalism existed alongside the imperial government
    2. The *samurai* military-social code was the *Bushido*, or Way of the Warrior
      a. Loyalty to his lord was the key to this code
      b. They came to constitute the local aristocracy and were expected to behave in a chivalrous manner

E. The Kamakura shogunate, 1185–1333
    1. Yoritamo's victory over the emperor meant the advance of feudalism

      a.   His government (*Bakufu*) at Kamakura consisted of three bodies of governing officials
      b.   These officials became hereditary, and thus independent
      c.   By 1219 the shogun had been reduced to a figurehead by the Hojo family
  2. Invasion of Japan in the thirteenth century led to the downfall of the Hojo family and its Kamakura shogunate
      a.   Kublai Khan's armies stormed Japan but were defeated by the *samurai*
      b.   Unrest and growth of the *samurai* class led to a victory for Takauji and the *samurai*

REVIEW QUESTIONS

Q-1. What were the major accomplishments of Chandragupta and Samudragupta?

Q-2. Describe Indian life in terms of work, marriage, and womanhood.

Q-3. India was both united and divided by the caste system. Explain.

Q-4. Describe the Muslim invasions of India. What were their most lasting results?

Q-5. Describe how Buddhism affected China and explain how China, in turn, influenced Buddhism.

Q-6. What important economic and political changes occurred in China during the T'ang rule?

Q-7. Describe the mandarin system. Why is it of great importance in Chinese society?

Q-8. Describe the economic state of China during the early Sung period. What contributed to this condition?

Q-9. What developments occurred in poetry, intellectual activity, and painting during the T'ang and Sung periods?

Q-10. How did the Mongols affect China? How did the Chinese respond to this?

Q-11. Describe the Yamato state in terms of its economic and political organization and its religion.

Q-12. How did Buddhism affect Japanese society, and how did Buddhism adjust and change to meet the needs of the Japanese people?

Q-13. Why did feudalism emerge in Japanese society? Compare and contrast Japanese and European feudalism.

Q-14. Describe the role of the *samurai* class in Japan. Was it responsible for the decline of the Kamakura shogunate?

STUDY-REVIEW EXERCISES

<u>Define</u> *the following key concepts and terms.*

mandarin system

Japanese *shoen* village and farmland capable of growing rice

samurai social class of skilled warriors

Japanese feudalism

Bushido military and social code of conduct of the samurai

<u>Identify</u> *each of the following and give its significance.*

T'ang dynasty Came out of Sui Dynasty - Conquered Turks Probably greatest dynasty in Chinese history. Invention of gunpowder

Sung dynasty Founded by Chao Kung yin - unified So. China Prosperity due to production of coal, iron, invention of

T'ai-tsung printing and block printing and 'abacus

Grand Canal

Samudragupta

Chandragupta II Most sig. exploit - overthrow of Shakas Son of Samudragupta

Kalidasa

White Huns

sati

Sabuktigin

Muhammed of Ghur

bhakti

gurus

bodhisattva Buddhis concept of "a buddha is coming. inspired rules to give good and humane government

Li Po Tang poet - member of litery circle - wrote 8 immortals of the wine cup

Wang An-shih

Jenghiz Khan

Kublai Khan annexed So. China . Found Yuan Dynasty Reunited China

Marco Polo

Yamato

Shinto

Kamakura shogunate

Explain the focus and appeal of each of the following new Buddhist sects in China.

T'ien-t'ai sect

Pure Land sect belief that one had to declare faith in Buddha to read paradise

True Word sect pop. in Japan - promised salvation through ritual

Ch'an sect

Explain the importance of each of the following in Japanese history.

Yamato

Prince Shotoku

Murasaki Shikibu

samurai skilled warriors Preferred death to dishonor

Test your understanding of this chapter by answering the following questions.

1. After the fall of the Guptas, the Indian caste system *proliferated*/*shrank*.
2. Marriage for Indian women was usually arranged *before*/*after* they reached puberty, and the betrothed husband was usually *about the same age*/*much older*.
3. The Muslim Turks who invaded India generally held to the practice of *destroying*/ *tolerating* non-Muslim religions.
4. The most lasting impact of the Muslim invasions of India was their effect on *religion*/*politics*.
5. The Mongol leader who conquered northern China in 1234 was

    _____Jenghiz Khan_____.

6. The Japanese prince who authored the Seventeen Article Constitution and who led the way in introducing Buddhist and Confucian thought into Japanese

    politics was _____Phrince Shotoku_____.
7. The greatest numbers of people converted to Islam lived in the

    _____Kampuchea_____ part of India.
8. The samurai, preferring death to dishonor, would commit what we erroneously

    call *harakiri*. The correct Japanese term is _____Seppuku_____.

MULTIPLE-CHOICE QUESTIONS

1. The major problem of Indian agriculture is
    a. flooding.
    b. locusts.
    c. poor soil.
    d. drought.

2. By about A.D. 800, the caste system had split Indian society into
    a. 4 groups.
    b. 1,000 groups.
    c. 3,000 groups.
    d. 500 groups.

3. Indians favored child marriage because
    a. they wanted women to start families early.
    b. it was an outlet for young male sex drives.
    c. young girls were thought to be fascinated by sex.
    d. older men were thought to be fascinated by young girls.

4. *Sati* in ancient India was
   a. the betrothal of young girls.
   b. the custom of widow suicide.
   c. a true and faithful wife.
   d. both b and c

5. Pregnant Indian women were
   a. segregated from men.
   b. pampered and treated with affection.
   c. forbidden to leave the home.
   d. thought to bring good luck.

6. The Srivijaya Empire's wealth was based on
   a. maritime trade.
   b. caravan routes.
   c. agriculture.
   d. mining.

7. The religion that suffered the most severe decline due to the Muslim invasion was
   a. Hinduism.
   b. Christianity.
   c. Buddhism.
   d. Taoism.

8. The Chinese discovery of printing led to the use of
   a. census records.
   b. counterfeiting.
   c. tax records.
   d. paper.

9. Kublai Khan was
   a. Mongol emperor of China.
   b. conqueror of southern Russia.
   c. Jenghiz Khan's brother.
   d. conqueror of India.

10. The Red Turbans were
   a. a monastic order distinguished by their headdress.
   b. an anti-Mongol Chinese secret society.
   c. Jenghiz Khan's elite military corps.
   d. an enterprising group of merchants.

11. The first successful invasion of Japan was made by
    a. China.
    b. the Mongols.
    c. Russia.
    d. the Americans in 1945.

12. *Shinto* is best described as
    a. the first Japanese capital.
    b. an early Japanese emperor.
    c. a native Japanese religion.
    d. the Japanese sun goddess.

13. Buddhism's Pure Land sect taught
    a. belief in the Eightfold Path.
    b. the importance of meditation.
    c. that Paradise could be reached through simple faith.
    d. the importance of ritual and magic.

14. An important Japanese contribution to literature is
    a. the epic poem.
    b. free verse.
    c. the short story.
    d. the novel.

15. Japan's civil disturbances in 1331 led to
    a. restoration of the emperor.
    b. a civil authority under the samurai.
    c. both a and b
    d. none of the above

16. An important contribution to mathematics made during Gupta times was
    a. the zero.
    b. geometry.
    c. calculus.
    d. algebra.

17. In ancient India the merchant class was
    a. respected.
    b. spurned for making profits.
    c. shunned as a lower caste.
    d. composed mostly of foreigners.

18. Women in ancient India
    a. were required to wear a veil.
    b. sometimes owned large tracts of land.
    c. had equal status within the Hindu religion.
    d. were distinctly inferior before the law.

19. The major weakness of the Chinese mandarin civil service system was that it
    a. discouraged independent thinking.
    b. produced educated men in small numbers.
    c. encouraged graft and corruption.
    d. fostered class consciousness.

20. Well-off families in Sung China bound the feet of their women
    a. so they could attract a wealthy husband.
    b. to symbolize the inferior status of women.
    c. to show they didn't have to work.
    d. because tiny feet were thought attractive.

21. The Japanese warrior aristocracy were called
    a. shogun.
    b. samurai.
    c. shoen.
    d. bushido.

22. *Bushido* was
    a. ritual suicide.
    b. the shogun's mandate to rule.
    c. an upper-class religious custom.
    d. the warrior's code of honor.

23. The founder of the Gupta Empire was
    a. Kalidasa.
    b. Chief Timur.
    c. Chandragupta.
    d. Samudragupta.

24. Buddhism found many converts in China because it
    a. appealed to different social groups.
    b. was forced on a conquered people.
    c. was strict and inflexible.
    d. offered no intellectual challenges.

25. Buddhism reached China
     a.   during the T'ang Dynasty.
     b.   with the invading Mongols.
     c.   from the north.
     d.   between the fall of the Han and the rise of the Sui.

26. The introduction of paper money in China led to
     a.   the downfall of the Sung Dynasty.
     b.   new monetary and banking systems.
     c.   massive crime and revolt.
     d.   a decrease in trade.

27. Li Po was a noteworthy T'ang
     a.   poet.
     b.   administrator.
     c.   emperor.
     d.   mathematician.

28. Korea was important to Japanese development because it
     a.   was an abundant source of slaves.
     b.   introduced the Shinto religion.
     c.   conquered Japan and imposed its political administration.
     d.   was the avenue through which Chinese culture came to Japan.

UNDERSTANDING HISTORY THROUGH READING AND THE ARTS

Because of the rapid advancement of the Chinese economy beginning around the tenth century, some modern scholars have come to see the Sung dynasty as the beginning of China's modern economic period. Likewise, in the field of painting this period is seen as being one of great change. On the economy, read Mark Elvin, *The Pattern of the Chinese Past* (1973), and on art, Michael Sullivan, *The Arts of China* (1979).

The T'ang era of nearly three hundred years witnessed an unrivaled florescence of the arts in China — particularly sculpture, painting, ceramics, and the decorative arts. This history, along with photographs, is traced in H. Scott, *The Golden Age of Chinese Art: The Lively T'ang Dynasty* (1967). For another period, the Yuan (A.D. 1279–1368), is explored in S. Lee and W. Ho, *Chinese Art Under the Mongols: The Yuan Dynasty* (1968).

PROBLEMS FOR FURTHER INVESTIGATION

Traditional Chinese social institutions, such as the extended family, and political institutions, such as authoritarian, centralized government, often seem harshly restrictive to modern Western students. However, you may find some rationale for these institutions in T. T. Ch'u, *Law and Society in Traditional China* (1965), and Etienne Balaza, *Chinese Civilization and Bureaucracy* (1964).

Japanese feudalism shared some similarities with its Western counterpart. Its feudal values, such as loyalty and discipline, were to play a crucial role in the nation's modernization in the later centuries. For more on Japanese culture in the Middle Ages see G. C. Sansom, *Japan: A Short Cultural History* (1962), and Edwin Reischauer, *Japan: The Story of a Nation* (1981).

The cult of Confucianism in China was fostered by the state and was limited to scholars and officials. Why was Confucianism never popular among the common people? What are the fundamental beliefs of Confucianism? To begin your study turn to J. K. Shryock, *The Origin and Development of the State Cult of Confucius* (1966).

READING WITH UNDERSTANDING
EXERCISE 3

LEARNING HOW TO IDENTIFY MAIN POINTS THAT ARE EFFECTS, RESULTS, CONSEQUENCES

In the introduction to this *Study Guide* and in Reading with Understanding Exercises 1 and 2 we noted that learning to underline properly plays an important part in college work. Underlining (or highlighting with a felt-tipped pen) provides a permanent record of what you study and learn. It helps you review, synthesize, and do your best on exams.

We suggested three simple guidelines for effective underlining or highlighting:*

1. Be selective; do not underline or highlight too much.
2. Underline or highlight the main points.
3. Consider numbering the main points.

These guidelines will help you in courses in many different subjects.

Cause and Effect in History

The study of history also requires learning to recognize special kinds of main points. These points are *explanatory* in nature. *They answer why and how questions*, thereby helping you to interpret and make sense of the historical record.

Two particularly important types of why and how questions focus on *cause* and *effect* in history. You are already familiar with questions of this nature, questions that provide much of history's fascination and excitement. "Why did the Roman Empire

---

*The guidelines for underlining are from *RSVP: The Houghton Mifflin Reading, Study, & Vocabulary Program*, second edition, by James F. Shepherd (Houghton Mifflin, 1984). We urge students to consult this very valuable book for additional help in improving their reading and study skills.

C-1

decline and fall?" That is, what *causes* explain the decline and fall of the Roman Empire? "What were the *effects* of the Black Death?" You should pay particular attention to questions of cause and effect. They give history meaning. They help you increase your ability to think and reason in historical terms.

Two other insights will help you greatly in identifying main points involving cause and effect. First, historians use a number of different words and verbal constructions to express these concepts. Thus "causes" often become "reasons" or "factors," or things that "account for," "contribute to," or "play a role in" a given development. "Effects" often become "results" or "consequences," or are "the product of an impact." In most cases students can consider such expressions as substitutes for cause and effect, although they should be aware that historians are not of one mind on these matters.

Second, cause and effect are constantly interrelated in the historical process. Yesterday's results become today's causes, which will in turn help bring tomorrow's results. To take examples you have studied, the *causes* of the fall of the Roman Empire (such as increasing economic difficulties) brought *results* (such as the self-sufficient agrarian economy) which contributed to—helped *cause*—the rise of Benedictine monasticism. In short, *a historical development can usually be viewed as a cause or an effect, depending on what question is being answered.*

Exercise A

Read the following passage once as a whole. Read it a second time to underline or highlight it in terms of main points identified as effects or results. Consider numbering the effects in the margin. Then do Exercise B at the end of the passage.

The effects of the invention of movable-type printing were not felt overnight. Nevertheless, within a half-century of the publication of Gutenberg's Bible of 1456, movable type brought about radical changes. The costs of reproducing books were drastically reduced. It took less time and money to print a book by machine than to make copies by hand. The press also reduced the chances of error. If the type had been accurately set, all the copies would be correct no matter how many were reproduced. The greater the number of pages a scribe copied, the greater the chances for human error.

Between the sixteenth and eighteenth centuries, printing brought about profound changes in European society and culture. Printing transformed both the private and the public lives of Europeans. Governments that "had employed the cumbersome methods of manuscripts to communicate with their subjects switched quickly to print to announce declarations of war, publish battle accounts, promulgate treaties or argue disputed points in pamphlet form. Theirs was an effort 'to win the psychological war.' " Printing made propaganda possible, emphasizing differences between various groups, such as crown and nobility, church and state. These differences laid the basis for the formation of distinct political parties.

Printed materials reached an invisible public, allowing silent individuals to join causes and groups of individuals widely separated by geography to form a common identity; this new group consciousness could compete with older, localized loyalties. Book shops, coffee shops, and public reading rooms gradually appeared and, together with print shops, provided sanctuaries and meeting places for intellectuals and wandering scholars. Historians have yet to assess the degree to which such places contributed to the rise of intellectuals as a distinct social class.

Printing also stimulated the literacy of lay people and eventually came to have a deep effect on their private lives. Although most of the earliest books and pamphlets dealt with religious subjects, students, housewives, businessmen, and upper- and middle-class people sought books on all subjects. Printers responded with moralizing, medical, practical, and travel manuals. Pornography as well as piety assumed new forms. Broadsides and flysheets allowed great public festivals, religious ceremonies, and political events to be experienced vicariously by the stay-at-home. Since books and printed materials were read aloud to the illiterate, print bridged the gap between written and oral cultures.

Exercise B

Study the last paragraph again. Can you see how it is a good example of the historical interaction of cause and effect? Do you see how a given development is an effect or a cause *depending on what historical question is being asked?* Be prepared for such "reversals" in the text, in lecture and class discussion, and on exams.

Hint: In the last paragraph, what is an *effect* of the invention of the printing press? (Ideas could be spread more rapidly.) What "stimulated"—helped *cause*—the spread of literacy? (The invention of the printing press. The author develops this point further in Chapter 14.)

CHAPTER 12

EUROPE IN THE EARLY AND HIGH MIDDLE AGES

CHAPTER OBJECTIVES

After reading and studying this chapter you should be able to answer the following questions:

Q-1. How did Charlemagne acquire and govern his empire?
Q-2. What was the Carolingian Renaissance?
Q-3. What was feudalism in the West, and how did it come about?
Q-4. What were the features of the eleventh-century revival in Europe and what were the social and political results of this revival?
Q-5. How did the relationship between church and state in Europe change during these periods?
Q-6. What were the Crusades?

CHAPTER SYNOPSIS

For about a century after the Franks defeated the Muslims at the battle of Tours in 733, Europe enjoyed a period of political and economic regeneration and unity. At the center of this regeneration was the Frankish Carolingian family. It was the Carolingian Charles Martel who won at Tours, and it was his son Pippin III and grandson Charlemagne who molded western Europe into a unified Christian empire — the Carolingian Empire.

This Carolingian era was a high point of stability and creativity in the early Middle Ages. The Carolingians struck up a mutually beneficial relationship with the church. They supported church missionaries and enforced Christian moral codes. In return, the pope recognized and strengthened Carolingian political authority. Charlemagne extended the boundaries of his empire and brought peace to Europe.

Within this climate of peace a renaissance in learning and the arts took place — with its center being northern Europe, not Italy.

While these changes were taking place, Europe continued to experience the economic-political transformation that historians call feudalism. Beginning as a response of insecure people to the disappearance of the protection that the strong Roman government had provided, feudalism became a means for communities to defend themselves. Over time freemen gave up their personal rights and their property to local lords. These lords provided protection, in return, and built their own little empires. Charlemagne was able to manage the feudal lords, but his grandsons could not keep control of the feudal system. When they divided Charlemagne's empire into three parts in 843, it was already soaked in blood because of the ambitions of petty lords. The division was an invitation to invasion from the outside. The Vikings, Magyars, and Muslims then threw Europe back into a period of violence and fear.

Around the year 1000, Europe began to recover from this long, bitter winter of violence. The two most important signs of that European springtime, political recovery and the spiritual and political revival of the church, were of great importance for the evolution of individual freedom and for the political and intellectual growth of Europe.

One of the earliest signs of revival was the success feudalism achieved — as in Normandy — in bringing peace and unity to Europe in the tenth and eleventh centuries. The reduced level of warfare in this period, together with favorable changes in climate, resulted in both population explosion and agricultural improvement, and explains why the German nobility was able to dominate German politics. Further, another testimony to the dynamism of the age was the Crusades. Growing out of the influence of the papacy and religion in medieval society, and the conflict in Spain, the Crusades provided an outlet for the spiritual and political energy of Europe.

A religious revival also began, with a monastic reform at the abbey of Cluny, and spread across Europe. When monastic life was subsequently threatened by materialism and lay interference, there were fresh demands for reform by the Cistercians. At the same time, and partly as a result of the Cistercian reforms, the papacy set out to purify itself and to redefine its relationship with the emperors, kings, and other lay political authorities. This led to the investiture controversy, which reached its height in the conflict between Pope Gregory VII and the German emperor Henry IV. The struggle between the popes and the emperors turned out to be one of the most important and long-lasting political conflicts in European history.

STUDY OUTLINE

I. The Frankish aristocracy and the rise of the Carolingian dynasty
   A. The Frankish kingdom under the Merovingians included most of France and the southwest of Germany
      1. Clovis, the Merovingian leader, made the Franks the most powerful people of Europe
      2. After Clovis's death in 511, the Merovingians fell into a long period of civil war
      3. Civil war was accompanied by the rise of a wealthy and powerful aristocracy
      4. Reconstruction of the Frankish kingdom began with Pippin of Landen, who was mayor of the East Frankish palace
   B. The rise of the Carolingian dynasty
      1. The Carolingian family under Martel and Pippin III built a vast power base in France, aided by missionaries
      2. Bishop Boniface organized the church and spread Christianity in central Europe
         a. He aided the German church and established the *Rule* of Saint Benedict
         b. With Pippin III's help he reformed the Frankish church
      3. Boniface and the Carolingians attacked pagan sexual customs and promoted respect for civil authority
   C. Monarchy and papacy
      1. Pippin III's acquisition of the kingship was aided by the pope
      2. Pippin created strong ties between the church and the Carolingian dynasty
II. The empire of Charlemagne and the Carolingian renaissance
   A. The warrior-ruler Charlemagne is described in Einhard's biography as strong and a good horseman and swimmer
   B. Territorial expansion
      1. Charlemagne continued the Carolingian tradition by building a large European kingdom
      2. He checked the Muslim expansion and conquered the Saxon German tribes
      3. His need for children (and wives and concubines) was partly a result of political and diplomatic considerations
      4. He added northern Italy to his Frankish kingdom, but his Spanish campaign had only literary significance
   C. The government of the Carolingian Empire
      1. The empire of Charlemagne was mainly a collection of agricultural estates of the Frankish aristocracy

   2. He made the *missi dominici*, or agents of the king, the link between the country and king
   3. Charles's empire was not a state in the modern sense
   4. The Carolingians sought a single, unified Christian society presided over by a Christian king
  D. The imperial coronation of Charlemagne in 800
   1. The church supported Charlemagne, and in 800 the pope crowned Charles the Roman Emperor
   2. Charles unified old Rome, Christianity, and Frankish practices
   3. The motives of both Charles and the pope are unclear; it is possible that each planned the coronation in order to increase his own power
   4. The coronation gave rise to theories of both imperial and papal supremacy
III. The Carolingian intellectual revival
  A. The revival of learning began with Irish-Celtic influence in Anglo-Saxon Britain
  B. Northumbrian culture in Britain
   1. Irish-Celtic culture permeated Roman Britain and Europe, partly by way of monastic missals, or books
   2. The Lindisfarne book is a high point in the Northumbrian artistic renaissance
   3. The monk Bede was one of the greatest scholars of the Middle Ages
   4. Bede wrote a history of early Britain — *The Ecclesiastical History of the English Nation* — that is the chief source of information about early Britain
   5. The poem *Beowulf* illustrates the complexities and contradictions within people and society and the importance of loyalty, fame, and warfare in medieval society
  C. The Carolingian renaissance
   1. Charlemagne fostered an intellectual revival that centered on his court at Aachen
   2. His scholars (the most important being Alcuin) encouraged interest in and preserved Greek and Roman knowledge
   3. Basic literacy was established among the clergy and Christianity was spread
IV. Health and medical care in the early Middle Ages
  A. No rational understanding of disease existed
  B. Drug prescription therapy was common
  C. "Physicians" knew little about disease, and their treatments were primitive and often harmful
  D. Christianity contributed to a better understanding of health, and later secular schools were founded for the study of medicine

E.   The Italian school at Salerno was an important medical center and several women physicians played a key role in medical writings

V.   The division and disintegration of the Carolingian Empire

A.   Without the unifying force of Charlemagne the empire fell

B.   Charlemagne's grandsons, Lothair, Louis, and Charles, agreed to divide the empire in 843 in the Treaty of Verdun

C.   The "middle kingdom" of Lothair became a disputed territory

D.   War among the Carolingians meant the growth of the feudal military system and disorder

VI.   Feudalism

A.   Early feudalism served the needs of medieval society

B.   The two levels of feudalism were retainers (knights) and counts

1.   Feudalism was a type of government in which power was considered as private and was divided among many lords

2.   Its two levels were armed knights at the bottom and great counts on a higher level

3.   Stirruped cavalry made the Carolingian use of armed retainers (knights) possible

4.   Retainers, or *vassals*, took an oath of *fealty*, and some were given estates by their lords

C.   Because of the premium placed on physical strength, women were subordinate to men, although they occasionally held positions of power and wealth

D.   Manorialism was the economic and social side of feudalism, which centered on the relationship between peasant (or serf) and the lord's estate

E.   Over time the free farmer (peasant) became a serf

VII.   The great invasions of the ninth century

A.   Disunity in Europe after Charlemagne's death was an invitation to aggression from the outside

B.   The Vikings from the north overran parts of France, Britain, and Russia, and elsewhere

C.   The Magyars pushed into Europe from the east, and the Muslims pushed up from the south

D.   These invasions accelerated the growth of feudalism

VIII.   Political revival in western Europe in the tenth and eleventh centuries

A.   The decline of invasion and civil disorder

1.   The Normans were Christianized and brought into France

2.   The Norman duke Rollo made Normandy a strong territory

3.   The Vikings slowly became assimilated into European society

4.   Beginning in 987 the Capetian kings strengthened their territory

5.   West Saxon victory in 878 led to English unity based on the *fyrd* and royal law

6. The Danish king Canute made England part of his empire
7. The German king Otto halted the Magyars and revived the Holy Roman Empire in central Europe (Germany and Italy)
   a. Otto brought peace and stability to Germany and Italy
   b. The base of his power was his alliance with the church, which he used to weaken the feudal lords
   c. His coronation in 962 advanced German interests
8. The Italian cities broke Muslim control of Mediterranean trade
B. Increasing population and mild climate
   1. The decline in war and disease meant a rise in population
   2. The warmer climate meant better agricultural production
IX. Revival and reform in the Christian church in the eleventh century
A. The monastic revival
   1. Monastic activity had declined as the Carolingian Empire disintegrated
   2. The abbey of Cluny led the way in a tenth-century monastic revival
      a. Cluny stood for reform of abuses such as *simony*, for high religious standards, and for sound economic management
      b. The Cluniac reform spread throughout Europe
   3. By the eleventh century, wealth and lay interference caused corruption
   4. The Cistercians (beginning in 1098) isolated themselves from laymen and elaborate ritual
      a. Their reform movement was widespread
      b. It centered on farming and a simple communal life
B. The reform of the papacy
   1. The tenth-century papacy was corrupt and materialistic and provided little leadership to the people of Europe
   2. Leo IX made the first sweeping reforms
   3. Later reforms, under the Lateran Synod of 1059, included decreeing that the college of cardinals would henceforth elect the pope
X. The Gregorian revolution in church reform
A. Pope Gregory VII's ideas for reform of the church
   1. Gregory believed that papal orders were the orders of God
   2. He wanted the church to be free from lay control
B. The controversy over lay investiture
   1. The church outlawed the widespread practice of lay investiture, but Germany presented certain problems
   2. Emperor Henry IV of the Holy Roman Empire protested Pope Gregory's stand on investiture
   3. Their conflict was resolved by Henry's submission to the pope at Canossa in 1075

        4. But the problem was not yet settled; a compromise was not reached until 1122
          a. The emperor surrendered the right to invest bishops
          b. But lay rulers retained a veto over ecclesiastical choices
        5. In the long run, the investiture crisis perpetuated the political division of Germany, and it encouraged the rise of noble dynasties

  C. The papacy in the High Middle Ages
        1. Pope Urban II laid the foundation for the papal monarchy
        2. The papal curia, which henceforth formulated church law for all of Europe, was established and became important
        3. Pope Innocent III brought the papacy to the height of its power

XI. The Crusades of the eleventh and twelfth centuries
  A. The Crusades reflect papal influence in the society and the fact that the military class had assumed an ecclesiastical function
  B. The Crusades, or holy wars, were seen as a reflection of the religious zeal and secular vitality of the High Middle Ages
        1. They grew out of the Christian-Muslim conflict in Spain
        2. The Eastern emperor appealed to the West for help against the Muslim Turks
        3. Many people responded to Pope Urban II's plea for a crusade to take Jerusalem from the Turks
  C. The results of the Crusades
        1. The First Crusade (1096) resulted in new feudal states — "Crusader kingdoms" — at Jerusalem, Edessa, Tripoli, and Antioch
        2. The Fourth Crusade, which resulted in Christians fighting Christians, was a disaster
        3. The Crusades brought few cultural changes
          a. Crusades were also used to purge Europe of its social enemies
          b. The Crusades encouraged greed and intolerance
          c. Deep bitterness between Christian and Muslim society was established, but the Christian West benefited from commercial contact with the Middle East

REVIEW QUESTIONS

Q-1. "Without Muhammad, Charlemagne would have been inconceivable." Explain and evaluate this statement.

Q-2. Define *feudalism* and describe its origins. How did it affect the peasants?

Q-3. Describe Germanic marriage and sexual practices. How did Christianity affect these customs? Who was responsible for the change?

Q-4. It has been said that Saint Boniface carried on the "Romanization of Europe." Explain this statement in the light of the missionary activities of this important figure.

Q-5.   What was the relationship between the Carolingians and the pope? How did both sides benefit from the relationship?

Q-6.   How successful was Charlemagne in expanding the power of the Frankish state?

Q-7.   What techniques and methods did Charlemagne use to govern his vast empire? How well did his empire function?

Q-8.   What were the probable reasons for Charlemagne's quest for the title of emperor? The results?

Q-9.   Describe the Northumbrian cultural revival. What were its sources of inspiration and its goals?

Q-10.   What was the "Carolingian renaissance"? Who were its participants and what did they accomplish?

Q-11.   In this early medieval period, a person of forty was considered old. Why did people die young? How much did people understand about disease, and what kind of health care existed?

Q-12.   Describe the Magyar, Muslim, and Viking invasions in terms of motives, areas terrorized, methods, and impact.

Q-13.   Was feudalism a blessing or a disaster for Europe? Did it bring order and stability or merely chaos and exploitation?

Q-14.   Describe the political revival that took place in the ninth and tenth centuries. Who were the chief participants in this revival and what did they accomplish?

Q-15.   What role did the church play in the recovery of Europe from a period of war and invasion?

Q-16.   Soon after about 1000 the population of Europe began to increase. Why?

Q-17.   What were the goals of the Cluniac reformers? Why were they interested in isolation from lay society?

Q-18.   Describe the condition of the clergy and church leadership prior to Leo IX's reform movement. What were its major abuses?

Q-19.   Was it inevitable that Pope Gregory would come into conflict with the monarchs of Europe? Explain.

Q-20.   What was the investiture controversy? Where did ultimate power in medieval society rest?

Q-21.   Describe the conflict between Pope Gregory VII and Henry IV. Who had the best weapons and what was the outcome?

Q-22.   In the long run who were the winners in the investiture controversy? How did this controversy affect the political development of Germany?

Q-23.   What were the reasons for the Crusades?

Q-24.   Were the Crusades a "steam valve" for late medieval society?

Q-25.   What changes did the Crusades bring to western European society? Did the benefits outweigh the disadvantages?

STUDY REVIEW EXERCISES

Define the following key concepts and terms.

feudalism political and social organization

manorialism involved services and obligations
of peasant classes

rex et sacerdos

missi dominici officials appointed by Charlemagne
Regulated crime, education, clergy

vassal

fealty

polygamy

ecclesiastical

Carolingian renaissance Sought single unified Christian society
Presided by Christian king Basic literacy estab.

Charlemagne's *marks*

excommunication Cut off from sacraments and all
Christian worship

investiture

Peace of God

Truce of God

laymen

curia

Identify each of the following and give its significance.

investiture controversy

First, Third, and Fourth Crusades

Cluniac reforms

Cistercians

Canossa

college of cardinals

Worms conference of 1122

Northumbrian cultural renaissance

Battle of Tours

Treaty of Verdun 843

Beowulf

Explain why the following people were important.

Venerable Bede

Pippin of Landen

Pippin III

Saint Boniface

Charles Martel

Charlemagne

Alcuin

Louis the Pious

Pope Leo

Louis the German

Charles the Bald

Lothair

Canute, king of England

Rollo, duke of Normandy

Henry IV, Holy Roman Emperor

Otto, king of Germany

Pope Leo IX

Pope Gregory VII

<u>*Test your understanding of the chapter by answering the following questions.*</u>

1. The author of *The Ecclesiastical History of the English Nation* was

    Bede

2. In general, the economic and political power and status of aristocratic women in the early Middle Ages tended to *increase/decrease*.
3. In the eighth and ninth centuries, the population of western Europe tended to become *more/less* free.
4. In general, the relationship between the Carolingian emperor Charles and the Christian church was *good/warlike*.
5. This Northumbrian was an important scholar and educator and the major

    advisor to Charlemagne: *Alcuin*

6. The foundation of a medical school at *Salerno*
    in the ninth century gave tremendous impetus to medical study.
7. The Crusades resulted in an *increase/decrease* in greed and social-religious intolerance, while it *improved/deteriorated* relations between Christians and Muslim societies.
8. It appears that between the ninth and eleventh centuries the European climate became significantly *warmer/cooler*.
9. The church law called the *Peace of God*
    proclaimed that certain people and places were to be protected from war.
10. The *increase/decrease* of warfare in the eleventh century led to an *increase/decrease* in the population of Europe.

11. The important monastic revival began in the tenth century at the abbey of
    Cluny _____ in Burgundy.

12. According to the Worms (1122) settlement, bishops were henceforth to be

    chosen by the ___*Clergy*_____,

    but veto power was to be held by the ___*emperor*_____.

MULTIPLE-CHOICE QUESTIONS

1. Saint Boniface, the missionary monk,
   a. refused to support the Carolingian kings.
   b. took the *Rule* of Saint Benedict to many monasteries.
   c. attacked Germanic sexual and marriage customs.
   d. was a staunch enemy of Roman ideas and Roman traditions.

2. The most important source of Northumbrian (and then Carolingian) cultural
   revival was
   a. Muslim society.
   b. Jewish society.
   c. Irish-Celtic society.
   d. Frankish society.

3. The *missi dominici* of Charlemagne were
   a. missionaries.
   b. peasant farmers.
   c. royal legal officials.
   d. military outposts.

4. Charlemagne was crowned emperor by
   a. himself.
   b. his father Pippin.
   c. the pope.
   d. the Frankish council.

5. The Northumbrian period of creativity was centered in
   a. Charlemagne's court.
   b. the monasteries of Britain.
   c. the courts of feudal lords.
   d. Pavia in Lombardy.

6. When Charlemagne's son, Louis the Pious, died, the empire
   - a. was divided three ways.
   - b. remained intact under Charles Martel.
   - c. was united with the Anglo-Saxon kingdoms.
   - d. remained a unified but weak state.

7. The monk-historian who wrote *The Ecclesiastical History of the English Nation* was
   - a. Louis the German.
   - b. Pippin III.
   - c. Bede.
   - d. Augustine.

8. Saint Boniface is famous as the
   - a. biographer of Charlemagne.
   - b. author of *Beowulf.*
   - c. Apostle of Germany.
   - d. author of a great medical treatise.

9. Historians consider the narrative poem *Beowulf* useful for
   - a. an illustration of early Germanic marriage laws.
   - b. its information on eighth-century monastic life.
   - c. an early example of Germanic fairy tales.
   - d. the picture it provides of Anglo-Saxon society and ideals.

10. The Carolingian Empire collapsed because
    - a. it was too large and lacked effective machinery of government.
    - b. it was overrun by Arabs and Turks.
    - c. Charlemagne's grandsons were lazy and incompetent.
    - d. Charlemagne failed to make a will.

11. The first major medical center in Europe was at
    - a. Aix-la-Chapelle.
    - b. Bologna.
    - c. Salerno.
    - d. Strasbourg.

12. Constantine the African advanced medical knowledge by
    - a. founding hospitals.
    - b. researching dental problems.
    - c. recommending heroin as an anesthetic.
    - d. translating Arabic medical treatises.

13. Viking expansion in the eighth century was probably due to
    a. overpopulation.
    b. the search for a warmer climate.
    c. the search for new trade and commercial outlets.
    d. all of the above.

14. The curia was the
    a. headquarters for the Italian bishops.
    b. papal financial office.
    c. location of the imperial court.
    d. papal bureaucracy and court of law.

15. The battle of Edington in 878 marked
    a. West Saxon political revival and unity.
    b. the rise of Normandy.
    c. Danish control of northern Europe.
    d. the fall of Anglo-Saxon law and culture in England.

16. The Danish ruler who made England the center of his empire was
    a. Otto.
    b. Edward the Confessor.
    c. Canute.
    d. Lothair.

17. The real winner in the eleventh-century investiture controversy was the
    a. nobility.
    b. papacy.
    c. emperor.
    d. college of cardinals.

18. The Truce of God
    a. disallowed any fighting on church land.
    b. ended the Magyar invasions.
    c. disallowed fighting on certain days.
    d. was enforced by all the monastic orders in Europe.

19. In 962 which German king was crowned Holy Roman Emperor, thereby
    reviving imperial authority in central Europe?
    a. William
    b. Otto
    c. Gregory
    d. Charles V

20. It was at which Burgundian abbey that the famous tenth-century monastic reform and religious revival had its origins?
    a. Cluny
    b. Canossa
    c. Flanders
    d. Worms

21. The system of papal election was changed in the eleventh century in order that henceforth the pope was elected by whom?
    a. Emperor
    b. College of cardinals
    c. Townspeople
    d. Roman citizens

22. The power of the German emperor Otto I rested on
    a. an alliance with William of Normandy.
    b. heavy taxation of the merchants of his territories.
    c. papal approval.
    d. the support of ecclesiastical officials in Germany.

23. The peace movements of the Christian church worked to
    a. establish Sunday as a day of rest.
    b. improve relations with the Muslims.
    c. end the chronic violence and destruction.
    d. secure a treaty with William of Normandy.

24. In the tenth and eleventh centuries, Nicolaites were
    a. reformed monks.
    b. married priests.
    c. priests who bought and sold church offices.
    d. none of the above.

25. Crusades originated as reaction to
    a. Christian-Muslim conflict in Spain.
    b. the decline of Christian influence in Turkey.
    c. the decline of Christian influence in Italy.
    d. new economic opportunities in southern Italy.

26. The goal of the Gregorian reform movement was the
    a. end of Philip I's adulterous marriage.
    b. abolition of simony.

    c. moral reform of the clergy and the centralization of the Catholic church under papal authority.
    d. excommunication of William of Normandy.

27. The German emperor Henry IV opposed Gregory VII because
    a. the pope was too inflexible.
    b. Gregory VII was a peasant.
    c. the pope wanted Henry's strict obedience.
    d. Henry relied on the services of churchmen whom the pope wanted to make responsible solely to papal authority.

28. The pontificate of Innocent III represents the high point of medieval papal authority because he
    a. launched the crusades.
    b. composed important legal treatises.
    c. exerted power all over Europe.
    d. secured the end of clerical marriage.

29. The crusade that resulted in Christian fighting Christian was the
    a. Fourth Crusade.
    b. Second Crusade.
    c. Eastern Crusade.
    d. First Crusade.

GEOGRAPHY

With the maps in the text as your guide, use the outline map on page 191 to complete the following questions.

1. Mark the geographic boundaries of Charlemagne's empire and then in the space below explain why it disintegrated after his death.

2. Mark the divisions of Charlemagne's empire as of the Treaty of Verdun in 843.

3. Mark the route of Viking, Magyar, and Muslim penetration into Europe. In the space below indicate *why* these invasions occurred.

4. Mark on the outline map the location of Jerusalem, Acre, Edessa, Constantinople, Venice, Paris, and Lyons; then mark the routes of the four crusades.

UNDERSTANDING HISTORY THROUGH READING AND THE ARTS

For a closer look at the architectural achievements of this age see K. Conant, *Carolingian and Romanesque Architecture, 800–1200** (1978), and a good general introduction to the illuminated manuscripts and religious treasures of the period is J. Beckwith, *Early Medieval Art** (1979).

     Going directly to the sources can be an interesting and rewarding enterprise. Paperback editions of several early medieval works are available: L. Sherley-Price, trans., *Bede: A History of the English Church and Peoples** (1962); M. Alexander, trans., *The Earliest English Poems** (1972); D. L. Sayers, trans., *The Song of Roland**; and D. Wright, trans., *Beowulf** (1957). The myths of any period are important because they make up the backbone of the culture. Seven myths and hero stories of the Middle Ages are retold in N. L. Goodrich, *The Medieval Myths** (1961).

PROBLEMS FOR FURTHER INVESTIGATION

What was the relationship between politics and religion in medieval society? Politics and royal justice? Begin your investigation with the standard work on medieval political ideas, J. Morrall, *Political Thought in Medieval Times* (1962). The success, glory, idealism, and political aspects of the religious crusades have fascinated historians for generations. Students interested in further research in this area should begin with *The Crusades** (1939), by J. A. Brundage.

     What was life like for the serfs of the early Middle Ages? This is one subject dealt with in the fascinating book *Medieval People** (1963) by E. Power. G. Barraclough's *Medieval Papacy** (1968) is an interesting study for anyone interested in the power of the papacy and the Cluniac movement.

*Available in paperback.

How did Merovingian and Carolingian government work? How did the concept of kingship evolve? Was Christianity as important as claimed? These and other questions are answered in P. Wormald et al., *Ideal and Reality in Frankish and Anglo-Saxon Society* (1984). What were the contributions of women in medieval society? Begin your inquiry with D. Baker, ed., *Medieval Women** (1981).

What were the motives of the pope and Charlemagne at the time of the coronation on Christmas Day in the year 800? Of what significance is the fact that the church gave the title to the king? These and other questions are considered in a collection of interpretations entitled *The Coronation of Charlemagne** (1959), edited by R. E. Sullivan. How much did the Islamic movement shape the course of European history? The classic statement on this is Henri Pirenne, *Mohammed and Charlemagne** (1958).

*Available in paperback.

CHAPTER 13

LIFE IN CHRISTIAN EUROPE IN THE HIGH MIDDLE AGES

CHAPTER OBJECTIVES

After reading and studying this chapter you should be able to answer the following questions:

Q-1. How did the peasants, nobles, and monks in Christian Europe in the Middle Ages live, and what were their interests?

Q-2. How much social mobility existed in the Middle Ages in the West?

CHAPTER SYNOPSIS

This chapter surveys life in European medieval society. It focuses on the three major classes within medieval society: the peasants, who worked; the nobles, who fought; and the monks, who prayed. Despite the rise of towns and the beginning of a merchant class, most of the people were peasants or serfs who lived and labored on the land. Men and women toiled on the land of the manors to scratch out a meager existence for themselves and to support their noble lords in noble fashion. The agricultural productivity of the average manor was low because there was a lack of fertilizer and it was necessary to leave as much as half of the land fallow each year. Between the ninth and thirteenth centuries, however, it appears that European agricultural productivity doubled — a remarkable achievement. Yet the diet of the peasantry was very limited and seldom adequate. A major problem of the Middle Ages was that the birthrate tended always to outpace the food supply.

The manor was the basic unit of medieval rural life in Europe, and Christianity was the center of the day-to-day world on the manor. The church provided an explanation for the meaning of life, and it also supplied the community with much of its entertainment and political leadership. Women held a pivotal position in the family and village economy.

The aristocratic nobility was a class with special power and legal status. It had its own lifestyle and goals. The size of noble families, aristocratic patterns of child-rearing, marriage, and sex, and women's role were determined by the fact that males were the holders of property.

The monasteries of Europe had a great civilizing influence. They contributed to both literacy and agricultural improvement in the Middle Ages, and they were important in providing careers for the children of the aristocracy. Monastic life varied from order to order and from district to district, but daily life in all monasteries centered around the liturgy.

STUDY OUTLINE

I. Life in Christian Europe: those who work
    A. The status of the peasantry varied widely all across Europe
    B. Slavery, serfdom, and upward mobility
        1. Slavery was not common in Europe
        2. Serfs had no freedom, but they could not be bought and sold
        3. All serfs were obligated to perform certain duties and pay levies
        4. Only freemen could move and live as they wished
        5. Serfs could obtain freedom in several ways: from their lord, by purchase by a third party, or by being in a town guild for a year and a day
        6. Settlement on new land meant social mobility and freedom
    C. The manor as the basic unit of medieval rural life
        1. The manor — the estate of the lord — was a farming community of varying size
        2. Both the peasant's and the lord's land were divided into strips
        3. Each manor usually had meadows and forests
    D. Agricultural methods
        1. Usually half the land was left fallow (the open-field system)
        2. Animal manure was the major form of fertilizer
        3. The increase in iron production after 1100 meant better tools
        4. The development of the horse collar led to the use of horses in agriculture and thus a great increase in productivity
        5. Yields were low, but they improved from the ninth to the thirteenth centuries
    E. Life on the manor
        1. Medieval village life was provincial but secure
        2. Family life was important, and women played a central economic role

      3. Diet was limited to grains and beer with possibly a great increase in meat consumption by the mid-thirteenth century.

      4. Children contributed to the family economy

  F. Popular religion

      1. The Christian religion influenced and regulated daily life

      2. Religious ritual and practice synthesized many elements — Jewish, pagan, Roman, and Catholic

      3. The church was the center of village social and political life

      4. The peasants believed strongly in a personal God, and pilgrimages were very popular

      5. In the eleventh century a great emphasis on the devotion to Mary evolved

      6. Religion offered the peasants hope and adventure in a world of gloom

II. Those who fight

  A. The legal and social status of the nobility varied from region to region

  B. The aristocratic nobility

      1. The nobility was an elite, self-conscious social class

      2. Nobles held political power and had a special legal status

      3. Nobles were professional fighters; all nobles were *knights* but some knights (like the German *ministerials*) never attained noble status

  C. Infancy and childhood in aristocratic families

      1. Ignorant medical care contributed to the high infant mortality rate

      2. It is unclear whether infanticide increased during this period

      3. Wet-nursing and swaddling were common practices

      4. Aristocrats had large families but *primogeniture* led to the favoring of the first-born son

      5. Aristocratic women married early, but many did not marry at all

      6. Aristocratic boys received a military education — which culminated in "knighthood" in France and England

  D. Power and responsibility in the aristocracy

      1. Adulthood meant property and authority

      2. Aristocrats saw lavish living as a sign of status and power, but it often meant debt

      3. Military and economic needs meant frequent travel

      4. Aristocratic women often had considerable power

III. Those who pray

  A. Prayer was a vital social service performed by monks; they also performed other important cultural and economic services

  B. Recruitment

      1. Many who became monks did so because of their parents' decision

      2. Monasteries provided careers for aristocratic children

      3. In the later Middle Ages the monasteries recruited from the middle class

   C. Prayer and other work
       1. Daily life centered around the liturgy
       2. The monasteries — often supported by manorial lords — engaged in
           farming, stock breeding, iron production, and so on
       3. Various responsibilities were divided among the monks
       4. Monks were often advisers to kings
       5. The monasteries contributed to learning and agricultural progress
   D. Economic difficulties
       1. Monasteries depended on lay endowments
       2. By the late Middle Ages many monasteries, such as Cluny, did not
           have enough income to support their lavish lifestyles

REVIEW QUESTIONS

Q-1.   What were the ways in which a serf (villein) could obtain his or her freedom?

Q-2.   Describe a medieval manor. How did it work and what agricultural methods
governed its existence? Was it "efficient"?

Q-3.   What was the role of women in medieval society? What evidence exists to
suggest that women might have held considerable power within the family unit?

Q-4.   How important was religion in medieval manor life?

Q-5.   What do you believe to have been the world-view of the average medieval
peasant? How would peasant men and women have thought about themselves and
their environment?

Q-6.   What was the function of the nobility? What were its characteristics as a class?

Q-7.   How did medieval people treat their children? What were some of the common
child-care practices?

Q-8.   Aristocratic men married late and aristocratic women married early. Why?

Q-9.   Aristocratic society was marked by sexual tension and generational conflict.
Why?

Q-10.   Discuss the responsibilities and lifestyles of adult aristocratic men and
women.

Q-11.   What was the social background of most medieval monks? How did this
tend to change in the later Middle Ages?

Q-12.   What were the major functions of the medieval monasteries? Were they
solely spiritual institutions?

Q-13.   Why was the monastic movement important to the aristocratic families
of Europe?

Q-14.   Describe the economic dilemma that many monasteries faced in the late
Middle Ages.

Q-15.   Medieval society is often described in terms of those who work, those who
fight, and those who pray. Explain.

STUDY-REVIEW EXERCISES

<u>Identify</u> *each of the following and give its significance.*

serf

manor

ministerials

Abbey of Cluny

demesne land

Cistercian Order

Orderic Vitalis

The Leech Book of Bald

chivalry

chevaliers

wet nurse

knighthood

Salve Regina

<u>Define</u> *the following key concepts and terms.*

villeins

serf

nobility

almoner

choir monks

lay brothers

open-field system

swaddling

Explain each of the following important aspects of medieval life.

"popular religion"

monastic recruitment

aristocratic "adulthood"

medieval agricultural system

aristocratic marriage patterns

medieval peasants' diet

Test your understanding of the chapter by answering the following questions.

1. The common practice in medieval society of binding up an infant, often strap-
    ping it to a board, is known as *swaddling* _____.
2. The evidence about infanticide makes it *certain*/*uncertain* that it increased in
    the Middle Ages.
3. The use of horses rather than oxen in farming meant *greater*/*less* productivity.
4. In medieval society, women *did/did not* play an important economic role in
    the medieval manor and the family.
5. The word ____ "*manor*" _____ derives from
    a Latin term meaning "dwelling," "residence," or "homestead."
6. In medieval society women were *frequently*/*never* raised to the nobility.
7. Formal military training for the medieval aristocratic boy was concluded with
    the ceremony of *knighthood* _____.
8. Slavery *was*/*was not* common in medieval European society.

9. Some scholars believe that the use of the ___horse_____
   in agriculture was one of the decisive ways in which Europe advanced over the
   rest of the world.

MULTIPLE-CHOICE QUESTIONS

1. In the twelfth century many of the older monastic houses found themselves
   in economic difficulties because
   a. they could no longer recruit monks.
   b. peasants refused to pay their levies.
   c. building and living expenses increased faster than revenue.
   d. a papal decree forbade them to tax peasants.

2. Generally, the monasteries recruited their members from the
   a. middle class.
   b. aristocracy.
   c. peasantry.
   d. village church schools.

3. For noble men, "adulthood" came with
   a. knighthood.
   b. the age of eighteen.
   c. the acquisition of property.
   d. the demonstration of military prowess.

4. The difference between a free person and a serf was that the
   a. free person was tied to the land and the serf was not.
   b. serf had no obligations to the lord, while the free person had many.
   c. serf paid rent to his lord, while the free person paid nothing at all.
   d. serf was bound to the land by the obligations he owed his lord, while
      the free person usually just paid rent.

5. Medieval farmers
   a. generally farmed the land in strips scattered throughout the manor.
   b. were too ignorant to use any kind of fertilizer.
   c. never used iron for tools.
   d. were unable to show any improvement in nearly a thousand years.

6. Medieval peasants
   a. traveled widely and visited many foreign countries.
   b. had a sense of community and a pride of place.

    c.   hardly every drank alcoholic beverages.
    d.   refused to let women work in the fields.

7. Monastic life in general was
    a.   a combination of attention to liturgy and manual work.
    b.   devoted exclusively to prayer.
    c.   so different from place to place that it is impossible to generalize about it.
    d.   centered exclusively on manufacturing and farming.

8. *Chevaliers* were
    a.   wealthy monks.
    b.   members of a religious order that stressed agricultural reform.
    c.   horsemen, or knights.
    d.   court painters and architects.

9. A medieval manor was a(n)
    a.   estate of at least ten villages.
    b.   plantation.
    c.   estate of a lord and his dependent tenants.
    d.   estate of at least three villages.

10. To provide food for all the people on the manor, the land had to yield at least
    a.   six times the amount seeded.
    b.   ten times the seed.
    c.   three times the seed.
    d.   five times the seed.

11. A person became a noble by
    a.   thrift, hard work, and sobriety.
    b.   clever business acumen.
    c.   birth or remarkable service to king or lord.
    d.   buying a patent of nobility.

12. Most of the education of medieval aristocrats was in the
    a.   Bible.
    b.   Latin classics.
    c.   canon law.
    d.   arts of war and chilvalry.

13. Until the fourteenth century, most monks were drawn from the
    a.   business classes.
    b.   peasantry.

    c. petty bourgeoisie.
    d. nobility.

14. Management of the monastic estate was the basic responsibility of the
    a. abbot.
    b. novices.
    c. cellarer.
    d. almoner.

15. The most important differences that should be kept in mind when discussing medieval society are
    a. religious differences.
    b. local differences.
    c. national differences.
    d. cultural differences.

16. Members of the nobility
    a. did not have a special legal status.
    b. were uninterested in military questions.
    c. generally inherited their privileges.
    d. seldom owned land.

17. The center of manorial life was the
    a. village church.
    b. manor house.
    c. commons.
    d. local pub.

18. Medieval people described society as being organized by
    a. churchmen, commercial people, and peasants.
    b. monks, nobles, and peasants.
    c. nobles, cardinals, and rich merchants.
    d. aristocrats, clerks at the British museum, and serfs.

19. The basic difference between a serf and a slave was that
    a. slaves did not have to pay inheritance taxes.
    b. serfs worked on the lord's land four days a week, slaves five.
    c. a slave could be bought and sold but a serf could not.
    d. a serf could be sold if he or she were black; a white slave could not.

20. Although all peasants participated in the cultivation of arable land, each individual possessed

      a. strips scattered throughout the manor.
      b. a plot near the forest.
      c. a piece of land for raising hogs and chickens.
      d. some land planted in oats, some in peas and beans.

21. Apart from bread, the medieval diet consisted primarily of
      a. chicken and fish.
      b. cabbage and roots, such as onions, turnips, and carrots.
      c. potatoes, tomatoes, and black-eyed peas.
      d. apples, pears, and cherries.

22. The social center of the medieval village was the
      a. alehouse.
      b. lord's castle.
      c. cemetery.
      d. church.

23. The nobility's set of values, involving generosity, graciousness, and courtesy, is generally known as
      a. the chivalric code.
      b. the Mosaic code.
      c. the Christian virtues.
      d. all of the above

24. Childbearing among medieval aristocrats tended to produce large families because
      a. they were oversexed.
      b. peasant girls were easily available.
      c. the death rate of children was very high, and lords wished to ensure continuation of their families.
      d. of many factors, but historians really cannot explain this phenomenon.

25. Military service to one's lord was eventually limited to
      a. a year and a day.
      b. forty days a year.
      c. three months a year.
      d. six months.

26. The most important service performed by the clergy for society was
      a. teaching the young.
      b. preaching.
      c. praying.
      d. performing marriages and baptisms.

27. Depending on local conditions and possibilities, monasteries engaged in which of the following economic activities?
    a. Mining
    b. Horse breeding
    c. Sheep farming
    d. Agriculture

GEOGRAPHY

Study the diagram of a local manor — Figure 13.1 in the text — and then answer the following questions.

1. How many fields existed, and why was one *not* planted? What percentage of planted land went to the lord?

2. What was the value of the forest or woodland?

3. What was the purpose of the meadowland and the common land?

4. Who would have lived in the manor house? The village? Why are the village houses enclosed?

UNDERSTANDING HISTORY THROUGH READING AND THE ARTS

Did the peasants really starve? What are some of the modern world's mistaken beliefs about sex, marriage, and family in medieval times? These and other questions are considered in a ground-breaking social history, *The World We Have Lost** (1965), by P. Laslett.

From the profoundly moral to the bawdy, the tales of an odd assortment of pilgrims in Geoffrey Chaucer's *The Canterbury Tales** reflect the manners and morals of medieval England.

"Carmina Burana" by C. Orff is a series of songs based on poems written in the thirteenth century by wandering students and disillusioned monks who celebrated their carousing and lovemaking in verse. The poems, written in medieval Latin, German, and French, were discovered in 1830 in the archives of the Benedictine monastery at Bevern near Munich. Orff put these intensely physical, scenic, and entertaining poems to vibrant music in 1937.

PROBLEMS FOR FURTHER INVESTIGATION

Did aristocratic women have any power in the churches or households of this military society? Were children maltreated in the medieval family? Historians are just beginning to investigate how childhood and the status of women in society have changed over the course of history. A good starting point for research on childhood is L. de Mause, ed., *The History of Childhood** (1974) and the journal *The History of Childhood Quarterly*. For medieval women see E. Power, *Medieval Women** (1976). Most of the work on medieval women is on women in the world of religion. The best of these works is J. Nichols and L. Shank, *Medieval Religious Women*, Vol. 1: "Distant Echoes" (1984). A good place to begin a study on women as mystics and the masculine-feminine issues in religion is C. Bynum, *Jesus as a Mother: Studies in the Spirituality of the High Middle Ages* (1982).

Did the emergence of urban life result in a clash between Christianity and urban values? Did urbanization force Christianity to reevaluate its traditional anti-materialistic position? A good place to begin your investigation is with an excellent synthesis of the new urban life and Christianity: L. Little, *Religion, Poverty, and the Profit Economy in Medieval Europe* (1978).

*Available in paperback.

CHAPTER 14

THE CREATIVITY AND VITALITY OF
THE HIGH MIDDLE AGES

CHAPTER OBJECTIVES

After reading and studying this chapter you should be able to answer the following questions:

Q-1.   How did medieval European towns originate, and how did they reflect radical change, including heresy?

Q-2.   How did medieval rulers in England, France, and Germany solve their problems of government and lay the foundations of the modern state?

Q-3.   How did European universities develop, and what needs of medieval society did they serve?

Q-4.   What does the Gothic cathedral reveal about the ideals, attitudes, and interests of medieval European people?

CHAPTER SYNOPSIS

The High Middle Ages — roughly, the twelfth and thirteenth centuries — were an era of remarkable achievement in law, the arts, philosophy, and education in Europe. Of central importance, the modern idea of the sovereign nation-state took root in this period. By means of war, taxation, and control over justice the kings of England and France were able to strengthen royal authority and establish a system of communication with all of their people.

The Normans were important in bringing a centralized feudal system to England by using the sheriff, the writ, and other devices to replace baronial rule with royal power. Out of this process emerged the concept of common law and, with the Magna Carta, the idea of supremacy of the law. The process, however, was not altogether smooth, as the conflict between Henry II and Becket illustrates. The evolution of the territorial state in France was not quite as rapid as in England. France was less of a geographical unit than England, and the creation of a strong royal authority involved more armed conflict between king and barons. And in Germany, royal power failed to develop at all, despite a strong start by Emperor Frederick Barbarossa. Part of the reason was the historic connection between Germany and Italy. The church-state struggle was also a major reason that royal authority in Germany was destined to remain weak.

The rise of the universities accompanied the emergence of the strong secular states because the new states needed educated administrators to staff their bureaucracies. The new universities became centers for the study of law and medicine. They were loosely organized institutions, where curriculum and faculty status were often dictated by rioting students.

Improvement in agriculture, coupled with a reopening of the Mediterranean to Christian traders, fostered a great, but gradual, rise of towns and commerce. Flanders and Italy led the way in this urban revival. The growth of towns was one of the most important developments in Western history. Towns meant a new culture and social order, increased economic opportunities, and the beginnings of modern capitalism.

Connected to this process of urbanization, the author claims, religious heresy grew up as the traditional Christian religion was unable to meet the needs of urban dwellers. The result of the heretical crisis was the evolution of several new religious orders of friars, which counteracted the heretical movement by putting emphasis on a nonmaterialistic clergy that could preach to the needs of the people and at the same time manage the Inquisition process of reconversion.

Few periods in history can make claim to artistic achievement as can the High Middle Ages. The Gothic cathedrals, shimmering in stone and glass, stand not only as spiritual and artistic testimony to the age but also as a reflection of the economic power and civic pride of the great cities. By 1300, the energy of the High Middle Ages had been spent.

STUDY OUTLINE

I. The medieval origins of the modern state
   A. The royal desire to extend authority and increase public order led to the modern state, which uses law, bureaucracy, and money to provide its citizens with order and protection
   B. Unification and communication in England
      1. England was unified earlier than other countries
      2. William the Conqueror used local people to enforce royal law
      3. Sheriffs, the writ, the Norman inquest, and *Domesday Book* were used to centralize royal power

  4. The English "Angevin empire" began with Henry II of England, whose father was the French duke of Anjou
C. Unification and communication in France (see Map 14.2)
  1. The cult of *Saint Denis* generated national devotion and loyalty to the French king
  2. Philip II began the process of unifying France
  3. By the end of the thirteenth century, the king of France was stronger than his nobles
  4. Philip Augustus devised a system of royal agents called baillis and seneschals to help enforce royal law
  5. Unlike England, where administration was based on unpaid local officials, royal administration in France rested on a professional class
D. Unification and communication in Germany (see Map 14.3)
  1. Germany was split into many states
  2. The German emperors were weak and lacked a strong royal domain to serve as a source of revenue and a power base
  3. Frederick Barbarossa tried to unify Germany by creating royal officials to enforce his will
  4. But he became involved in Italian affairs, which were costly and caused disorder at home
  5. At the battle of Legnano his feudal cavalry was defeated by bourgeois infantrymen
  6. By 1187 the princes were able again to block the centralized monarchy
E. The financial problems of medieval kings
  1. Henry I of England established a state finance bureau called the Exchequer to keep track of income
  2. French kings relied on royal taxes, mostly from the church, the *tallage*, and the conversion of feudal dues to cash payments
  3. Medieval society believed that royal taxation should be imposed only at times of emergency
  4. The Sicilian state is a good example of an efficient financial bureaucracy
    a. Roger de Hauteville introduced feudalism to the island
    b. Frederick II Hohenstaufen centralized royal power in Sicily
    c. He received the permission of his people to tax them regularly
F. Law and justice in medieval Europe
  1. A system of royal justice, founded by Louis IX, unified France
  2. Beginning with Henry II the English kings developed and extended the *common law*, which was accepted by the whole country
  3. King John's conflict with church and barons led to the Magna Carta (1215), which claimed that everyone, including the king, must obey the law
  4. The English common law system was strikingly different from the system of continental (Roman) law

     5. Various factors led to prejudice against homosexuals, so that by 1300 homosexuality, which had heretofore been treated with indifference, was declared illegal

II. Economic revival

    A. The rise of towns in the tenth and eleventh centuries

       1. Some historians believe that towns began as fortifications, while the historian Henri Pirenne claimed that towns resulted from trade

       2. Others believe that towns sprang up around religious centers

       3. All towns had a few common characteristics: a town wall, a central market, a legal system, and a monetary system

       4. The *bourgeoisie*, or *burghers*, or townspeople, became a new class in medieval society

       5. Many towns benefited from having a literate and industrious Jewish population

    B. Town liberties

       1. Townspeople worked hard to acquire social, political, and legal freedoms

       2. Merchant and craft guilds evolved, and their members bargained for town liberty from local lords or the king

       3. Women played an important role in the household, the guilds, and the town economy

       4. Townspeople's great wealth bought them liberty but also new taxes, such as *tallage*, imposed by kings

    C. Town life

       1. Medieval towns served as places of trade and protection

       2. Towns grew without planning or regulation

       3. Church building was an important symbol of bourgeois wealth

    D. The revival of long-distance trade in the eleventh century

       1. Italian and Flemish cities dominated the trade market

          a. Venice led the West in trade and controlled the oriental market

          b. Flanders controlled the cloth trade

          c. Bruges, Ghent, and Ypres became cloth manufacturers

       2. England was the major supplier of wool for Flanders

          a. Wool was the cornerstone of the English economy

          b. Eventually cloth manufacture was taken up in English towns

    E. The commercial revolution of the eleventh through thirteenth centuries

       1. The growth of medieval commerce meant the rise of capitalist ideas and practices

       2. The Hanseatic League developed new trade routes and established new "factories" and business techniques (see Map 14.5)

       3. The commercial revolution meant a higher standard of living, new practices, changes in taste, and new opportunities

       4. Kings allied with the middle classes to defeat feudal lords and build modern states, while many serfs used the commercial revolution to improve their social position

III. Medieval universities

    A. Origins

       1. Prior to the twelfth century, only monasteries and cathedral schools existed

       2. Universities grew up along with interest in law and medicine

       3. The first universities were at Bologna and Salerno in Italy (see Map 14.6)

       4. The learning community at Paris was made a *universitas* — an educational guild — in 1200

       5. Peter Abélard, a teacher in Paris, became popular because of his emphasis on reason and doubt

    B. Instruction and curriculum

       1. The scholastic method of teaching was used

          a. In this method of reasoning and writing, questions were raised and authorities cited on both sides of the question

          b. It applied Aristotelian axioms to science and theology

          c. The scholastics sought to organize all knowledge into *summa*, or reference books

          d. Aquinas used reason to obtain knowledge of everything, including the existence of God

       2. The lecture and the gloss, or interpretation of a reading, were the main learning methods

       3. Oral examinations came at the end of a period of study

IV. Gothic art

    A. Medieval church building was innovative and reflected the wealth, pride, and religious faith of the townspeople

    B. From Romanesque gloom to "uninterrupted light"

       1. Eleventh-century peace encouraged church building

       2. The Gothic style was created by the abbot of St.-Denis

       3. The Gothic style has several distinct features: the pointed arch, the ribbed vault, the flying buttress, and interior brightness

    C. The creative outburst of cathedral building

       1. Bishops, nobility, and the commercial classes supported cathedral building

       2. Cathedrals became symbols of civic pride

       3. Cathedrals served many purposes

          a. They were used on feast days

          b. Local guilds met in them

          c. Political meeting were held in them

       4. Architecture became a means of religious instruction

       5. Tapestry making and drama were first used to convey religious themes to ordinary people

V. Heresy and the friars

    A. Heresy flourished most in the most economically advanced and urbanized areas

       1. Neither traditional Christian theology nor the isolated monastic orders addressed the problems of mercantile society

       2. Townspeople desired a pious clergy who would meet their needs

    B. Heresy, originally meaning "individual choosing," was seen as a threat to social cohesion and religious unity

       1. The Gregorian injunction against clerical marriage made many priests vulnerable to Donatist and other claims of immorality

       2. Various heretics, such as Arnold of Brescia, Peter Waldo, the Albigensians, and others denounced wealth, the sacraments, and material things

       3. The Albigensian heresy grew strong in southern France and was the subject of a political-religious crusade against it

    C. As a response to heretical cults, two new religious orders (the friars) were founded

       1. The Spaniard Saint Dominic's mission to win back the Albigensians led to the founding of a new religious order of preaching friars (the Dominicans)

       2. Francis of Assissi founded an order (the Franciscans) based on preaching and the absolute poverty of the clergy

       3. These new orders of friars were urban, based on the idea of poverty, and their members were drawn from the burgher class

    D. The friars met the spiritual and intellectual needs of urban people

       1. The friars stressed education and intellectual pursuits

       2. Their emphasis on an educated and nonmaterialistic clergy won them the respect of the bourgeoisie

       3. The friars administered the Inquisition process so successfully that heresy was virtually extinguished

REVIEW QUESTIONS

Q-1. Define the "modern state." What are its characteristics and goals?

Q-2. Describe the unification and centralization of royal power in England. Who were the participants and what methods did they use?

Q-3. What problems did the French kings face in unifying France under royal authority? What techniques did they use?

Q-4.   Why was unification in Germany so much more difficult than in England and France? What were the factors that weakened and divided Germany?

Q-5.   Evaluate the work of Frederick Barbarossa. In what did he succeed, and why, in the end, did he fail?

Q-6.   Why was Frederick II Hohenstaufen called "The Transformer of the World"? What was so modern about him? What effect did he have on Germany?

Q-7.   Describe the evolution of common law and royal justice in England. Who were the important participants and what were their methods and accomplishments?

Q-8.   What were the principal reasons for the rise of urban society in the eleventh century?

Q-9.   Evaluate the various theories advanced to explain the rise of towns in late medieval society. Which do you believe to be the most plausible?

Q-10.   How did the new townspeople manage to gain political status and liberty for their towns?

Q-11.   Why did Venice and the Flemish towns come to lead in the long-distance trade?

Q-12.   How did the rise of towns and the so-called commercial revolution affect the way people lived?

Q-13.   Describe the purpose and the origins of the medieval universities.

Q-14.   Who were the medieval scholastics? What were their basic beliefs about knowledge and education and what were their methods of acquiring knowledge?

Q-15.   Describe the Gothic style. What were its chief features?

Q-16.   The cathdrals became symbols of civic pride. Explain.

Q-17.   The author claims that in the High Middle Ages architecture became the servant of theology. What does he mean? Give examples.

Q-18.   What were the reasons for the rise of heretical cults? Why and how were they extinguished?

Q-19.   "Beginning in the late twelfth century . . . a profound change occurred in public attitudes toward homosexual behavior." Explain.

Q-20.   In what ways did the Dominican and Franciscan orders differ significantly from the older monastic orders? What were the objectives of Francis of Assissi?

STUDY-REVIEW EXERCISES

Define the following key concepts and terms.

Gothic

scholasticism

universitas

common law

Roman law

faubourg or suburb

Ile-de-France

the modern state

Hanseatic League

Explain each of the following terms and tell how it contributed to the evolution of the modern state.

writ

sheriff

baillis and seneschals

Exchequer

tallage

Magna Carta

Identify each of the following and give its significance.

the cult of Saint Denis

heresy

Frederick II Hohenstaufen

Philip II of France

Saint Thomas Aquinas

Suger, abbot of St.-Denis

King John of England

Peter Abélard

Louis IX of France

John of Salisbury

Saint Dominic

Saint Francis of Assissi

Explain what the following were and why they are important in understanding the High Middle Ages.

Domesday survey

crusade against the Albigensians

University of Bologna

Frederick Barbarossa's Italian wars

William of Normandy's conquest of England

conflict between Pope Boniface VIII and King Philip the Fair of France

church building activity of the twelfth and thirteenth centuries

changing attitude toward homosexuals by 1300

Test your understanding of the chapter by answering the following questions.

1. The letter that declared that everyone must submit to the papacy was the
   Unam Sanctam .

2. The English royal bureau of finance was the *Exchequer* .

3. The emperor _Frederick Barbarossa_ of Germany tried to unite Germany.

4. William the Conqueror's survey of English wealth was _Domesday Book_ .

5. The European country best known for its common law was _England_ .

6. The area that underwent development by Frederick II Hohenstaufen was _Sicily_ .

7. The _Magna Carta_ was the document that implied that in English society the law is above the king.

8. The French cathedral school famous for its curriculum and students was _Chartes_ .

9. The architectural style of _Romanesque_ reflects Roman and early Christian models.

10. Medieval reference books were _Summa_ .

11. A league of German cities with its center at Lübeck was _Hanseatic League_ .

12. A Paris teacher, _Peter Abelard_ , was the author of *Sic et Non*.

13. The _Parlement of Paris_ was a kind of French supreme court.

MULTIPLE-CHOICE QUESTIONS

1. Historians maintain that medieval towns probably developed from
   a. old Roman army camps.
   b. fortifications.
   c. ecclesiastical centers.
   d. all of the above.

2. By origin and definition, a burgher or bourgeois was a person
   a. involved in trade or commerce.
   b. who lived within town walls.
   c. who resided in Hamburg, Germany.
   d. who lived on hamburgers.

3. The modern historian who identified the growth of medieval towns with the development of trade was
   a. Josiah Cox Russell.
   b. Eileen Power.
   c. Henri Pirenne.
   d. Marc Bloch.

4. *Town liberty* meant
   a. citizenship.
   b. the right to buy and sell in the town.
   c. personal freedom.
   d. all of the above.

5. Artisans and craftspeople in medieval towns formed
   a. courts to try corrupt businessmen.
   b. craft guilds.
   c. merchant guilds.
   d. the AFL-CIO.

6. The French government, as conceived by Philip Augustus, was characterized by
   a. centralization at the local level and diversity at the top.
   b. diversity at the local level and centralization at the top.
   c. complete local government.
   d. a system identical to England's.

7. Frederick Barbarossa's success in restoring order to the Holy Roman Empire was spoiled by his involvement in
   a. France.
   b. Germany.
   c. England.
   d. Italy.

8. The principle implied in Magna Carta was
   a. democracy.
   b. that all people, even the king, are subject to the law.
   c. that the king is above the law.
   d. that the people rule the monarch.

9. The surge of cathedral building in the twelfth and thirteenth centuries was closely associated with
    a. the increase of university-trained architects.
    b. financial hard times, which caused people to turn to faith.
    c. the low cost of building materials.
    d. the growth of towns and the increase of commercial wealth.

10. The goal of the medieval rulers of France, England, and the Holy Roman Empire was to
    a. be totally subject to the pope.
    b. split their power with the pope.
    c. strengthen and extend royal authority within their territories.
    d. go on crusade.

11. The university in the Europe of the High Middle Ages was
    a. borrowed from the Muslims.
    b. a unique contribution of western Europe.
    c. copied from the Greek model.
    d. copied from the Roman model.

12. The duties of sheriffs in Norman England included
    a. maintaining law and order.
    b. collecting taxes when instructed by the king.
    c. raising infantry at the king's request.
    d. all of the above

13. Heresy flourished in
    a. the most economically advanced and urbanized areas.
    b. backward rural areas.
    c. only southern France.
    d. urban areas suffering from plague and economic depression.

14. The two European states that first developed efficient state bureaucracies were
    a. England and Sicily.
    b. England and France.
    c. England and Italy.
    d. Sicily and France.

15. Which of the following financial problems eventually forced England's King John to sign the Magna Carta?
    a. The debts incurred from Richard the Lionhearted's crusading zeal

b. The ransom paid for Richard the Lionhearted
c. The war debt caused by John in his attempt to regain Normandy from France
d. All of the above

16. The first European universities were located in
a. England.
b. France.
 c. Italy.
d. Germany.

17. Prior to the systematization of law in the thirteenth century, homosexuality was
a. socially accepted.
b. outlawed.
c. uncommon.
d. unknown.

18. The majority of university students in the Middle Ages came from the
a. peasantry.
b. middle class.
c. aristocracy.
d. none of the above

19. Common law differed from the system of Roman law in that
a. common law was applied only to the peasant class.
b. common law was more permanent and static.
c. it relied on precedents.
d. it relied heavily on torture.

20. Peter Abélard's method of learning was to
a. accept whatever his professors said.
b. work on his own, with no discussion.
c. pose questions.
d. seek divine revelation.

21. An outstanding difference between the English sheriff and the French baillis was that the French baillis
a. lacked many of the sheriff's powers.
b. lacked judicial jurisdiction in his district.
c. was never a native of his district, as the sheriff was.
d. represented the king, unlike the sheriff, who represented only the people of his shire or county.

22. The major opposition to Frederick of Sicily's unification of Italy came from
     a. the Holy Roman Empire.
     b. the papacy.
     c. France.
     d. England.

23. In the early Middle Ages education was the responsibility of
     a. secular universities.
     b. feudal manorial schools.
     c. monasteries or cathedral schools.
     d. none of the above

24. The university most famous for the study of medicine was
     a. Paris.
     b. Oxford.
     c. Bologna.
     d. Salerno.

25. The many Gothic cathedrals, abbeys, and parish churches constructed in
     Europe during the High Middle Ages reflected
     a. bourgeois wealth.
     b. civic pride.
     c. strong Christian faith.
     d. all of the above

26. The first Gothic church was built in
     a. France.
     b. Italy.
     c. the Holy Roman Empire.
     d. England.

27. The scholastics of the medieval universities argued and taught from reference
     books called
     a. indulgences.
     b. theological texts.
     c. *summa.*
     d. none of the above

GEOGRAPHY

Using the outline map on page 222 and the text Map 14.2 as your guide:

1. Mark the location of the *Ile-de-France*, and give its significance in the history of the centralization of France.

2. Mark the location of Artois, Vermandois, and Normandy, and explain how these regions came under the control of the French king.

3. Mark the location of Anjou, and discuss how it became the center of an English Angevin empire.

4. Mark the location of Poitou, Provence, and Languedoc. How were these provinces added to the domain of the French kings?

5. How did the system of baillis and seneschals work to tie all of these provinces together?

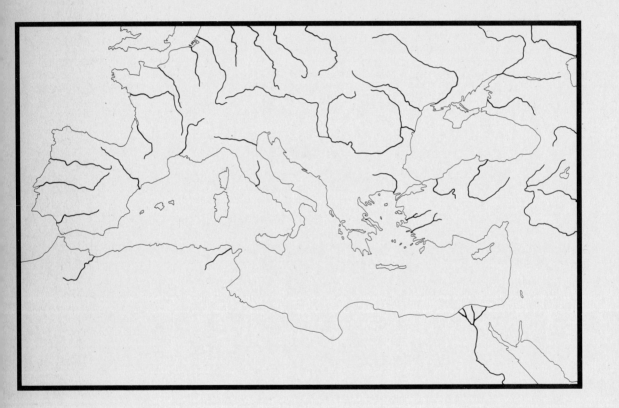

UNDERSTANDING HISTORY THROUGH READING AND THE ARTS

One of the most fascinating women of the Middle Ages was Eleanor of Aquitaine, wife to the king of France and the king of England and mother to two kings of England. She is the subject of a spellbinding biography, *Eleanor of Aquitaine and the Four Kings** (1950), by A. Kelly.

Those interested in medieval cathedral building will want to see J. Harvey, *The Medieval Architect* (1972). And by the same author is one of the most readable surveys of Gothic architecture, *The Master Builders* (1971). See also Chapters 3 and 4 of N. Pevsner, *An Outline of European Architecture** (7th ed., 1963).

PROBLEMS FOR FURTHER INVESTIGATION

What caused the rise of "individualism" in European life? How did the cult of individualism affect European society? The best book on this subject is M. Colin, *The Discovery of the Individual, 1050-1200** (1973). See also R. Hanning, *The Individual in Twelfth Century Romance* (1977).

New interpretations and ideas for research on the rise of the modern state are found in a collection of essays edited by H. Lubasz, *The Development of the Modern State** (1964). The success, glory, idealism, and political aspects of the religious crusades have fascinated historians for generations. Students interested in further research in this area should begin with *The Crusades** (1939) by J. A. Brundage, a book in the Heath series on historical problems. Many possible research and term-paper topics are suggested in T. M. Jones, ed., *The Becket Controversy* (1970).

*Available in paperback.

CHAPTER 15

THE CRISIS OF THE
LATER MIDDLE AGES

CHAPTER OBJECTIVES

After reading and studying this chapter you should be able to answer the following questions:

Q-1.   What were the causes and the effects of the fourteenth-century disasters in Europe — namely, plague, war, social upheaval, crime, and violence?
Q-2.   Was war a catalyst for change?
Q-3.   What provoked the division in the church in the fourteenth century?

CHAPTER SYNOPSIS

The fourteenth century was a time of disease, war, crime, and violence. The art and literature of the period are full of the portrayal of death, just as the historical accounts are full of tales of conflict and violence. There were several major causes for this century of human suffering. Natural disasters — including changes in climate and horrible new diseases — attacked Europe. A long series of wars between France and England not only brought death and economic ruin but increased personal violence and crime as well. In addition, a serious shortage of labor, created by the bubonic plague, resulted in intense social conflict between landlords and peasants. Economic crisis during the century also resulted in a bitter struggle between urban workers and their guild masters.

Amid such violence the church lost power and prestige, partly because of the religious disillusionment that accompanied the plague. In short, the institutional church failed to fill the spiritual vacuum left by the series of disasters. A more immediate reason for the decline of the church's influence and prestige was the Babylonian captivity and the Great Schism. The call for reform, often in the form of the conciliar movement, by people such as Marsiglio of Padua and John Wyclif, was a signal of things to come in the sixteenth-century Reformation.

But the century of disaster was also a century of change, some of it for the good of ordinary people. It is in this light that the chapter examines some important changes in marriage practices, family relations, and the life of the people. The decline in population meant that those who survived had better food and higher wages. Peasants in western Europe used the labor-shortage problem to demand higher wages and freedom from serfdom. These demands often resulted in conflict with their lords. The disillusionment with the organized church also led to greater lay independence and, ultimately, ideas of social and political equality. The wars actually fostered the development of constitutionalism in England. All in all, it was a period of disaster but of disaster that brought with it important changes.

STUDY OUTLINE

I. Death and disease in the fourteenth century
   A. Prelude to disaster
      1. Climate changes and inflation caused economic decline
      2. Diseases killed many people and animals
      3. The population was undernourished, and population growth came to a halt
      4. Weak governments were unable to deal with these problems
   B. The Black Death
      1. Genoese ships brought the plague — the Black Death — to Europe in 1347
      2. This bubonic bacillus lived in fleas that infested black rats
      3. Unsanitary and overcrowded cities were ideal breeding grounds for the black rats
      4. Most people had no rational explanation for the disease, and out of ignorance and fear many blamed it on Jews
      5. The disease, which killed millions, recurred often and as late as 1700
   C. The social and psychological consequences of the Black Death
      1. The plague hit the poor harder than the rich, but all classes suffered
      2. The decline in population meant labor shortages; thus wages went up and social mobility increased
      3. The psychological consequences of the plague were enormous: depression, gross sensuality, flagellantism, and obsession with death
II. The Hundred Years' War (ca 1337–1453)
   A. The causes of the war
      1. Edward III of England, the grandson of the French king Philip the Fair, claimed the French crown, and French barons used Edward's claim as a way to check their king

2. Flemish wool merchants supported the English claim to the crown
3. Both the French and the English saw military adventure as an excuse to avoid domestic problems
4. The French barons passed the crown to Philip Valois and not Edward III
5. Royal propaganda for war and plunder was strong on both sides
   B. The Indian summer of medieval chivalry during the Hundred Years' War
1. Chivalry was a code of conduct for the knightly class
   a. Knights were supposed to be brave, loyal, courteous, and generous
   b. Chivalry and feudal society glorified war
2. Chivalry enjoyed its final days of glory during the war
   C. The course of the war to 1419
1. The battles took place in France and the Low Countries
2. At the battle of Crécy (1346), the English disregarded the chivalric code and used new military tactics: the longbow and cannon
   D. Joan of Arc and France's victory
1. Joan of Arc's campaigns meant a turning point and victory for France
2. Joan was turned over to the English, and a French church court burned her as a heretic
   E. Costs and consequences
1. The war meant economic and population decline for France and England
2. War financing caused a slump in the English wool trade
3. In England, returning soldiers caused social problems
4. The war encouraged the growth of parliamentary government, particularly in England
5. The war generated feelings of nationalism in England and France
III. Vernacular literature
   A. The emergence of national consciousness is seen in the rise of literature written in national languages — the vernacular
   B. Three literary masterpieces manifest this new national pride
1. Dante's *Divine Comedy*, a symbolic pilgrimage to the City of God, embodies the psychological tensions of the age and contains bitter criticism of some church authorities
2. Chaucer, in his *Canterbury Tales*, uses a religious setting to depict the materialistic and worldly interests of a variety of English people in the fourteenth century
3. Villon used the language of the lower classes to talk about the reality, beauty, and hardships of life here on earth
IV. The decline of the church's prestige
   A. The Babylonian Captivity (1309–1377)
1. The pope had lived at Avignon since the reign of King Philip the Fair of France and thus was subject to French control

2. This Babylonian Captivity damaged papal power and prestige
3. Pope Gregory XI brought the papacy back to Rome in 1377, but then a split occurred when the newly elected Urban VI alienated the church hierarchy in his zeal to reform the church
4. A new pope, Clement VII, was elected, and the two popes both claimed to be legitimate (the Great Schism)

B. The Great Schism lasted until 1417
1. England and Germany recognized Pope Urban VI
2. France and others recognized Pope Clement VII

C. The conciliar movement was based on the idea of reform through a council of church leaders
1. Marsiglio of Padua claimed that authority within the church should rest with a church council and not the pope
2. The English teacher John Wyclif and his "Lollard" followers attacked papal authority and called for even more radical reform of the church
3. Wyclif's ideas were spread to Bohemia by John Hus
4. Finally, the council at Constance (1414–1418) ended the schism with the election of Pope Martin V and condemned Hus to death

V. The life of the people in the fourteenth and fifteenth centuries
A. Marriage and the family
1. Economic factors, rather than romantic love, usually governed the decision to marry
2. Marriage usually came very early for women and later for men; divorce did not exist
3. Many people, however, did not observe church regulations and married without a church ceremony

B. Life in the parish
1. The land and the religion were the centers of life
2. Mobility within guilds declined in the fourteenth century, and strikes and riots within guilds became frequent
3. Cruel sports, such as bullbaiting, and drunkenness reflect the violence and frustrations of the age
4. Lay people increasingly participated in church management

C. Peasants' revolts
1. Peasants revolted in France in 1358 and in England in 1381
2. One cause was the lords' attempt to freeze wages
3. In general, the revolts were due to rising expectations
4. The 1381 revolt in England began as a protest against taxes
5. As in England, workers in Italy, Germany, and Spain revolted

D. Conclusion: catalysts for change
1. The crises and wars of the fourteenth and fifteenth centuries altered traditional ways of life

2. Rising social consciousness, changes in government, and advances in technology were some of the changes brought by the events of the times

REVIEW QUESTIONS

Q-1.   What were the causes of the European population decline that began in the early fourteenth century?

Q-2.   What was the source of the bubonic plague, and why did it spread so rapidly in Europe?

Q-3.   How did the plague affect wages and the demand for labor? Can you guess what happened to land values?

Q-4.   Describe the psychological effects of the plague. How did people explain this disaster?

Q-5.   What were the immediate and other causes of the Hundred Years' War?

Q-6.   In your opinion, did feudalism tend to encourage or prevent war? Explain.

Q-7.   What were the results of the Hundred Years' War? Who were the winners and losers within both countries?

Q-8.   Why did a national representative assembly emerge in England?

Q-9.   Drawing on the writings of Dante, Chaucer, and Villon, describe vernacular literature in terms of its form and subject matter. What makes it "modern"?

Q-10.   The Babylonian Captivity greatly weakened the power and prestige of the church. Explain.

Q-11.   In 1409 there were three popes. Why? Who were they, and how and why did this situation occur?

Q-12.   What was the conciliar movement, and who were its advocates? Was this a revolutionary idea?

Q-13.   Why was Wyclif a threat to the institutional church? Even many powerful and rich lords feared the Lollards. Why?

Q-14.   Did peasant conditions improve or deteriorate in the fourteenth and fifteenth centuries? Explain.

Q-15.   What were the reasons for the French *Jacquerie* of 1358 and the English Peasants' Revolt of 1381?

Q-16.   Who was Joan of Arc, and how did she affect French history?

Q-17.   Describe the marriage patterns of late medieval people in terms of when and why people married and the influence that the Church had on marriage.

Q-18.   What is meant by the idea of the Indian summer of medieval chivalry?

STUDY-REVIEW EXERCISES

Define each of the following key concepts and terms.

English Statute of Labourers

conciliar movement

Pasteurella pestis

vernacular

craft guild

Identify each of the following and give its significance.

Marsiglio of Padua

Battle of Crécy (1346)

Martin V

Joan of Arc

Babylonian Captivity

Margaret Paston

Lollards

Edward III

John Hus

John Wyclif

Jacquerie

Explain the importance of each of the follwoing concepts in late medieval life and describe what changes it was subject to in this period.

pluralism

marriage and womanhood

feudal chivalry

individual Christian faith

leisure time

nationalism

Provide approximate dates for the following important events.

1. The first instance of the bubonic plague in Europe

2. The Babylonian Captivity

3. The Hundred Years' War

4. The Council of Constance

5. The battle of Crécy

6. The French *Jacquerie* revolt

7. Dante's *Divine Comedy*

Test your understanding of the chapter by answering the following questions.

1. In reaction to the calls for reform in the fourteenth century, the church *did/ did not* enter into a period of reform and rejuvenation.
2. Prior to the plague in 1348, Europe experienced a period of unusually *good/bad* harvests.
3. The Hundred Years' War was between the kings of *France*

   and *England*.

4. The followers of the English theologian Wyclif were called _Lollards_.
5. Up to the nineteenth century, *economic/romantic* factors usually determined whom and when a person married.
6. For the most part, job mobility within the late medieval guilds tended to *increase/decrease.*

MULTIPLE-CHOICE QUESTIONS

1. The conciliar movement was a (an)
   a. effort to give the pope the power to use councils to wipe out heresy.
   b. effort by the French lords to establish a parliament.
   c. new monastic order vowing poverty.
   d. attempt to place ultimate church authority in a general council.

2. The plague was probably brought into Europe by
   a. Chinese soldiers.
   b. Spanish warriors returning from South America.
   c. English soldiers pushing into France.
   d. Genoese ships from the Crimea.

3. In general, farm laborers who survived the bubonic plague faced
   a. higher wages.
   b. food shortages.
   c. the need to migrate.
   d. excommunication from the church.

4. Most people in the fourteenth century believed that the plague (Black Death) was caused by
   a. bad air.
   b. poor sanitation and housing.
   c. a bacillus living in fleas.
   d. black rats.

5. One reason for peasant-landlord conflict in the fourteenth century was
   a. peasants' opposition to declining wages and inflation.
   b. landlords' attempts to legislate wages.
   c. land scarcity.
   d. peasants' refusal to be drafted for war service.

6. The author of *Defensor Pacis* and proponent of the idea that authority in the Christian church rested in a general council rather than in the papacy was
   a. Cardinal Robert of Geneva.

      b. Pope Urban V.

      c. John Wyclif.

      (d.) Marsiglio of Padua.

7. After 1347, the Black Death generally moved from
    a. north to south.
    b. west to east.
    c. south to north.
    d. east to west.

8. Initially the Hundred Years' War was fought over
    a. Aquitaine.
    b. King Edward III's claim to the French crown.
    c. the control of the Flemish wool trade.
    d. religion.

9. English military innovation(s) during the Hundred Years' War included
    a. the crossbow.
    b. the cannon and the longbow.
    c. cavalry.
    d. the pike.

10. Who of the following was not a writer of vernacular literature?
    a. Dante
    b. Villon
    c. Clement VII
    d. Chaucer

11. For the French, the turning point of the Hundred Years' War was the
    a. relief of Paris.
    b. defeat of the English fleet in the English Channel.
    c. relief of Orleans.
    d. battle of Poitiers.

12. The condition(s) that made Europeans susceptible to the Black Death included
    a. devastating weather.
    b. crop failure.
    c. typhoid epidemic.
    d. all of the above.

13. The chivalric code applied to
    a. knights.
    b. peasants.

    c.   infantry.
    d.   all of the above.

14. The majority of the battles in the Hundred Years' War were fought in
    a.   France and the Low Countries.
    b.   England.
    c.   Germany.
    d.   Ireland.

15. The greatest gain made by England from the Hundred Years' War was
    a.   Aquitaine.
    b.   the growth of parliamentary power.
    c.   Normandy.
    d.   royal absolutism.

16. Of the following social groups, which probably had the highest mortality rate
    as a result of the plague?
    a.   Knights
    b.   Doctors
    c.   Clergy
    d.   Merchants

17. The reason many men fought for England against France was
    a.   national honor and hatred of the French.
    b.   the opportunity provided them to display knightly virtue and the chivalric
        code.
    c.   the chance provided them to collect the spoils of war.
    d.   all of the above.

18. Which of the following statements about the fourteenth century is true?
    a.   The population increased.
    b.   The standard of living fell drastically.
    c.   The power of the church declined.
    d.   War between England and France was infrequent.

19. Generally, the plague disaster of the fourteenth century resulted in which of
    the following?
    a.   Higher wages for most workers
    b.   A sharp increase in the number of German clergymen
    c.   A decline in flagellantism
    d.   Little concern about death

20. The Hundred Years' War had which of the following effects on English society?
    a. It encouraged representative government.
    b. It caused nationalism to decline.
    c. It increased the amount of arable land in England.
    d. It created a manpower surplus.

21. Which of the following was a social consequence of the agricultural catastrophes of the fourteenth century?
    a. Earlier marriage
    b. Full employment
    c. Decrease in crime
    d. Increased serfdom

22. Which of the following statements characterizes marriage during the Middle Ages?
    a. Marriages were never made privately.
    b. Women tended to marry in their late twenties.
    c. Divorce did not exist.
    d. Marriages were determined by romantic love.

23. Which of the following was true of Joan of Arc?
    a. She was unpatriotic.
    b. The English king was her greatest supporter.
    c. She was accused of being a heretic and burned.
    d. She was from an aristocratic family.

24. Which of the following statements about the Babylonian Captivity is true?
    a. The papacy was moved to Paris.
    b. The papacy lost its prestige.
    c. The papacy concentrated only on spiritual matters.
    d. Rome experienced an economic boom.

25. Which of the following was a major point expressed by Marsiglio of Padua in his *Defensor Pacis*?
    a. The church should acquire more property.
    b. The church was subordinate to the state.
    c. The pope's authority could not be overruled.
    d. The Scriptures should be the only basis of Christian belief and practice.

26. Which of the following had become the main purpose of craft guilds in the fourteenth century?
    a. To supply entertainment to members

b. To maintain a monopoly on its product
c. To ensure high standards for products
d. To greatly increase membership

27. The English Statute of Labourers unsuccessfully tried to address the problem of
   a. poor working conditions.
   b. the manpower surplus.
   c. high wages.
   d. declining workmanship.

28. Whose vision was the most "modern" of the medieval vernacularists?
   a. Chaucer
   b. Dante
   c. Villon
   d. St. Augustine

GEOGRAPHY

A. Using Map 15.2 in the text
   1. Locate the extent of the English possessions in France from about 1337 to 1453. What were the origins of English claims to French land?

   2. Why was it unlikely that England could have held these territories permanently?

B. Using Map 15.3 in the text
   1. Locate the main centers of popular revolt in France and England.
   2. Why were so many of the English revolts in the highly populated and advanced areas of the country?

UNDERSTANDING HISTORY THROUGH READING AND THE ARTS

One of the results of the Black Death was a revival of Christian mysticism — a search for meaning in life through a personal relationship with God. One of the most popular books of this movement was *The Imitation of Christ** by Thomas à Kempis.

An excellent introduction to the music of this period is a recording, *Instruments of the Middle Ages and Renaissance*, with an accompanying illustrated book by David Munro (Angel recording number SB2-3810 [1976]), and for the French chansons and the English Madrigals listen to the recording titled *The King's Singers Sing of Courtly Pleasures*, which includes text and translations (Angel recording number s-37025 [1974]).

Students interested in the history of disease in general or in the plague in particular should check the chapter bibliography. Three interesting accounts of the subject are G. C. Coulton, *The Black Death* (1929); P. Zeigler, *The Black Death* (1960); and W. McNeill, *Plagues and Peoples* (1976). E. Perroy, *The Hundred Years' War** (1951), is a good start for anyone interested in that subject. Boccaccio's *Decameron* is a series of bawdy tales told by a group of Florentine men and women who fled to the countryside to escape the plague.

PROBLEMS FOR FURTHER INVESTIGATION

What was the cause of the conflict between Philip the Fair of France and the pope? Was the French king out to destroy the power of the papacy? These and other questions are debated by a number of historians in C. T. Wood, ed., *Philip the Fair and Boniface VIII** (1967).

What were the causes and results of the English peasants' revolt? Begin your investigation with R. Hilton, *Bond Men Made Free: The Medieval Peasant Movements and the English Rising of 1381* (1973).

*Available in paperback.

READING WITH UNDERSTANDING
EXERCISE 4

LEARNING TO CLASSIFY INFORMATION ACCORDING TO SEQUENCE

As you know, a great deal of historical information is classified by sequence, in which things follow each other in time. This kind of *sequential order* is also known as *time order* or *chronological order*.

Attention to time sequence is important in the study of history for at least two reasons.

1. It helps us organize historical information effectively.

2. It promotes historical understanding. If the student knows the order in which events happened, he or she can think intelligently about questions of cause and effect. The student can begin to evaluate conflicting interpretations.

Since time sequences are essential in historical study, the authors have placed a number of timelines in the text to help you organize the historical information.

Two Fallacies Regarding Time Sequences

One common fallacy is often known by the famous Latin phrase *post hoc, ergo propter hoc:* "after this, therefore because of this." This fallacy assumes that one happening that follows another *must* be caused by the first happening. Obviously, some great development (such as the Protestant Reformation) could come after another (the Italian Renaissance) without being caused by it. *Causal relationships must be demonstrated, not simply assumed on the basis of the "after this, therefore because of this" fallacy.*

A second common, if old-fashioned, fallacy assumes that time sequences are composed only of political facts with precise data. But in considering social, intellectual, and economic developments, historians must often speak with less chronological exactitude—in terms of decades or even centuries, for example. Yet they still use time sequences, and students of history must recognize them. For example, did you realize that the sections on "The Scientific Revolution" and "The Enlightenment" in Chapter 18 are very conscientious about time sequence, even though they do not deal with political facts?

Exercise

Reread the large section in Chapter 18 on "The Scientific Revolution" with an eye for dates and sequential order. Then take a sheet of notebook paper and with the book open make a "Timeline for the Scientific Revolution." Pick out at least a dozen important events and put them in the time sequence, with a word or two to explain the significance when possible.

Suggestion: Do not confine yourself solely to specific events with specific dates. Also, integrate some items from the subsection on the causes of the Scientific Revolution into the sequence. You may find that constructing timelines helps you organize your study.

After you have completed your timeline, compare it with the one on the following page, which shows how one of the authors of the text did this assignment.

Timeline on the Scientific Revolution

(1300-1500)	Renaissance stimulates development of mathematics
early 1500s	Aristotle's ideas on movement and universe still dominant
1543	Copernicus publishes *On the Revolution of the Heavenly Spheres*
1572, 1577	New star and comet create more doubts about traditional astronomy
1546-1601	Tycho Brache—famous astronomer, creates mass of observations
1571-1630	Johannes Kepler—his three laws prove Copernican theory and demolish Aristotle's beliefs
1589	Galileo Galilei (1564-1642) named professor of mathematics
1610	Galileo Galilei studies moon with telescope and writes of experience
1561-1626	Francis Bacon—English scientific enthusiast, advocates experimental (inductive) method
1596-1650	René Descartes—French philosopher, discovers analytical geometry in 1619 and advocates theoretical (deductive) method
to about 1630	All religious authorities oppose Copernican theory
about 1632	Galileo tried by papal inquisition
1622	Royal Society of London founded—brings scientists and practical men together
1687	Isaac Newton publishes his *Principia*, synthesizing existing knowledge around idea of universal gravitation
to late 1700s	Consequences of Scientific Revolution primarily intellectual, not economic

CHAPTER 16

AFRICA AND THE AMERICAS
BEFORE EUROPEAN INTRUSION,
CA 400–1500

CHAPTER OBJECTIVES

After reading and studying this chapter you should be able to answer the following questions:

Q-1.   What sources of information help us to understand Africa in history?
Q-2.   What patterns of social and political organization prevailed among the peoples of Africa and Central and South America?
Q-3.   What types of agriculture and commerce did African and American peoples engage in?
Q-4.   What values do their art, architecture, and religion express?
Q-5.   What internal difficulties among American and African peoples contributed to their conquest by Europeans?

CHAPTER SYNOPSIS

The social and political organization of medieval Africa and pre-Columbian America has received little attention from historians. Until recently we knew virtually nothing about the history of the interior of Africa — and thus held an incomplete picture of the beginning of agricultural civilization. By 1500 Africa, the second-largest continent in the world, supported a variety of very different societies and civilizations. A network of caravan routes connected the Mediterranean coast with the Sudan, bringing Islam to West Africa and stimulating gold mining, trade in slaves, and urbanization. It was the kingdom of Ghana that emerged as one of Africa's richest and most powerful states. By controlling the southern end of the caravan route, the semidivine Ghanaian king and the Ghanaian farmers built an agricultural and gold-rich state with its capital at Kumbi. Likewise, Mali had for centuries carried on a brisk trade in salt, gold, and slaves; significantly, as in much of Africa, this trade introduced the Africans to Islam, which in turn led to the conversion of rulers to Islam, the growth of intellectual centers such as Timbuktu, and the strong influence of Muslim *ulemas*. The city-states of the East African coast conducted complicated mercantile activities with the Muslim Middle East, India, and China. By far, the most important foreign influence was Islam. In Ethiopia the city of Axum became the capital of an important civilization that held to a special brand of Christianity, that of Coptic Christianity, and in South Africa a society evolved that was based on new farming techniques gained from Bantu peoples and the mining of gold.

In America before European intrusion the Aztec, Maya, and Inca societies provide us with several of the most interesting (and puzzling) chapters in human history. By 1500 these cultures had passed their intellectual peaks, as their history became chapters in the history of European imperialism. The Aztec built a unified civilization based heavily on their Toltec heritage and distinguished by sophisticated achievements in engineering, sculpture, and architecture and a military-religious system that demanded enormous human sacrifice. The Inca state revealed a genius for organization — being unique at the time in assuming responsibility for the social welfare of all its people. The Maya used agricultural advancement to support a large population and invented a calendar, writing, and mathematics. After setting forth a variety of possible explanations, the author argues that the primary reason for the failure of the Incas to meet the Spanish challenge was political weakness and inferior military skills.

STUDY OUTLINE

I. The land and peoples of Africa
    A. The geography of Africa
        1. Five geographical zones divide this continent, which covers 20 percent of the earth's land surface
            a. The Mediterranean and southwestern coasts have fertile land, good rainfall, and dense vegetation
            b. The dry steppe country of the inland, the Sahel, in the north has little plant life
            c. From here stretch the great deserts — the Sahara in the north and the Namib and Kalahari in the south
            d. The equatorial regions of central Africa have dense, humid, tropical rain forest
            e. The savanna lands that extend from west to east across the widest part of Africa make up one of the richest habitats in the world
            f. Each of these ecological zones has encouraged different economic activity

    2. The climate of Africa is tropical; rainfall is seasonal and is sparse in the desert and semidesert areas

    3. Five peoples inhabited Africa by 3000 B.C.

       a. The Berbers inhabited North Africa

       b. The Egyptians were a cultural rather than a racial group

       c. Black Africans inhabited the region south of the Sahara

       d. Pygmies inhabited the equatorial rain forests

       e. The Khoisans lived south of the equatorial rain forests

  B. Early African societies

    1. Africa was one of the sites of the beginning of agriculture

       a. It spread south from Ethiopia

       b. Agricultural development led to strong extended-family life

       c. Ironworking was introduced by 1000 B.C.

       d. The Bantu moved to Central Africa, where they grew as a result of their agricultural life

       e. Thin topsoil and scarcity of water led to migratory agriculture — that is, the shift of cultivation from place to place

    2. The western Sudan

       a. The Sudan is the area bounded by Egypt, the Red Sea, Ethiopia, Uganda, Zaire, Chad, and Libya

       b. Here a series of kingdoms emerged

       c. The Marde and Chadic peoples of western Sudan grew and prospered as a result of settled agriculture

       d. Religions were largely animistic and centered around family ritual cults

    3. The trans-Saharan trade

       a. The introduction of the camel had a profound economic and social impact in West Africa

         (1) Between A.D. 200 and A.D. 700, a network of caravan trade routes developed between the Mediterranean and the Sudan

         (2) Manufactured goods and foods were exchanged for raw materials and slaves

         (3) Caravan trade stimulated gold mining, slavery, and the slave trade

    4. Export of slaves was largely to Muslim societies

    5. Urban centers grew and Muslim culture, law, and religion became important

    6. Because of Islam, West Africa advanced in the fields of culture, government, and construction

II. African kingdoms and empires

  A. The medieval kingdom of Ghana, ca 900–1100, was a wealthy state

    1. The Soninke people called their ruler *ghana*, or war chief

    2. Ghana's farms supported a large population

    3. The war chief captured the southern portion of the caravan route in 992

    4. The king was considered semisacred, his power was absolute, and he attained the crown through matrilineal heredity

B. The court, influenced by Muslim ideas and run by a bureaucracy, was situated at Kumbi — which contained two sections

    1. Muslims lived in their own quarter, or "town" — with their own religious-political authority

    2. The king resided in another "town"

    3. The royal court was extravagant and rich

C. Ghana's juridical system was based on appeal to the supernatural — but the king could also be appealed to

D. The royal estates, the tribute from chiefs, gold mining, and trade duties enabled the king to support a lavish court

E. Ghanaian society consisted of several ranks

    1. The governing aristocracy (king, court, officials) occupied the highest rank

    2. Next were merchants, followed by the middle classes: farmers, miners, craftsmen, and weavers

    3. At the bottom was a small slave class

    4. Apart from these classes was the army

F. The kingdom of Mali, ca 1200–1450

    1. The kingdom of Ghana split into smaller kingdoms — one of which was Kangaba, which became Mali

        a. Mali owed its greatness to its agriculture and its two great military rulers: Sundiata and Mansa Musa

        b. The Mandinke people were successful at agriculture, and they profited from the West African salt and gold trade

    2. Sundiata encouraged trade and expanded the Mali state

        a. He transformed his capital, Niani, into an important financial and trading center

        b. He conquered the former Ghana territories in addition to Gao, Jenne, and Walata

    3. The Mansa, or emperor, Musa continued these expansionist policies

        a. He extended his influence northward to Berber cities in the Sahara, east to Timbuktu and Gao, and west to the Atlantic

        b. Royal control over the trans-Saharan trade brought great wealth; the empire grew to 8 million people

        c. Musa appointed members of the royal family as governors to rule provinces and dependent kingdoms

        d. He turned from animism to the Muslim religion, and Islamic practices and influence multiplied

      e. Musa's visit to Egypt illustrated his great wealth, but his spending and gifts caused inflation

      f. His pilgrimage to Mecca furthered relations among Mali, the Mediterranean states, and Islamic culture

      g. Timbuktu was transformed into a commercial, intellectual, and artistic center, to become known as the Queen of the Sudan

    4. The mix between Arabic trade, Muslim culture, and African peoples encouraged a high degree of cosmopolitanism and racial toleration

G. The East African city-states

    1. Commercial activity fostered the establishment of great city-states along the East African coast

      a. Many of the natives were called "Ethiopian," or black

      b. The relationship between Arab traders and native black people is unclear — although Islam did not overtake African religions

      c. Asian, African, and Islamic characteristics were established by the intermarriage of Arabs, Persians, and blacks

      d. This culture was called Swahili — a Bantu language

      e. Ibn-Battuta, a traveler, has left a written account of the great cities of Mombasa, Pemba, Kilwa, and Mogadishu

      f. The city of Kilwa was large and elegant, and the farmland produced rich yields

    2. By 1300 a ruler, or *sheikh*, had arisen, and Kilwa was the most powerful city on the coast

      a. Kilwa's prosperity rested on the gold trade and on the export of animal products

      b. Swahili cities traded these products for goods from China, India

    3. Slaves were bought for military, agricultural, maritime, and other purposes — including domestic work

H. Ethiopia: the Christian Kingdom of Axum

    1. The Kingdom of Ethiopia had close ties with the early Christian rulers of Nobatia, a Nubian state, and the Roman and Byzantine worlds

      a. The Ethiopian city of Axum, the center of this civilization, adopted Monophysite Christianity, which held that Christ was divine only, not divine and human

      b. Axum was the major military and political power in East Africa

      c. Economic contact with the Muslim world, along with the Abyssinian mountain range, caused Axum to sever ties with the Byzantine Empire

      d. The special brand of Christianity (Coptic Christianity) that developed here is the most striking feature of Ethiopia between 500 and 1500

I. South Africa

    1. This region is bordered on the northeast by the Zambesi River (see

Map 16.2), has a Mediterranean-type climate, and the land varies from desert to temperate grasslands

2. Until the arrival of the Portuguese (late 15th century) South Africa, unlike the rest of Africa, remained isolated from the outside
   a. Only the Bantu ironworking and farming skills reached South Africa — this occurred by the year 1000 A.D. in what is now Zimbabwe, Orange Free State, and the Transvaal, and by 1500 in the western coastal region
   b. In the west were Khosian-speaking farmers and in the east Bantu-speaking farmers who practiced polygamy
   c. The city of Great Zimbabwe, built entirely of granite between the eleventh and fifteenth centuries, was over sixty acres in area, with great decoration, a temple, and an encircling wall
      (1) This city was the capital of a vast empire consisting of the Zambezi-Limpopo region, and its wealth rested largely on gold mining
      (2) Great Zimbabwe declined in the fifteenth century and a new empire, also based on gold trade, was built in the Mazoe Valley under the Mwene Mutapa rulers

J. All early African societies were stateless societies — in that their social and political organization was an outgrowth of clan bonds

K. The eastern region of Africa (East Africa) and the western region (the western Sudan) were similar in that they were shore cultures that had in common some word roots, cross-cultural interaction with the Muslim world, and a slave trade

III. The geography and peoples of the Americas
A. The concept of the "New World" was a European invention that had no basis in European thought
B. The name "America" applies to the entire continent
   1. It is about 9,000 miles in length, with a mountain range from Alaska to the tip of South America that crosses Central America from northwest to southwest
   2. Mexico is dominated by high plateaus bounded by coastal plains: The plateau regions are "Cold Lands," whereas the valleys are "Temperate Lands" and the coasts are "Hot Lands"
   3. The Central American coast is characterized by jungle, heavy rainfall, and heat; the uplands are better for agriculture and habitation
   4. South America contains twelve nations and is a continent of extremely varied terrain
      a. The western coast is edged by the Andes Mountains
      b. On the east coast is the range called the Brazilian highlands
      c. Three-quarters of the continent is plains

d. The Amazon River bisects the north-central part of the continent and creates dense and humid jungle lands

5. Immigrants — including Amurians and Mongoloids — crossed the Bering Straits as long as 20,000 years ago

    a. Amerinds, or the American Indians, were a hybrid of these two groups

    b. They practiced migratory agriculture, but some settled in villages

    c. These newcomers spread out to make diverse linguistic and cultural groups

    d. By about 2500 B.C. they had learned how to domesticate plants

6. The Mexicans built *chinampas*, whereas the land was terraced in Peru

IV. Mesoamerican civilizations from the Olmec to the Toltec

A. The Olmec civilization (ca 1500 B.C. to A.D. 300) was the first Mesoamerican civilization

1. All subsequent Mesoamerican cultures have rested on the Olmec

    a. Olmec society revolved around groups of large stone buildings that housed the political and religious elite

    b. Peasants inhabited the surrounding countryside

    c. A hereditary elite governed the mass of workers

    d. Around 900 B.C. power shifted from San Lorenzo to LaVenta

2. The Great Pyramid at LaVenta was the center of the Olmec religious cult

3. When LaVenta fell around 300 B.C., Tres Zapotes became the leading Olmec site

B. The Maya of Central America

1. Between A.D. 300 and 900 the Maya of Central America built one of the world's highest cultures

    a. The first Maya emigrated from North America

        (1) The Cholan-speaking Maya apparently created the Maya culture

        (2) Its economic base was agriculture, which supported a large population, and trade between cities evolved

    b. Sharply defined social classes characterize the Maya culture

        (1) No distinct mercantile class existed

        (2) The hereditary nobility possessed the land and acted as warriors, merchants, and priests

        (3) The rest were free workers, serfs, and slaves

    c. Maya hieroglyphic writing has been deciphered, allowing us to understand the history and art of the Maya

    d. The Maya invented a calendar and devised systems of mathematics and writing

C. Teotihuacan and Toltec civilizations lasted from about A.D. 300 to A.D. 900 and were the "Classic Period"

       1. New people from the Mexico Valley built the city of Teotihuacan, which reached a population of over 200,000
          a. Its inhabitants were stratified into the powerful elite and ordinary workers
          b. It was the center for Mesoamerican trade and culture as well as its ceremonial center
          c. At its center were the Pyramids of the Sun and Moon, while other gods were worshipped at lesser temples
       2. In the valley of Oaxaca, the Zapotecan peoples established a great religious center
       3. Teotihuacan society collapsed before invaders around A.D. 700
       4. This was followed by "the Time of Troubles" — a period of disorder, militarism, and emphasis on militant gods and warriors
   D. The Toltec confederation rose up during "the Time of Troubles"
       1. The Toltecs assimilated into the Teotihuacan culture
       2. Under Toliptzin, or Quetzalcoatl, the Toltecs came to control most of central Mexico from coast to coast
       3. According to legend, the rich and powerful Quetzalcoatl went into exile when the god Tezcatlipoca won the battle over sacrifice
          a. The promise of Quetzalcoatl to return confused the emperor Montezuma and the Mexicans when the Spanish conquerors arrived
          b. Drought, weak rulers, and northern invasions brought trouble to the Toltecs
          c. In 1224 the Chichimec peoples of the north captured the Toltec capital of Tula
          d. The last of these Chichimec were the Aztecs, who absorbed the Olmec-Teotihuacan-Toltec culture
V. Aztec society: religion and war
   A. The early Aztecs founded a poor city on the swamps of Lake Texcoco in 1325
       1. By the time of Cortes in 1520, the Aztecs had risen to control all of central Mexico
       2. The Aztecs attributed their success to their god Huitzilopochtli and to their own will power; equally important, the Aztec state was geared for war
   B. War and human sacrifice in Aztec society
       1. War was the dominant cultural institution in Aztec society
          a. The Aztecs believed that the sun needed human blood as its fuel
          b. Victim-gladiators were sacrificed to the sun god
          c. At times thousands of victims were sacrificed, then eaten
       2. Anthropologists have proposed a variety of explanations for these practices

      a.   Human sacrifice served to regulate population growth

      b.   Protein deficiency turned the Aztecs to cannibalism

      c.   State terrorism used human sacrifice to control the people

C. The life of the people

   1. The early Aztecs made no sharp social distinctions

   2. By 1500 a stratified social structure existed

      a.   Legend claims that the first king, a Toltec, fathered a noble class

      b.   By 1500 warriors dominated the state

      c.   The highest generals were great lords, or *tecuhtli*

      d.   Provincial governors functioned much like the feudal lords in medieval Europe

      e.   Beneath the nobility of soldiers were the common warriors

      f.   Male children were instructed in the art of war and sought to become *tequiua* (nobility)

   3. A *maceualti*, or working class, made up the backbone of society

      a.   Members of this class were assigned work, but some of them enjoyed certain rights

   4. The lowest class was the *thalmaitl*, which was made up of the landless workers or serfs

      a.   They were bound to the soil

      b.   They had some rights and often performed military service

   5. Alongside all of these were the temple priests, who performed the sacrifice rituals and predicted the future

   6. At the very top was the emperor, who was selected by a small group of priests, warriors, and officials

      a.   He lived in great luxury and ceremony

      b.   He was expected to be a great warrior and the lord of men (*tlacatecuhtli*)

D. The cities of the Aztecs

   1. Tenochtitlan, or Mexico City, was one of the largest and greatest cities in the world at the time of Diaz

      a.   Built on salt marshes and connected to the mainland by four highways, it had a population of half a million

      b.   Streets and canals crisscrossed the city and were lined with stucco houses

      c.   The Spanish marveled at the city's aqueduct, public squares, and marketplace with its variety of goods

      d.   The pyramid-temple of Huitzilopochtli dominated the city's skyline and was surrounded by a wall and many towers

      e.   In spite of their paganism, Cortes found these people remarkable in their accomplishments

VI. The Incas of Peru

  A. The Inca civilization was established in the six fertile valleys of Peru

    1. Its culture rested on agriculture based on hill farming and guano fertilizing

        a. By the fifteenth century, the farms could support a large number of warriors and industrial workers

B. Inca imperialism

    1. The Incas ascribed divine origin to their earliest king, Manco Capac

    2. The king Pachacuti Inca and his son Topa Inca launched the imperialistic phase of Incan civilization

        a. He extended Incan rule north to modern Ecuador and Colombia and to the Maule river in the South

        b. Pachacuti made Quechua the official language

        c. By imperial colonization (*mitima*) — language, religion, politics, and communication — the Incas controlled their subjects

C. Incan society

    1. The *ayllu*, or clan, was the central unit of early Incan society

        a. The chief, or *curacau*, of the clan was used by kings Pachacuti and Topa to unify society

        b. Eventually a new noble class was created by the king-emperors

        c. Peasants were required to work for the nobility and the state

    2. Marriage was required of all and was often decided by the state; polygamy was common

    3. Daily life was regimented but all people were cared for

        a. Although it had some socialist appearances, society was not based on equal distribution of wealth

        b. The great nobility, the ones called big ears, and the lesser nobility were exempt from work

D. The fall of the Incas

    1. The Incan empire, with the emperor as a benevolent despot, fell easily to the Spanish under Pizarro

        a. Isolation and legendary beliefs — such as the return of the legendary god Virocha — kept the Incas from taking prompt action

        b. Pizarro came at a time of civil war

        c. Pizarro wisely captured the emperor, Atahualpa

REVIEW QUESTIONS

Q-1. Name and briefly describe the five groups of people who had inhabited Africa by 8000 B.C.

Q-2. What have been the sources of our knowledge of Africa?

Q-3. Describe the Bantu agricultural achievements. Why did the Bantu adopt the practice of migratory agriculture?

Q-4.   What were the cultural and religious features of life in the western Sudan and how did the introduction of the camel affect West African life?

Q-5.   What was the economic base of the Ghanaian state and what sort of political organization did it exhibit?

Q-6.   Describe the reigns of Sundiata and Mansa Musa in Mali. What did they accomplish?

Q-7.   Discussing the economic, intellectual, and artistic features of the East African states, explain why this area can be described as highly cosmopolitan, rich, and racially tolerant.

Q-8.   Where was the location of the Kingdom of Axum, and in what way did its form of Christianity differ from that of the orthodox West?

Q-9.   Why was South Africa "far removed" from the outside world, and how was it influenced by Bantu-speaking peoples?

Q-10.   Describe the city of Great Zimbabwe. What was its economic base?

Q-11.   Early African societies are described as stateless societies. Explain.

Q-12.   What role did religion play in the Olmec civilization? How did architecture complement this?

Q-13.   Describe Teotihuacan-Toltec civilization in terms of its class structure and religion.

Q-14.   What was the legend of Quetzalcoatl's exile, and what role may it have played in later Mexican history?

Q-15.   To what features of Aztec culture do you attribute its success in building a great empire?

Q-16.   Why was human blood sacrifice an integral part of Aztec culture? What explanation is most plausible to you?

Q-17.   Describe the social structure of Aztec society. Who were the *tecuhtl*, the *maceualti*, and the *thalmaitl*? Who was the *tlacatecuhtli*?

Q-18.   Who were the Mayans and how was their society organized?

Q-19.   What did the Mayans accomplish?

Q-20.   Compare and contrast the agricultural-economic system and the political system of the Mayans and the Incas.

Q-21.   The Incan emperor has been described as a benevolent despot. Explain. Was Incan society an early socialist state?

Q-22.   Explain why the Inca civilization fell so easily to the Spanish under Pizarro.

Q-23.   Compare and contrast the Mayan and Aztec military systems and their methods of warfare.

STUDY-REVIEW EXERCISES

Define the following key concepts and terms.

trans-Saharan trade

ulemas

ghana

Swahili

"New World"

chinampas

Mesoamerican

tecuhtl

Incan policy of *mitima*

ayllu

sheikh

stateless societies

Identify each of the following and give its significance.

Tenochtitlan

Amerigo Vespucci

Mansa Musa

Timbuktu

Ibn-Battuta

Kingdom of Axum

Kilwa

Toliptzin-Quetzalcoatl

Huitzilopochtli

Francisco Pizarro

Atahualpa

Pachacuti Inca and Topa Inca

the *Periplus*

Ras Assir

Manco Capac

Montezuma II

Hernando Cortes

Aztec "gladiator"

Explain the main features and characteristics *(social, political, economic, and religious) of the following civilizations.*

Olmec

Teotihuacan-Toltec

Aztec

Incan

Mayan

Ghanaian

Mali

early South Africa

Test your understanding of the chapter by answering the following questions.

1. The great Mali emperor whose lavish spending during a visit to Egypt caused terrible inflation as well as world recognition was *Mansa Musa* .

2. The Soninke people of Africa called their ruler *Ghana* , meaning war chief.

3. The most powerful city of the East-African city-states was *Kilwa* .

4. Bantu agricultural achievements rested on (a) settled agriculture, (b) migratory agriculture. *(b)*

5. The early Aztecs founded their city *Tenochtitlan* on the swamps of *Lake Texcoco* in 1325.

6. The secret of the Incan imperial system seems to be its (a) military terrorism, (b) benevolent despotism. *(b)*

7. The great pyramid-temple that dominated the Tenochtitlan city was the temple of *Huitzilopochtli* .

8. In early times, the term *Ethiopian* referred to *"black"* .

MULTIPLE-CHOICE QUESTIONS

1. The Berbers inhabited
   a. South Africa.
   b. the Congo region.
   c. North Africa.
   d. the Gold Coast.

2. Most of Africa's interior was not explored by Europeans until the
   a. 1800s.
   b. 1700s.
   c. 1500s.
   d. 1900s.

3. The Bantu people originally inhabited
   a. South Africa.

    b. Rhodesia.
    c. Nigeria.
    d. Ethiopia.

4. By A.D. 400, the Western Sudan's population had increased dramatically as the result of
    a. changes in climate.
    b. increased concern for hygiene.
    c. increase in food production.
    d. the practice of polygamy.

5. The religious beliefs of animism center on the
    a. worship of animals.
    b. sacredness of cows.
    c. idea that *anima*, or spirits, reside in almost everything.
    d. idea that the gods assume animal forms.

6. Trans-Saharan trade was made possible by
    a. the canteen.
    b. the camel.
    c. coined money.
    d. caravans.

7. The slave population of West Africa was composed of
    a. those guilty of civil or religious offenses.
    b. persons of certain ethnic groups.
    c. peoples captured in war.
    d. debtors who sold themselves into slavery.

8. The line of succession in the kingdom of Ghana was
    a. elective.
    b. matrilineal.
    c. patrilineal.
    d. none of the above

9. The Ghanaian king's top officials were
    a. eunuchs.
    b. Muslims.
    c. Europeans.
    d. Arabs.

10. Mansa Musa created a stir in Egypt with his
    a. enormous armies.

    b.   generosity.
    c.   fabulous wealth in gold.
    d.   both b and c

11.   At its peak, Timbuktu was
    a.   a trade center.
    b.   an intellectual center.
    c.   a cosmopolitan, tolerant city.
    d.   all of the above.

12.   The Swahili language blends both Bantu and
    a.   Indonesian.
    b.   Mali.
    c.   Malagasy.
    d.   Arabic.

13.   Arab influence in eastern Africa
    a.   extended deep into the interior.
    b.   spelled the end for animist religion.
    c.   was mostly confined to coastal ports.
    d.   left few permanent traces.

14.   The Indians of Mexico used *chinampas* in
    a.   human sacrifice.
    b.   the growing of corn.
    c.   military campaigns.
    d.   religious observances.

15.   The potato originated in
    a.   West Africa.
    b.   South America.
    c.   eastern Europe.
    d.   India.

16.   The earliest American civilization was the
    a.   Aztec.
    b.   Incan.
    c.   Mayan.
    d.   Olmec.

17.   The central institution of the Aztec state was the
    a.   priesthood.
    b.   army.

    c.   peasantry.
    d.   great landed estates.

18. The Aztecs believed that without human sacrifice the
    a.   corn would not grow.
    b.   rain would cease.
    c.   gods would take revenge.
    d.   sun's orbit would stop.

19. The text suggests that the social purpose of human sacrifice and cannibalism was to
    a.   control population.
    b.   alleviate a scarcity of meat.
    c.   terrorize and subdue the population.
    d.   control bloodthirsty impulses.

20. The Mayans were most advanced in their
    a.   mathematics.
    b.   literature.
    c.   agriculture.
    d.   architecture.

21. In the Inca empire, *mitima* was the
    a.   colonization of conquered areas.
    b.   paying of tribute to the King.
    c.   cult of the sun-god.
    d.   system of roads.

22. An Inca man "courted" a girl by
    a.   sending her gifts.
    b.   getting permission from the governor to marry.
    c.   hanging around her house and sharing in the work.
    d.   formally asking her father for permission to marry.

23. The Incas had been weakened previous to Pizarro's arrival by a (an)
    a.   civil war.
    b.   terrible epidemic.
    c.   earthquake.
    d.   provincial rebellion.

24. *Tuaregs*, the caravan's greatest enemy, were
    a.   hallucinations caused by heat and glare.

b. sandstorms.
c. poisoned wells.
d. nomadic robbers.

25. Muslim law regarding slaves decreed that
a. children of slaves be freed.
b. slaves be freed on their master's death.
c. slaves be treated humanely at all times.
d. runaway slaves be severely punished.

26. Bananas were introduced into Africa from
a. Europe.
b. the Middle East.
c. South and Central America.
d. Southeast Asia.

27. Between the eleventh and fifteenth centuries, the gold trade wealth of the
Zambezi-Limpopo region was centered at the city of
a. Axum.
b. Great Zimbabwe.
c. Sofala.
d. Meroe.

28. The Teotihuacan civilization inhabited
a. central Mexico.
b. the Panamanian isthmus.
c. southern Florida.
d. Peru.

GEOGRAPHY

A. Using the outline map provided and referring to the text Map 16.1 as your
guide:
1. Indicate the geographic features that define the five distinct geographical
zones that divide Africa. In the space below describe the climatic features
of these zones, and explain how geography has shaped the lives of African
peoples.

2. Indicate the location and chief characteristics of the following early African societies:

Kingdom of Ghana

Western Sudan

Kingdom of Mali

East African city-states

Kingdom of Axum

South Africa

3. Indicate the location of the trans-Saharan trade routes. What was the importance of these routes to the history of Africa?

B. Using Maps 16.4 and 16.5 in the text on pages 476 and 484 as a guide, answer the following questions about South America.
1. Identify the major South American mountain range and river.
2. Describe the geography of Incan Peru in terms of (1) its impact on Incan contact with the outside world, (2) its agriculture, and (3) the Incan imperial road system.
3. Describe the variety of Central American geography. In which of these areas did the Aztec and Mayan civilizations evolve?

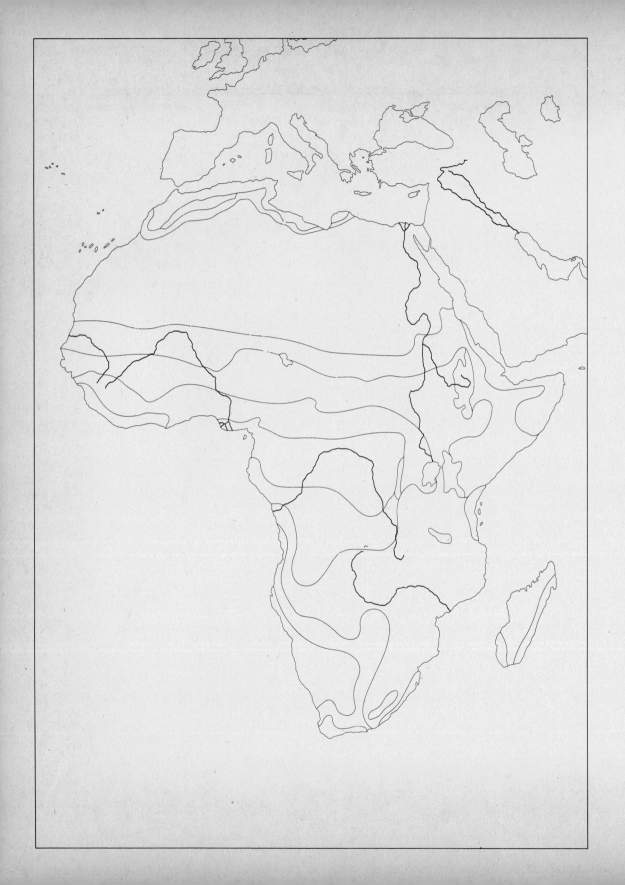

UNDERSTANDING HISTORY THROUGH READING AND THE ARTS

For untold centuries before the Spanish conquest of Central America, the peoples of Central America developed an art and architecture of their own, particularly in ceramics, gold work, and city building. How and why were the fabled cities of the Aztecs and Incas built? Begin your investigation with Leopoldo Castedo's *A History of Latin American Art and Architecture* (1969).

PROBLEMS FOR FURTHER INVESTIGATION

This chapter describes the bloody rituals of human sacrifice practiced by the Aztecs. For further investigation into why the Aztec society was based on war and human sacrifice, see G. Vaillant, *Aztecs of Mexico* (1979), as an initial source.

Why was Islam the major intellectual force in much of Africa in its earlier history? How did Islam help shape African society? Begin your research with J. Trimingham, *A History of Islam in West Africa* (1970) and *Islam in East Africa* (1974).

CHAPTER 17

EUROPEAN SOCIETY IN THE AGE OF THE
RENAISSANCE AND REFORMATION

CHAPTER OBJECTIVES

After reading and studying this chapter you should be able to answer the following
questions:

Q-1. What does the term *Renaissance* mean?
Q-2. How did the Renaissance influence politics, government, and social organization in Europe?
Q-3. Why did Luther's ideas trigger political, social, and economic reactions, and
how did the Catholic church respond to these changes?

CHAPTER SYNOPSIS

The Renaissance is difficult to define but usually is regarded as an era of intellectual
and artistic brilliance unsurpassed in European history. Many educated people in this
era saw themselves living in an age more akin to that of the bright and creative
ancient world than that of the recent dark and gloomy Middle Ages. Although
many of the supposedly "new" Renaissance ideas are actually found in the Middle
Ages, scholars generally agree that the Renaissance was characterized by a number
of distinctive ideas about life and humanity — individualism, secularism, humanism,
materialism, and hedonism.

    The Renaissance began in Florence, Italy, in the fourteenth century. It sub-
sequently spread to the rest of Italy — particularly Rome — and then to northern
Europe, where it developed somewhat differently. The best-known manifestations
of the bold new Renaissance spirit can be seen in the painting, sculpture, and
architecture of the period. But new attitudes were also found in education, politics,
and philosophy and in northern Europe in ideas of social reform. Although the

Renaissance brought some benefits to the masses of people, such as the printing press, it was basically an elitist movement. One negative feature of the age was a deterioration in the power and position of women in society.

The political side of the Renaissance expressed itself in an approach to power and the state that historians often call the theory and practice of "new monarchies." The best known theoretician of this school was Niccolo Machiavelli. Its most able practitioners are the fifteenth- and sixteenth-century monarchs of France, England, and Spain. In Italy, the city-state system led to wealthy and independent cities that were marvelously creative but also vulnerable to invasion and control from the outside by powerful Spanish and French kings.

A great religious upheaval called the Protestant Reformation ended the centuries-long religious unity of Europe and resulted in a number of important political changes. Cries for reform were nothing new, but in the sixteenth century they resulted in revolution. There were a number of signs pointing to the need for moral and administrative reform. For example, it was the granting of indulgences (remissions from the penalties for sin) that propelled Martin Luther into the movement for doctrinal change in the church. Luther had come to the conclusion that salvation could not come by good works or indulgences, but only through faith. This was to be one of the fundamental tenets of Protestantism and one of the ideas that pushed Luther and the German nobility to revolt against not only Rome but Rome's secular ally, the Holy Roman Emperor.

Luther's challenge to the authority of the church and to Catholic unity in Europe invited and supported an attack on the emperor by the German nobility. The pope and the emperor, as separate powers and allies, represented religious and political unity and conformity in Germany. Thus, the victory of Luther and the nobility was a victory for decentralized authority; it meant the collapse of Germany as a unified power in Europe. This is one reason that Catholic France usually supported the German Protestants in their quarrel with Rome.

Outside of Germany the Protestant reformer Calvin's harsh and dogmatic religion spread from Geneva into northern Europe, England, and Scotland. It was England, in fact, that eventually became the political center of Protestantism. Initiated by Henry VIII, the English Protestant Reformation was at first motivated by the personal and political interests of the king himself. The type of Protestantism eventually adopted by the Church of England was much more moderate — and closer to Catholicism — than that of Scotland.

With the Council of Trent of 1545–1563, the Catholic church launched a massive and somewhat successful Counterreformation to convince dissidents to return to the church.

STUDY OUTLINE

I. The evolution of the Italian Renaissance
   A. The "Renaissance" was a period of cultural achievement in two phases —
       from 1050 to 1300 and from 1300 to about 1600
       1. The wealth of the northern Italian cities was a cause of the Renais-
           sance; it was an artistic and intellectual movement sustained by urban
           wealth
       2. Florence, the first city of the Renaissance, was a banking and manu-
           facturing center
   B. Communes and republics
       1. In the Italian cities of Milan, Florence, Genoa, Siena, and Pisa the
           feudal nobility and the commercial aristocracy merged and ruled
           a. The *popolo*, or middle class, was excluded from power
           b. Popolo-led republican governments failed — which led to the rule
               of despots or oligarchies
           c. In the fifteenth century, the princely courts of the rulers were
               centers of wealth and art
   C. The balance of power among the Italian city-states
       1. Italy had no political unity; it was divided into city-states such as
           Milan, Venice, and Florence, a papal area, and a kingdom of Naples in
           the south (see map 17.1)
       2. The political and economic competition among the city-states was
           damaging and weakened Italy
       3. After 1494 a divided Italy became a European battleground, beginning
           with an invasion by Charles VIII of France
II. Intellectual hallmarks of the Renaissance
   A. Many, like the poet and humanist Petrarch, saw the fourteenth century
       as a new age and a revival of ancient Roman culture
   B. Individualism stressed personality, genius, and uniqueness
   C. The revival of antiquity was one important feature of the Renaissance and
       led to humanism
       1. Italians copied the ancient Roman lifestyle
       2. The study of the classics led to humanism, or an emphasis on human
           beings
           a. Humanists sought to understand human nature through a study of
               pagan antiquity *and* Christian thought
           b. The humanist writer Pico della Mirandola believed that there were
               no limits to what human beings could accomplish
       3. Ancient Latin style was considered superior to medieval Latin
   D. Secular spirit
       1. *Secularism* means a concern with materialism rather than religion

    2. Unlike medieval people, Renaissance people were most concerned about money and the accumulation of wealth

    3. They were also interested in pleasure and the enjoyment of life on earth

    4. The church did little to combat secularism; in fact, many popes were Renaissance patrons and participants

III. Art and the artist

    A. The *quattrocento* and the *cinquecento* saw great artistic activity as the center of activity shifted from Florence to Rome

    B. Art and power

        1. Art served a social function during the Renaissance

            a. It was patronized by corporate groups such as guilds and religious bodies and by rich individuals

            b. It was a means of glorifying politicians and rich families

        2. The purpose and style of art changed in the fifteenth century

            a. It became more secular

            b. Painting and sculpture became more naturalistic and realistic

            c. The human body was glorified in art — for example, by Michelangelo

            d. A new "international style" emphasized color, decoration, and curvilinear rhythms

    C. The status of the artist

        1. The status of the artist improved during the Renaissance; most work was done by commission from a prince

        2. The creative genius of the artist was recognized

        3. The Renaissance was an elitist movement that cared little for ordinary people and thus maintained the gulf between the educated few and the multitude

IV. Social change

    A. Education and political thought

        1. Vergerio's humanism represents the Renaissance concern for education

        2. The Renaissance man was well rounded

        3. Castiglione's *The Courtier* describes the model Renaissance gentleman as a man of many talents, including intellectual and artistic skills

        4. Machiavelli's *The Prince* describes how to acquire political power

            a. Machiavelli believed that the politician may use any means to gain power

            b. He viewed the state not as a utopia but as an amoral force

    B. The printed word

        1. The invention of movable type by Gutenberg, Fust, and Schöffer — all at Mainz, Germany — revolutionized life

        2. Printing brought about new possibilities for propaganda, encouraged wider "common identity," and improved literacy

      3. It meant the spread of ideas — ideas that were often critical of the existing order

C. Women in Renaissance society

    1. The status of upper-class women declined during the Renaissance

    2. Nevertheless, the Renaissance meant improved educational opportunities for women

    3. Women's position declined with regard to sex and love

    4. The rape of women by upper-class men was frequent and not considered serious

    5. Infanticide and abandonment of children was frequent and eventually led to the establishment of foundling hospitals

D. Blacks in Renaissance society

    1. Beginning in the fifteenth century, black slaves were brought into Europe in large numbers

    2. Black slaves filled a variety of positions, from laborers to dancers and musicians

    3. The Europeans perceived blacks from both positive and negative religious perspectives

V. The Renaissance in the north of Europe

A. The Renaissance in the north began about 1475 and was more Christian than the Renaissance in Italy; it stressed social reform based on Christian ideals

B. Christian humanists sought to create a more perfect world

    1. Humanists like Lefèvre believed that the use of the Bible by common people would bring about social improvement

    2. Thomas More, the author of *Utopia*, set forth the new idea that society, not people, needed improving

    3. The Dutch monk Erasmus best represents Christian humanism in his emphasis on education and inner Christianity

C. French humanist writers were more secular; Rabelais satirized social institutions and behavior while he promoted individual instinct and enjoyment of life

D. Northern art and architecture were more religious than in Italy and less influenced by classical themes and motifs

    1. Van Eyck painted realist works based on human themes

    2. Bosch used religion and folk legends as themes

VI. Politics and the state in the Renaissance (ca 1450–1521)

A. The "new" monarchs

    1. The fifteenth century saw the rise of many powerful and ruthless rulers interested in the centralization of power and the elimination of disorder and violence

    2. Many of them seemed to be acting according to Machiavelli's principles

      3. The ideas of the new monarchs were not entirely original — some of them had their roots in the Middle Ages

  B. France after the Hundred Years' War

      1. Charles VII ushered in an age of recovery of the monarchy

      2. He ended civil war, established a royal army, and made the church subject to the state

      3. Louis XI, the "Spider King," expanded the French state and laid the foundations of later French absolutism

  C. England

      1. Feudal lords controlled England in the fifteenth century, leading to the Wars of the Roses

      2. Edward IV and his successors began to restore royal power

      3. The English Parliament had become a power center for the aristocracy but was manipulated by Henry VII (Tudor) into becoming a tool of the king

         a. Henry VII used the royal council and the Court of Star Chamber to check aristocratic power

         b. He rebuilt the monarchy and restored the economy — relying on middle class support and the local justices of the peace

  D. Spain

      1. The marriage of Ferdinand and Isabella united Spain into a loose confederation

      2. They used the *hermandades*, or local police forces, to administer royal justice

      3. The royal council checked aristocratic power

      4. The church was used to strengthen royal authority

      5. Ferdinand and Isabella completed the *reconquista* — the expulsion or conversion of Arabs and Jews

      6. Anti-Semitic riots were frequent

  E. Germany and the rise of the Habsburg dynasty

      1. In the Holy Roman Empire (the German states) the Golden Bull of 1356 gave each of the seven Electors virtual sovereignty

         a. This form of localism gave the nobility the power to strengthen their territories

         b. Chronic disorder also helped the nobility

      2. The rise of the Habsburgs, particularly with the marriage of Maximilian I of Austria and Mary of Burgundy in 1477, gave unity to much of Europe

         a. Charles V, their grandson, dominated Europe

         b. He was committed to the idea of its religious and political unity

VII. The condition of the church (ca 1400–1517)

  A. The declining prestige of the Church was due to the Great Schism, while the Humanists satirized and denounced moral corruption within the Church

B. Signs of disorder in the early sixteenth century
1. Critics wanted moral and administrative reform in three areas
   a. Clerical immorality created a scandal among the faithful
   b. The lack of education of the clergy was condemned by Christian humanists
   c. The absenteeism, pluralism (holding of several *benefices*, or offices), and wealth of the greater clergy bore little resemblance to Christian gospel
2. The prelates and popes of the period lived like secular princes; they did not set a good example

C. Signs of vitality in the late fifteenth and early sixteenth centuries
1. Sixteenth-century Europe remained deeply religious
2. New organizations were formed to educate and minister to the poor
3. Thomas à Kempis and the Brethren of the Common Life urged ordinary people to achieve spiritual perfection by means of the simple life
4. The Italian Oratorians devoted themselves to ministering to society
5. Pope Julius II summoned an ecumenical council on reform in the church called the Lateran Council (1512–1527)

VIII. Martin Luther and the birth of Protestantism
A. Luther was a German miner's son trained as a monk and a professor of religion; he concluded that faith was central to Christianity and the only means to salvation

B. Luther's Ninety-five Theses (October 1517)
1. Luther's opposition to the sale of indulgences (remissions of penalties for sin) prompted his fight with Rome
2. His Ninety-five Theses, or propositions on indulgences, raised many theological issues and initiated a long period of debate in Europe
3. Luther was excommunicated by the pope and declared an outlaw by Charles V at Worms in 1521

C. Protestant thought (1520–1530)
1. Protestant thought was set forth in the Confession of Augsburg, in which Luther raised four basic theological issues
   a. He believed that salvation derived through faith alone
   b. He stated that religious authority rests with the Bible, not the pope
   c. He believed that the church consists of the entire community of Christian believers
   d. And he believed that all work is sacred and everyone should serve God in his or her individual vocation
2. Protestantism, therefore, was a reformulation of Christian beliefs and practices

D. The social impact of Luther's beliefs
  1. By 1521 Luther's religious ideas had a vast following among all social classes and eventually led to social revolt
     a. Luther's ideas were popular because of popular resentment of clerical wealth
     b. Prosperous burghers encouraged preaching of sermons while peasants found in Luther a reason to demand land
     c. In the end Luther did not support them; he believed in obedience to civil authority
     d. Widespread peasant revolts were brutally crushed but some land was returned to common use
     e. Luther's greatest weapon was his mastery of the language, and his words were spread by the advent of printing
        (1) Zwingli and Calvin were greatly influenced by his writings
        (2) The publication of Luther's translation of the New Testament in 1523 democratized religion
  2. Luther held enlightened views on sex and marriage — although he claimed that women should be no more than efficient housewives
  3. The political impact of Luther's beliefs
     a. The Protestant Reformation stirred nationalistic feelings in Germany against the wealthy Italian papacy
     b. Luther's appeal to patriotism earned him the support of the princes, who used religion as a means of gaining more political independence
     c. Thus, Luther's teachings prevailed, despite his condemnation by the pope and the Holy Roman Emperor
     d. Charles V did not understand or take any interest in the Luther issue
        (1) The Turkish threat blocked Charles V's position in Germany
        (2) He was also involved in numerous wars against France, which kept Germany a divided and weakened royal power
     e. By the Peace of Augsburg of 1555, Charles recognized Lutheranism as a legal religion
IX. The growth of the Protestant Reformation
  A. Calvinism
     1. Calvin believed that God selects certain people to do His work and that he was selected to reform the city of Geneva
     2. Under Calvin, Geneva became a theocracy, in which the state was subordinate to the church
     3. Calvin's central idea was his belief in the omnipotence of God and the insignificance of humanity
        a. People lacked free will

        b. God decided ahead of time who would be saved (the doctrine of predestination)

    4. Austere living and intolerance characterized Calvin's Geneva

    5. The city was the model for international Protestantism, and Calvinism became the most dynamic and influential form of Protestantism

B. The Anabaptists

    1. This Protestant sect believed in adult baptism, revelation, and the separation of church and state

    2. Their beliefs and practices were humane but too radical for the times, and they were bitterly persecuted

C. The English Reformation

    1. As early as the fourteenth century the English Lollards stressed the idea of a direct relationship between the individual and God

    2. Wolsey's career represents corruption in the English church

    3. Henry VIII desired a divorce from his queen, Catherine, daughter of Ferdinand and Isabella of Spain

    4. Pope Clement VII and emperor Charles V blocked the divorce

    5. The pro-Protestant Archbishop Cranmer engineered an annulment

    6. The result was the nationalization of the English church and a break with Rome as Henry used Parliament to legalize the Reformation

        a. Henry needed money so he dissolved the monasteries and confiscated their lands

        b. Some traditional Catholic practices, such as confession and the doctrine of transubstantiation, were maintained, however

        c. Nationalization of the church led to a new form of government

    7. Under Edward VI, Henry's heir, England shifted closer to Protestantism

    8. Mary Tudor attempted to bring Catholicism back to England

    9. Under Elizabeth I a religious settlement — mainly Protestant — was made

D. The establishment of the Church of Scotland

    1. Scotland was an extreme case of church abuse

    2. John Knox brought Calvinism to Scotland from Geneva

    3. The Presbyterian Church became the national church of Scotland

E. Protestantism in Ireland

    1. The English ruling class in Ireland adopted Protestantism

    2. The Irish people defiantly remained Catholic

F. Lutheranism in Scandinavia

    1. In Sweden, Norway, and Denmark the monarchy led the religious reformation

    2. The result was Lutheran state churches

X. The Catholic and counterreformations

A. The slowness of institutional reform

      1. Too often the popes were preoccupied with politics and material pleasures
      2. Also, popes feared conciliarism because it would limit their authority, so they resisted calls for reform councils
   B. The Council of Trent
      1. Pope Paul III called the Council of Trent, which met from 1545 to 1563
         a. An attempt to reconcile with the Protestants was made, but it failed
         b. International politics hindered the theological debates and the attempts at reconciliation
   C. New religious orders within the Catholic Church
      1. The Ursuline order was dedicated to combating heresy
      2. The Jesuits, under Loyola, sought to fight heresy and reform the Church
   D. The Sacred Congregation of the Holy Office
      1. The Roman Inquisition — founded in 1542 by Pope Paul III — was an arm of the Counterreformation empowered to combat heresy
      2. Under the direction of religious fanatics, it had the power to arrest, imprison, and execute
      3. Its influence was confined to Italy

REVIEW QUESTIONS

Q-1. How do Valla and Boccaccio illustrate and represent what Renaissance people were like?

Q-2. Do you believe that it is possible, through education, to perfect mankind? What did the Renaissance thinkers believe the keys to this process to be?

Q-3. According to Vergerio, what is the purpose of education? Was he a humanist?

Q-4. How does Castiglione's *The Courtier* define the "perfect Renaissance man"? How does this book represent the philosophy of humanism?

Q-5. In what ways does Machiavelli represent a Renaissance thinker? What were his suggestions for and philosophy of the acquisition and meaning of political power?

Q-6. Explain why the invention of movable type revolutionized European life.

Q-7. What were the similarities and differences between the Renaissance in northern Europe and that of Italy?

Q-8. Discuss Christian humanism by describing the works and ideas of Thomas More and Desiderius Erasmus.

Q-9. Describe the make-up of the Italian city-state political system. How well did it work?

Q-10. "After 1494, Italy became a battleground for the European superpowers." Explain.

Q-11.   What were the obstacles to royal authority faced by the kings of France in the fifteenth century? How did Charles VII and his successors strengthen the French monarchy?

Q-12.   What devices did Henry VII of England use to check the power of the aristocracy and strengthen the monarchy?

Q-13.   The reign of Ferdinand and Isabella is one of the most important in Spanish history. Why? What were their achievements in the areas of national power and national expansion?

Q-14.   Why were blacks valued in Renaissance society? What roles did they play in the economic and social life of the times?

Q-15.   What were some of the signs of disorder within the early sixteenth-century church? How did church wealth affect the condition of the church?

Q-16.   What were some of the signs of religious vitality in fifteenth- and early sixteenth-century society?

Q-17.   Describe the circumstances that prompted Luther to post his Ninety-five Theses.

Q-18.   Describe the practice of indulgence selling. What authority did Luther question, and on what argument did he base his position?

Q-19.   What were Luther's answers, as delineated in the Confession of Augsburg, to the four basic theological issues?

Q-20.   What effect did Luther's concept of state authority over church authority have on German society and Cerman history?

Q-21.   Calvin's Geneva was called "the city that was a church." Explain. What is a theocracy?

Q-22.   In what ways were the Anabaptists radical for their time? Why did many of their beliefs cause them to be bitterly persecuted?

Q-23.   Explain the causes and results of the English Reformation. What was the Elizabethan Settlement?

Q-24.   Compare and contrast the religious settlements made in Scotland and Ireland. Why was Protestantism in one place a source of national strength and in the other a source of national weakness?

Q-25.   What were the repercussions of the marriage of Maximilian and Mary? How did this marriage affect France?

Q-26.   Charles V has been considered a medieval emperor. In what respects is this true? What were the origins of his empire?

Q-27.   Why was the condemnation of Luther in 1521 at Worms not enforced by the German nobility? What was the result?

Q-28.   What were the goals and methods of the Ursuline order and the Society of Jesus?

Q-29.   Why was reform within the Catholic church often unwelcome and slow in coming?

Q-30.   What were the achievements of the Council of Trent? What circumstances surrounding the calling of the council made its task difficult and its goal of reconciliation with Protestantism unattainable?

STUDY-REVIEW EXERCISES

Define the following key concepts and terms.

oligarchies

signori

Brethren of the Common Life

John Knox

Pope Paul III

Archbishop Cranmer

Martin Luther

Henry VIII

Charles V

Mary Tudor

Pope Alexander VI

Council of Trent

Elizabethan Settlement

Act of Restraint of Appeals

pluralism

benefices

Peace of Augsburg

Ninety-five Theses

Spanish *conversos*

communes

reconquista

Renaissance

humanism

secularism

individualism

materialism

"Machiavellian"

Explain the importance of each of the following.

English Royal Council and Court of Star Chamber

Habsburg-Valois wars

Brunelleschi's Foundling Hospital in Florence

Spanish anti-Semitic riots of the fourteenth century

Identify each of the following people and give his significance.

Pico della Mirandola

Desiderius Erasmus

Thomas More

Donatello

Baldassare Castiglione

Niccolo Machiavelli

Johann Gutenberg

Jacques Lefèvre d'Etaples

Saint John Chrysostom

François Rabelais

Explain why each of the following is often considered to be a "new monarch."

Louis XI of France

Henry VII of England

Ferdinand and Isabella of Spain

Charles VII of France

Cesare Borgia

Define the basic beliefs of the following Christian religions and churches.

Roman Catholicism

Lutheranism

Calvinism

Anabaptism

Church of England

Presbyterian Church of Scotland

Test your understanding of the chapter by answering the following questions.

1. He was the author of a best-selling political critique called *The Prince*.

   _____

2. Renaissance humanists tended to be *more/less* concerned about religion than about people.

3. In the fifteenth century, infanticide *increased/decreased*.

4. He was an important English humanist and the author of *Utopia*.

   _____

5. Generally, the legal status of upper-class women *improved/declined* during the Renaissance.

6. It *is/is not* clear that the economic growth and the material wealth of the Italian cities were direct causes of the Renaissance.

7. The Council of Trent *did/did not* reaffirm the seven sacraments, the validity of tradition, and transubstantiation.

8. The English Supremacy Act of 1534 declared the _____ to be the Supreme Head of the Church of England.

9. For the most part, the English Reformation under Henry VIII dealt with *political/theological* issues.

10. He wrote: 'How comes it that we Germans must put up with such robbery and such extortion of our property at the hands of the pope?"

    _____

11. This pope's name became a synonym for moral corruption.

    _____

12. Mary Tudor, the English queen and daughter of Henry VIII, *was/was not* interested in the restoration of Catholicism in England.

13. In general, Protestantism tended to *strengthen/weaken* Germany as a political unit.

14. During the reign of Elizabeth, the English church moved in a moderately *Protestant/Catholic* direction.

MULTIPLE-CHOICE QUESTIONS

1. The Renaissance began in
   a. the Low Countries.
   b. Rome.
   c. France.
   d. Florence.

2. The patrons of the Renaissance were mostly
   a. churchmen.

    b.   the popes.
    c.   the common people.
    d.   merchants and bankers.

3. The king who began French economic and political recovery in the early fifteenth century was
    a.   Henry Tudor.
    b.   Charles VII.
    c.   Philip the Fair.
    d.   Louis XI.

4. It appears that in Renaissance society blacks were
    a.   valued as soldiers.
    b.   valued as servants and entertainers.
    c.   considered undesirable and were not allowed in society.
    d.   treated equally with whites.

5. A major difference between northern and Italian humanism is that northern humanism stressed
    a.   economic gain and materialism.
    b.   social reform.
    c.   pagan virtues.
    d.   popular education.

6. Local groups in Spain that were given royal authority to administer justice were the
    a.   *conversos.*
    b.   liberals.
    c.   *hermandades.*
    d.   royal tribunals.

7. The Court of Star Chamber in England was
    a.   a common law court.
    b.   under the control of the barons in the House of Lords.
    c.   done away with by the powerful Tudors.
    d.   used to check aristocratic power.

8. The superiority of the French monarch over the church was the object of the
    a.   Pragmatic Sanction of Bourges.
    b.   Habsburg-Valois wars.
    c.   Declaration of Calais.
    d.   Hundred Years' War.

9. Most of the northern Renaissance thinkers agreed that
   a. democracy, not monarchy, was the only workable political system.
   b. humanity is basically sinful.
   c. Christianity is unacceptable.
   d. society is perfectible.

10. The late-fifteenth-century ruler of England who ended the civil war and strengthened the crown was
    a. John I.
    b. William III.
    c. Henry II.
    d. Henry VII.

11. The High Renaissance masterpiece, the dome of St. Peter's in Rome, is considered to be the greatest work of
    a. Brunelleschi.
    b. Donatello.
    c. Michelangelo.
    d. Ghiberti.

12. The term *Renaissance* means
    a. a rise in the average standard of living among the masses.
    b. a resurgence of art and culture out of a concern for individualism and study of the ancients.
    c. an increase in the population after the ravaging effects of the "Four Horsemen of the Apocalypse."
    d. the recovery of the church from economic and moral decline.

13. The financial and military strength of the towns of northern Italy was directly related to
    a. their wealth, which enabled them to hire mercenary soldiers to protect their commercial interests.
    b. their contractual and marital alliances with the rural nobility.
    c. protections provided them by the Holy Roman Emperor.
    d. their alliance with the papacy.

14. Erasmus advocated
    a. paganism.
    b. Christian education for moral and intellectual improvement.
    c. monastic life of contemplation and divorce from the material world.
    d. obedience to church doctrine and ritual.

15. The Renaissance artist of talent and ability often lived a life
     a. of economic desperation.
     b. of economic security through patronage.
     c. of luxury, but without social status.
     d. like that of the masses.

16. The most influential book on Renaissance court life and behavior was
     a. Castiglione's *The Courtier.*
     b. Machiavelli's *The Prince.*
     c. Augustine's *The City of God.*
     d. Boccaccio's *Decameron.*

17. The Wars of the Roses were
     a. civil wars between the English ducal houses of York and Lancaster.
     b. between England and France.
     c. civil wars between the English king, Henry VI, and the aristocracy.
     d. minor disputes among English gentry.

18. Just before the advent of Ferdinand and Isabella, the Iberian peninsula could best be described as a
     a. homogeneous region sharing a common language and cultural tradition.
     b. heterogeneous region consisting of several ethnic groups with a diversity of linguistic and cultural characteristics.
     c. culturally poor and backward region.
     d. region dominated equally by Arabs and Jews in both numbers and political power.

19. Under the Presbyterian form of church government, the church is governed by
     a. bishops.
     b. the king of Scotland.
     c. ministers.
     d. the people.

20. According to Luther, salvation comes through
     a. good works.
     b. faith.
     c. indulgences.
     d. a saintly life.

21. The cornerstone of Calvin's theology was his belief in
     a. predestination.
     b. indulgences.

   c. the basic goodness of man.
   d. religious tolerance and freedom.

22. John Knox and the Reformation movement in Scotland were most influenced by which of the following theological positions?
   a. Catholicism
   b. Calvinism
   c. Lutheranism
   d. Church of England

23. Overall, Henry VIII's religious reformation in England occurred for
   a. strictly economic reasons.
   b. religious reasons.
   c. mostly political reasons.
   d. mostly diplomatic reasons.

24. The Reformation in Germany resulted in
   a. a politically weaker Germany.
   b. a politically stronger Germany.
   c. no political changes of importance.
   d. a victory for imperial centralization.

25. The great Christian humanists of the fifteenth and sixteenth centuries believed that reform could be achieved through
   a. the use of violent revolution.
   b. education and social change.
   c. mass support of the church hierarchy.
   d. prayer alone.

26. Luther tacked his Ninety-five Theses to the door in Wittenberg as a response to the
   a. sale of indulgences and papal wealth.
   b. revelation he experienced instructing him to start a new church.
   c. illiteracy of the clergy.
   d. oppressive rule of Frederick of Saxony.

27. By 1555 the Protestant Reformation had spread to all but
   a. England.
   b. Scandinavia.
   c. Spain.
   d. Scotland.

28. The chief center of the Protestant Reformers in the sixteenth century was
    a. Paris.
    b. Geneva.
    c. Zurich.
    d. Cologne.

29. The Anabaptists appealed to the
    a. nobility.
    b. poor, uneducated, and unemployed.
    c. intellectuals.
    d. merchant classes.

30. Henry VIII dissolved the monasteries largely because
    a. they were corrupt and mismanaged.
    b. they were symbolic of papal authority.
    c. he needed the wealth they would bring.
    d. they were a burden on the state.

31. The Scandinavian countries were most influenced by the religious beliefs of
    a. Martin Luther.
    b. John Knox.
    c. Roger Brown.
    d. the Jesuits.

32. A vow of the Jesuit order making it uniquely different from others was
    a. poverty.
    b. chastity.
    c. obedience to the pope.
    d. pacifism.

UNDERSTANDING HISTORY THROUGH READING AND THE ARTS

The music of the European Renaissance is introduced in the recordings *From the Renaissance* (STL-150) and *From the Renaissance-Concert* (STL-160) in the Time-Life series *The Story of Great Music* (1967), which includes a book with a good introduction to the period and its musical styles, art, and history. Another good introduction to Renaissance music is H. Brown, *Music in the Renaissance** (1976).

One of the best ways to understand the Renaissance is to read the works of its participants. Three works dealt with in this chapter are Niccolo Machiavelli, *The*

*Available in paperback.

Prince* (a number of paperback translations are available); Baldassare Castiglione, *The Courtier**, Charles Singleton, trans. (1959); and Thomas More, *Utopia**.

Few men in history have been the subject of more biographies than Martin Luther, the German reformer. One of the most important is a psychological study by E. Erikson entitled *Young Man Luther: A Study in Psychoanalysis and History** (1962). Other books about Luther include R. Bainton, *Here I Stand** (1950); E. Schwiebert, *Luther and His Times* (1952); G. Forel, *Faith Active in Love* (1954); and J. Atkinson, *Martin Luther and the Birth of Protestantism** (1968).

King Henry VIII of England is the subject of a number of interesting biographies. Three of the best are L. B. Smith, *Henry VIII* (1971); A. F. Pollard, *Henry VIII** (1905); and J. Scarisbrick, *Henry VIII* (1968). Henry's marital problems, as seen from his wife's side, are the subject of the fascinating and exciting *Catherine of Aragon** (1941) by G. Mattingly.

PROBLEMS FOR FURTHER INVESTIGATION

Students interested in women in the Renaissance in Europe should begin with M. Rose et al., *Women in the Middle Ages and the Renaissance: Literary and Historical Perspectives* (1986).

The Swiss historian Jakob Burckhardt called the Renaissance the "mother" of our modern world. Was the Renaissance as important as Burckhardt and others have claimed? Did it dramatically change the way people acted and the direction history was to take? These and other questions are considered in several historical debates on the Renaissance: D. Hay, ed., *The Renaissance Debate** (1965); B. Tierney, et al., *Renaissance Man — Medieval or Modern?** (1959). How did Renaissance thinking affect the arts? Fine illustrations and a discussion of new directions in the arts are woven into a number of interesting essays on the age in D. Hay, *The Renaissance* (1967).

Students interested in further study of the religious revolution of the sixteenth century will find some of the problems of interpretation and investigation relative to that subject set out in L. W. Spitz, ed., *The Reformation** (1972), and K. Sessions, ed., *Reformation and Authority: The Meaning of the Peasants' Revolt** (1968). The relationship between the Protestant religion and economic growth has long interested historians. This historical problem is defined in R. Green, ed., *Protestantism, Capitalism, and Social Science* (1973). Students interested in the Counterreformation should begin with E. M. Burns, *The Counter Reformation** (1964), and those interested in the political implications of Calvinism should see R. Kingdon, *Calvin and Calvinism: Sources of Democracy** (1970).

*Available in paperback.

CHAPTER 18

THE AGE OF EUROPEAN EXPANSION
AND RELIGIOUS WARS

CHAPTER OBJECTIVES

After reading and studying this chapter you should be able to answer the following questions:

Q-1.   Why and how did Europeans gain control over distant continents?
Q-2.   How did overseas expansion affect Europe and conquered societies?
Q-3.   What were the causes of religious wars in France, the Netherlands, and Germany, and how did the religious wars affect the status of women?
Q-4.   How and why did African slave labor become the dominant form of labor organization in the New World?
Q-5.   What religious and intellectual developments led to the growth of skepticism?
Q-6.   What literary masterpieces did this period produce?
Q-7.   How did the invading Spaniards overcome the powerful Aztec and Incan Empires in America?

CHAPTER SYNOPSIS

In this chapter we see how the trends in the High Middle Ages in Europe toward centralized nations ruled by powerful kings and toward territorial expansion were revitalized. The growth of royal power and the consolidation of the state in Spain, France, and England accompanied and supported world exploration and a long period of European war.

The Portuguese were the first to push out into the Atlantic, but it was Spain, following close behind, that built a New World empire that provided the economic basis for a period of Spanish supremacy in European affairs. In the short run, Spanish gold and silver from the New World made the Spanish Netherlands the financial and manufacturing center of Europe, and Spain became Europe's greatest military power. In the long run, however, overseas expansion ruined the Spanish economy, created massive European inflation, and brought the end of Spain's empire in Europe.

The fall of the Aztec and Incan nations to the Spanish was due to a variety of reasons — internal struggle, legendary beliefs, and technological and military backwardness are four. The takeover of the Americas led to the first world seaborne empires, first by the Portuguese and the Spanish and then by the Dutch. The Spanish concentrated in the Philippines, the Portuguese in the Indian Ocean, and the Dutch in Indonesia.

The attempts by Catholic monarchs to re-establish European religious unity and by both Catholic and Protestant monarchs to establish strong centralized states led to many wars among the European states. Spain's attempt to keep religious and political unity within her empire led to a long war in the Netherlands — a war that pulled England over to the side of the Protestant Dutch. There was bitter civil war in France, which finally came to an end with the reign of Henry of Navarre and the Edict of Nantes in 1598. The Thirty Years' War in Germany from 1618 to 1648 left that area a political and economic shambles.

The sixteenth century also saw a vast increase in witch-hunting and the emergence of modern racism, sexism, and skepticism. Generally, the power and status of women in this period did not change. Protestantism meant a more positive attitude toward marriage, but the revival of the idea that women were the source of evil and the end of the religious orders for women caused them to become increasingly powerless in society. North American slavery and racism had their origins in the labor problems in America and in Christian and Muslim racial attitudes. Skepticism was an intellectual reaction to the fanaticism of both Protestants and Catholics and a sign of things to come, while the Renaissance tradition was carried on by Shakespeare's work in late sixteenth-century England.

STUDY OUTLINE

I. Discovery, reconnaissance, and expansion (1450–1650)
  A. Overseas exploration and conquest
    1. The spread of the Ottoman Turks frightened the Europeans and overshadowed their international exploits at first
    2. Political centralization in Spain, France, and England prepared the way for expansion
    3. The Portuguese, under the leadership of Prince Henry the Navigator, pushed south from North Africa
      a. Da Gama, Diaz, and Cabral set routes to India
      b. The Portuguese gained control of the Indian trade by overpowering Muslim forts in India

> 4. Spain began to play a leading role in exploration and exploitation
>   a. Columbus sailed under the Spanish flag and discovered the Caribbean
>   b. Spanish exploitation in the Caribbean led to the destruction of the Indian population
>   c. Magellan sailed southwest across the Atlantic for Charles V of Spain, and his expedition circumnavigated the earth
>   d. Pizarro crushed the Inca empire in Peru and opened the Potosi mines to Spanish use
>   e. New Spain brought great wealth to Spain
> 5. The Low Countries, particularly the cities of Antwerp and Amsterdam, became the center of European trade
>   a. The Dutch East India Company became the major organ of Dutch imperialism
>   b. The Dutch West India Company gained control of much of the African and American trade
> 6. France and England made sporadic efforts at exploration and settlement

B. The explorers' motives
   1. The desire to Christianize the Muslims and pagan peoples played a central role in European expansion
   2. Limited economic and political opportunity for upper class men in Spain led to emigration
   3. Government encouragement was also important
   4. Renaissance curiosity caused people to seek out new worlds
   5. The economic motive — the quest for material profit — was the basic reason for European exploration and expansion

C. Technological stimuli to exploration
   1. The development of the cannon aided European expansion
   2. New sailing and navigational developments — such as the caravel ship and the compass — also aided the expansion

D. The conquest of Aztec Mexico and Incan Peru
   1. The strange end of the Aztec nation at the hands of the Spanish is one of history's most fascinating events
      a. Cortes gained control of the capital in less than two years
      b. One reason was that the Aztecs were preoccupied with harvesting their crops at the time of invasion
      c. A comet raised the specter of the return of Quetzalcoatl
      d. Many people under Aztec rule welcomed the Spanish as liberators
      e. The emperor Montezuma's vacillation led to his being taken hostage by Cortes
      f. The major reason for the collapse of the empire lies in the Aztec notion of warfare and its low level of technology
   2. The Incan empire, with the emperor as a benevolent despot, fell easily to the Spanish under Pizarro

      a.   Isolation and legendary beliefs kept the Incas from taking prompt action

      b.   Pizarro came at a time of civil war

      c.   Pizarro wisely captured the emperor, Atahualpa

E. The South American Holocaust

    1.   The Spanish settlers in the New World established the *encomiendas* system

      a.   The Spanish needed laborers to work their mines and agricultural estates

      b.   The *encomiendas* system was a legalized form of slavery

      c.   Millions of Indians died as a result of this system

    2.   Scholars have debated the causes of this devastating slump in population

      a.   The long isolation of the Indians made them susceptible to diseases brought from Europe

      b.   Indians in Mexico and Peru fell victim to smallpox

      c.   The Spanish murdered thousands of others

      d.   Missionaries such as Las Casas fought for Indian rights and the end of *encomiendas* abuse

      e.   Some argue that much death was due to mass suicide and infanticide

F. Colonial administration

    1.   The Spanish monarch divided his new world into four viceroyalties, each with a viceroy and *audiencia*

    2.   Spanish economic policy toward its colonies was that of mercantilism

    3.   Portuguese administration and economic policy was similar

G. The economic effects of Spain's discoveries in the New World

    1.   Enormous amounts of American gold and silver poured into Spain

    2.   It is probable that population growth and not empire building caused inflation in Spain

    3.   Spanish gold caused European inflation, which hurt the poor the most

H. Seaborne trading empires

    1.   The first global seaborne trade was the result of the linking of the newly discovered Americas and the Pacific with the rest of the world

      a.   The sea route to India came under Portuguese control — with their major bases at Goa and Malacca

      b.   The Portuguese traded in a variety of goods, including slaves and sugar

      c.   The Spanish built a seaborne empire that stretched across the Pacific, with Manila its center

      d.   Manila became rich from the Spanish silk trade

    2.   In the later seventeenth century the Dutch overtook Spanish dominance in world trade

      a.   The new Dutch East India Company led the Dutch to Indonesia, where it established a huge trading empire

       b. The Dutch, Portuguese, and Spanish all paved the way for the French and the British

II. Politics, religion, and war

    A. The Spanish-French wars ended in 1559 with a Spanish victory, thus leading to a variety of wars centering on religious and national issues

        1. These wars used bigger armies, with gunpowder, and with a need for better financial administration

        2. Governments had to use various propaganda devices, including the printing press, to arouse public opinion

        3. The Peace of Westphalia (1648) ended religious wars but also ended the idea of a unified Christian society

    B. The origins of difficulties in France (1515-1559)

        1. By 1500, France was recovering from plague and disorder, and the nobility began to lose power

        2. The French kings, such as Francis I and Henry II, continued the policies of centralization but spent more money than they raised

        3. The wars between France and Emperor Charles V — the Habsburg-Valois wars — were costly

        4. To raise money, Francis signed the Concordat of Bologna (1516), in which he recognized the supremacy of the papacy in return for the right to appoint French bishops

           a. This settlement established Catholicism as the national religion

           b. It also perpetuated corruption within the French church

           c. The corruption made Calvinism attractive to Christians eager for reform: some clergy and members of the middle and artisan classes

    C. Religious riots and civil war in France (1559-1589)

        1. The French nobility, many of them Calvinist, attempted to regain power

        2. Frequent religious riots symbolized the struggle for power

        3. The Saint Bartholomew's Day massacre of Calvinists led to the War of the Three Henrys, a conflict for secular power

        4. King Henry IV's Edict of Nantes (1598) saved France from further civil war by allowing Protestants to worship

    D. The Netherlands under Charles V

        1. The Low Countries were part of the Habsburg empire and enjoyed relative autonomy

        2. Charles V divided his empire between his brother Ferdinand and his son, King Philip of Spain

    E. The revolt of the Netherlands (1556-1587)

        1. Regent Margaret attempted to destroy Protestantism by establishing the Inquisition in the Netherlands

        2. Popular support for Protestantism led to the destruction of many Catholic churches

3. The Duke of Alva and his Spanish troops were sent by Philip II to crush the disturbances in the Low Countries
4. Alva's brutal actions only inflamed the religious war, which raged from 1568 to 1578
5. The Low Countries were finally split into the Spanish Netherlands in the south and the independent United Provinces of the Netherlands in the north
    a. The north was Protestant and ruled by the commercial aristocracy
    b. The south was Catholic and ruled by the landed nobility
6. Elizabeth I of England supported the northern, or Protestant, cause as a safeguard against Spain's attacking England
    a. This was for economic reasons
    b. She had her rival, Mary Queen of Scots, beheaded

F. Philip II and the Spanish Armada
1. Philip II planned war on England for several reasons
    a. He wanted to keep England in the Catholic fold
    b. He believed he would never conquer the Dutch unless he defeated England first
2. The failure of the Spanish invasion of England — the armada of 1588 — did not mean the end of the war, but it did prevent Philip from forcibly unifying western Europe
3. In 1609, Philip III agreed to a truce, recognizing the independence of the United Provinces

G. The Thirty Years' War (1618-1648)
1. Protestant Bohemian revolt over religious freedom led to war in Germany
2. The Bohemian phase was characterized by civil war in Bohemia for religious liberty and political independence from the Habsburgs; the Catholics won
3. The Danish phase led to further Catholic victory
4. The Swedish phase ended the Habsburg plan to unite Germany
5. The French phase ended with a destroyed Germany and an independent Netherlands

H. Germany after the Thirty Years' War
1. The war was economically disastrous for Germany
2. The war led to agricultural depression in Germany, which in turn encouraged a return to serfdom for many peasants

III. Changing attitudes
A. The status of women
1. Literature on women and marriage called for a subservient wife with the household as her first priority and a protective, firm-ruling, and loyal husband

      a. Catholic marriages could not be dissolved while Protestants held that divorce and remarriage were possible

      b. Women did not lose their identity or meaningful work, but their subordinate status did not change — although a few women (like Bess of Hardwick) gained wealth and power

  2. Sexual indulgence was popular and widespread; prostitution was common — as brothels were licensed — but Protestant moralists fought it

  3. Protestant reformers believed that convents were antifeminist

      a. They felt that women should be free to marry and enjoy sex

      b. However, it was understood even by Protestants that religious orders for women provided upper class women with an outlet for their talents

B. The great European witch-hunt

  1. Growth in religion and advent of religious struggle led to a rise in the belief in the evil power of witches

  2. The thousands of people executed as witches represent society's drift toward social and intellectual conformity

  3. Reasons varied but all in all witch-hunting reflects widespread misogyny

C. European slavery and the origins of American racism

  1. Black slavery originated with the end of white slavery (1453) and the widespread need for labor, particularly in the new sugar-producing settlements

  2. Africans were brought to America to replace the Indians

  3. A few, like Las Casas, called for the end of slavery

  4. North American racist ideas originated in Christian and Muslim ideas

D. The origins of modern skepticism: Michel de Montaigne

  1. Skeptics doubt whether definitive knowledge is ever attainable

  2. Montaigne is the best representative of early modern skepticism

      a. He was a humanist graced with open-mindedness and tolerance

      b. He believed that the beginning of wisdom lies in the confession of ignorance

  3. Montaigne's skepticism represents a sharp break with the past; it is a forerunner of modern attitudes

IV. Elizabethan and Jacobean literature

A. The golden age of English literature was the late sixteenth and early seventeenth centuries

B. Shakespeare reflects the Renaissance in that his great plays express national consciousness and human problems

C. The Authorized Bible of King James I is a masterpiece of English vernacular writing

REVIEW QUESTIONS

Q-1.   Describe the Portuguese explorations. Who were the participants, and what were their motives?

Q-2.   Describe the American-Spanish-Dutch economic arrangement. How did it work? Who were the winners and who were the losers?

Q-3.   The sixteenth century was a century of money inflation. Why?

Q-4.   What role did technology play in European expansion?

Q-5.   Overall, what do you believe to be the major reasons for European expansion in the fifteenth and sixteenth centuries?

Q-6.   How did Protestantism affect the economic and political development of France? Why is the Edict of Nantes an important event in French history?

Q-7.   What were the causes and consequences of the French civil war of 1559-1589? Was it chiefly a religious or a political event?

Q-8.   Discuss the origins and the outcome of the war between the Netherlands and Spain in the late sixteenth and early seventeenth centuries.

Q-9.   What were the circumstances surrounding Elizabeth's decision to aid the United Netherlands in their war against Spain? What was the Spanish reaction?

Q-10.   Why did Catholic France side with the Protestants in the Thirty Years' War?

Q-11.   What were the political, religious, and economic consequences of the Thirty Years' War in Europe?

Q-12.   Describe the social status of women between 1560 and 1648.

Q-13.   What were the origins of North American racism?

Q-14.   What is skepticism? Why did faith and religious certainty begin to come to an end in the first part of the seventeenth century?

Q-15.   What were the major literary masterpieces of this age? In what ways can the English playwright Shakespeare be regarded as a true Renaissance man?

Q-16.   What do the witch-hunts tell us about social attitudes toward women?

Q-17.   What peoples built the first global seaborne trading empire, and what were the reasons for their success?

Q-18.   What was the function of the Dutch East India Company? How successful were the Dutch in the field of international trade?

Q-19.   Why did the Aztec and Incan empires fall to the Europeans? Which explanation, to you, is the most plausible? Why?

Q-20.   What is meant by the South American holocaust? Discuss it in terms of causes and results.

STUDY-REVIEW EXERCISES

Identify and give the significance of each of the following.

politiques

Elizabeth I of England

Huguenots

Philip II of Spain

Prince Henry the Navigator

Michel de Montaigne

Christopher Columbus

Bartholomew Diaz

Portuguese cities of Goa and Malacca

Dutch East India Company

Hernando Cortez

Elizabeth Hardwick

Council of Blood

Habsburg-Valois wars

quinto

audiencia

corregidores

Thirty Years' War

defeat of the Spanish Armada

Concordat of Bologna

Peace of Westphalia

Saint Bartholomew's Day massacre

War of the Three Henrys

Edict of Nantes

Pizarro

Define the following key concepts and terms.

encomiendas

mercantilism

inflation

sexism

racism

skepticism

misogyny

Spanish American holocaust

Test your understanding of the chapter by answering the following questions.

1. The war that brought destruction and ensured division in Germany was

    _____ .

2. The Spanish explorer _____ conquered the Aztecs.
3. The Spanish priest and defender of the American Indians was

    _____ .

4. The law of 1598 that granted religious freedom to French Protestants was

   _____ .

5. Spain's golden century was _____ .

6. King _____ of Sweden intervened in the Thirty Years'
   War.

7. After 1551, the seven northern provinces of the Netherlands were called

   _____ .

8. The city of _____ became the financial capital of Europe
   by 1600.

9. The monarch of Britain at the time of the Spanish Armada was

   _____ .

10. The idea that nothing is completely knowable is

    _____ .

11. _____ was the emperor who divided the Habsburg empire
    into two parts.

12. The 1516 compromise between church and state in France was

    _____ .

13. _____ was the first European country to establish sea
    routes to the east.

MULTIPLE-CHOICE QUESTIONS

1. Beginning in 1581, the northern Netherlands revolted against their political
   overlord,
   a. France.
   b. Spain.
   c. Elizabeth I of England.
   d. Florence.

2. North American racist attitudes toward African blacks originated in
   a. South America.

    b. Spain.

    c. France.

    d. England.

3. In the Thirty Years' War, France supported
    a. the German Catholics.
    b. the Holy Roman Emperor.
    c. Spain.
    d. the German Protestants.

4. The nation that considered itself the international defender of Catholicism was
    a. France.
    b. Spain.
    c. Italy.
    d. England.

5. Columbus, like many of his fellow explorers, was principally motivated by
    a. a desire to discover India.
    b. a desire to Christianize the Americans.
    c. the desire of Spain to control the New World.
    d. the Spanish need to control the Mediterranean.

6. The earliest known explorers of North America were the
    a. Spanish.
    b. Vikings.
    c. Italians.
    d. English.

7. In order to gain control of the spice trade of the Indian Ocean, the Portuguese were thrown into direct competition with
    a. Spain.
    b. England.
    c. the Muslims.
    d. France.

8. The main contribution of Cortez and Pizarro to Spain was the
    a. tapping of the rich silver resources of Mexico and Peru.
    b. Christianizing of the New World peoples.
    c. further exploration of the Pacific Ocean.
    d. discovery of South Africa.

9. France was saved from religious anarchy when religious principles were set aside for political necessity by the new king,
   a. Henry III.
   b. Francis I.
   c. Henry IV of Navarre.
   d. Charles IX.

10. The vast palace of the Spanish monarchs, built under the direction of Philip II, was called
    a. Versailles.
    b. the Escorial.
    c. Tournai.
    d. Hampton Court.

11. The Treaty of Westphalia, which ended the Thirty Years' War (1618–1648),
    a. further strengthened the Holy Roman Empire.
    b. completely undermined the Holy Roman Empire as a viable state.
    c. maintained that only Catholicism and Lutheranism were legitimate religions.
    d. refused to recognize the independence of the United Provinces of the Netherlands.

12. Of the following, the best representative of early modern skepticism is
    a. Las Casas.
    b. James I.
    c. Calvin.
    d. Montaigne.

13. The Portuguese explorer who first reached India was
    a. Bartholomew Diaz.
    b. Prince Henry the Navigator.
    c. Vasco da Gama.
    d. Hernando Cortez.

14. The origin of racial attitudes found in North America was
    a. England.
    b. Spain.
    c. Catholic teaching.
    d. the Dutch.

15. The fundamental driving force of European expansion and exploration was
    a. religious zeal.
    b. curiosity stirred up by the Renaissance.

c. the desire for wealth and material gain.
d. the need for spices that improved the blandness of food.

16. The Calvinists in the Low Countries initially rebelled against Spanish oppression by
a. guerrilla war tactics.
b. large military confrontations.
c. destroying those images and symbols they considered false.
d. attacking the Spanish verbally through political and religious pamphlets.

17. The defeat of the Spanish Armada in 1588
a. brought Spanish power in Europe to an end.
b. cut off the supply of gold and silver from the New World.
c. kept Philip II from uniting western Europe by force or conquering England.
d. resulted in the invasion of Spain by an English fleet.

18. During the fifteenth century Europe was threatened by the
a. Ottoman Empire.
b. Chinese Empire.
c. Indian Empire.
d. Black Death.

19. Generally, between 1560 and 1648, the status of women
a. improved because of new economic opportunities.
b. improved only for Protestant women.
c. declined because of increased sexism.
d. changed little from previous generations.

20. Although his early life is unknown, Christopher Columbus was originally a
a. Portuguese seaman.
b. Genoan mariner.
c. Florentine banker.
d. Venetian merchant.

21. Columbus always thought that
a. he had discovered islands off the coast of India.
b. he had discovered a vast new continent.
c. he had failed in his quest for a new route to India.
d. none of the above.

22. French Calvinists were called
a. Huguenots.

    b. Conversos.
    c. Gallicans.
    d. Jesuits.

23. The seaborne commercial empires of the Portuguese and the Spanish were succeeded by the
    a. Ottoman Turks.
    b. English.
    c. French.
    d. Dutch.

24. What group of people did Pope Pius IV expel from Rome in 1566, only to rescind his order because of the financial depression it caused in the city?
    a. Prostitutes
    b. Artisans
    c. Calvinists
    d. Jews

25. Calvinism appealed to the middle classes for which of the following reasons?
    a. Its emphasis away from morals
    b. Its stress on leisure and ostentatious living
    c. Its anti-intellectual emphasis
    d. Its approval of any job well done, hard work, and success

26. Which of the following statements is true about the Spanish Armada in 1588?
    a. It was the end of a long war with England.
    b. It achieved its objective.
    c. It prevented Philip II from reimposing unity on Western Europe by force.
    d. It made possible Spanish conquest of the Netherlands.

27. Which of the following statements about Protestantism in France is true?
    a. Its theological source was Luther.
    b. It attracted many people of the middle class.
    c. It was universally rejected by the nobility.
    d. It was particularly appealing to the French peasantry.

28. Which of the following was true concerning the status of women during the Restoration?
    a. Women were thought to be clearly equal to men.
    b. Their primary role was to produce heirs.
    c. Women from all social classes made their mark in the world.
    d. Women could obtain a divorce without much difficulty.

GEOGRAPHY

A. Using Map 18.1 in the text as a guide:
    1. Show on the outline map the exploration routes of da Gama, Columbus, and Magellan.
    2. Mark the location of the Aztec and Inca empires and locate and label the following places.

Ceuta	Cape of Good Hope	Amsterdam	Guinea Coast of Africa
Calicut	Cape Horn	London	Lisbon
Goa	Antwerp	Mexico City	Moluccas

3. Why did the Spanish and Portuguese gain an early lead in European expansion? What were the goals of the early explorers, such as Columbus?

4. Explain, in geographic and economic terms, the reasons for the growth of the Flemish (Netherland) towns such as Antwerp and Amsterdam.

5. Explain the important economic relationship that developed among Spain, the Americas, and the Netherlands.

B. Using Map 18.5 in the text as a reference, list below the areas that were the main sources of African slaves and the main areas of slave importation into the New World. Do the latter areas illustrate the economic origins of the slave trade?

UNDERSTANDING HISTORY THROUGH READING AND THE ARTS

Those interested in skepticism and the life of its finest representative will want to read M. Lowenthal, ed., *Autobiography of Michel de Montaigne* * (1935). There were a number of extremely important and powerful women of the sixteenth century whose biographies make for fascinating reading: R. Roeder, *Catherine de Medici and the Lost Revolution* * (1937); J. E. Neal, *Queen Elizabeth I* * (1934, 1966); and A. Fraser, *Mary Queen of Scots* * (1969). An interesting seventeenth-century woman is Gustavus Adolphus's daughter, whose life is told in G. Masson, *Queen Christina* (1968); N. Harvey, *The Rose and the Thorn* (1977), is an account of the lives and times of Mary and Margaret Tudor.

PROBLEMS FOR FURTHER INVESTIGATION

Those interested in doing work in the area of European expansion should begin with D. L. Jensen, ed., *The Expansion of Europe: Motives, Methods, and Meaning* (1967). A discussion of some of the problems faced in studying the religious conflict in France is found in J. H. M. Salmon, *The French Wars of Religion* * (1967), and anyone interested in research on the Thirty Years' War should begin with S. H. Steinberg, *The Thirty Years' War and the Conflict for European Hegemony, 1600–1660* * (1966) and T. K. Rabb, *The Thirty Years' War* * (1964). Those interested in understanding how the vast Spanish Empire worked will want to see C. H. Haring, *The Spanish Empire in America* * (1947, 1963). This book includes an excellent bibliography on the subject.

*Available in paperback.

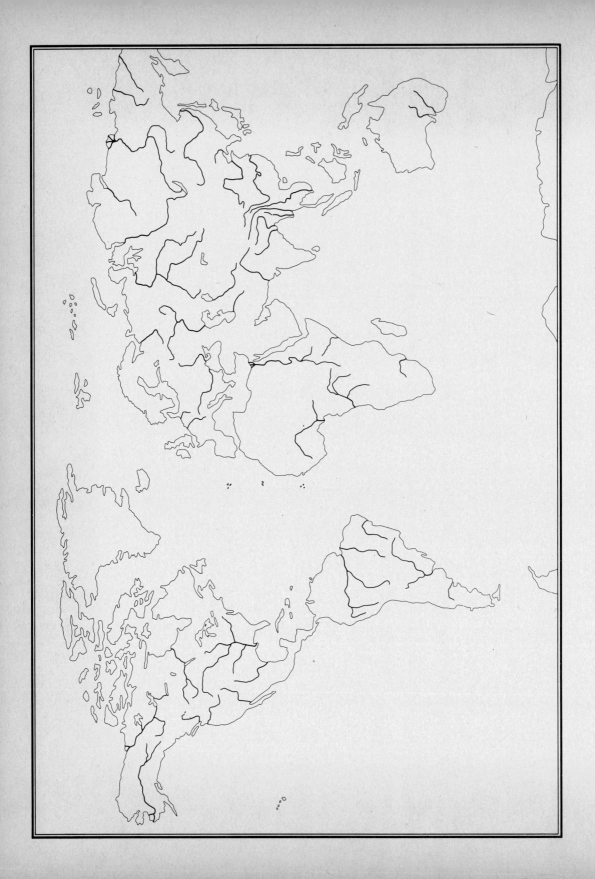

CHAPTER 19

ABSOLUTISM AND CONSTITUTIONALISM
IN WESTERN EUROPE (CA 1589–1715)

CHAPTER OBJECTIVES

After reading and studying this chapter you should be able to answer the following questions:

Q-1. In what ways are absolutism and constitutionalism "modern" political systems?

Q-2. How did absolute monarchy and constitutionalism differ from the feudal and dynastic monarchies of earlier centuries?

Q-3. Which countries best represent absolutism and constitutionalism?

CHAPTER SYNOPSIS

This chapter examines how the political system of absolutism succeeded gloriously in France and failed dismally in England in the seventeenth century. Few kings have been as successful in establishing complete monarchial sovereignty as the great Sun King of France, Louis XIV. Louis gave Europe a masterful lesson on how to reduce the power of the class that historically had been a constant competitor of the monarchy, the nobility. He was a superb actor and propagandist, who built on the earlier achievements of Henry IV and Richelieu and used his magnificent palace of Versailles to imprison the French nobility in a beautiful golden cage. He succeeded in expanding France at the expense of the Habsburgs, and his patronage of the arts helped form the great age of French classicism. However, the economic progress he first made was later checked by his policy of revoking religious toleration.

While the France of Louis was the classic model of modern absolutism, Spain was the classic case of imperial decline. By 1600 Spain was in trouble, and by 1700 it was no longer a major European power. Not only did the silver and labor of

America run out, but this great American wealth ruined the Spanish economic and social structure. War with the Dutch, the English, and the French also helped turn Spain into a backwater of Europe.

England and the United Provinces of the Netherlands provide a picture of constitutionalism triumphing over absolutism. For England, the seventeenth century was a long period of political conflict, complete with a bitter civil war and a radical experiment with republicanism. The causes of this era of conflict were varied, but it is clear that by 1689 the English army and Parliament had destroyed the Stuart quest for divine-right absolutism. The period that followed witnessed some important changes in the way the state is managed.

The Netherlands was important not only because it became the financial and commercial center of Europe, but also because it provided the period's third model of political development — a loosely federated, middle-class constitutional state.

STUDY OUTLINE

I. Absolutism
  A. Absolutism defined
    1. Under absolutism, sovereignty resided in kings — not the nobility or the parliament — who considered themselves responsible to God alone
    2. Absolute kings created new state bureaucracies and armies, and they regulated all the institutions
    3. However, the ambitions of absolute monarchs were limited and not the same as those of leaders of modern totalitarian states
  B. The cornerstone of French absolutism: Louis XIII and Richelieu
    1. Cardinal Richelieu, the ruler of France under King Louis XIII, broke the power of the French nobility
    2. He also brought about administrative reform that helped centralize the state's power
    3. However, his financial actions were unsound and created problems for the future
    4. Richelieu regarded the Protestant Huguenots as a source of aristocratic power
    5. Under Richelieu, France sought to break the Habsburg power
    6. Mazarin's policies gave rise to the *Fronde*, which was a noble movement in opposition to the crown
  C. The absolutism of Louis XIV
    1. Louis the "Sun King" was selfish, an insatiable eater, a great actor, and fearful of the nobility
    2. He made the court at Versailles a fixed institution and used it as a means of preserving royal power and as the center of French absolutism

     a. Showmanship and the court ceremonials at Versailles were devices to ruin the power of the aristocracy

     b. The architecture and art of Versailles were means of carrying out state policy

     c. The French language and culture became the international style

D. Economic management under Louis XIV: Colbert

  1. The tax burden fell most heavily on the poor peasants

  2. Mercantilism is a collection of governmental policies for the regulation of the economy by the state

  3. Louis XIV's finance minister, Colbert, tried to achieve a favorable balance of trade and make France self-sufficient so the flow of gold to other countries would be halted

     a. Colbert encouraged French industry, enacted high tariffs, and created a strong merchant marine

     b. He hoped to make Canada part of a French empire

     c. Though France's industries grew, its agricultural economy declined

E. The revocation of the Edict of Nantes

  1. In 1685, Louis revoked the Edict of Nantes, which had given religious freedom to French Protestants

  2. This revocation caused many Protestants to flee the country; but it had little effect on the economy and it caused fear and hatred abroad

F. Louis XIV's wars

  1. The French army under Louis XIV was modern because it employed mercenaries rather than nobles

  2. Louis XIV's foreign policy was expansionist

  3. The height of French expansion was reached in 1678 with victory over Spain and the Holy Roman Empire

  4. Louis then fought the new Dutch king of England, William III, and the League of Augsburg

  5. The War of the Spanish Succession (1701–1713) involved the issue of the succession to the Spanish throne: Louis claimed Spain but was opposed by the Dutch, English, Austrians, and Prussians

     a. The war was also an attempt to check French economic growth in the world

     b. The war was concluded by the Peace of Utrecht in 1713, which forbade the union of France and Spain

     c. The war left France on the brink of bankruptcy with widespread misery

G. The decline of absolutist Spain in the seventeenth century

  1. Several factors contributed to Spain's decline

     a. Fiscal disorder, political incompetence, population decline, intellectual isolation, and psychological malaise contributed to the decline

      b. The defeat of the "Invincible Armada" in 1588 was a crushing blow to Spain's morale

      c. Spain's economy began to decline by 1600

        (1) Royal expenditure increased, but income from the Americas decreased

        (2) Business and agriculture suffered

      d. Spanish kings lacked force of character and could not deal with all these problems

      e. Spain could not escape from her past: military glory, Roman Catholicism, and easy money from America

II. Constitutionalism in England and the Netherlands

  A. Constitutionalism defined

    1. Under constitutionalism, the state must be governed according to law, not royal decree

      a. It implies a balance between the power of the government and the rights of the subjects

      b. A nation's constitution may be written or unwritten, but the government must respect it

    2. Constitutional government is not the same as full democracy because not all of the people have the right to participate

  B. The decline of royal absolutism in England (1603–1649)

    1. The Stuart kings of England lacked the political wisdom of Elizabeth I

    2. James I was devoted to the theory of rule by divine right

    3. His absolutism ran counter to English belief

    4. James I faced a new, educated merchant-gentry class that opposed absolutism

    5. This new class controlled the House of Commons, which the Stuarts attempted to control

    6. The Protestant or "capitalist ethic" and the problem of religion in England

      a. Many English people were attracted by the values of hard work, thrift, and self-denial implied by Calvinism; these people were called Puritans

      b. The Puritans, who were dissatisfied with the Church of England, saw James I as an enemy

      c. Charles I and his archbishop, Laud, appeared to be pro-Catholic

    7. The English Civil War (1642–1649)

      a. Charles I had ruled without Parliament for eleven years

      b. A revolt in Scotland over the religious issue forced him to call a new Parliament into session to finance an army

        (1) The Commons passed an act compelling the king to summon Parliament every three years

(2) It also impeached Archbishop Laud

(3) Religious differences in Ireland led to a revolt there, but Parliament would not trust Charles with an army

c. Charles initiated military action against Parliament

(1) The Civil War revolved around the issue of whether sovereignty should reside in the king or in Parliament

(2) The problem was not resolved, but Charles was beheaded in 1649

8. Puritanical absolutism in England: Cromwell and the Protectorate

a. Kingship was abolished in 1649 and a commonwealth proclaimed

b. In actuality, the army — led by Cromwell — controlled the government

c. Cromwell's Protectorate became a military dictatorship, but it ended when Cromwell died in 1658

C. The restoration of the English monarchy (1660–1688)

1. The restoration of the Stuart kings failed to solve the problems of religion and authority in society

2. Charles II's Cabal was the forerunner of the cabinet system, and it helped create good relations with the Parliament

3. Charles's pro-French policies led to a Catholic scare

4. James II violated the Test Act, which prevented Catholics from holding government posts

5. Fear of Catholicism led to the expulsion of James II and the *Glorious Revolution*

D. The Triumph of England's Parliament: Constitutional Monarchy and Cabinet Government

1. The Bill of Rights of 1689 stated that sovereignty henceforth resided with Parliament

a. Locke argued that all people have natural rights — including that of rebellion

b. Locke's ideas served as the foundation of English and American liberalism

2. The cabinet system, which developed in the eighteenth century, reflects the victory of aristocratic government over absolutism

E. The Dutch republic in the seventeenth century

1. The Dutch republic emerged from the sixteenth-century struggle against Spain

2. Power in the republic resided in the local Estates

a. The republic was a confederation: a weak union of strong provinces

b. The republic was based on middle-class ideas and values

3. Religious toleration fostered economic growth

4. The province of Holland became the commercial and financial center of Europe

REVIEW QUESTIONS

Q-1.   In what way does the French minister Richelieu symbolize absolutism? What were his achievements?

Q-2.   It has been said that the palace of Versailles was a device to ruin the nobility of France. Explain. Was Versailles a palace or a prison?

Q-3.   Define *mercantilism*. What were the mercantilist policies of the French minister Colbert?

Q-4.   The revocation of the Edict of Nantes has been considered a great error on the part of Louis XIV. Why?

Q-5.   What were the reasons for the fall of the Spanish Empire?

Q-6.   Discuss the foreign policy goals of Louis XIV. Was he successful?

Q-7.   Define *absolutism*. How does it differ from totalitarianism?

Q-8.   How did Louis XIV's wars affect the French economy and French society?

Q-9.   What were the causes of the War of the Spanish Succession? How did William III of England affect European events after about 1689?

Q-10.   What was constitutionalism? How does it differ from democratic form of government?

Q-11.   Discuss John Locke's political theory. Why is it said that Locke was the spokesman for the liberal English Revolution of 1689 and for representative government?

Q-12.   What were the attitudes and policies of James I that made him so unpopular with his subjects?

Q-13.   Who were the Puritans? Why did they come into conflict with James I?

Q-14.   What were the immediate and the long-range causes of the English Civil War of 1642–1649? What were the results?

Q-15.   Why did James II flee from England in 1688? What happened to the kingship at this point?

Q-16.   Were the events of 1688–1689 a victory for English democracy? Explain.

Q-17.   Compare and contrast constitutionalism and absolutism. Where does sovereign power reside in each system?

Q-18.   What accounts for the phenomenal economic success and political stability of the Dutch republic?

STUDY-REVIEW EXERCISES

Define the following key concepts and terms.

mercantilism

absolutism

totalitarianism

republicanism

constitutionalism

cabinet government

sovereign power

commonwealth

Identify each of the following and give its significance.

Versailles

Dutch Estates General

intendants

Count Olivares of Spain

Spanish Armada of 1588

Peace of Utrecht

Cabal of Charles II

Instrument of Government

Puritans

Long Parliament

Oliver Cromwell

Cardinal Richelieu

Louis XIV of France

James II of England

Glorious Revolution in England

English Bill of Rights

John Churchill

Philip II of Spain

Thomas Hobbes

Richelieu's *Dictionary*

William Laud

<u>Explain</u> *what each of these men believed about the placement of authority within society.*

James I of England

Thomas Hobbes

Louis XIV of France

John Locke

<u>Explain</u> *what the following events were and why they were important.*

revocation of the Edict of Nantes

Scottish revolt of 1640

War of the Spanish Succession

Glorious Revolution

English Civil War of 1642–1649

Treaty of the Pyrenees

<u>*Test*</u> *your understanding of the chapter by answering the following questions.*

1. The highest executive office of the Dutch republic was _____ .

2. Louis XIV's able minister of finance was _____ .
3. During the age of economic growth in Spain, a vast number of Spaniards *entered/ left* religious orders.
4. For Louis XIV of France the War of the Spanish Succession was a *success/disaster.*
5. The Englishman who inflicted defeat on Louis XIV at Blenheim was

    _____ .

6. The archbishop whose goal was to enforce Anglican unity in England and Scot-

    land was _____ .

MULTIPLE-CHOICE QUESTIONS

1. French Protestants tended to be
    a. poor peasants.
    b. the power behind the throne of Louis XIV.
    c. a financial burden for France.
    d. clever business people.

2. The War of the Spanish Succession began when Charles II of Spain left his territories to
    a. the French heir.
    b. the Spanish heir.
    c. Eugene of Savoy.
    d. the archduke of Austria.

3. This city was the commercial and financial capital of Europe in the seventeenth century.
    a. London
    b. Hamburg
    c. Paris
    d. Amsterdam

4. Of the following, the country most centered on middle-class interests was
    a. England.
    b. Spain.
    c. France.
    d. the Netherlands.

5. Which of the following Englishmen was a Catholic?
   a. James II
   b. Oliver Cromwell
   c. Archbishop Laud
   d. William III

6. Cardinal Richelieu's most notable accomplishment was
   a. the creation of a strong financial system for France.
   b. the creation of a highly effective administrative system.
   c. winning the total support of the Huguenots.
   d. allying the Catholic church with the government.

7. The statement "There are no privileges and immunities which can stand against a divinely appointed king" forms the basis of the
   a. Stuart notion of absolutism.
   b. Stuart notion of constitutionalism.
   c. English Parliament's notion of democracy.
   d. English Parliament's notion of constitutionalism.

8. The English Long Parliament
   a. enacted legislation supporting absolutism.
   b. supported the Catholic tendencies of Charles I.
   c. supported Charles I as a military leader.
   d. enacted legislation against absolutism.

9. Cromwell's government is best described as a
   a. constitutional state.
   b. democratic state.
   c. military dictatorship.
   d. monarchy.

10. One way in which Louis XIV controlled the French nobility was by
    a. maintaining standing armies in the countryside to crush noble uprisings.
    b. requiring the presence of the major noble families at Versailles for at least part of the year.
    c. periodically visiting the nobility in order to check on their activities.
    d. none of the above.

11. When Archbishop Laud directed the Presbyterian Scots to accept the Anglican Book of Common Prayer, the Scots
    a. revolted.
    b. reluctantly accepted the directive.

    c. ignored the directive.
    d. willingly agreed to the directive.

12. Acting as spokesman for the landowning class and proponent of the idea that the purpose of government is to protect life, liberty, and property was
    a. Thomas Hobbes.
    b. William of Orange.
    c. John Locke.
    d. Edmund Burke.

13. After the United Provinces of the Netherlands won independence from Spain, their structure of government was a
    a. strong monarchy.
    b. centralized parliamentary system.
    c. weak union of strong provinces.
    d. democracy.

14. The Dutch economy was based on
    a. fishing and the merchant marine.
    b. silver mining in Peru.
    c. export of textiles.
    d. copper mining in central America.

15. The decline of Spain in the seventeenth century was caused primarily by
    a. a strong monarchy that drove Spain to disaster.
    b. a program of modernization that was too costly.
    c. economic depression caused by a decrease of bullion coming from the colonies.
    d. revolts by the aristocracy.

16. Louis XIV's modern standing army consisted largely of
    a. the bourgeoisie.
    b. the French peasants.
    c. foreign mercenaries, many of whom were from Protestant countries.
    d. the nobility.

17. James I of England believed that royal power
    a. should be shared with Parliament.
    b. should be shared with the people.
    c. was absolute and God-given.
    d. was given to the monarch by the people.

18. After the long and difficult struggle for independence, the Dutch
    a. were intolerant of religions except for Calvinism.
    b. persecuted all Catholics.
    c. permitted religious freedom.
    d. were wary of all religions.

19. As an economic system, mercantilism
    a. was indistinguishable from militarism.
    b. advocated a favorable balance of trade.
    c. was adopted in France but not elsewhere.
    d. claimed that state power was based on land armies.

20. The Peace of Utrecht in 1713
    a. decreased the size of the British Empire significantly.
    b. reflected the balance of power principle.
    c. began Spain's role as a major power in Europe.
    d. marked the beginning of French expansionist policy.

21. Cardinal Richelieu consolidated the power of the French monarchy by which
    of the following?
    a. Erecting castles for the nobility
    b. Ruthlessly treating conspirators who threatened the monarchy
    c. Placing nobles in high government offices
    d. Eliminating the "intendant" system of local government

22. By revoking the Edict of Nantes, Louis XIV
    a. granted liberty of conscience to French Huguenots.
    b. provided political rights to French Calvinists.
    c. attempted to achieve religious unity in France.
    d. encouraged religious dissidents to come to France.

23. Which of the following was part of Colbert's mercantile scheme?
    a. A self-sufficient France
    b. Low tariffs
    c. The decolonization of Canada
    d. A large export trade

24. Which of the following is a characteristic of the English House of Commons in
    the seventeenth century?
    a. The Commons guarded the pocketbook of the nation.
    b. The members were not well educated.
    c. The Commons supported the Stuart monarchy.
    d. The Commons wanted no voice in the expenditure of taxes.

25. Which of the following statements about the Glorious Revolution is true?
    a. It was quite bloody.
    b. It was democratic.
    c. It was initiated by the fear of having a Catholic monarch.
    d. It restored the Stuart monarchy.

26. Who became known as England's first "prime" minister?
    a. Sir Robert Walpole
    b. Oliver Cromwell
    c. William Laud
    d. The duke of Marlborough

27. The independence of the Dutch republic was confirmed in 1648 by the
    a. Glorious Revolution.
    b. Peace of Utrecht.
    c. Edict of Nantes.
    d. Peace of Westphalia.

GEOGRAPHY

1. Using Map 19.1 in the text as a guide, on the outline map shade in the territory added to France as a result of the wars and foreign policy of King Louis XIV.
2. Explain how each of the territories was acquired and from whom.

3. Louis XIV declared in 1700 that "the Pyrenees no longer exist." What did he mean?

4. What changes in the balance of power came about as a result of the Treaty of
    Utrecht in 1713?

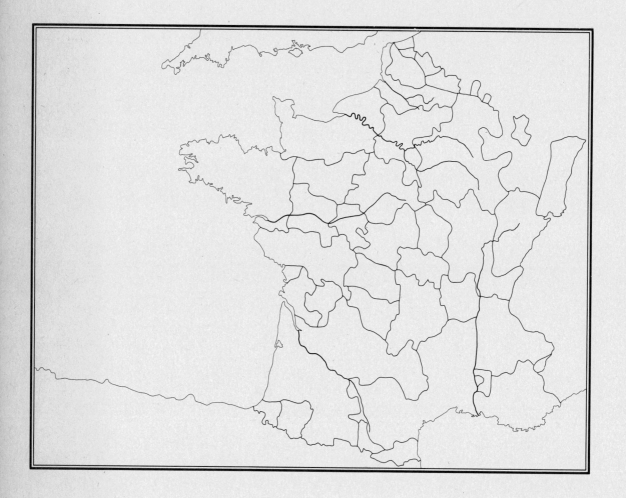

UNDERSTANDING HISTORY THROUGH READING AND THE ARTS

Louis XIV and the magnificence of his court at Versailles are re-created with color and spirit in W. H. Lewis, *The Splendid Century** (1953), and a vivid picture of life of the English upper classes — how they ran their estates, entertained, and when possible ran the country — is found in Mark Girouard, *Life in the English Country House: A Social and Architectural History* (1979).

The seventeenth century was a period of architectural splendor in France and in England. Some of the great achievements of this period are discussed in Chapter 7 of N. Pevsner, *An Outline of European Architecture* (7th ed., 1963). The splendor of Versailles and French and British baroque painting and architecture are the subjects of Chapter 7, "The Baroque in France and England," in H. W. Janson, *History of Art* (1962).

Much good reading is found in the literature of the seventeenth century. The great comic writer of the age was Molière, whose *Tartuffe* is still a source of entertainment. LaFontaine's *Fables* are a lively reworking of tales from antiquity and Cervantes's *Don Quixote* continues to inspire its readers. The greatest writer to emerge from the Puritan age in England was John Milton, whose *Paradise Lost* is a classic.

PROBLEMS FOR FURTHER INVESTIGATION

James Stuart was a successful king in Scotland but a failure in England. Why? See D. Willson, *King James VI and I** (1956). Was the Glorious Revolution of 1688–1689 in England a victory for modern political democracy or a palace revolution by a group of aristocrats? This and other problems surrounding this political event are discussed in G. M. Straka, ed., *The Revolution of 1688 and the Birth of the English Political Nation** (rev. ed., 1973). Some of the problems in interpretation of the crucial period 1642 to 1649 in Britain are considered in P. A. M. Taylor, ed., *The Origins of the English Civil War** (1960), L. Stone, ed., *Social Change and Revolution in England, 1540-1640** (1965) — and B. Manning deals with popular participation in the wars and revolution in *The English People and the English Revolution* (1976).

Students interested in research on absolutism and Louis XIV in France will want to consider H. G. Judge, ed., *Louis XIV* (1965); William F. Church, ed., *The Greatness of Louis XIV: Myth or Reality?** (rev. ed., 1972); and R. F. Kierstead, ed., *State and Society in Seventeenth-Century France** (1975). The best biography of Louis XIV is *Louis XIV* (1968) by J. Wolf.

*Available in paperback.

READING WITH UNDERSTANDING
EXERCISE 5

LEARNING HOW TO IDENTIFY MAIN POINTS THAT ARE CAUSES OR REASONS

In Exercise 3 we considered cause and effect and underlined a passage dealing with effects or results. This exercise continues in this direction by focusing on causes or reasons.

Exercise

Read the following passage as a whole. Reread it and underline or highlight each cause (or factor) contributing to the Industrial Revolution in England.

Note that there are several causes and that they are rather compressed. (This is because the author is summarizing material presented in previous chapters before going on to discuss other causes or factors—notably technology and the energy problem—in greater detail.) Since several causal points are presented in a short space, this is a very good place to number the points (and key subpoints) in the margin. After you have finished, compare your underlining or highlighting with that in the suggested model on pages E-4 to E-5.

Eighteenth-Century Origins

The Industrial Revolution grew out of the expanding Atlantic economy of the eighteenth century, which served mercantilist England remarkably well. England's colonial empire, augmented by a strong position in Latin America and in the African slave trade, provided a growing market for English manufactured goods. So did England itself. In an age when it was much cheaper to ship goods by water than by land, no part of England was more than twenty miles from navigable water. Beginning in the 1770s, a canal building boom greatly enhanced this natural advantage (see Map 22.1). Nor were there any tariffs within the country to hinder trade, as there were in France before 1789 and in politically fragmented Germany.

Agriculture played a central role in bringing about the Industrial Revolution in England. English farmers were second only to the Dutch in productivity in 1700, and they were continuously adopting new methods of farming as the century went on. The result, especially before 1760, was a period of bountiful crops and low food prices. The ordinary English family did not have to spend almost everything it earned just to buy bread. It could spend more on other items, on manufactured goods—leather shoes or a razor for the man, a bonnet or a shawl for the woman, toy soldiers for the son, and a doll for the daughter. Thus, demand for goods within the country complemented the demand from the colonies.

England had other assets that helped give rise to the Industrial Revolution. Unlike eighteenth-century France, England had an effective central bank and well-developed credit markets. The monarchy and the aristocratic oligarchy, which had jointly ruled the country since 1688, provided stable and predictable government. At the same time the government let the domestic economy operate fairly freely and with few controls, encouraging personal initiative, technical change, and a free market. Finally, England had long had a large class of hired agricultural laborers, whose numbers were further increased by the enclosure movement of the late eighteenth century. These rural wage earners were relatively mobile—compared to village-bound peasants in France and western Germany, for example—and along with cottage workers they formed a potential industrial labor force for capitalist entrepreneurs.

All these factors combined to initiate the Industrial Revolution, which began in the 1780s—after the American war for independence and just before the French Revolution. Thus the great economic and political revolutions that have shaped the modern world occurred almost simultaneously, though they began in different countries. The Industrial Revolution was, however, a longer process. It was not complete in England until 1830 at the earliest, and it had no real impact on continental countries until after the Congress of Vienna ended the era of revolutionary wars in 1815.

Eighteenth-Century Origins

causes

1

a

b

c

2

a

b

c

3

4

5

6

The Industrial Revolution grew out of the expanding Atlantic economy of the eighteenth century, which served mercantilist England remarkably well. England's colonial empire, augmented by a strong position in Latin America and in the African slave trade, provided a growing market for English manufactured goods. So did England itself. In an age when it was much cheaper to ship goods by water than by land, no part of England was more than twenty miles from navigable water. Beginning in the 1770s, a canal building boom greatly enhanced this natural advantage (see Map 22.1). Nor were there any tariffs within the country to hinder trade, as there were in France before 1789 and in politically fragmented Germany.

Agriculture played a central role in bringing about the Industrial Revolution in England. English farmers were second only to the Dutch in productivity in 1700, and they were continuously adopting new methods of farming as the century went on. The result, especially before 1760, was a period of bountiful crops and low food prices. The ordinary English family did not have to spend almost everything it earned just to buy bread. It could spend more on other items, on manufactured goods—leather shoes or a razor for the man, a bonnet or a shawl for the woman, toy soldiers for the son, and a doll for the daughter. Thus, demand for goods within the country complemented the demand from the colonies.

England had other assets that helped give rise to the Industrial Revolution. Unlike eighteenth-century France, England had an effective central bank and well-developed credit markets. The monarchy and the aristocratic oligarchy, which had jointly ruled the country since 1688, provided stable and predictable government. At the same time the government let the domestic economy operate fairly freely and with few controls, encouraging personal initiative, technical change, and a free market. Finally, England had long had a large class of hired agricultural laborers, whose numbers were further increased by the enclosure movement of the late eighteenth century. These rural wage earners were relatively mobile—compared to village-bound peasants in France and western Germany, for example—and a along with cottage workers they formed a potential industrial labor force for capitalist entrepreneurs.

All these factors combined to initiate the Industrial Revolution, which began in the 1780s—after the American war for independence and just before the French Revolution. Thus the great economic and political revolutions that have shaped the modern world occurred almost simultaneously, though they began in different countries. The Industrial Revolution was, however, a longer process. It was not complete in England until 1830 at the earliest, and it had no real impact on continental countries until after the Congress of Vienna ended the era of revolutionary wars in 1815.

CHAPTER 20

ABSOLUTISM IN EASTERN EUROPE
TO 1740

CHAPTER OBJECTIVES

After reading and studying this chapter you should be able to answer the following questions:

Q-1. Why did the basic structure of society in eastern Europe move away from that in western Europe?

Q-2. How and why did the rulers of Austria, Prussia, and Russia manage to build more durable absolute monarchies than that of Louis XIV of France?

Q-3. How did the absolute monarchs' interactions with artists and architects contribute to the achievements of baroque culture?

CHAPTER SYNOPSIS

This chapter discusses why monarchial absolutism developed with greater lasting strength in eastern Europe than in western Europe. In Russia, Prussia, and Austria monarchs became more powerful as the peasants were pushed back into serfdom. That is, peasants gradually lost the personal and economic freedoms they had built up over several hundred years during the Middle Ages. At the same time that eastern nobles gained greater social and economic control over the enserfed peasants, they lost political power to the rising absolute monarchs. The author concludes that while there were some economic reasons for the re-emergence of serfdom in the east, it was essentially for political reasons that this strong authoritarian tradition emerged. As opposed to western Europe, it was the common people — the peasants — who were the great losers in the power struggle between nobility and monarchy.

Absolutism in Russia, Austria, and Prussia emerged because of war, foreign invasion, and internal struggle. For example, the Austrian monarchs solved the problems

317

arising from external conflicts and a multicultural state by building a strong, centralized military state. Prussian absolutism — intended to check the power of the nobility
— was achieved by the Hohenzollern monarchs, while Russian absolutism was largely
the outgrowth of the Mongol conquest and internal power struggles.

Some of the absolute monarchs were enlightened reformers, but their good
intentions were often thwarted by internal problems. But if reform from above was
not overly effective, the absolute monarchs' use of architecture and urban planning
— much of which was in the so-called baroque form — to enhance their images was a
noteworthy success. They created buildings and cities that reflected their growing
power, and they hired baroque painters and musicians such as Rubens and Bach to
glorify them and to fill their palaces with paintings and music.

STUDY OUTLINE

I. Lords and peasants in eastern Europe
   A. The medieval background (1400-1650)
      1. Personal and economic freedom for peasants increased between 1050
         and 1300
      2. Thus, living conditions improved and serfdom was reduced
      3. After 1300, powerful lords in eastern Europe reinstituted serfdom to
         combat their economic problems
      4. Laws restricted freedom, and labor obligations were increased in eastern
         Europe
   B. The consolidation of serfdom
      1. The re-establishment of hereditary serfdom took place in Poland,
         Prussia, and Russia between 1500 and 1650
      2. This was a result of the growth of estate agriculture
         a. Lords seized peasant land for their own estates
         b. They then demanded unpaid serf labor on those estates
   C. Political reasons for changes in serfdom in eastern Europe
      1. Serfdom increased because of political, not economic, reasons
      2. Weak monarchs could not resist the demands of the powerful noble
         landlords
      3. The absence of the Western concept of sovereignty meant that the king
         did not think in terms of protecting the people of the nation
      4. Overall, the peasants of the East were weaker than those of the West,
         and the urban middle class was undermined by the landlords
II. The rise of Austria and Prussia (1650-1750)
   A. Austria and the Ottoman Turks
      1. After the end of the Thirty Years' War in 1648, the Austrian Habsburgs,
         having failed to destroy Protestantism, turned inward and eastward to
         unify their holdings

    2. Austria became absorbed in a war against the Turks for the conquest of Hungary and Transylvania

    3. Under Suleiman the Magnificent the Ottoman Turks built the most powerful empire in the world, which included part of central Europe

    4. The Turkish attack on Austria in 1683 was turned back, and the Habsburgs conquered all of Hungary and Transylvania

    5. The Habsburg possessions consisted of Austria, Bohemia, and Hungary, which were joined in a fragile union

       a. The Pragmatic Sanction (1713) stated that the possessions should never be divided

       b. The Hungarian nobility resisted accepting Habsburg rule

  B. Prussia in the seventeenth century

    1. The Hohenzollern family ruled the electorate of Brandenburg but had little real power

    2. The Thirty Years' War weakened the representative assemblies of the realm and allowed the Hohenzollerns to consolidate their absolutist rule

    3. Frederick William (the Great Elector) used military force and taxation to unify his holdings into a strong state

  C. The consolidation of Prussian absolutism

    1. Frederick William I encouraged Prussian militarism and created the best army in Europe plus an efficient bureaucracy

    2. The nobility — the Junker class — became the military elite

III. The development of Russia

  A. The Vikings and the Kievan principality

    1. Eastern Slavs moved into Russia between the fifth and ninth centuries

    2. Slavic-Viking settlements grew up in the ninth century

    3. The Vikings unified the eastern Slavs politically and religiously, creating a ruling dynasty and accepting Eastern Orthodox Christianity for themselves and the Slavs

    4. A strong aristocracy (the boyars) and a free peasantry made it difficult to strengthen the state

  B. The Mongol yoke and the rise of Moscow

    1. The Mongols conquered the Kievan state in the thirteenth century and unified it under their rule

    2. The Mongols used Russian aristocrats as their servants

       a. The princes of Moscow served the Mongols well and became the hereditary great princes

       b. Ivan I served the Mongols while using his wealth and power to strengthen the principality of Moscow

       c. Ivan III stopped acknowledging the Mongol Khan and assumed the headship of Orthodox Christianity

    C. Tsar and people to 1689
        1. By 1505, the prince of Moscow — the tsar — had emerged as the divine-right ruler of all the lands of the eastern Slavs
        2. The tsars and the boyars struggled over who would rule the state, and the tsars won
        3. Ivan the Terrible was an autocratic tsar who expanded Muscovy and further reduced the power of the boyars
            a. He murdered leading boyars and confiscated their estates
            b. Many peasants fled his rule to the newly conquered territories, forming groups called Cossacks
            c. Businessmen and artisans were bound to their towns and jobs
        4. The Time of Troubles (1598–1613) was a period characterized by internal struggles and invasions
            a. There was no heir
            b. Cossack bands slaughtered many nobles and officials
            c. Swedish and Polish armies invaded
        5. Michael Romanov was elected tsar by the nobles (1613), and he re-established tsarist autocracy
        6. The Romanovs brought about the total enserfment of the people
        7. A split in the church over religious reforms led to mass protests by the peasants, and the church became dependent on the state for its authority
    D. The reforms of Peter the Great
        1. Peter wished to create a strong army for protection and expansion
            a. He forced the nobility to serve in the army or in the civil service
            b. He created schools to train technicians for his army
        2. Army and government became more efficient and powerful as an interlocking military-civilian bureaucracy was created and staffed by talented people
        3. Russian peasant life under Peter became more harsh
        4. Modest territorial expansion took place under Peter, and Russia became a European Great Power
        5. Peter borrowed many western ideas
IV. Absolutism and the Baroque
    A. Baroque art and music
        1. Baroque art fulfilled the needs of the Catholic Church and the absolute rulers
        2. In painting, the baroque is best seen in the work of Rubens; in music it reached its height with Bach
    B. Palaces and power
        1. Architecture played an important role in politics because it was used by kings to enhance their image and awe their subjects
        2. The royal palace was the favorite architectural expression of absolutist power

   3. The dominant artistic style of the age of absolutism was baroque — a dramatic and emotional style
C. Royal cities
   1. The new St. Petersburg is an excellent example of the tie among architecture, politics, and urban development
   2. Peter the Great wanted to create a modern, baroque city from which to rule Russia; the city became a showplace for the tsar, paid for by the Russian nobility and built by the peasants
D. The growth of St. Petersburg
   1. During the eighteenth century, St. Petersburg became one of the world's largest and most influential cities
   2. The new city was modern or "baroque" in its layout and design
   3. All social groups, including the peasants, paid heavily in the construction of the city
   4. Tsarina Elizabeth and architect Rastrelli crowned the city with great palaces

REVIEW QUESTIONS

Q-1. What were the reasons for the re-emergence of serfdom in eastern Europe in the early modern period (1400–1650)? Build a case for either an economic or political explanation.

Q-2. In western Europe the conflict between the king and his vassals resulted in gains for the common man. Why did this not happen in eastern Europe?

Q-3. Why would the reign of the Great Elector be regarded as "the most crucial constitutional struggle in Prussian history for hundreds of years"? What did he do to increase royal authority? Who were the losers?

Q-4. Prussia has traditionally been considered one of the most militaristic states in Europe. How do you explain this development? Who or what was responsible?

Q-5. How did war (the Thirty Years' War) and invasion (by the Ottoman Turks) help the Habsburgs consolidate power?

Q-6. What was the Pragmatic Sanction and why were the Hungarian and Bohemian princes opposed to it?

Q-7. What role, if any, did war play in the evolution of absolutism in eastern Europe?

Q-8. Use the following to illustrate the relationship between baroque architecture and European absolutism: St. Petersburg, Karlsruhe, Upper and Lower Belvedere, Schönbrunn. Was it simply that "every fool likes his own hat"? Explain.

Q-9. It has been said that the common man benefited from the magnificent medieval cathedrals as much as the princes. Can the same be said about the common man and the building projects of the absolute kings and princes? Explain.

Q-10.   Discuss the influence of the Vikings and the Mongols on Russian history.

Q-11.   Why do you think the history of Russia is more a history of servitude than of freedom? How do you account for the enormous amount of violence in Russian history?

Q-12.   Why was territorial expansion "the soul of tsardom"?

Q-13.   Trace the fortunes and political power of the boyar class in Russia from the time of the Kievan state to the death of Peter the Great.

Q-14.   Peter the Great of Russia and Frederick William I of Prussia are often viewed as heroes and "reformers" in the histories of their own countries. How valid is this assessment in terms of the peasants of the early eighteenth century?

STUDY-REVIEW EXERCISES

Identify the following people and explain their importance.

Bartolomeo Rastrelli

Suleiman the Magnificent

Frederick the Great

Charles VI of Austria

Jenghiz Khan

Ivan the Terrible

J. S. Bach

Peter the Great

Frederick William, the Great Elector

Ivan III

Peter Paul Rubens

Define the following key concepts and terms.

absolutism

baroque

Prussian Junkers

Hohenzollern

kholops

Romanov

boyar

autocracy

Vikings

Habsburg

Mongol yoke

Pragmatic Sanction

Explain and describe baroque architecture by referring to the pictures in the textbook.

Explain what the following events were, who participated in them, and why they were important.

Building of the Winter Palace of St. Petersburg

Siege of Vienna, 1683

War of the Austrian Succession

Time of Troubles

Battle of Poltava

Test your understanding of the chapter by answering the following questions.

1. The founder of the new Russian city on the coast of the Baltic Sea was

    _____ .

2. The unsurpassed master of baroque music is _____ .
3. After 1500, serfdom in eastern Europe *increased/decreased.*
4. The Ottoman Turkish leader who captured Vienna in 1529 was

    _____ .

5. In the struggle between the Hungarian aristocrats and the Austrian Habsburgs,
    the Hungarian aristocrats *maintained/lost* their traditional privileges.
6. The Prussian monarch who doubled the size of Prussia in 1740 by taking Silesia

    from Austria was _____ .
7. Number the following events in correct chronological order.

    _____ The election of the first Romanov tsar

    _____ The establishment of the Kievan state

    _____ The Time of Troubles

    _____ Invasion by the Mongols

    _____ The building of St. Petersburg

    _____ The battle of Poltava

8. The monarchs of eastern Europe in the sixteenth and seventeenth centuries were
    generally *stronger/weaker* than the kings of western Europe.

MULTIPLE-CHOICE QUESTIONS

1. The unifiers and first rulers of the Russians were the
   a. Mongols.
   b. Turks.
   c. Romanovs.
   d. Vikings.

2. By the seventeenth century, in Russia commercial activity, manufacturing, and mining were owned or controlled by
   a. rising urban capitalists.
   b. the Cossacks.
   c. the tsar.
   d. foreign investors.

3. The principality called the "sandbox of the Holy Roman Empire" was
   a. Brandenburg-Prussia.
   b. Hungary.
   c. Sweden.
   d. Austria.

4. Ivan the Terrible
   a. failed to conquer Kazan.
   b. was afraid to call himself tsar.
   c. monopolized a great deal of mining and business activity.
   d. abolished the system of compulsory service for noble landlords.

5. The dominant artistic style of the seventeenth and early eighteenth centuries was
   a. Gothic.
   b. Romantic.
   c. impressionistic.
   d. baroque.

6. The noble landowners of Prussia were known as
   a. boyars.
   b. Junkers.
   c. Vikings.
   d. Electors.

7. Apparently the most important reason for the return to serfdom in eastern Europe from about 1500 to 1650 was

a. political.
b. economic.
c. military.
d. religious.

8. After the disastrous defeat of the Czech nobility by the Habsburgs at the battle of White Mountain in 1618, the
   a. old Czech nobility in great numbers accepted Catholicism.
   b. majority of Czech noble land was given to soldiers who had fought for the Habsburgs.
   c. conditions of the enserfed peasantry improved.
   d. Czech nobility continued their struggle effectively for many years.

9. After the Thirty Years' War and the creation of a large standing army, Austria turned its attention to control of
   a. northern Italy.
   b. Prussia.
   c. Hungary.
   d. Poland.

10. The result of the Hungarian nobility's struggle against Habsburg oppression was that
    a. they suffered a fate similar to the Czech nobility.
    b. they gained a great deal of autonomy compared with the Austrian and Bohemian nobility.
    c. they won their independence.
    d. their efforts were inconclusive.

11. In 1742, as a result of the War of Austrian Succession, Maria Theresa
    a. was forced to abdicate.
    b. was forced to give up the province of Silesia to Prussia.
    c. gained Prussian possessions.
    d. was unable to keep Hungary in the Austrian Empire.

12. The Viking invaders in early Russian history were principally interested in
    a. controlling vast new lands politically.
    b. spreading their religion.
    c. establishing and controlling commercial interests.
    d. developing cultural exchanges.

13. The Muscovite princes gained their initial power through
    a. services rendered to the Vikings.

    b.   strategic marriages.
    c.   services rendered to the Mongols.
    d.   a pagan religious cult.

14.   The rise of the Russian monarchy was largely a response to the external threat of the
    a.   French monarchy.
    b.   Asiatic Mongols.
    c.   Prussian monarchy.
    d.   English monarchy.

15.   The Time of Troubles was caused by
    a.   a dispute in the line of succession.
    b.   Turkish invasions.
    c.   Mongol invasions.
    d.   severe crop failures resulting in starvation and disease.

16.   The real losers in the growth of eastern Europe absolutism were the
    a.   peasants.
    b.   peasants and middle classes.
    c.   nobility.
    d.   nobility and the clergy.

17.   A basic social reality on which the absolutist states of eastern Europe rested was
    a.   an oppressed and enserfed peasantry.
    b.   a weak nobility.
    c.   a powerful middle class.
    d.   well-developed urban centers.

18.   Frederick William I was especially fond of
    a.   beautiful women.
    b.   gourmet food.
    c.   the French language.
    d.   tall soldiers.

19.   The greatest obstacle to attempts of the eastern European monarchs to establish absolutism was a (an)
    a.   weak middle class.
    b.   weak nobility.
    c.   oppressed peasantry.
    d.   strong nobility.

20. The first Russian tsar to use an elite corps of service nobility to crush opposition was
    a. Ivan I.
    b. Peter the Great.
    c. Catherine the Great.
    d. Ivan III.

21. Peasants who were drafted into the army of Peter the Great
    a. served a ten-year term.
    b. served for life.
    c. had excellent chances for advancement.
    d. served twenty-five-year terms.

22. The largest empire in the world in the sixteenth century was the
    a. French Empire.
    b. Ottoman Empire.
    c. Spanish Empire.
    d. Habsburg Empire.

23. The eastern European nobility gained power from struggling monarchs during the late Middle Ages because of
    a. a lack of wars during the period.
    b. undisputed royal successions.
    c. aristocratic loyalty to the monarch.
    d. the absence of a well-developed concept of sovereignty.

24. The royal family of Brandenburg-Prussia were the
    a. Hohenzollerns.
    b. Habsburgs.
    c. Hanovers.
    d. Bourbons.

25. Hungarian nobles revolted against the absolute rule of the
    a. Ottoman Turks.
    b. Hohenzollerns.
    c. Habsburgs.
    d. Mongols.

26. The Kievan principality was originally established by
    a. Mongol invaders.
    b. Turkish invaders.
    c. German invaders.
    d. Viking invaders.

27. The reforms of Peter the Great were for the most part
     a. economic and commercial.
     b. political and constitutional.
     c. social and humanitarian.
     d. militaristic and bureaucratic.

28. Which of the following characterizes the peasantry in the sixteenth and seventeenth centuries?
     a. The number of free peasants increased.
     b. Peasants acquired land from their lords.
     c. Peasants became veritable forced laborers.
     d. Peasants gained more freedom of movement.

GEOGRAPHY

1. Show on the outline map the area covered by the principality of Moscow in 1300. Was the principality of Moscow an important state at that time?

2. Shade in with different colors the territories acquired by the principality of Moscow from 1300 to 1689. How successful was Moscow in expanding before 1689?

3. Shade in the acquisitions of Peter the Great. How do these acquisitions suggest that Russia was becoming more western and European and less eastern and Asiatic during Peter the Great's reign?

4. Using your knowledge of Russian geography and the information in the text-book, explain how Russia's history has been influenced by its geography. For example, does Russia's geographic setting contribute to its absolutism?

5. Looking at Map 20.1 in the text, identify the three territorial parts of the Habsburg (Austrian) state and explain how they came to be united. Do these geographic facts help explain the development of absolutism and militarism in Austria?

UNDERSTANDING HISTORY THROUGH READING AND THE ARTS

For centuries the Moscow Kremlin was the axis of Russian culture — that is, it was the place where works of great historical and artistic significance were amassed. Many examples of painting and applied art of the Kremlin are discussed and illustrated in *Treasures of the Kremlin**** published by the Metropolitan Museum of Art, New York (1979). See also, T. Froncek, ed., *The Horizon Book of the Arts of Russia* (1970), and G. Hamilton, *The Art and Architecture of Russia* (1975).

Baroque music, the dominant musical style in the age of absolutism, was often written for a particular monarch or princely court. The mathematical and harmonic emphasis of baroque music and its aristocratic patronage are illustrated in the six Brandenburg Concertos by Johann Sebastian Bach, written for the margrave of Brandenburg in the early eighteenth century, and in George F. Handel's *Water Music*, written for George I of England at about the same time. Both of these are available on numerous recordings. For the history of baroque music see M. F. Bukofzer, *Music in the Baroque Era* (1947).

*Available in paperback.

PROBLEMS FOR FURTHER INVESTIGATION

The personality and reign of Tsar Peter the Great have generated considerable controversy for many years. Many ideas for further research can be found in M. Raeff, *Peter the Great* (rev. ed., 1972), and in L. J. Oliva, ed., *Russia and the West from Peter to Khrushchev* (1965).

CHAPTER 21

TOWARD A NEW WORLD-VIEW IN THE WEST

CHAPTER OBJECTIVES

After reading and studying this chapter you should be able to answer the following questions:

Q-1. Why did the world-view of the educated classes in Europe change during the seventeenth and eighteenth centuries from a primarily religious one to one that was primarily secular and scientific?

Q-2. How did this new outlook on life affect Western society and politics?

CHAPTER SYNOPSIS

This chapter shows how the educated classes in the West moved from a world-view that was basically religious to a world-view that was primarily secular in the course of the seventeenth and eighteenth centuries. The development of scientific knowledge was the key cause of this intellectual change. This change was momentous because it laid the groundwork for both enlightened absolutism and the spirit of revolution.

Until about 1500, Western scientific thought reflected the Aristotelian-medieval world-view, which taught that a motionless earth was at the center of a universe made up of planets and stars in ten crystal spheres. These and many other beliefs showed that science was primarily a branch of religion. Beginning with Copernicus, who taught that the earth revolved around the sun, Europeans slowly began to reject Aristotelian-medieval scientific thought. They developed a new conception of a universe based on natural laws, not on a personal God. Isaac Newton, standing on the shoulders of earlier mathematicians, physicists, and astronomers,

333

formulated the great scientific synthesis: the law of universal gravitation. Newton's work was the culminating point of the scientific revolution.

The chapter examines the causes of the scientific revolution in the West, its relationship to religion, and its impact on nonscientific thought. The new science was more important for intellectual development than for economic activity or everyday life, for above all it promoted critical thinking. Nothing was to be accepted on faith; everything was to be submitted to the rational, scientific way of thinking. This critical examination of everything, from religion and education to war and politics, was the program of the Enlightenment and the accomplishment of the philosophes, a group of thinkers who propagandized the new world-view across Europe and the North American colonies.

The philosophes were reformers, not revolutionaries. Yet reform of European society from the top down — that is, by the absolute monarchs through what is called "enlightened absolutism" — proved to be impossible because the enlightened monarchs could not ignore the demands of their conservative nobilities. In the end, it was revolution, not enlightened absolutism, that changed and reformed Western society.

Enlightened absolutism had its greatest effect in Prussia, Russia, France, and Austria, where new-style monarchs spread the cultural values of the Enlightenment, undertook state-building reforms, and expanded their boundaries. The "Greats" — Frederick of Prussia and Catherine of Russia — best illustrate these movements. Frederick expanded the size and power of Prussia (largely at the expense of Maria Theresa's Austria), while Catherine deposed her husband, adopted Enlightenment ideas and reforms, extended serfdom, and pushed Russia into the West at the expense of Turkey and Poland. In France, Louis XV used Maupeou, his chancellor, to counterattack the growing and well-entrenched aristocracy who had used the Parlement of Paris to check royal power. Louis's efforts came to an end with his death and the succession of the young Louis XVI, who sought popular favor by reinstating the old Parlement of Paris. In Austria, Joseph II continued the state-building of his mother, Maria Theresa (who had limited Church power, strengthened the central government, and reformed serfdom), by granting religious reform and — temporarily — abolishing serfdom.

STUDY OUTLINE

I. The scientific revolution: the origin of the modern Western world
   A. Historians now recognize that the history of science and the history of society must be brought together
   B. Scientific thought in 1500
      1. Until the early 1500s, European ideas about the universe were based on Aristotelian-medieval ideas

      a.   Central to this view was the belief in a motionless earth fixed at the center of the universe

      b.   Around the earth moved ten crystal spheres

      c.   Beyond the spheres was heaven

   2.   Aristotle's scheme fit into Christianity because it made human beings the center of the universe and established a home for God

C. The Copernican hypothesis

   1.   Copernicus, a Polish astronomer, claimed that the earth revolved around the sun — that the sun was the center of the universe

   2.   This heliocentric theory was a great departure from the medieval system

   3.   Copernicus's theory created doubts about traditional religion

D. From Tycho Brahe to Galileo

   1.   Brahe set the stage for the modern study of astronomy by building an observatory and collecting data

   2.   His assistant, Kepler, formulated three laws of planetary motion that described the precise relationship among planets in a sun-centered universe

   3.   Galileo discovered the laws of motion using the experimental method — the cornerstone of modern science

   4.   Galileo was tried by the Inquisition for heresy and forced to recant his views

E. Newton's synthesis

   1.   Newton integrated the astronomy of Copernicus and Kepler with the physics of Galileo

      a.   He formulated a set of mathematical laws to explain motion and mechanics

      b.   The key feature in his synthesis was the law of universal gravitation

F. Causes of the scientific revolution

   1.   Medieval European universities provided the framework for the new science

   2.   The Renaissance stimulated science by rediscovering ancient Greek mathematics

   3.   The navigational problems of sea voyages generated scientific research

   4.   New ways of obtaining knowledge improved scientific methods

      a.   Bacon advocated empirical, experimental research

      b.   Descartes stressed mathematics and deductive reasoning

   5.   After the Reformation the Catholic church discouraged science while Protestantism tended to favor it

G. Some consequences of the scientific revolution in Europe

   1.   There arose a scientific community whose primary goal was the expansion of knowledge

   2.   A modern scientific method arose that rejected traditional knowledge and logic

3. Because the link between pure science and applied technology was weak, the scientific revolution was more an intellectual than material revolution

II. The Enlightenment in the West
   A. Enlightenment ideas
      1. Natural science and reason can explain all aspects of life
      2. The scientific method can explain the laws of human society
      3. It is possible to create better societies and better people
   B. The emergence and results of the Enlightenment
      1. The French philosophes popularized Enlightenment ideas
      2. The Enlightenment and the scientific revolution were directly connected — the former popularized the latter
      3. The Enlightenment encouraged the growth of uncertainty about religious truth, cultural superiority, and the role of experience in learning
   C. The philosophes and their ideas
      1. The philosophes acquainted the elite of western Europe with the ideas of the new world-view
      2. They were committed to the reformation of society and humanity, although they often had to cloak attacks on church and state in satire
         a. Montesquieu used social satire to criticize existing practices
         b. He proposed that power be divided and shared by all classes by adopting the principle that "power checks power"
         c. Voltaire challenged traditional Catholic theology and exhibited a characteristic philosophe belief in a distant God who let human affairs take their own course
         d. Diderot and d'Alembert edited a great encyclopedia that attempted to examine all of human knowledge and to teach people how to think critically and rationally
            (1) The *Encyclopedia* exalted science and knowledge over religion
            (2) As a summary of the Enlightenment world-view it was extremely influential
   D. The later Enlightenment built rigid and dogmatic systems
      1. D'Holbach argued that humans were completely controlled by outside forces
      2. Hume's skepticism argued that the mind can contain only empirical knowledge
      3. Rousseau attacked rationalism and civilization and claimed that children needed to be protected from society
      4. His *Social Contract* centered on the idea of the general will of the people
   E. The social setting of the Enlightenment
      1. Enlightenment ideas were spread by salons of the upper classes

       2. The salons were often presided over by women like the brilliant Geoffrin and Deffand

III. The evolution of the "Greats": absolutism

   A. Many believed that "enlightened" reform would come by way of "enlightened" monarchs

   B. Frederick II and Catherine II of Russia

       1. Frederick II used the War of the Austrian Succession to expand Prussia into a Great Power

       2. Renewed conflict in 1756 (the Seven Years' War, 1756–1763) saw Prussia aligned against Austria and Russia

       3. Frederick allowed religious freedom and promoted education

       4. He reformed the legal system and bureaucracy and encouraged agriculture and industry to improve the life of his subjects

       5. Catherine imported Western culture to Russia and corresponded with the philosophes

          a. Her ideas about reforming serfdom changed after Pugachev's uprising in 1773, however, and she restricted the serfs even more

          b. She defeated the Turks

          c. Catherine also succeeded in annexing part of Poland while the rest of Poland was taken by Austria and Prussia

   C. Absolutism in France and Austria

       1. With the duke of Orleans and the Parlement of Paris the French nobility enjoyed a revival of power following the death of Louis XIV, and the monarchy lost the power of taxation

       2. The French minister began the restoration of royal absolutism under Louis XV

       3. With the reign of Louis XVI royal absolutism once again declined and noble power revived

       4. The Austrian emperor Joseph II was a dedicated reformer who abolished serfdom, taxed all his subjects equally, and granted religious freedom

       5. Joseph failed, however, because of aristocratic opposition; his reforms were short-lived

   D. An overall evaluation

       1. In France, the rise of judicial and aristocratic opposition combined with a public educated in liberalism put absolutism on the defensive

       2. In eastern Europe, however, the results of "enlightened absolutism" were modest and therefore absolutism remained entrenched

       3. By combining state-building with the Enlightenment these absolutists underscored the long tradition of the dominant role of the state in European society

REVIEW QUESTIONS

Q-1.   Contrast the old Aristotelian-medieval world-view with that of the new science of the sixteenth and seventeenth centuries in the West. What were the contributions of Copernicus, Brahe, Kepler, Galileo, and Newton? What is meant by Newton's "synthesis"?

Q-2.   How did the new scientific theory and discoveries alter the concept of God and religion? Did science, in fact, come to dictate humanity's concept of God?

Q-3.   The author tells us that Copernicus hit on "an old Greek idea being discussed in Renaissance Italy." How does this help explain the origins of the new science?

Q-4.   Discuss the origins and the momentum of the scientific revolution in terms of (a) its own "internal logic" and (b) external and nonscientific causes.

Q-5.   How did Bacon and Descartes contribute to the development of the modern Western scientific method?

Q-6.   Did the Catholic and Protestant churches retard or foster scientific investigation? Explain.

Q-7.   What are the consequences of the rise of modern science?

Q-8.   Were the philosophes interested in popular rule by or the political education of the people? Were their dreams of reform from above utopian?

Q-9.   What was the effect of Catherine's reign on (a) the Russian nobility, (b) the Russian serfs, and (c) the position of Russia in the European balance of power?

Q-10.   Describe the nature of the power struggle in France following the death of Louis XIV in 1715.

Q-11.   Discuss: "Joseph II [of Austria] was a heroic but colossal failure."

Q-12.   Because the enlightened absolutists in the West tried but failed to make life better for common men and women, who were the real enemies of the people? Why was the system of absolutism resistant to change?

STUDY-REVIEW EXERCISES

Define the following key concepts and terms.

deductive reasoning

rationalism

the idea of progress

skepticism

Parlement of Paris

Enlightenment

enlightened absolutism

Aristotelian world-view

empirical method

Identify each of the following and give its significance.

Gresham College

Diderot

Bayle

Kepler

Galileo

Partition of Poland

Newton

Montesquieu

Voltaire

Copernicus

Brahe

Catherine the Great

Frederick the Great

Louis XV

Joseph II

philosophes

Bacon

Descartes

D'Holbach

Explain the general significance of the following books and indicate how these works and their authors influenced one another.

On the Revolutions of the Heavenly Spheres, Copernicus

New Astronomy or Celestial Physics, Kepler

Two New Sciences, Galileo

Principia, Newton

Test your understanding of the chapter by answering the following questions.

1. According to Aristotle, the sublunar world was made up of four elements: air,

    fire, _____, and _____ .
2. Copernicus *did/did not* attempt to disprove the existence of God.
3. Galileo claimed that *motion/rest* is the natural state of all objects.

4. The key feature in Newton's synthesis was the law of _____ .
5. In the medieval European universities, science emerged as a branch of

    _____ .

6. The method of finding latitude came out of study and experimentation in the

    country of _____ .
7. The idea of progress *was/was not* widespread in the Middle Ages.
8. In the seventeenth and eighteenth centuries a close link between pure (theoretical) science and applied technology *did/did not* exist.

9. A _____ is one who believes that nothing
    can ever be known beyond all doubt.

10. Voltaire believed that _____ was history's greatest
    man because he gave humanity truth.
11. Overall, Joseph II of Austria *succeeded/failed* as an enlightened monarch.

MULTIPLE-CHOICE QUESTIONS

1. "Enlightened" monarchs believed in
   a. reform.
   b. democracy.
   c. urbanization.
   d. all of the above

2. Geoffrin and Deffand were
   a. scientific writers.
   b. religious leaders.
   c. "enlightened" women.
   d. leaders of the serf uprising.

3. The philosophes were
   a. mainly university professors.
   b. generally hostile to monarchial government.
   c. enthusiastic supporters of the Catholic church.
   d. satirist writers who wished to reform society and humanity.

4. The social setting of the Enlightenment
   a. excluded women.
   b. was characterized by poverty and boredom.
   c. was dominated by government officials.
   d. was characterized by witty and intelligent conversation.

5. Catherine the Great
   a. believed the philosophes were dangerous revolutionaries.
   b. freed the serfs to satisfy Diderot.
   c. increased the size of the Russian Empire.
   d. established a strong constitutional monarchy.

6. According to medieval thought, the center of the universe was the
   a. sun.
   b. earth.
   c. moon.
   d. heaven.

7. Copernicus' theory of a sun-centered universe
   a. suggested the universe was small and closed.
   b. challenged the idea that crystal spheres moved the stars around the earth.
   c. ruled out the belief that the worlds of heaven and earth were different.
   d. suggested an enormous and possibly infinite universe.

8. The first astronomer to prove his theories through the use of mathematical equations was
   a. Galileo.
   b. Johannes Kepler.
   c. Tycho Brahe.
   d. Isaac Newton.

9. D'Holbach, Hume, and Rousseau are examples of the later Enlightenment trend toward
   a. rigid systems.
   b. social satire.
   c. religion.
   d. the idea of absolutism.

10. The French philosopher who rejected his contemporaries and whose writings influenced the romantic period was
    a. Rousseau.
    b. Voltaire.
    c. Diderot.
    d. Condorcet.

11. The gathering ground for many who wished to discuss the ideas of the French Enlightenment was the
    a. salon.
    b. lecture hall.
    c. palace at Versailles.
    d. University of Paris.

12. Frederick II was considered an enlightened despot because he
    a. freed the serfs.
    b. wrote poetry, allowed religious freedom, and improved the legal and bureaucratic systems.
    c. kept the Junkers in a dominant position socially and politically.
    d. avoided war.

13. Catherine the Great of Russia hardened her position on serfdom after the _____ rebellion.

a. Pugachev
b. Moscow
c. Polish
d. "Five Year"

14. He used the War of the Austrian Succession to expand Prussia into a great power.
    a. Joseph II
    b. Frederick II
    c. William I
    d. Frederick William I

15. The imperialist aggressiveness of Prussia, Austria, and Russia led to the disappearance of this eastern European kingdom from the map after 1795.
    a. Hungary
    b. Sweden
    c. Brandenburg
    d. Poland

16. Francis Bacon's great contribution to scientific methodology was
    a. the geocentric theory.
    b. the notion of logical speculation.
    c. the philosophy of empiricism.
    d. analytic geometry.

17. This man set the stage for the modern study of astronomy by building an observatory and collecting data.
    a. Darwin
    b. Hume
    c. Newton
    d. Brahe

18. Developments in these two sciences were at the heart of the scientific revolution:
    a. physics and astronomy
    b. chemistry and medicine
    c. theology and mathematics
    d. biology and politics

19. According to the revised Aristotelian view of the early sixteenth century,
    a. the stars revolved around the sun.
    b. only the moon and sun revolved around the earth.
    c. the earth revolved around the sun.
    d. the sun, moon, planets, and stars revolved around the earth.

20. The religion that never discouraged scientific experimentation and writing was
    a. Catholicism.
    b. Protestantism.
    c. Judaism.
    d. Russian Orthodoxy.

21. The Enlightenment thinkers clashed with the established churches because they
    a. renounced their faith in God.
    b. believed it was possible to improve society.
    c. said that theological sources, such as the Bible, should be examined in the light of reason.
    d. wanted to continue the wars of religion.

22. The Enlightenment reached its peak about
    a. 1687.
    b. 1750.
    c. 1810.
    d. 1715.

23. Before Copernicus, people were primarily dependent on the work of the great astronomer of antiquity
    a. Galileo.
    b. Archimedes.
    c. Plato.
    d. Ptolemy.

24. The mathematician who first used controlled experiments to test the movement of objects was
    a. Galileo.
    b. Tycho Brahe.
    c. Copernicus.
    d. Isaac Newton.

25. The French writer who translated the complicated science of his day into entertaining, instructive literature was
    a. Voltaire.
    b. Descartes.
    c. Fontenelle.
    d. Diderot.

26. Generally speaking, the philosophes
    a. concentrated on educating the masses.

    b. distrusted the masses.
    c. believed that democracy was the best road to progress.
    d. held to the doctrines of the Roman Catholic church.

27. In general, the immediate successors of Louis XIV were
    a. inadequate leaders.
    b. competent monarchs.
    c. even more absolute than Louis XIV.
    d. able to dominate the nobility.

28. Which of the following is true of Joseph II of Austria?
    a. He abolished serfdom.
    d. He demanded strict religious conformity.
    c. He taxed only the nobility.
    d. He placed education under the control of the Catholic church.

GEOGRAPHY

Using Map 21.1 in the text as your guide, describe below the "partition of Poland."
Who were the participants, when did it occur, and why did it occur?

UNDERSTANDING HISTORY THROUGH READING AND THE ARTS

The upsurge of creativity in the arts in Europe in the seventeenth and eighteenth
centuries, which was greatly influenced by the Enlightenment, is known as the age
of the baroque. The meaning of this highly creative and dynamic style and the
achievements of its great artists are discussed in M. Kitson, *The Age of the Baroque*
(1966). See also Chapter 6 in N. Pevsner, *An Outline of European Architecture*
(7th ed., 1963). Few artists captured English life as well as did the painter Hogarth,
whose *Rake's Progress* and *Harlot's Progress* point to the consequences of moral
decay. Hogarth's paintings can be seen and studied in W. Gaunt, *The World of
William Hogarth* (1978), and D. Bindman, *Hogarth* * (1981).

*Available in paperback.

The two greatest philosophes of the age of Enlightenment were Rousseau and Voltaire. Rousseau's ideas on education and natural law are interestingly set forth in his *Emile*, and Voltaire's most-praised work is *Candide*, a funny and sometimes bawdy parody on eighteenth-century life and thought. Much of the new fiction writing of the eighteenth century reflects, often in satire, the spirit of the new world-view — Jonathan Swift, *Gulliver's Travels*; Daniel Defoe, *Moll Flanders*; and Henry Fielding, *Tom Jones*, are just a few. In Germany, the *Sturm und Drang* (storm and stress) movement, which produced works such as Lessing's *Nathan the Wise* which stressed a universal religion, was devoted to the ideas of the Enlightenment and romanticism.

PROBLEMS FOR FURTHER INVESTIGATION

Those interested in pursuing the topic of the Enlightenment will want to begin with two books that set forth some of the major issues and schools of interpretation on the subject: B. Tierney et al., eds., *Enlightenment — The Age of Reason** (1967), and R. Wines, ed., *Enlightened Despotism** (1967).

Why was it not until the seventeenth century that rational science emerged in the West? What has been the relationship between science and religion in Western society? What ideas did Darwin and modern biology draw from the Scientific Revolution of 1500–1800? These are just a few of the questions asked by scholars of the subject. Begin your investigation with a general reference and bibliography such as G. Sarton, *Introduction to the History of Science* (1927–1948, 5 vols.), and L. Thorndike, *History of Magic and Experimental Science* (1923–1958). On particular figures in science see F. S. Taylor, *Galileo and the Freedom of Thought* (1938), A. Armitage, *Copernicus, the Founder of Modern Astronomy* (1938), M. Casoar, *Johannes Kepler* (1959, trans. C. Hellman), L. T. More, *Isaac Newton* (1934), and I. Cohen, *Franklin and Newton* (1956).

*Available in paperback.

CHAPTER 22

THE LIFE OF THE PEOPLE IN EUROPE

CHAPTER OBJECTIVES

After reading and studying this chapter you should be able to answer the following questions about the peasant masses and the urban poor:

Q-1.   What changes occurred in agriculture and population in eighteenth-century Europe?

Q-2.   Why did traditional marriage and sex practices begin to change in Europe in the late eighteenth century?

Q-3.   What was it like to be a child in European preindustrial society?

Q-4.   How adequate was the diet and health care of eighteenth-century Europeans? Were there any signs of improvement?

Q-5.   What influence did religion hold in everyday life in Europe and what was *pietism*?

CHAPTER SYNOPSIS

Until recently the aspects of everyday life, such as family relations, sex, marriage, health, and religion, took a secondary place in history. As a result, much of our understanding of these subjects is often based on myth rather than on solid historical research and interpretations.

The chapter begins with three important and interrelated subjects. First, the centuries-old open-field system of agricultural production, a system that was both inefficient and unjust, is described. The second topic is the explosive growth of European population in the eighteenth century. This growth, still imperfectly understood, was probably due largely to the disappearance of the plague and to new and better food, such as the potato. Doctors and organized medicine played a

347

very minor role in the improvements in health. Third, the chapter discusses the movement of manufacturing from urban shops to cottages in the countryside. Rural families worked there as units in the new domestic system, particularly in the textile industry, which provided employment for many in the growing population.

Contrary to early belief, it appears that in western Europe the nuclear family was very common among preindustrial people. Furthermore, preindustrial people did not marry in their early teens, and illegitimacy was not as common as usually thought, and certainly less so than today. The concept of childhood as we know it hardly existed. The author shows that the diet of poor people was probably almost as nutritionally sound as that of rich people — when the poor got enough to eat. As for medical science, it probably did more harm than good in the eighteenth century. Also explained in this chapter are the reasons for a kind of "sexual revolution" beginning in mid-eighteenth-century Europe — with young people engaging in sex at an earlier age and with illegitimacy on the rise.

In the area of religion the West in the eighteenth century witnessed a tug of war between the Enlightenment's attempt to demystify Christianity and place it on a more rational basis and a popular movement to retain traditional ritual, superstition, and religious mysteries. In Protestant and Catholic countries alike, rulers and religious leaders sought to purify religion by eliminating many ritualistic practices. The response to this "reform" by the common people in Catholic countries was a resurgence of religious ritual and mysticism, while in Protestant Germany and England there occurred a popular religious revival based on piety and emotional "conversion." Meanwhile, most of Europe — Catholic and Protestant — saw the state increase its control over the church.

STUDY OUTLINE

I. Agriculture and population in eighteenth-century Europe
    A. Frequent poor harvests and bad weather led to famine and disease and a search for new sources of food and income
    B. Working the land
        1. The medieval open-field system divided the land into a few large fields, which were then cut up into long, narrow strips
        2. The fields were farmed jointly, a portion of the arable land was always left fallow, and output was low
        3. Common lands were set aside for community use
        4. The labor and tax system throughout Europe was unjust, but eastern European peasants suffered the most
        5. By the eighteenth century most peasants in western Europe were free from serfdom and many owned some land
        6. Crop rotation eliminated the need for fallowing and broke the old cycle of scarcity; more fodder meant more animals, which meant more food

   7. Enclosure of the open fields to permit crop rotation also meant the disappearance of common land
   C. The balance of numbers
   1. The traditional checks on growth were famine, disease, and war
   2. The use of "famine foods" made people weak and susceptible to illness and epidemics
   3. These checks kept Europe's population growth rate fairly low
   4. Quarantine of ports and the victory of the brown rat helped reduce the bubonic plague
   5. The basic cause of population growth was fewer deaths, partly owing to the disappearance of the plague
   6. An increase in the food supply meant fewer famines and epidemics
   D. The growth of cottage industry
   1. Population increase caused the rural poor to take in manufacturing work to supplement their income
   2. This cottage industry challenged the monopoly of the urban craft guilds
   3. It was based on rural workers' producing cloth in their homes for merchant-capitalists, who supplied the raw materials and paid for the finished goods
   4. This system reduced the problem of rural unemployment and provided cheap goods
   5. The textile industry in England was an example of the putting-out system
II. Marriage and the family in preindustrial European society
   A. Extended and nuclear families
   1. Contrary to popular belief, the extended family was not common in western Europe
   2. Also, early marriage was not common prior to 1750, and many people never married at all
   3. Marriage was commonly delayed because of poverty and/or local law and tradition
   B. Work away from home
   1. Many boys left home to work as craftsmen or laborers
   2. Girls left to work as servants
   C. Premarital sex and birth-control practices
   1. Illegitimate children were not common in preindustrial society
   2. Premarital sex was common, but marriage usually followed
   3. Coitus interruptus was the most common form of birth control
   D. New patterns of marriage and illegitimacy after about 1750
   1. The growth of cottage industry resulted in people marrying earlier — and for love
   2. The explosion of births and the growth of prostitution from about 1750 to 1850 had several causes

       a. Increasing illegitimacy signified rebellion against laws that limited the right of the poor to marry

       b. Pregnant servant girls often turned to prostitution, which also increased illegitimacy

    E. The question of sexual emancipation for women

       1. Women in cities and factories had limited economic independence

       2. Poverty kept many people single — leading to premarital sex and illegitimate births

III. Women and children in preindustrial European society

    A. Child care and nursing

       1. Infant mortality was very high

       2. Breast-feeding of children was common among poor women

       3. Middle- and upper-class women hired wet nurses

       4. The occupation of wet-nursing was often exploitative of lower-class women

    B. Foundlings and infanticide

       1. "Killing nurses" and infanticide were forms of population control

       2. Foundling hospitals were established but could not care for all the abandoned babies

    C. Attitudes toward children

       1. Attitudes toward children in preindustrial society were different from those of today

         a. Parents and doctors were generally indifferent to children

         b. Children were often neglected or treated brutally

       2. The Enlightenment brought about more humane treatment of children

    D. Schools and education

       1. The beginnings of education for common people lie in the seventeenth and eighteenth centuries

       2. Protestantism encouraged popular education

       3. Literacy increased, especially in France and Scotland, between 1700 and 1800

IV. Food and medicine

    A. The life span of Europeans increased from twenty-five years to thirty-five years between 1700 and 1800 — but why?

    B. Diet and nutrition

       1. The major improvements were in the area of prevention, or "preventive medicine"

       2. The diet of ordinary people improved

         a. Poor people ate mainly grains and vegetables

         b. Milk and meat were rarely eaten

       3. Rich people ate quite differently from the poor

        a. Their diet was rich in meat and wine

        b. They avoided fruits and vegetables

C. The impact of diet on health

    1. There were nutritional advantages and disadvantages to the diet of the poor

        a. Their breads were very nutritious

        b. Their main problem was not getting enough green vegetables and milk

    2. The rich often ate too much rich food

D. New foods and new knowledge about diet

    1. The potato substantially improved the diet of the poor

    2. There was a growth in market gardening and an improvement in food variety in the eighteenth century

    3. There was some improvement in knowledge about diet, although Europeans did not entirely cast off their myths

    4. Greater affluence caused many to turn to less nutritious food, such as white bread and sugar

E. The medical professionals

    1. The demonic view of disease was common, and faith healers were used to exorcise the demons

    2. Pharmacists sold drugs that were often harmful to their patients

    3. Surgeons often operated without anesthetics and surrounded by dirt

    4. Physicians frequently bled or purged people to death

F. Hospitals and mental illness

    1. Patients were crowded together, often several to a bed

    2. There was no fresh air or hygiene

    3. Mental illness was misunderstood and treated inhumanely

    4. Some attempts at reform occurred in the late eighteenth century

G. Medical experiments and research

    1. Much medical experimentation was creative quackery

    2. The conquest of smallpox was the greatest medical triumph of the eighteenth century

        a. Jenner's vaccination treatment, begun in 1796, was a great medical advance

        b. Smallpox soon declined drastically in Europe

V. Religion and Christian churches

A. The institutional church

    1. Despite the critical spirit of the Enlightenment, the local parish church remained important in daily life in Europe

    2. The Protestant belief in individualism in religion was tempered by increased state control over the church and religion

B. Catholic piety

    1. In Catholic countries the old religious culture of ritual and superstition remained popular

      2. Catholic clergy reluctantly allowed traditional religion to survive
  C. Protestant revival
      1. Pietism stressed religious enthusiasm and individualism
      2. In England, Wesley was troubled by religious corruption, decline, and uncertainty
      3. His "Methodist" movement rejected Calvinism and stressed salvation through faith
      4. Wesley's ministry brought on a religious awakening, particularly among the lower classes

REVIEW QUESTIONS

Q-1. How did the open-field system work? Why was much of the land left uncultivated while the people sometimes starved?

Q-2. What changes brought the open-field system to an end?

Q-3. Where did the modern agricultural revolution originate? Why?

Q-4. What is meant by "enclosure"? Was this movement a great swindle of the poor by the rich, as some have claimed?

Q-5. It is often believed that the typical preindustrial family in Europe consisted of an extended family. Do you agree? Define extended and nuclear family.

Q-6. In *Romeo and Juliet*, Juliet was just fourteen and Romeo was not too many years older. Is this early marriage typical of preindustrial society? Why did so many people not marry at all?

Q-7. When did the custom of late marriage begin to change? Why?

Q-8. Did preindustrial men and women practice birth control? What methods existed?

Q-9. How do you explain that prior to 1750 there were few illegitimate children but that there was a growth of illegitimacy thereafter?

Q-10. It is often claimed that factory women, as opposed to their rural counterparts, were sexually liberated. Is this claim correct? Explain.

Q-11. How and why did life expectancy improve in the eighteenth century?

Q-12. What were the differences in the diets of the rich and the poor in the eighteenth century? What nutritional deficiencies existed?

Q-13. How important was the potato in the eighteenth century? Is it important enough to merit more attention from historians?

Q-14. How did the "revolution in the animal kingdom" break the force of the deadly bubonic plague?

Q-15. What improvements in the eighteenth century contributed to the decline of disease and famine?

Q-16. How important were the eighteenth-century advances in medical science in extending the life span?

Q-17.   What was the demonic view of disease?

Q-18.   It is said that when it came to medical care, the poor were better off than the rich because they could not afford doctors or hospitals. Why might this have been true?

Q-19.   Why was there so much controversy over the smallpox inoculation? Was it safe? What contribution did Edward Jenner make to the elimination of this disease?

Q-20.   How was mental illness regarded and treated in the eighteenth century?

Q-21.   What effect did changes in church-state relations have on the institutions of the church?

Q-22.   The movement of production from town to country is commonly known as the growth of the domestic, or putting-out, system. Using textile production as an example, explain how the system worked and why it grew.

Q-23.   Describe the forms in which popular religious culture persisted in Catholic Europe.

Q-24.   Define *pietism* and describe how it is reflected in the work and life of John Wesley.

STUDY-REVIEW EXERCISES

Define the following key concepts and terms.

extended family

foundlings

demonic view of disease

nuclear family

illegitimacy explosion

Methodists

famine foods

common land

open-field system

enclosure

cottage industry

putting-out system

purging

"killing nurses"

Jesuits

Pietism

Identify each of the following and give his or her significance.

Saint Vincent de Paul

Lady Mary Montague

Edward Jenner

James Graham

Joseph II

John Wesley

Test your understanding of the chapter by answering the following questions.

1. It is apparent that the practice of breast-feeding *increased/limited* the fertility of lower-class European women in the eighteenth century.
2. The teenage bride *was/was not* the general rule in preindustrial Europe.
3. Prior to about 1750, premarital sex usually *did/did not* lead to marriage.

4. In the eighteenth century, the _____ was the primary new food in Europe.
5. People lived *longer/shorter* lives as the eighteenth century progressed.
6. The key to Jenner's inoculation discovery was the connection between immunity

   from smallpox and _____ , a mild and not contagious disease.

7. In Catholic countries it was largely *the clergy/the common people* who wished to hold on to traditional religious ritual and superstition.

8. The Englishman who brought religious "enthusiasm" to the common folk of

    England was _____ .

MULTIPLE-CHOICE QUESTIONS

1. One of the chief deficiencies of the diet of both rich and poor Europeans was the absence of sufficient
    a. meat.
    b. fruit and vegetables.
    c. white bread.
    d. wine.

2. A family in which three or four generations live under the same roof under the direction of a patriarch is known as a (an)
    a. nuclear family.
    b. conjugal family.
    c. industrial household.
    d. extended family.

3. Prior to about 1750 in Europe, marriage between two persons was more often than not
    a. undertaken freely by the couple.
    b. controlled by law and parents.
    c. based on romantic love.
    d. undertaken without economic considerations.

4. The establishment of foundling hospitals in the eighteenth century was an attempt to
    a. prevent the spread of the bubonic plague.
    b. isolate children from smallpox.
    c. prevent willful destruction and abandonment of newborn children.
    d. provide adequate childbirth facilities for rich women.

5. It appears that the role of doctors and hospital care in bringing about improvement in health in the eighteenth century was
    a. very significant.
    b. minor.
    c. helpful only in the area of surgery.
    d. helpful only in the area of ophthalmology.

6. In the seventeenth and early eighteenth centuries European people usually married
    a. surprisingly late.
    b. surprisingly early.
    c. almost never.
    d. with enormous frequency.

7. The overwhelming reason for postponement of marriage was
    a. that people didn't like the institution of marriage.
    b. lack of economic independence.
    c. the stipulation of a legal age.
    d. that young men and women valued the independence of a working life.

8. Which of the following statements best describes the attitude toward children in the first part of the eighteenth century?
    a. They were protected and cherished.
    b. They were never disciplined.
    c. They were treated as they were — children living in a child's world.
    d. They were ignored, often brutalized, and often unloved.

9. Most of the popular education in Europe of the eighteenth century was sponsored by
    a. the church.
    b. the state.
    c. private individuals.
    d. parents, in the home.

10. Which of the following would most likely be found in an eighteenth-century hospital?
    a. Isolation of patients
    b. Sanitary conditions
    c. Uncrowded conditions
    d. Uneducated nurses and poor nursing practices

11. The greatest medical triumph of the eighteenth century was the conquest of
    a. starvation.
    b. smallpox.
    c. scurvy.
    d. cholera.

12. The practice of sending one's newborn baby to be cared for by a poor woman in the countryside was known as

    a. the cottage system.

    b. infanticide.

    c. wet-nursing.

    d. all of the above

13. It appears that the chief dietary problem of European society was the lack of an adequate supply of
    a. vitamins A and C.
    b. vitamin B complex.
    c. meat.
    d. sugar.

14. Most probably the best thing an eighteenth-century sick person could do with regard to hospitals would be to
    a. enter only if an operation was suggested by a doctor.
    b. enter only if in need of drugs.
    c. enter only a hospital operating under Galenic theory.
    d. stay away.

15. The country that led the way in the development of universal education was
    a. Britain.
    b. Prussia.
    c. France.
    d. Italy.

16. The agricultural improvements of the mid-eighteenth century were based on the elimination of
    a. livestock farming.
    b. the open-field system.
    c. rotation of fields.
    d. nitrogen-producing plants, such as peas and beans.

17. Which of the following prevented eighteenth-century peasants from making a profit on their land?
    a. The combination of oppressive landlords and poor harvests
    b. The plague
    c. The relatively light taxes imposed on them by landlords
    d. Their reliance on crop rotation

18. A fair description of population fluctuation figures before 1700 in Europe would be that the
    a. population was remarkably uniform in its growth.

    b.   population increased steadily on account of very young marriages and large families.

    c.   population decreased slightly on account of war, famine, and disease.

    d.   population grew slowly and erratically.

19.   Rural workers who participated in the putting-out system
    a.   did so to pass abundant free time.
    b.   became experts in the manufacture of luxury items.
    c.   were highly regulated.
    d.   usually sold their labor for much less than urban workers.

20.   Which of the following is true about preindustrial society's attitudes toward children?
    a.   Parents often treated their children with indifference and brutality.
    b.   Children were not allowed to work in the early factories.
    c.   Doctors were the only people interested in the welfare of children.
    d.   Killing of children by parents or nurses became very rare.

21.   The "illegitimacy explosion" of the late eighteenth century in Europe was encouraged by which of the following?
    a.   The laws, especially in Germany, concerning the poor's right to marry
    b.   The immobility of young rural workers
    c.   The influence of the French Revolution, which repressed freedom in sexual and marital behavior
    d.   The respectful treatment of girls in the servant class

22.   In the second half of the eighteenth century in Europe, the earlier patterns of marriage and family life began to change. Which of the following was a result of this change?
    a.   Decrease in the number of illegitimate births
    b.   Later marriages
    c.   Weakening of the urban subculture of habitual illegitimacy
    d.   Marriages for love

23.   The diet of the European poor consisted mostly of
    a.   fruit.
    b.   grains and vegetables.
    c.   milk and dairy products.
    d.   meat and eggs.

24.   After the decline of the bubonic plague, the dominant infectious disease in Europe was

a. measles.
b. tuberculosis.
c. smallpox.
d. syphilis.

25. The major health problem linked to the diet of the poor was
   a. constipation.
   b. disorders associated with a deficiency of the vitamin B complex.
   c. scurvy.
   d. gout.

26. The potato first took hold as a dietary staple in
   a. France.
   b. England.
   c. Germany.
   d. Ireland.

27. Which of the following statements best characterizes the medical profession in the eighteenth century?
   a. Medicine played only a very small role in improving the health of the population.
   b. The number of doctors declined steadily.
   c. For the most part, people placed little value on the services of doctors.
   d. The practice of bloodletting was abandoned.

28. Pietism's appeal can be explained by its
   a. isolation of the clergy as agents of God.
   b. emotionalism and enthusiasm.
   c. disdain for "reborn" Christians.
   d. attempt to take religion out of everyday life.

UNDERSTANDING HISTORY THROUGH READING AND THE ARTS

The relationship between people and agriculture makes for interesting reading. For more on the agricultural life in Britain the reader should start with J. D. Chambers and G. E. Mingay, *The Agricultural Revolution (1750–1880)* (1966). For Europe in general, F. Huggett, *The Land Question and European Society Since 1650** (1975), presents a picture of how agricultural changes have affected the development of European society.

*Available in paperback.

Was the enclosure a blessing or a great swindle for the British farmer? This question has been debated by historians and social commentators since the movement toward business agriculture began in sixteenth-century England. The general argument against enclosure was first set out on the sixteenth century by Sir Thomas More, who claimed (in his book *Utopia*) that it resulted in rural unemployment and rural crime. It is the enclosures between 1750 and 1850, however, that are the most controversial. The best contemporary coverage of the debate is G. E. Mingay, *Enclosure and the Small Farmer in the Age of the Industrial Revolution** (1968), which also contains a useful bibliography.

Painting is one of the major sources of information for the history of childhood. Preindustrial childhood is the subject of *Children's Games*, by Pieter Brueghel the Elder. It is a lively and action-packed painting of over two hundred children engaged in more than seventy different games, and it is the subject of an interesting article by A. Eliot, "Games Children Play," *Sports Illustrated* (January 11, 1971): 48–56.

Tom Jones, eighteenth-century England's most famous foundling, was the fictional hero of Henry Fielding's *Tom Jones* and the subject and title of director Tony Richardson's highly acclaimed, award-winning film version of Fielding's novel. Starring Albert Finney, Susannah York, and Dame Edith Evans, the film re-creates, in amusing and satirical fashion, eighteenth-century English life. A more recent film adaptation is Richardson's *Joseph Andrews*, based on another Fielding novel.

London was the fastest-growing city in the eighteenth century. How people lived in London is the subject of two highly readable and interesting books: M. D. George, *London Life in the Eighteenth Century** (3rd ed., 1951), and R. J. Mitchell and M. D. R. Leys, *A History of London Life** (1963).

Few men in preindustrial society earned enough to support a family. This, in part, explains why and when women married, and why most women worked. The preindustrial woman, therefore, was not in any modern sense a homemaker. The subject of women and the family economy in eighteenth-century France is discussed by O. Hufton in *The Poor of Eighteenth-Century France* (1974).

PROBLEMS FOR FURTHER INVESTIGATION

Did medical science contribute to an improvement in eighteenth-century life? Until about twenty-five years ago, it was fashionable to believe that the population explosion was due to improvements made by medical science. Although this theory is generally disclaimed today, it appears to be enjoying a slight revival. For both sides, read the following journal articles (which also have bibliographies): T. McKeown and R. G. Brown, "Medical Evidence Related to English Population Change," *Population*

*Available in paperback.

Studies 9 (1955); T. McKeown and R. G. Record, "Reasons for the Decline in Mortality in England and Wales During the Nineteenth Century," *Population Studies* 16 (1962); and P. Razzell, "Population Change in Eighteenth-Century England: A Reinterpretation," *Economic History Review*, 2nd series, 18-2 (1965); and on the history of disease see D. Hopkins, *Princes and Peasants: Smallpox in History* (1977).

CHAPTER 23

AFRICA, THE MIDDLE EAST, AND INDIA,
CA 1400–1800

CHAPTER OBJECTIVES

After reading and studying this chapter you should be able to answer the following questions:

Q-1.   What were the features of Ottoman society and government and those of Safavid Persia? Why did these states decline?

Q-2.   How did Muslim reform and art affect the dominant Hindu population of India? How and why did the British gain power over India?

Q-3.   How did the slave trade affect African kingdoms?

CHAPTER SYNOPSIS

By 1500 Africa consisted of a number of kingdoms as well as a number of societies that were held together by family or kinship ties: the Senegambian states on the West African coast, the kingdom of Songhay that dominated much of the Sudan, Kanem-Bornu and Hausa city-states, and the Swahili city-states on the east coast of Africa. This chapter argues that the overall effect of the slave trade was slight. Although French culture influenced the coastal fringes of Senegal, the English maintained factories along the Gold Coast, and the Portuguese held Angola and Mozambique, by 1800 European influence had hardly penetrated the African interior.

The Mughal leader Babur and his successors conquered the Indian subcontinent and Mughal rule inaugurated a period of radical administrative reorganization and the flowering of intellectual and architectural creativity. Babur's grandson, Akbar, gave India one of its greatest periods in history. During this period, India, the prize of European commercial interests, began to experience British political domination. Meanwhile in Turkey another Islamic empire emerged, that of the Ottoman Turks. Stressing the holy war and military organization, the Ottomans established a wealthy empire that stretched from the Balkans in Europe through the Near East and along the West African coast. The reign of Suleiman the Magnificent demonstrated the power and splendid creativity of the Ottomans under the Safavids. Safavid power reached its height under Shah Abbas, whose military achievements — based on the Ottoman model, support for trade and commerce, and endowment of the arts — earned him the title "the Great."

STUDY OUTLINE

I. African kingdoms and societies, ca 1500–1800
   A. Senegambia and Benin
      1. The Senegambian states of the West African coast possessed a homogeneous culture
         a. They served as a center in the trade from North Africa and the Middle East
         b. They became the most important center for the slave trade
      2. Ghana and Mali controlled much of Senegambia, but other states remained independent
      3. Senegambian social and political structure
         a. The three Senegambian states (and language groups) were Wolof, Seere, and Pulaar
         b. Wolof and Seere culture had defined classes: royalty, nobility, warriors, peasants, artisans, and slaves
         c. Senegambian slavery was different from Western slavery
         d. The Wolof nobility elected the king who appointed village chiefs
         e. In stateless societies, age-grade societies evolved
         f. The typical Senegambian community was the self-supporting agricultural village made up of family farms
      4. The forest kingdom of Benin (now southern Nigeria) emerged in the fifteenth and sixteenth centuries
         a. A balance of power between the king (*oba*) and the nobility had evolved under Ewuare
         b. Ewuare expanded the state east to the Niger river, west to Yoruba country, and south to the Atlantic
         c. The capital, Benin City, was large and wealthy
         d. From 1485 on, the Portuguese and other Europeans tried unsuccessfully to influence Benin
         e. Reasons for its decline remain a mystery
   B. The Sudan: Songhay, Kanem-Bornu, and Hausaland

1. Songhay dominated the Niger region of western and central Sudan
   a. Muhammad Toure tried to introduce political centralization and Muslim reforms into Songhay
   b. His death left the country weak and it fell to Moroccan armies
2. Kanem-Bornu thrived under Idris Alooma's leadership
   a. A strong feudal military-feudal state was established
   b. Agriculture and trade with North Africa flourished
   c. Idris Alooma's great feats were described by the historian Ibn Fartua
   d. He introduced Muslim religion and law into Kanem-Bornu
3. The Hausa were agricultural people who lived in city-states
   a. Trade with North Africa resulted in the establishment of Hausa city-states such as Katsina and Kano
   b. Kano and Katsina became Muslim intellectual centers
   c. King Muhammad Rimfa of Kano introduced the practice of wife seclusion and the use of eunuchs

C. Ethiopia
1. The East African Christian kingdom of Ethiopia faced numerous invaders
   a. The state of Adal defeated Emperor Lebna Dengel and then devastated the land and forced many to convert to Islam
   b. The Adal Muslims were defeated by the Portuguese
   c. The Galla peoples occupied parts of Ethiopia and the Ottoman Turks seized Massawa and other coastal cities
2. Portuguese Jesuits tried to replace the Coptic Christian tradition with Roman Catholic Christianity
   a. In spite of these conflicts, the Coptic Christian church remained the cornerstone of Ethiopian national identity
   b. The Jesuits were expelled

D. The Swahili city-states
1. The Swahili city-states prospered until Portuguese intrusion
2. Mogadishu, Mombasa, Kilwa, and Sofala traded ivory, gold, and slaves with Arabian and Persian Gulf ports and the Far East
3. Kilwa dominated the cities, which were cosmopolitan and wealthy
4. In 1498 the Portuguese, under da Gama, conquered the city-states
5. The Swahili people responded by deserting their cities
6. Portugal established a hundred-year East African foothold called Fort Jesus near Mombassa in 1589

E. Africa and the transatlantic slave trade
1. The slave trade began with Spanish and Portuguese exploration
2. Portugal dominated the slave trade from 1493 to 1600; it sent many slaves to Brazil

3. From 1690 to 1807, England was the leading carrier of African slaves
4. Most slaves were intended for sugar and coffee plantations
5. The 400 years of slave trade was a brutal and exploitive process
    a. At the ports they were treated brutally and given poor food
    b. They were branded a number of times
    c. In ships they were packed below deck and received little food
6. The main sources were downward from the West African coast
    a. At first the Senegambian coast and the mouth of the Congo River yielded the greatest numbers
    b. Then the Ivory Coast, the Bight of Benin, and the Gold Coast became large suppliers
    c. The Portuguese took most of their slaves from Angola
    d. Most slaves were carried to the sugar and coffee plantations of Latin America
    e. Luanda and Benguela were the major slave ports to which slaves were brought from the interior
7. The Portuguese slave trade was dominated by its colony of Brazil
    a. Ships, capital, and goods for the trade came from Brazil
    b. Rio de Janeiro commanded the Brazil trade and the slave market with Angola
8. The British slave trade was dominated by London, Bristol, and Liverpool; the British traded textiles, gunpowder and flint, and liquor for slaves
9. European traders and African dealers all looked for profits
    a. The "sorting" was the system of trading goods for slaves
    b. The Europeans had fort-factories as centers for slave trade
    c. But the shore method of trading was more popular
10. A northbound trade in slaves went across the Sahara to Algiers, Tripoli, and Cairo — surviving into the twentieth century
11. The economic, social, and political impact of this trade on African societies
    a. The trade did not lead to the economic development of Africa because slave-trade income was usually spent on luxury and consumer goods or firearms
    b. The trade encouraged slavery within Africa, encouraged population growth, and resulted in a *métis* or mulatto class
    c. The *métis* came to exercise considerable economic and social power
    d. Political and social consequences varied greatly from state to state
12. Although it caused great misery and affected millions, the overall impact of the slave trade on Africa was slight

II. The Ottoman and Safavid empires
   A. The Ottoman military state
      1. The first Ottoman Turkish state expanded out of western Anatolia
      2. Its rulers were the leaders of the Ghazis, fighters in the holy war
      3. The principle of *jihad*, or holy war, was central to the Ottoman state
      4. The Ottomans pushed into the Balkans of Europe, and under Mehmed II they conquered Constantinople
         a. The conquest of Constantinople inaugurated the imperial phase of the Ottomans
         b. They threatened Italy and conquered much of the territory surrounding the Mediterranean
         c. They crushed the Hungarians and attacked Vienna
      5. Under Suleiman the Magnificent (1520-1566), Ottoman militarism reached classic form
         a. The military was viewed as the source of the state's existence
         b. Members of the ruling class held landed estates only for their lifetimes
         c. Much of the civil service and military was run by slaves loyal to the sultan
         d. Authority flowed from the sultan to his *pashas*
      6. Suleiman represents the peak of Ottoman influence and culture
         a. He used his great wealth to adorn Constantinople with palaces and mosques
         b. Pasha Sinan's architecture illustrates the creativity and the devotion to Islam that characterized Suleiman's empire
         c. Following Suleiman, the *janissaries* weakened the sultan's power and became a hereditary feudal class
         d. Under Muhammad Kuprili the Ottomans' position improved and an aggressive foreign policy was pursued — although their defeat at Vienna (1683) led to their decline in the European Balkan area
   B. The Persian theocratic state
      1. Shah Ismail founded the Safavid dynasty and united all of Persia
         a. He declared the Shi'ite form of religion the state religion
         b. Shi'ites oppose the traditional, or "Sunni," Islamic branch
         c. The Shi'ites claim to be descended from Ali and that they alone possess the correct interpretation of the Qur'an
         d. The Safavid state was a theocratic and puritanical state
      2. The Safavid state reached its height under Shah Abbas (1587-1629)
         a. He built an army on the Ottoman model and used it effectively
         b. He improved trade by encouraging the growth of carpetweaving and tile making
         c. Isfahan was reconstructed to become a city of active trade and great beauty

       d. Shah Abbas's successors were inept, and the state fell into the hands of religious leaders — later to be carved up by foreigners

III. India: from Mughal domination to British domination, ca 1498–1805

    A. The rule of the Mughals

       1. Mughal, or Muslim, rule in India began with Babur's conquests

       2. Babur's grandson, Akbar, gave the Indian Mughal state its form, although his father, Humayun, gave it a strong artistic base

          a. As *badshah*, the young Akbar was assisted by the military leader Bairam Khan

          b. Akbar continued Bairam Khan's expansionist policy — adding Mala, Gondwana, Gujarat, and Bengal to the Empire

          c. Akbar developed an efficient bureaucracy, including a bureau of finance and a royal mint

          d. He appointed *mansabdars* to administer imperial policy at the local level

       3. Akbar sought universal religious tolerance, or *sulahkul*

          a. He worked for the mutual assimilation of Hindus and Muslims

          b. Under the principle of *sulahkul*, he assumed responsibility for all his subjects

          c. He abolished taxes (jizya) on non-Muslims, married Hindu women, and employed Hindus in his government

          d. From his mediation of religious disputes he created the *Din-i-Ilahi*, which was a mix of a number of religions

          e. With Akbar as the philosopher-king, Din-i-Ilahi created serious Muslim rebellions

          f. Akbar built a great new city, Fatehpur-Sikri, which combined Muslim and Hindu traditions

          g. He supported artists and writers

       4. Akbar was followed by his son Jahangir and his grandson Shah Jahan

          a. Jahangir consolidated rule in Bengal and supported the arts

          b. Shah Jahan moved the court to Delhi and built the Peacock Throne and the Taj Mahal — a *pairidaeza*, or walled garden

       5. The absence of procedure for imperial succession led to Aurangzeb's puritanical rule

          a. He reimposed laws and taxes against the non-Muslim majority

          b. His religious policies proved unpopular with the Hindus

          c. His attempt to conquer the south was only partly successful

          d. After Aurangzeb's death the provincial governors began to rule independently

          e. The Marathas revolted and fought the Afghans, who were led by the Persian Nadir Shah

    B. European rivalry for the Indian trade

1. From their port of Goa, the Portuguese used piracy and terrorism to push the Muslims from the Indian and Arabian oceans and claimed that international law did not apply to non-Westerners
2. The Dutch and British formed East India trading companies
   a. The Dutch East India Company sought profits in the spice trade
   b. Madras and Bombay became British trade centers
   c. The British pushed the Portuguese out of the India trade, while Indonesia came under Dutch control
C. Factory-fort societies
   1. A "factory" was a European trade settlement
      a. At first the British company discouraged involvement in local politics
      b. With local disorder, the company came to exert political control over its factory-forts and surrounding territory
      c. The one-way nature of the trade led to demands in England to prohibit the import of certain goods, particularly Indian cloth
D. The rise of the British East India Company
   1. Colbert's French East India Company established factories in India in the 1670s
   2. Joseph Dupleix advocated use of *sepoys* and alliances with princes to accomplish the French hegemony
      a. India was a battleground in the French-British struggle
      b. British seapower, along with Clive's victory at Plassey, led to British control of India
   3. Hastings implemented the parliamentary legislation that transferred some power from the East India Company to a governor
      a. Hastings laid the foundations for the civil service, instituted reforms, and checked Indian coalition
      b. After his resignation, the British imposed a new property system on India and tightened control over the local princes
   4. At the beginning of the nineteenth century, Britain controlled India through Indian princes, the sepoys, and the civil service

REVIEW QUESTIONS

Q-1. Describe the Senegambian political and social structure.

Q-2. What was the extent of Benin territory, what was its political structure, and why was it attractive to the Portuguese invaders?

Q-3. What were Muhammad Toure's goals in Songhay, and did he succeed? Explain.

Q-4. Describe Idris Alooma's accomplishments in the state of Kanem-Bornu.

Q-5. Who were the Hausa people, and what was their culture like?

Q-6.   What external threats faced the Ethiopians in the sixteenth century, and what was the outcome?

Q-7.   Describe the conomic basis of the Swahili prosperity. Why did the Swahili city-states crumble?

Q-8.   Describe the African slave trade in terms of its origins, the European countries involved, and the African areas of supply.

Q-9.   Describe the relationship between Portugal, its colony Brazil, and the African slave trade.

Q-10.   What was the economic and demographic impact of the slave trade on African societies?

Q-11.   Describe the role that religion and militarism played in the Ottoman Turkish state.

Q-12.   What were the chief accomplishments of Suleiman the Magnificent? What role did the janissaries play in Turkish history?

Q-13.   Describe the relationship between Shah Abbas and the Shi'ite religion. What were the accomplishments of Abbas?

Q-14.   Trace the religious and political policies and accomplishments of the Mughal Indian state under Akbar. What were the additions and contributions of Jahangir and Shah Jahan?

Q-15.   Why is Aurangzeb's rule described as "puritanical"? What was his attitude toward his grandfather's policies of religious toleration?

Q-16.   Describe the goals, interests, and trade practices of the Dutch and British East India companies.

Q-17.   What were Dupleix's ideas of colonial policy in India? Describe how the British adopted these policies under Hastings.

STUDY-REVIEW EXERCISES

Define the following key concepts and terms.

métis

jihad

janissaries

pashas

factory-forts

Identify each of the following and give its significance.

Jesuit missionaries in Latin America

sepoys of India

Las Casas

Benin City

Taj Mahal

Robert Clive

British East India Company

Coptic Christianity

Rio de Janeiro

Battle of Plassey

Dutch East India Company

Warren Hastings

Explain why each of the following was important.

Oba Ewaure of Benin

Muhammad Toure of Songhay

Idris Alooma of Kanem-Bornu

Mehmed II, the Ottoman Sultan

Shah Abbas of Persia

Akbar, *badshah* of India

Suleiman the Magnificent of Turkey

Shah Jahan of Mughal India

Test your understanding of the chapter by answering the following questions.

1. The Portuguese slave trade was dominated by the Portuguese colony of

   _____.

2. From 1690 to 1807, the country that led in the slave trade was

   _____.

3. The principle of *jihad*, meaning _____,
   was the cornerstone of Ottoman political theory and the Ottoman state.

4. The class of slave recruits in Ottoman Turkey who rose to secure permanent
   military and administrative influence was known as the

   _____ class.

5. Shah Jahan's most well-known building is the _____.

MULTIPLE-CHOICE QUESTIONS

1. In the kingdom of Benin, the *Oba* was the
   a. clan system.
   b. king.
   c. supreme god.
   d. priesthood.

2. Benin's political history was marked by struggles between the king and
   a. European slave traders.
   b. the nobility.
   c. Muslim traders.
   d. the peasants.

3. In the Sudanese kingdoms, the religion of Islam
   a. was embraced by the masses.
   b. was popular primarily with the rulers.
   c. made deep changes in the legal system.
   d. was forbidden by royal decree.

4. The Coptic church is an ancient branch of
    a. Hinduism.
    b. Islam.
    c. Christianity.
    d. animism.

5. The nation most deeply involved in the slave trade was
    a. Portugal.
    b. England.
    c. the United States.
    d. Holland.

6. Most Portuguese slave ships were bound for
    a. the United States.
    b. the West Indies.
    c. Brazil.
    d. Argentina.

7. European trade with the Africans
    a. led to technological progress for the Africans.
    b. soaked up the Africans' surplus wealth.
    c. increased the African standard of living.
    d. brought badly needed gold to Europe.

8. The *métis* were
    a. French slave traders.
    b. blacks who spoke French.
    c. mulattoes.
    d. ex-slaves.

9. Which of the following was a consequence of the slave trade?
    a. African kingdoms broke down.
    b. Populations were depleted and economics destroyed.
    c. The trade enriched and strengthened economies.
    d. Consequences varied from place to place.

10. The janissaries were originally
    a. provincial governors.
    b. a slave army.
    c. Ottoman officials.
    d. Muslim monks.

11. An important point of Akbar's policy was
    a. religious toleration.
    b. territorial expansion.
    c. strong central government.
    d. suppression of Hinduism.

12. Sepoys were
    a. native soldiers.
    b. Muslim wise men.
    c. concubines.
    d. Indian-born Europeans.

13. Which of the following was *not* a basis for British rule in India?
    a. Support of the Indian princes
    b. The British navy
    c. The sepoys
    d. The civil service

14. The source of more New World slaves than any other African region was
    a. Ghana.
    b. Mali.
    c. Sudan.
    d. Senegambia.

15. In the fifteenth and sixteenth centuries, a great forest kingdom emerged in what is now southern Nigeria. It is known as the kingdom of
    a. Senegambia.
    b. Oba.
    c. Benin.
    d. Songhay.

16. The militaristic king of the Kanem-Bornu who replaced tribal customs with Islamic rule was
    a. Muhammad Toure.
    b. Idris Alooma.
    c. Legna Dengel.
    d. Ahman ibn Ghazi.

17. The Swahili city-states were on the
    a. east coast of Africa.
    b. north coast of Africa.
    c. south coast of Africa.
    d. west coast of Africa.

18. Portuguese merchants in Angola and Brazil sought to keep the flow of slaves at only a trickle from Africa to Brazil because they did not
    a. want to depopulate Angola too quickly.
    b. approve of the slave trade and wanted to eventually stop it for good.
    c. want to depress the American market.
    d. want to pay exorbitant transportation costs.

19. The slave trade that lasted late into the nineteenth century and even into the twentieth century was the
    a. North Atlantic trade.
    b. Angola-Brazil trade.
    c. northbound trade across the Sahara.
    d. eastbound trade via the Indian Ocean.

20. The slave trade produced the greatest demographic losses to the slaving coast of
    a. Angola.
    b. South Africa.
    c. the Gold Coast.
    d. Mali.

21. The Ottomans captured Constantinople during the reign of
    a. Mehmed II.
    b. Suleiman the Magnificent.
    c. Mustafa Naima.
    d. Muhammad Kuprili.

22. The military leader of the Ottoman Empire who tried unsuccessfully to capture Vienna in 1683 was
    a. Suleiman the Magnificent.
    b. Muhammad Kuprili.
    c. Mehmed II.
    d. Kara Mustafa.

23. The founder of the Safavid Dynasty, a Shi'ite state in Persia, was
    a. Shah Abbas.
    b. Shah Ismail.
    c. Babur.
    d. Suleiman II.

24. Babur was a
    a. Mongol.
    b. Safavid.

    c. Turk.

    d. Mughal.

25. Which of the following characterizes Akbar's great empire in India?

    a. He developed an efficient bureaucracy.

    b. He employed only Muslim officials.

    c. He demanded religious conformity.

    d. He instituted the jizya, a tax on non-Muslim adult males.

26. The decline of the Mughal state began under Aurangzeb, whose unsuccessful reforms were basically

    a. economic in nature.

    b. bureaucratic in nature.

    c. religious in nature.

    d. political in nature.

27. Britain fought for control of India with

    a. France.

    b. Portugal.

    c. Spain.

    d. Holland.

28. The British governor general of India who defeated the Mysore was

    a. Charles Cornwallis.

    b. Richard Wellesley.

    c. Warren Hastings.

    d. Robert Clive.

GEOGRAPHY

1. On the accompanying outline map and using Maps 16.1 and 23.1 on pages 455 and 711 in the text as a reference, locate the following:

    a. The kingdoms of Kanem-Bornu and Hausaland

    b. The Hausa city-states of Katsina and Kano

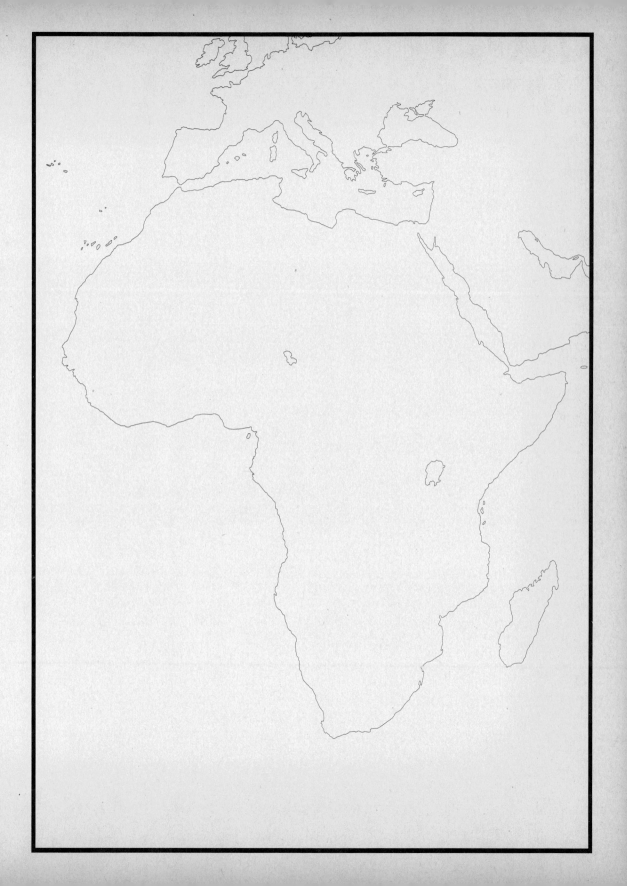

   c. The kingdom of Ethiopia

   d. The Swahili city-states of Mogadishu, Mombasa, Kilwa, and Sofala

2. In the spaces above, describe briefly the kinds of products each of these areas traded and the directions in which its trade flowed.

PROBLEMS FOR FURTHER INVESTIGATION

With ships and seamen no better than those of any other country in Europe, why did the Portuguese succeed where their Mediterranean predecessors failed? How did the unique combination of crusading zeal, desire for Guinea gold, the quest of Prester John, and the search for spices combine to spell success? Begin your investigation with C. R. Boxer, *Four Centuries of Portuguese Expansion* (1969).

     Reading biographies is an excellent way of furthering your understanding of a particular period. The period covered in this chapter abounds with interesting personalities. Several good biographies are M. Edward, *Clive, The Heaven-Born General* (1977), L. Binyon, *Akbar* (1932), and H. Lamb, *Suleiman the Magnificent — Sultan of the East* (1951).

CHAPTER 24

CHINA AND JAPAN TO 1800

CHAPTER OBJECTIVES

After reading and studying this chapter you should be able to answer the following questions:

Q-1. What features characterized the governments of the Ming and Ch'ing in China and the Tokugawa shogunate in Japan?

Q-2. How were Chinese and Japanese societies affected by agricultural and commercial developments?

Q-3. How did Chinese thinkers interpret and explain the shift from the Ming to the Ch'ing?

Q-4. What were the Chinese and Japanese attitudes toward western Christian missionary efforts?

CHAPTER SYNOPSIS

In China the Ming dynasty replaced Mongol rule. Under the Ming, China experienced a remarkable upsurge in agricultural and commercial development. A remarkable and important agricultural revolution took place between 1370 and 1398, which included not only agricultural innovations and new crops but land reclamation (see Table 24.1), reforestation, and repopulation of devastated regions. This revolution encouraged advancements in culture and economics as well, and the state became highly centralized and rested on rule by bureaucracy (often to the dismay of the emperors), which, in the end, fell to corruption and greed. The founder of the Ming dynasty in 1368 was Hung Wu, who centralized government, instituted land reform, strengthened the civil service, and extended the Great Wall. The extravagances of Yung Lo and his court, his neglect of the merchant classes, high taxes, and a weakened military provoked riots and foreign intervention. The invading Manchus became the new Ch'ing dynasty in 1644. In turn, the Ch'ing replaced the Ming, which brought a long period of peace, prosperity, and population expansion. The Ch'ing Empire supported a population of 380 million in 1812, compared to only 193 million in all of Europe in 1800. China was also geographically larger than present-day China, and by the eighteenth century it enjoyed a favorable balance of trade, which brought to it a large portion of the bullion from Latin American mines. However, by the early nineteenth century China was stagnating under an excessive bureaucracy, graft, an extravagant court, and the opium trade.

At about the same time Japan was reaping the rewards of two centuries of peace and social order. Steady economic growth and improved agricultural technology had swelled the population. This chapter outlines the important aspects of Japanese feudalism and shows how the great samurai Nobunaga won control of most of Japan by the sword and went on to unite Japan with a central government and a policy of conciliation. Nobunaga was followed by the Tokugawa regime, which inaugurated a long era of peace while it sealed Japan's borders from the outside world. Prosperity led to urbanization and population increase, while the samurai class was transformed into urban consumers and bureaucrats.

Much of this chapter is devoted to Chinese and Japanese life. More than anywhere else, the family in China exercised great social control. Marriages were arranged, and education and employment were determined by the family. Life was very much influenced by agriculture, although important new jobs were created in the textile and porcelain-making industries. Women held an inferior position within China, but China did not have the hard-and-fast social lines found in Europe. Christianity's influence was limited, although the Jesuits were important agents in a scientific-mathematical exchange between Europe and China. Ordinary life in Japan is best seen in that of the oppressed peasant, although by 1800 a class of rich peasants existed and many peasants had turned to manufacture and urban life. The nobility were stripped of much of their power, the samurai lifestyle emerged, as did an important urban-merchant class.

STUDY OUTLINE

I. China: from the Ming dynasty to the mid-Manchu, ca 1368–1795
    A. Hung Wu, founder of the Ming dynasty, pushed the Mongols out of China
    B. The Ming agricultural and commercial revolutions
        1. The Ming agricultural revolution was in part a recovery from the economic chaos of the Mongol rule
            a. Improvements in rice production, such as Champa rice, led to two yearly harvests
            b. Irrigation pumping, fish stocking, and new crops also resulted in increased food supply

      c. Land reclamation, repopulation, and reforestation led to agricultural growth as well

    2. The social consequences were threefold

      a. A population boom began in about 1550

      b. An intensification of labor and lower income per capita

      c. Towns and small cities multiplied; here the marketplaces dominated commercial life

C. The government of Hung Wu

    1. Hung Wu founded the Ming dynasty in 1368 and instituted reform

      a. He centralized his rule by confiscating noble and religious land and giving it to the peasants

      b. He relied on land taxes and carried out a land survey and population census

      c. All members of the three hereditary classes — peasants, artisans, and soldiers — had to provide service to the state

      d. The emperor was absolute and all power was dispersed from his court

      e. Later, Hung Wu divided China into principalities run by his sons

      f. The civil service was reformed by the creation of an exclusive and arduous examination system based on the classics, literary abilities, and lack of originality

      g. After 1426 the emperor's eunuchs came to hold much state power

    2. In foreign affairs Hung Wu sought to strengthen China

      a. He strengthened and extended the Great Wall

      b. He demanded that foreign traders pay him tribute

      c. However, Mongols and Japanese violated Chinese traditions

D. Maritime expansion

    1. The Ming era is also marked by important naval accomplishments under Yung Lo between 1405 and 1433.

    2. They resulted in new trade, new tribute, navigational publications, and Chinese emigration into Asia and India

E. Decline of the Ming dynasty

    1. After Hung Wu died his son Yung Lo won a struggle for the throne, but the extravagances of his court hurt China's economy

      a. Yung Lo moved the capital north to Peking and continued his father's policies

      b. This, along with Yung Lo's extravagance, displeased the new gentry and mercantile groups

      c. The emperor and his court lived in splendor in the Forbidden City, surrounded by the Imperial City

    2. Yung Lo's successors had difficulties in foreign affairs

      a. They could not hold back the Mongol invaders, and in 1449 the emperor was captured

        b.   Chinese invasion of Vietnam led to a Vietnamese liberation movement

        c.   Japan accelerated her raids on the China coast

        d.   The army was weak because taxes were not paid by the people

   3.   Nevertheless, Chinese trade with the West resulted in prosperity, as China exchanged her goods for the Europeans' silver

        a.   Silver became the medium of exchange

        b.   Foreign trade flourished

        c.   Large silk- and cotton-weaving and paper-making industries grew up

   4.   By 1600 China faced grave political and economic problems

        a.   The treasury was drained by war, royal extravagance, and enormous allowances for the extended imperial family

        b.   The military was weak and corrupt

        c.   New taxes provoked riots, and the eunuchs brought on terrorism and factionalism

        d.   The civil bureaucracy was faction-ridden and greedy and blocked imperial reform

   5.   Confucian theory has it that the Mings had forfeited the Mandate of Heaven because their own greed and self-interest had passed on to their officials — all of which invited unrest and eventual downfall

   6.   Under Nurhachi, the Manchus conquered Ming China

F.   Manchu rule

   1.   The Manchus established the Ch'ing dynasty in 1644

        a.   By 1681 their military control of China was complete

        b.   They purged the civil service of factions and eunuchs

        c.   Eighteenth-century China covered much of Asia, including Manchuria, Mongolia, Tibet, and Sinkiang, and received tribute from other states such as Burma, Laos, and Korea

   2.   Manchu rule rested on traditional Chinese methods

        a.   The emperor was supreme and ruled by the Mandate of Heaven

        b.   The central bureaucracy (civil service) continued to manage the state, but the Manchus kept themselves separate and above the Chinese

        c.   Ming and Manchu agricultural improvements continued to encourage population explosion (see Table 24.2), but by 1800 population was outpacing agriculture

        d.   Under Emperor K'ang-hsi, the emperorship was revitalized, domestic revolt crushed, and the Mongolian threat eliminated

        e.   K'ang-hsi's literary encyclopedia was a collection of all Chinese literature

        f.   K'ang-hsi encouraged literary and artistic work as China became a center for fine goods — including *china*

G.   The life of the people
1.   The family exercised greater social influence than elsewhere
   a.   The family directed education of children, marriage, religious life, and welfare services
   b.   Whereas poor families were "nuclear," middle- and upper-class families were "extended"; power in both rested with the father
   c.   Marriages were arranged between parents; the bride became a part of the husband's family and was expected to bear sons
   d.   Divorce was open only to men, and men held a higher position in society than women; girl babies were unwanted
   e.   Young brides came under the control of their mothers-in-law, who were often cruel and severe
   f.   Age was respected; wealthy women had little to do, whereas poor women worked in the fields
2.   The educational system during the Ming and Ch'ing periods had both virtues and weaknesses
   a.   The village schools for boys stressed preparation for civil service examinations, but the curriculum was limited
   b.   Still, they produced a highly literate society
   c.   Girls received training that prepared them to be wives and mothers
3.   Unlike Europe, China did not have hard-and-fast social lines based on hereditary rights
   a.   Upward mobility was possible for intelligent children
   b.   Scholars held the highest rank in the social order
4.   The Chinese had a variety of forms of relaxation and recreation
   a.   Gambling at cards, frequenting the tea houses, using alcoholic drink, and patronizing theaters were common entertainments
   b.   Athletics and racing were looked down on
5.   Christian missionaries had little effect on the masses but were influential among the intellectual elite
   a.   The Jesuit missionary Matteo Ricci found favor at the imperial court in the seventeenth and eighteenth centuries
   b.   Christianity was rejected for a variety of reasons, including its stress on absolutes and its corrupting of Chinese morals
   c.   A dispute between the Jesuits and other Catholic orders weakened the influence of the missionaries
6.   Christian missionaries (Jesuits) brought on the rebirth of mathematics and encouraged science, while Europeans took home ideas on bridge building, electrostatics, and magnetism
II.   Japan, ca 1400–1800
A.   During the Ashikaga shogunate (fourteenth to sixteenth centuries) Japan was thrust into civil war among the *daimyos*, or lords; historians call this an era of feudalism

B.   Feudalism in Japan
  1.   Feudalism in Japan, unlike that in Europe, evolved in complete isolation from outside forces
  2.   Two elements of Japanese feudalism appeared between the eighth and twelfth centuries
       a.   The shoen, or land, with its *shiki*, or rights
       b.   The military warrior clique — with its samurai warriors
  3.   By 1550 the number of shoen decreased, while the *daimyos* consolidated their territories
  4.   The nature of warfare changed as the cannon and musket made the mounted *samurai* obsolete
C.   Nobunaga and national unification
  1.   The *samurai* Nobunaga slowly extended his power and emerged ruler of central Japan by 1568
       a.   1568–1600 is the "period of national unification" during which Nobunaga subdued most of Japan by force
       b.   To do so, he had to destroy Japan's most powerful Buddhist monastery
       c.   He augmented his conquests by force with able rule and a policy of reconciliation
       d.   Trusted *damyos* were favored, castles were built, and his reforms encouraged economic growth
  2.   Nobunaga was succeeded by his general, Hideyoshi
       a.   Hideyoshi brought the province of Mori and the island of Kyushu under his domination
       b.   He reduced the threat of the *daimyos*
       c.   He extended his control over agriculture and peasants through a great land survey and through taxes
D.   The Tokugawa regime
  1.   This regime was fashioned by Ieyasu
       a.   He left the emperor rich and sovereign in theory, but real power resided in his Tokugawa shogunate
       b.   The *daimyos* became his hostages at his capital at Edo
       c.   He used many devices similar to those used by Louis XIV and William the Conqueror in limiting the power of the nobility
       d.   Taxes were imposed on villages, not individuals
       e.   Class mobility ended, and class stratification was encouraged
  2.   *Sakoku*, or the closed country policy, was instituted by Ieyasu's descendants
       a.   To maintain stability and peace, the Japanese were not allowed to leave; foreigners were excluded
       b.   Because of Catholic peasant revolts Christianity was associated with domestic disorder and was accordingly repressed

E. The life of the people
    1. Japanese life changed profoundly in the seventeenth and eighteenth centuries
        a. Stripped of power, the nobility passed their lives in the pursuit of pleasure
        b. This warrior class was gradually ruined by overindulgence in drink, sex, and costly living
        c. The *kabuki* theater, with its crude and bawdy skits, was a favorite pastime of the nobility
        d. Homosexuality, long accepted in Japan, was practiced by the samurai warrior class
    2. Peasants were sometimes severely oppressed and led miserable lives
        a. Peasant village life was highly regulated by the state
        b. In the eighteenth century, 50 percent of the peasant rice crop was paid in taxes
        c. Low rice prices and overpopulation led to frequent peasant revolts, such as in Iwaki in 1739
        d. Famines in the 1780s and 1830s made the peasants' lot worse
    3. The peasant society was not homogeneous
        a. By the early 1800s, a large class of wealthy and educated peasants existed
        b. A shortage of farm labor reflected the fact that many peasants worked in manufacturing
    4. In theory the urban merchant class occupied the bottom rung of the social ladder
        a. Merchants had no political power but accumulated great wealth
        b. The growing cities offered social mobility to the poor peasants
        c. Population growth, the *samurai* lifestyle, and urbanization encouraged the production of consumer goods and the formation of guilds and banks

REVIEW QUESTIONS

Q-1. Describe the various factors that gave rise to the so-called Ming Agricultural Revolution. What were the social consequences of this revolution?

Q-2. How did Hung Wu strengthen and reform China? Compare and contrast the new and old Chinese methods of governing.

Q-3. Why did the Ming Dynasty decline after Hung Wu's death? In what ways did the nation's economy reflect both decay and prosperity?

Q-4. Describe the Forbidden City. In what ways does it symbolize China after Hung Wu's death?

Q-5. What changes did the Manchus bring to China, and how successful were they in making China powerful?

Q-6. Describe Chinese life during the Ming and Ch'ing periods by discussing Chinese marriage customs and family life, education, social status and entertainment.

Q-7. What caused the civil war in Japan during the Ashikaga shogunate and by what term is this period known?

Q-8. Briefly describe the evolution of feudalism in Japan, particularly the two distinctive elements that appeared between the eighth and twelfth centuries.

Q-9. Who unified Japan and how did he encourage economic growth? Why did he have to destroy Japan's most powerful Buddhist monastery?

Q-10. Compare the regime of Ieyasu and his Tokugawa shogunate with his European counterparts Louis XIV and William the Conqueror. What was the fate of Christianity during this period and why?

Q-11. Why did Japanese life change profoundly during the seventeenth and eighteenth centuries? Describe the somewhat contradictory position of the urban merchant class.

STUDY-REVIEW EXERCISES

Define the following key concepts and terms.

Ming Agricultural Revolution

Mandate of Heaven.

china manufacture

Chinese civil service examinations

chinese family

Japanese *samurai*

harakiri

kabuki

sakoku policy

Japan's "period of national unification"

Identify each of the following and give its significance.

Forbidden City

Ming Dynasty

Ch'ing Dynasty

Emperor Hung Wu

Emperor K'ang-hsi

Matteo Ricci

Nobunaga

Japanese *daimyos*

Japanese *shoen*

Hideyoshi

Tokugawa shogunate

Describe each of the following and note how each illustrates how Japanese nationalism was both alike and different from that of other Asian countries — such as China.

Japan's "semi-divine mission"

Zaibatsu

Japanese "ultranationalism"

Japanese economy

Test your understanding of the chapter by answering the following questions.

1. The peasant founder of China's Ming Dynasty was _____.
2. Under the later Ming rulers, such as Yung Lo, the costs of the imperial court *increased/decreased*, while the balance of trade between China and Europe grew *more/less* favorable.

3. Compared to Europe at the time, China during the Ming and Ch'ing periods *was/was not* a society of hard-and-fast social lines.
4. Homosexuality *was/was not* accepted in Japan.
5. The eighteenth century was a period of economic and demographic *growth/decay* in both Japan and China.

MULTIPLE-CHOICE QUESTIONS

1. During the Ming era in China, there was a proliferation of
   a. towns.
   b. small cities.
   c. large cities.
   d. both a and b

2. In Ming times the entire Chinese population was divided into three categories according to
   a. place of residence.
   b. occupation.
   c. religion.
   d. wealth.

3. Ming China regarded foreigners as
   a. pirates.
   b. curiosities.
   c. barbarians.
   d. enemies.

4. The flow of silver into China caused a(n)
   a. abandonment of the gold standard.
   b. prospering of the wealthy merchant class.
   c. decline in the value of paper money.
   d. sharp drop in the price of silver.

5. Emperor Wan-Li was unable to accomplish his ends because
   a. bureaucracy and precedent stood in his way.
   b. war interrupted his reforms.
   c. he died very young.
   d. the nobility opposed him.

6. Under the Tokugawa government, Japan was ruled by the
   a. emperor.

b.   shogun.
c.   Tokugawa regent.
d.   council of *samurai*.

7.   *Kabuki* theater usually depicted
     a.   crude love and romance.
     b.   historical events.
     c.   scenes from court life.
     d.   folk tales.

8.   In more recent times, female roles in the *kabuki* theater were played by
     a.   boys.
     b.   prostitutes.
     c.   eunuchs.
     d.   divorcees.

9.   It may be generally said that during the Tokugawa era in Japan that
     a.   the country enjoyed peace and development.
     b.   the country suffered continuous civil strife.
     c.   people lost their faith in the monarchy.
     d.   the standard of living declined.

10.   The shogun Ieyasu kept effective control over the feudal lords by
      a.   executing their prominent leaders.
      b.   forcing them to spend alternate years in the capital.
      c.   imposing heavy taxes.
      d.   requiring their personal oath of loyalty.

11.   Japan expelled Christian missionaries because they
      a.   were spies for European nations.
      b.   encouraged Japanese Christians to participate in feudal revolts.
      c.   preached the overthrow of the shogun.
      d.   interfered with Japan's traditional culture.

12.   The founder of the Ming Dynasty and leader of the Red Turbans was
      a.   Hung Wu.
      b.   Wan-Li.
      c.   Wu Ti.
      d.   Wang Chih.

13.   The Ming agricultural and commercial revolutions were closely linked with
      a.   an expansion of foreign trade.
      b.   dramatic improvements in rice production.

c. deurbanization.
d. new methods of government spending.

14. "Fish farming" refers to
    a. big net fishing off the Chinese coast.
    b. fish hatching in government aquariums.
    c. farming for half the year and fishing the other half.
    d. planting fish in the rice paddies.

15. Hung Wu moved the Chinese capital to
    a. Peking.
    b. Nanking.
    c. Chungking.
    d. Shanghai.

16. Hung Wu's most enduring reform was his
    a. reorganization of the state ministry.
    b. implementation of a yearly census.
    c. reinstatement of civil service examinations.
    d. hereditary categories.

17. The naval expeditions of Yung Lo during the Ming period reached as far as
    a. the east coast of India.
    b. the east coast of Africa.
    c. the west coast of India.
    d. southeast Asia.

18. Yung Lo moved the capital to
    a. Peking.
    b. Nanking.
    c. Hong Kong.
    d. Shanghai.

19. The Forbidden city was built by
    a. Hung Wu.
    b. Yung Lo.
    c. Wan-Li.
    d. Liu Chin.

20. During the later Ming Dynasty
    a. China avoided all foreign trade.
    b. China achieved peace with her northern invaders.

    c. costs of the imperial court decreased.

    d. China became involved in the world economy.

21. The Ch'ing Dynasty was established by the
    a. Manchus.
    b. Mongols.
    c. Japanese.
    d. Vietnamese.

22. Early on, the Ch'ing gained the support of
    a. peasants.
    b. intellectuals.
    c. eunuchs.
    d. landowners.

23. The zenith of the Ch'ing Dynasty was achieved during the reign of
    a. K'ang-hsi.
    b. Wan-Li.
    c. Wang Chih.
    d. Liu Chin.

24. The greatest controversy between papal authority and the Christian converts in China, which resulted in the missionaries' being expelled from China, surrounded
    a. the use of Chinese in liturgical services.
    b. the Chinese practice of ancestor worship.
    c. the act of footbinding.
    d. imperial religious authority.

25. The code by which the samurai lived was called
    a. harakiri.
    b. seppuku.
    c. Bushido.
    d. shoen.

26. The leader who began the Japanese period of national unification was
    a. Ieyasu.
    b. Tokugawa.
    c. Nobunaga.
    d. Ashikaga.

27. In Tokugawa Japan the commercial class
    a. were outlawed.
    b. were considered lowly.
    c. were highly esteemed.
    d. rose to great power.

28. To maintain dynastic stability and internal peace, the Japanese imposed measures called *Sakoku*, which
    a. introduced the concept of primogeniture.
    b. limited the power of the samurai.
    c. was a closed-country policy.
    d. outlawed Buddhism.

UNDERSTANDING HISTORY THROUGH READING AND THE ARTS

Trade between China and the West is currently attracting much interest. But the movement of Chinese goods — including paintings, china ware, and the decorative arts — has been considerable and goes back many centuries. C. L. Crossman's *The China Trade** (1972) looks at the export of furniture and other objects from China, and M. Tregear's *Chinese Art** (1985) examines Chinese art since 5000 B.C., and Japan's art history is told in Stanley Baker, *Japanese Art** (1984).

PROBLEMS FOR FURTHER INVESTIGATION

Both the Meiji Restoration and the fall of the Manchus are now a part of global history. They should be read in the context of both Western imperialism and Japan and China's domestic problems of the nineteenth century. To begin this cross-cultural investigation, read G. B. Sansom, *The Western World and Japan* (1958), and F. Wakeman, *The Fall of Imperial China* (1975).

Japanese feudalism shared some similarities with its Western counterparts, and Japan's feudal values, such as loyalty and discipline, were to play a crucial role in the nation's modernization in the nineteenth century. For further investigation see G. B. Sansom, *Japan: A Short Cultural History* (1962), and E. Reischauer, *Japan: The Story of a Nation* (1981).

The rapid advancement of the Chinese economy around the tenth century led to important developments in Chinese art. For further investigation see M. Sullivan, *The Arts of China* (1979).

*Available in paperback.

READING WITH UNDERSTANDING
EXERCISE 6

LEARNING HOW TO MAKE HISTORICAL COMPARISONS

An important part of studying history is learning how to *compare* two (or more) related historical developments. Such comparisons not only demonstrate a basic understanding of the two objects being compared, but also permit the student-historian to draw distinctions that indicate real insight.

For these reasons, "compare-and-contrast" questions have long been favorites of history professors, and they often appear on essay exams. Even when they do not, they are an excellent study device for synthesizing historical information and testing your understanding. Therefore, as the introductory essay suggests, *try to anticipate* what compare-and-contrast questions your instructor might ask. Then work up your own study outlines that summarize the points your essay answer would discuss and develop. The preparation of study outlines of course is also a useful preparation for essay questions that do not require you to compare and contrast.

Exercise

Read the brief passage below. Reread it and underline or highlight it for main points. Now study the passage in terms of "compare and contrast." Prepare a brief outline (solely on the basis of this material) that will allow you to compare and contrast the Russian and German revolutions (of 1917-1919). After you have finished, compare your outline with the model on page F-3. Remember: the model provides a *good* answer, not the *only* answer.

The German Revolution of November 1918 resembled the Russian Revolution of March 1917. In both cases a genuine popular uprising toppled an authoritarian monarchy and established a liberal provisional republic. In both countries liberals and moderate socialists took control of the central government, while workers' and soldiers' councils formed a "countergovernment." In Germany, however, the moderate socialists won and the Lenin-like radical revolutionaries in the councils lost. In communist terms, the liberal, republican revolution in Germany in 1918 was only "half" a revolution: a "bourgeois" political revolution without a communist second installment. It was Russia without Lenin's Bolshevik triumph.

There were several reasons for the German outcome. The great majority of Marxian socialist leaders in the Social Democratic party were, as before the war, really pink and not red. They wanted to establish real political democracy and civil liberties, and they favored the gradual elimination of capitalism. They were also German nationalists, appalled by the prospect of civil war and revolutionary terror. Moreover, there was much less popular support among workers and soldiers for the extreme radicals than in Russia. Nor did the German peasantry, which already had most of the land, at least in western Germany, provide the elemental force that has driven all great modern revolutions, from the French to the Chinese.

Of crucial importance also was the fact that the moderate German Social Democrats, unlike Kerensky and company, accepted defeat and ended the war the day they took power. This act ended the decline in morale among soldiers and prevented the regular army with its conservative officer corps from disintegrating. When radicals headed by Karl Liebknecht and Rosa Luxemburg and their supporters in the councils tried to seize control of the government in Berlin in January, the moderate socialists called on the army to crush the uprising. Liebknecht and Luxemburg were arrested and then brutally murdered by army leaders. Finally, even if the moderate socialists had taken the Leninist path, it is very unlikely they would have succeeded. Civil war in Germany would certainly have followed, and the Allies, who were already occupying western Germany according to the terms of the armistice, would have marched on to Berlin and ruled Germany directly. Historians have often been unduly hard on Germany's moderate socialists.

Comparison of Russian and German Revolutions (1917-1918)

Similarities

1. Both countries had genuine liberal revolutions.
   a. Russia—March 1917
   b. Germany—November 1918

2. In both countries moderate socialists took control.

Differences

1. Russia had a second, radical (Bolshevik) revolution; Germany did not.

2. In Germany workers and peasants gave radicals less support than in Russia.

3. In Germany the moderate Socialists stopped the war immediately and therefore the German army, unlike the Russian army, remained intact to put down radical uprisings.

CHAPTER 25

THE REVOLUTION IN POLITICS,
1775-1815

CHAPTER OBJECTIVES

After reading and studying this chapter you should be able to answer the following questions:

Q-1.   What were the causes of the political revolutions between 1775 and 1815 in America and France?
Q-2.   What were the ideas and objectives of the revolutionaries in America and France?
Q-3.   Who won and who lost in these revolutions?

CHAPTER SYNOPSIS

The French and American revolutions were the most important political events of the eighteenth century. They were also a dramatic conclusion to the Enlightenment, and both revolutions, taken together, formed a major turning point in human history. This chapter explains what these great revolutions were all about.

The chapter begins with liberalism — the idea of popular sovereignty, individual rights, and self-determination. Liberalism was the fundamental ideology of the revolution in politics. It called for freedom and equality at a time when monarchs and aristocrats took their great privileges for granted. The author sees the immediate origins of the American Revolution in the British effort to solve the problem of war debts, which was turned into a political struggle by the American colonists, who already had achieved considerable economic and personal freedom. The American Revolution stimulated reform efforts throughout Europe.

It was in France that the ideas of the Enlightenment and liberalism were put to their fullest test. The bankruptcy of the state gave the French aristocracy the chance to grab power from a weak king. This move backfired, however, because the middle class grabbed even harder. It is significant that the revolutionary desires of the middle class depended on the firm support and violent action of aroused peasants and poor urban workers. It was this action of the common people that gave the revolution its driving force.

In the first two years of the French Revolution, the middle class, with its allies from the peasantry and urban poor, achieved unprecedented reforms. The outbreak of an all-European war against France in 1792 then resulted in a reign of terror and a dictatorship by radical moralists, of whom Robespierre was the greatest. By 1795, this radical patriotism wore itself out. The revolutionary momentum slowed and the revolution deteriorated into a military dictatorship under the opportunist Napoleon. Yet until 1815 the history of France was that of war, and that war spread liberalism to the rest of Europe. French conquests also stimulated nationalism. The world of politics was turned upside down.

STUDY OUTLINE

I. The new ideas of liberty and equality
  A. In the eighteenth century in the West, *liberty* meant human rights and freedoms and the sovereignty of the people
  B. *Equality* meant equal rights and equality of opportunity
  C. The roots of liberalism
    1. The Judeo-Christian tradition of individualism, reinforced by the Reformation, supported liberalism
    2. Liberalism's modern roots are found in the Enlightenment's concern for freedom and legal equality
    3. Liberalism was attractive to both the aristocracy and the middle class, but it lacked the support of the masses
II. The American Revolution (1775–1789)
  A. Some argue that the American Revolution was not a revolution at all but merely a war for independence
  B. The origins of the revolution are difficult to ascertain
    1. The British wanted the Americans to pay their share of imperial expenses
      a. Parliament passed the Stamp Act (1765) to raise revenue
      b. Vigorous protest from the colonies forced the act's repeal (1766)
    2. Many Americans believed they had the right to make their own laws
    3. The issue of taxation and representation ultimately led to the outbreak of fighting
  C. The independence movement was encouraged by several factors
    1. The British refused to compromise, thus losing the support of many colonists

  2. The radical ideas of Thomas Paine, expressed in the best-selling *Common Sense*, greatly influenced public opinion in favor of independence
  3. The Declaration of Independence, written by Thomas Jefferson and passed by the Second Continental Congress (1776), further increased the desire of the colonists for independence
  4. Although many Americans remained loyal to Britain, the independence movement had wide-based support from all sections of society
  5. European aid, especially from the French government and from French volunteers, contributed greatly to the American victory in 1783
D. The Constitution and Bill of Rights consolidated the revolutionary program of liberty and equality
  1. The federal, or central, government was given important powers — the right to tax, the means to enforce its laws, the regulation of trade — but the states had important powers too
  2. The executive, legislative, and judicial branches of the government were designed to balance one another
  3. Some people (the Anti-Federalists) feared that the central government had too much power; to placate them, the Federalists wrote the Bill of Rights, which spells out the rights of the individual
E. The American Revolution encouraged European revolution
III. The French Revolution: the revolution that began the modern era in politics
A. The influence of the American Revolution
  1. Many French soldiers, such as Lafayette, served in America and were impressed by the ideals of the revolution
  2. The American Revolution influenced the French Revolution, but the latter was more violent and more influential
B. The breakdown of the old order
  1. By the 1780s, the government was nearly bankrupt
  2. The French banking system could not cope with the fiscal problems, leaving the monarchy with no choice but to increase taxes
C. Legal orders and social realities: the three estates
  1. The first estate, the clergy, had many privileges and much wealth, and it levied an oppressive tax on the peasantry
  2. The second estate, the nobility, also had great privileges, wealth, and power, and it too taxed the peasantry
  3. The third estate, the commoners, was a mixture of a few rich members of the middle class, urban workers, and the mass of peasants
D. The formation of the National Assembly of 1789
  1. Louis XVI's economic reform plan to tax landed property was opposed by the nobles
  2. Louis called for a meeting of the Estates General, the representative body of the three estates

        a. Traditionally, historians have viewed the bourgeoisie's class and economic interests as pushing it into a revolutionary role

        b. Revisionist historians, however, claim that the bourgeoisie's interests did not differ from the interests of the upper class

        c. The nobility represented both conservative and liberal viewpoints

        d. The third estate representatives were largely lawyers and government officials

        e. The third estate wanted the three estates to meet together so the third estate would have the most power

    3. The dispute over voting in the Estates General led the third estate to break away and form the National Assembly

    4. Louis tried to reassert his monarchial authority and assembled an army

  E. The revolt of the poor and the oppressed

    1. Rising bread prices in 1788–1789 stirred the people to action

    2. Fearing attack by the king's army, angry Parisians stormed the Bastille (July 14, 1789)

        a. The people took the Bastille, and the king was forced to recall his troops

        b. The uprising of the masses saved the National Assembly

    3. The peasants revolted, forcing the National Assembly to abolish feudal dues, and won a great victory

  F. A limited monarchy established by the bourgeoisie

    1. The National Assembly's Declaration of the Rights of Man (1789) proclaimed the rights of all citizens and guaranteed equality before the law and a representative government

    2. Meanwhile, the poor women of Paris forced the king and government to move to Paris

    3. The National Assembly established a constitutional monarchy and passed major reforms of France's laws and institutions

    4. The National Assembly attacked the power of the church by seizing its land and subjugating the church to the state

    5. This attack on the church turned many people against the revolution

IV. World war and republican France (1791–1799)

  A. War began in April 1792

    1. The European attitude toward the French Revolution was mixed

        a. Liberals and radicals such as Priestley and Paine praised it as the triumph of liberty

        b. Conservatives like Burke and Gentz predicted it would lead to tyranny

    2. Fear among European kings and nobility that the revolution would spread resulted in the Declaration of Pillnitz (1791), which threatened the invasion of France by Austria and Prussia

3. In retaliation, the patriotic French deputies declared war on Austria in 1792, but France was soon retreating before the armies of the First Coalition

4. In 1792 a new assembly (the National Convention) proclaimed France a republic

B. The "second revolution" and rapid radicalization in France

1. Louis XVI was tried and convicted of treason by the National Convention and guillotined in early 1793

2. French armies continued the "war against tyranny" by declaring war on nearly all of Europe

3. In Paris, the republicans — divided between the Girondists and the Mountain — struggled for political power

4. The *sans-culottes* — the laboring poor — allied with the Mountain and helped Robespierre and the Committee of Public Safety gain power

C. Total war and the Reign of Terror (1793–1794)

1. Robespierre established a planned economy to wage total war and aid the poor

2. The Reign of Terror was instituted to eliminate opposition to the revolution, and many people were jailed or executed

3. The war became a national mission against evil within and outside of France

D. The "Thermidorian reaction" and the Directory (1795–1799)

1. Fear of the Reign of Terror led to the execution of its leader, Robespierre

2. The period of the "Thermidorian reaction" following Robespierre's death was marked by a return to bourgeois liberalism

   a. Economic controls were established

   b. The Directory, a five-man executive body, was established

   c. Riots by the poor were put down

3. The poor lost their fervor for revolution

4. A military dictatorship was established in order to prevent a return to peace and monarchy

V. The Napoleonic era (1799–1815)

A. Napoleon's rule

1. Napoleon appealed to many, like Abbé Sieyès, who looked for authority from above

2. Napoleon became the center of a plot to overturn the weak Directory and was named first consul of the republic in 1799

3. He maintained order and worked out important compromises

   a. His civil code of 1804 granted the middle class equality under the law and safeguarded their right to own property

   b. He confirmed the gains of the peasants

      c. He centralized the government, strengthened the bureaucracy, and granted amnesty to nobles
      d. He signed the Concordat of 1801, which guaranteed freedom of worship for Catholics
    4. He betrayed the ideals of the revolution by violating the rights of free speech and press, and free elections
  B. Napoleon's wars and foreign policy
    1. He defeated Austria (1801) and made peace with Britain (1802)
    2. Another war (against the Third Coalition — Austria, Russia, Sweden, and Britain) resulted in British naval dominance at the battle of Trafalgar (1805)
    3. Napoleon used the fear of a conspiracy to return the Bourbons to power to get himself elected emperor
    4. The Third Coalition collapsed at Austerlitz (1805), and Napoleon gained much German territory
    5. In 1806, Napoleon defeated Prussia and gained even more territory
    6. Napoleon's Grand Empire meant French control of continental Europe
    7. The beginning of the end for Napoleon came with the Spanish revolt and the British blockade
    8. The French invasion of Russia in 1812 was a disaster for Napoleon
    9. He was defeated by the Fourth Coalition and abdicated his throne in 1814 — only to be defeated again at Waterloo in 1815
VI. Was the French Revolution a success?
  A. Yes, the liberal revolution in France succeeded in giving great benefits to the people
  B. Although the revolution brought the Reign of Terror and a dictatorship, the old order was never reestablished, and thus a substantial part of the liberal philosophy survived

REVIEW QUESTIONS

Q-1. Define *liberalism*. What did it mean to be a liberal in Europe in the eighteenth and nineteenth centuries? How does this compare to twentieth-century liberalism?
Q-2. Were great differences in wealth contradictory to the revolutionaries' idea of equality? Explain.
Q-3. How did the writers of the Enlightenment differ on the method of establishing liberty?
Q-4. According to Locke, what is the function of government?
Q-5. Think back to the English Revolution of 1688 (Chapter 19). How does Locke's theory justify the English action of getting rid of one king and contracting for a new one?

Q-6.   Which side, American or British, had the better argument with regard to the taxation problem? How do the Seven Years' War, the Stamp Act, and the Boston Tea Party fit into your explanation?

Q-7.   Why is the Declaration of Independence sometimes called the world's greatest political editorial?

Q-8.   What role did the European powers play in the American victory? Did they gain anything?

Q-9.   What was the major issue in the debate between the Federalists and the Anti-Federalists?

Q-10.   How did Americans interpret *equality* in 1789? Has it changed since then? Are the definitions of *liberalism* and *equality* unchangeable, or do they undergo periodic redefinition?

Q-11.   Did the American Revolution have any effect on France?

Q-12.   Why was there fear in France that the tax-reform issue would have "opened a Pandora's box of social and political demands"?

Q-13.   Describe the three estates of France. Who paid the taxes? Who held the wealth and power in France?

Q-14.   With the calling of the Estates General, "the nobility of France expected that history would repeat itself." Did it? What actually did happen?

Q-15.   Discuss the reforms of the National Assembly. Did they display the application of liberalism to society?

Q-16.   What were the cause and the outcome of the peasants' uprising of 1789?

Q-17.   What role did the poor women of Paris play in the revolution?

Q-18.   Why were France and Europe overcome with feelings of fear and mistrust?

Q-19.   Why did the revolution turn into war in 1792?

Q-20.   What effect did the war have on the position of the French king and aristocracy?

Q-21.   Were the French armies conquerors or liberators?

Q-22.   Who were the sans-culottes? Why were they important to radical leaders such as Robespierre? What role did the common people play in the revolution?

Q-23.   Why did the Committee of Public Safety need to institute a Reign of Terror?

Q-24.   What event led to the takeover by Napoleon?

Q-25.   Was Napoleon a son of the revolution or just another tyrant? Explain.

Q-26.   Describe the Grand Empire of Napoleon. Was he a liberator or a tyrant?

Q-27.   What caused Napoleon's downfall?

STUDY-REVIEW EXERCISES

Define the following key concepts and terms.

liberalism

Montesquieu's "checks and balances"

natural or universal rights

republican

popular sovereignty

tithe

Estates General

Identify each of the following and give its significance.

Stamp Act

battle of Trafalgar

American Bill of Rights

American Loyalists

American Constitutional Convention of 1787

Jacobins

Reign of Terror

National Assembly

Declaration of the Rights of Man

Bastille

Declaration of Pillnitz

sans-culottes

assignats

First Coalition

September Massacres

National Convention

Girondists

the Mountain

Thermidorian reaction

Explain who the following people were and give their significance.

"the baker, the baker's wife, and the baker's boy"

Lord Nelson

Thomas Paine

Edmund Burke

Marie Antoinette

Marquis de Lafayette

Thomas Jefferson

Maximilien Robespierre

John Locke

Abbé Sieyès

Test your understanding of the chapter by answering the following questions.

1. Napoleon's plan to invade England was made impossible by the defeat of the French and Spanish navies in the battle of

   _____ in 1805.

2. Overall, the common people of Paris played *a minor/an important* role in the French Revolution.

3. The author of the best-selling radical book *Common Sense* was

   _____ .

4. The French philosophe who argued for dividing government into legislative,

   judicial, and executive branches was _____ .

5. The sans-culottes *were/were not* the aristocratic supporters of the king in France.

6. The king who was executed in 1793 in France was _____ .

7. Most liberal thinkers of the eighteenth century *favored/opposed* the idea of democracy.

8. The radical and democratic faction of the Jacobins in revolutionary France was

   known as the _____ .

9. Napoleon's influence on European society resulted in the *decrease/increase* of serfdom.

10. The peasant uprising of 1789 in France ended in *victory/defeat* for the peasant class.

11. By the mid 1790s, people like Sieyès were increasingly looking to *the people/ a military ruler* to bring order to France.

MULTIPLE-CHOICE QUESTIONS

1. Eighteenth-century liberals laid major stress on
   a. economic equality.
   b. equality in property holding.
   c. equality of opportunity.
   d. racial and sexual equality.

2. Which came first?
   a. Formation of the French National Assembly
   b. Execution of King Louis XVI

c. American Bill of Rights
d. Seven Years' War

3. The French Jacobins were
a. aristocrats who fled France.
b. monarchists.
c. priests who supported the Revolution.
d. revolutionary radicals.

4. The French National Assembly was established by
a. the middle class of the Third Estate.
b. King Louis XVI.
c. the aristocracy.
d. the sans-culottes.

5. The National Assembly did all but which one of the following?
a. Nationalized church land
b. Issued the Declaration of the Rights of Man
c. Established the metric system of weights and measures
d. Brought about the Reign of Terror

6. In 1789 the influential Abbé Sieyès wrote a pamphlet in which he argued that France should be ruled by the
a. nobility.
b. clergy.
c. people.
d. king.

7. In the first stage of the Revolution the French established a (an)
a. constitutional monarchy.
b. absolutist monarchy.
c. republic.
d. military dictatorship.

8. Edmund Burke's *Reflections on the Revolution in France* is a defense of
a. the Catholic church.
b. Robespierre and the Terror.
c. the working classes of France.
d. the English monarchy and aristocracy.

9. Most eighteenth-century demands for liberty centered on
a. the equalization of wealth.

    b. a classless society.

    c. better welfare systems.

    d. equality of opportunity.

10. Americans objected to the Stamp Act because the tax it proposed
    a. was exorbitant.
    b. was required of people in Britain.
    c. would have required great expense to collect.
    d. was imposed without their consent.

11. The American Revolution
    a. had very little impact on Europe.
    b. was supported by the French monarchy.
    c. was not influenced by Locke or Montesquieu.
    d. was supported by almost everyone living in the United States.

12. The first successful revolt against Napoleon began in 1808 in
    a. Spain.
    b. Russia.
    c. Germany.
    d. Italy.

13. The major share of the tax burden in France was carried by the
    a. peasants.
    b. bourgeoisie.
    c. clergy.
    d. nobility.

14. The participation of the common people of Paris in the revolution was initially attributable to
    a. their desire to be represented in the Estates General.
    b. the soaring price of food.
    c. the murder of Marat.
    d. the large number of people imprisoned by the king.

15. For the French peasants, the revolution of 1789 meant
    a. a general movement from the countryside to urban areas.
    b. greater land ownership.
    c. significant political power.
    d. few, if any, gains.

16. The group that announced that it was going to cut off Marie Antoinette's head, "tear out her heart, [and] fry her liver" was the

a. National Guard.
b. Robespierre radicals.
c. revolutionary committee.
d. women of Paris.

17. The group that had the task of ridding France of any internal opposition to the revolutionary cause was the
    a. Revolutionary Army.
    b. secret police.
    c. republican mob of Paris.
    d. Committee of Public Safety.

18. Between 1789 and 1792, the revolutionary assemblies in France
    a. abolished free trade within France.
    b. worked harmoniously with the Catholic church.
    c. declared war on Austria.
    d. none of the above

19. During the Reign of Terror, Robespierre and his followers
    a. allowed Louis XVI to emigrate to Britain.
    b. controlled the price of bread.
    c. weakened French armies.
    d. failed to use French nationalism.

20. In 1765 the British government attempted to defray the costs of war by imposing on its colonies the
    a. income tax.
    b. Poll Tax.
    c. Intolerable Tax.
    d. Stamp Tax.

21. The Americans who remained loyal to the British crown at the time of the British-American colonial conflict tended to be
    a. urban workers.
    b. poor farmers.
    c. upper-class colonists.
    d. political radicals.

22. Most of the members elected to represent the third estate in the Estates General of 1789 were
    a. peasants.
    b. artisans and day laborers.

c. clergy.
d. lawyers and government officials.

23. One reason that the French middle class was opposed to the Roman Catholic church was that
    a. they advocated a national Protestant church.
    b. the pope outlawed the charging of interest by the middle class.
    c. the pope wanted to reorganize the church.
    d. they had accepted the idea of the philosophes that the established religion was a "superstitious religion."

24. After 1795 women and the laboring poor demanded
    a. peace and a return to religion.
    b. cheaper food.
    c. land reform.
    d. all of the above

25. Napoleon's strongest support came from the
    a. upper class.
    b. middle class.
    c. urban working class.
    d. peasants.

26. The class that benefited most from the French Revolution was the
    a. nobility.
    b. peasants.
    c. middle class.
    d. urban workers.

27. Liberalism
    a. tried to break the shackles of Judeo-Christian tradition.
    b. opposed religious toleration.
    c. supported individual human rights.
    d. demanded democracy in government.

28. In 1794, in reaction to the Reign of Terror, a new French government with a five-man executive was established. This government lasted until 1799, and is known as the
    a. Committee for Public Safety.
    b. Directory.
    c. Second Coalition.
    d. Mountain.

GEOGRAPHY

1. Show on the outline map the boundaries of France before the outbreak of war in 1792. Now shade in the areas acquired by France by 1810. Was Napoleon successful in 1810 in expanding the boundaries of France? Who inhabited the territories newly acquired by France?

2. Shade in the dependent states in 1810. What nationalities inhabited these states? Were these large, powerful states?

3. Look closely at Map 25.1. Can you find the four small British fortified outposts scattered throughout Europe? How were these outposts necessary to and a reflection of Britain's military power? What did these outposts mean for smugglers and Napoleon's efforts to stop British trade with continental countries?

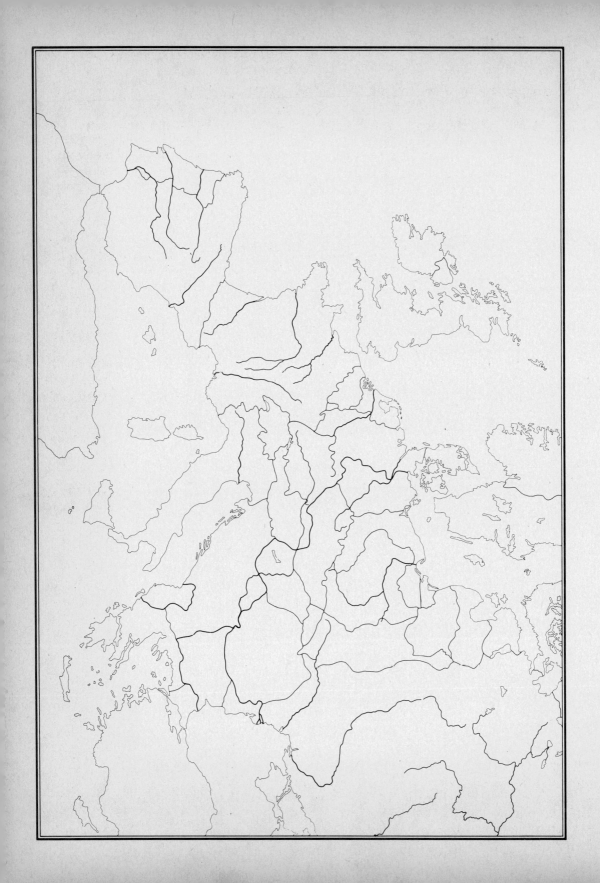

PROBLEMS FOR FURTHER INVESTIGATION

This era of revolution is ideal for the study of both individual and group actions. The various arguments of scholars over the motives and contributions of Napoleon are brought together in D. H. Pinkney, ed., *Napoleon: Historical Enigma** (1969), and the story of Admiral Lord Nelson, Britain's hero and victor of great sea battles is interestingly told in R. Hough, *Nelson, A Biography* (1980). King George III of England has often been viewed, in American history, as the arch-enemy of liberty and constitutionalism. Is this a fair assessment? The debate over his role has gone on for a number of years and is the subject of a book of collected opinions, *George III: Tyrant or Constitutional Monarch?** (1964), edited by E. A. Reitan.

Group action in a revolution makes for an equally interesting study. The role of women in the revolution in France (and in other times) is well handled in E. Boulding, *The Underside of History: A View of Women Through Time* (1976). The "people" (which includes the Paris mob) who participated in the revolution in France are the subject of the interesting study by G. Rudé, *The Crowd in the French Revolution** (1959).

Students interested in the origins of the French revolution will want to check R. W. Greenlaw, ed., *The Economic Origins of the French Revolution** (1958), and those interested in political theory may want to consider a study of liberalism beginning with H. Schultz, ed., *English Liberalism and the State — Individualism or Collectivism?** (1972).

*Available in paperback.

ANSWERS TO OBJECTIVE QUESTIONS

CHAPTER 1

Test your understanding.

1. Charles Darwin
2. Hammurabi
3. pharaoh
4. Hyskos
5. Akhenaten

6. Egyptian and Hittite
7. Babylon
8. were
9. could

10. Neolithic
11. Tigris, Euphrates
12. was
13. Nile

Number the following events.

1. 6
2. 3

3. 5
4. 2

5. 4
6. 1

Multiple-choice questions.

1. c
2. b
3. d
4. b
5. c
6. a
7. c

8. b
9. a
10. a
11. b
12. d
13. b
14. b

15. a
16. c
17. d
18. a
19. b
20. d
21. b

22. b
23. d
24. a
25. b
26. d
27. b
28. b

CHAPTER 2

Test your understanding.

1. (a)	4. Medes, Persians	7. was
2. more	5. east	8. Persians
3. Yahweh	6. satrapies	9. did not

Multiple-choice questions.

1. c	8. a	15. c	22. a
2. a	9. b	16. c	23. b
3. b	10. a	17. d	24. b
4. a	11. d	18. b	25. b
5. d	12. c	19. d	26. c
6. d	13. b	20. d	27. a
7. b	14. c	21. b	28. a

CHAPTER 3

Test your understanding.

1. Aryans	5. "true happiness"	8. Siddhartha Gautama
2. (d)	6. Pakistan and	9. Eightfold
3. outcastes	Afghanistan	10. (a)
4. Chandragupta	7. Ganges, Indus	11. Ashoka

Multiple-choice questions.

1. c	8. a	15. b	22. c
2. b	9. c	16. b	23. a
3. b	10. c	17. b	24. d
4. b	11. b	18. b	25. a
5. c	12. b	19. d	26. c
6. b	13. c	20. d	27. b
7. c	14. c	21. c	28. c

CHAPTER 4

Test your understanding.

1. was not	5. Han	8. noble
2. Shang	6. Mandate of Heaven	9. paper
3. (b)	7. Ssu-ma-ch'ien	10. Great Wall
4. Yellow		

Multiple-choice questions.

1. d	8. c	15. b	22. c
2. b	9. c	16. d	23. b
3. c	10. d	17. d	24. c
4. c	11. c	18. a	25. c
5. c	12. c	19. a	26. d
6. d	13. b	20. a	27. a
7. c	14. b	21. b	28. c

CHAPTER 5

Fill in the blank lines.

1. f	3. b	5. c	7. h
2. d	4. a	6. e	

Test your understanding.

1. Athens, Sparta, Thebes
2. were
3. did
4. Philip of Macedonia
5. divine law
6. were
7. supported

Multiple-choice questions.

1. c	8. b	15. b	22. b
2. a	9. d	16. b	23. b
3. a	10. d	17. c	24. a
4. d	11. c	18. c	25. b
5. b	12. d	19. c	26. c
6. a	13. a	20. d	27. b
7. d	14. b	21. c	28. c

CHAPTER 6

Test your understanding.

1. no
2. Stoicism
3. discard
4. Antisthenes
5. did not
6. 324 B.C.
7. did not
8. Alexander the Great
9. Hellenism
10. Persian
11. Isis
12. increase
13. fate, chance, or doom
14. tolerant
15. Isis

Multiple-choice questions.

1. c	8. a	15. c	22. b
2. d	9. d	16. c	23. a
3. b	10. a	17. a	24. d
4. b	11. d	18. d	25. a
5. b	12. b	19. d	26. b
6. c	13. b	20. a	27. b
7. c	14. c	21. a	

CHAPTER 7

Test your understanding.

1. Carthage	4. did not	7. realistic
2. did	5. more	8. did not
3. Sicily, Carthage	6. Jupiter	9. patricians

Number the following events.

1. 3	3. 1	5. 5
2. 6	4. 4	6. 2

Multiple-choice questions.

1. b	8. b	15. b	22. c
2. a	9. c	16. d	23. c
3. d	10. c	17. b	24. b
4. c	11. d	18. b	25. d
5. d	12. a	19. d	26. a
6. b	13. d	20. b	27. c
7. a	14. c	21. a	28. d

CHAPTER 8

Test your understanding.

1. did	4. 380	7. minor
2. Constantinople	5. did	8. expansion
3. increase	6. increase	

Number the following events.

1. 5	3. 2	5. 4
2. 3	4. 1	6. 6

Multiple-choice questions.

1.	d	8.	b	15.	d	22.	d
2.	b	9.	c	16.	c	23.	c
3.	d	10.	a	17.	b	24.	a
4.	a	11.	c	18.	d	25.	c
5.	d	12.	a	19.	c	26.	b
6.	b	13.	d	20.	c	27.	d
7.	b	14.	b	21.	a	28.	b

CHAPTER 9

Test your understanding.

1.	did	5.	was	8.	retarded
2.	Constantine	6.	St. Augustine	9.	City of God
3.	wergeld	7.	the Pope	10.	patriarch
4.	east				

Multiple-choice questions.

1.	c	8.	d	15.	b	22.	a
2.	d	9.	b	16.	d	23.	b
3.	a	10.	d	17.	b	24.	b
4.	c	11.	c	18.	b	25.	d
5.	b	12.	b	19.	a	26.	b
6.	d	13.	c	20.	a	27.	c
7.	b	14.	a	21.	d	28.	d

CHAPTER 10

Test your understanding.

1.	Qur'an	4.	*jihad*
2.	more	5.	Baghdad
3.	*dhimmis*	6.	*Arabian Nights* or *Thousand and One Nights*

Multiple-choice questions.

1.	b	8.	b	15.	c	22.	a
2.	c	9.	c	16.	a	23.	b
3.	a	10.	b	17.	c	24.	c
4.	c	11.	d	18.	c	25.	b
5.	d	12.	a	19.	d	26.	d
6.	d	13.	d	20.	a	27.	c
7.	a	14.	b	21.	d	28.	a

CHAPTER 11

Test your understanding.

1. proliferated
2. before, much older
3. destroying
4. religion
5. Jenghiz Khan
6. Prince Shotoku
7. Kampuchea
8. northwestern
9. *seppuku*

Multiple-choice questions.

1. d	8. b
2. c	9. a
3. c	10. b
4. d	11. d
5. b	12. c
6. a	13. c
7. c	14. d

15. c	22. d
16. a	23. c
17. a	24. a
18. d	25. d
19. a	26. b
20. c	27. a
21. b	28. d

CHAPTER 12

Test your understanding.

1. Bede
2. increase
3. less
4. good
5. Alcuin
6. Salerno
7. increase, deteriorated
8. warmer
9. Peace of God
10. decrease, increase
11. Cluny
12. clergy, emperor

Multiple-choice questions.

1. c	8. c
2. c	9. d
3. c	10. a
4. c	11. c
5. b	12. d
6. a	13. d
7. c	14. d

15. a	22. d
16. c	23. c
17. a	24. b
18. a	25. a
19. b	26. c
20. a	27. d
21. b	28. c
	29. a

CHAPTER 13

Test your understanding.

1. swaddling
2. uncertain
3. greater
4. did
5. "manor"
6. never
7. knighthood
8. was not
9. horse

Multiple-choice questions.

1. c	8. c	15. d	22. d
2. b	9. c	16. c	23. d
3. c	10. c	17. a	24. d
4. d	11. c	18. b	25. b
5. a	12. d	19. c	26. c
6. b	13. d	20. a	27. d
7. a	14. c	21. b	

CHAPTER 14

Test your understanding.

1. *Unam Sanctam*
2. Exchequer
3. Frederick Barbarossa
4. *Domesday Book*
5. England
6. Sicily
7. Magna Carta
8. Chartres
9. Romanesque
10. *summa*
11. Hanseatic League
12. Peter Abelárd
13. Parlement of Paris

Multiple-choice questions.

1. d	8. b	15. d	22. b
2. b	9. d	16. c	23. c
3. c	10. c	17. a	24. d
4. d	11. b	18. b	25. d
5. b	12. d	19. c	26. a
6. b	13. a	20. c	27. c
7. d	14. a	21. c	

CHAPTER 15

Provide approximate dates.

1. 1348
2. 1309–1377
3. 1337–1453
4. 1414–1418
5. 1346
6. 1358
7. 1321

Test your understanding.

1. did not
2. bad
3. England, France
4. Lollards
5. economic
6. decrease

Multiple-choice questions.

1. d	8. b	15. b	22. c
2. d	9. b	16. c	23. c
3. a	10. c	17. d	24. b
4. a	11. c	18. c	25. b
5. b	12. d	19. a	26. b
6. d	13. a	20. a	27. b
7. c	14. a	21. d	28. c

CHAPTER 16

Test your understanding.

1. Mansa Musa
2. *ghana*
3. Kilwa
4. (b)
5. Tenochtitlan (Mexico City), Lake Texcoco
6. (b)
7. Huitzilopochtli
8. "black"

Multiple-choice questions.

1. c	8. b	15. b	22. c
2. a	9. b	16. d	23. a
3. c	10. c	17. b	24. d
4. c	11. c	18. d	25. a
5. c	12. d	19. c	26. d
6. b	13. c	20. a	27. b
7. c	14. b	21. a	28. a

CHAPTER 17

Test your understanding.

1. Niccolo Machiavelli
2. less
3. increased
4. Thomas More
5. declined
6. is not
7. did
8. king
9. political
10. Martin Luther
11. Alexander VI
12. was
13. weaken
14. Protestant

Multiple-choice questions.

1.	d	9.	d	17.	a	25.	b
2.	d	10.	d	18.	b	26.	a
3.	b	11.	c	19.	c	27.	c
4.	b	12.	b	20.	b	28.	c
5.	b	13.	b	21.	a	29.	b
6.	c	14.	b	22.	b	30.	c
7.	d	15.	b	23.	c	31.	a
8.	a	16.	a	24.	a	32.	c

CHAPTER 18

Test your understanding.

1. Thirty Years' War
2. Cortes
3. Las Casas
4. Edict of Nantes
5. sixteenth
6. Gustavus Adolphus
7. the United Provinces of the Netherlands
8. Amsterdam
9. Elizabeth I
10. skepticism
11. Charles V
12. Concordat of Bologna
13. Portugal

Multiple-choice questions.

1.	b	8.	a	15.	c	22.	a
2.	d	9.	c	16.	c	23.	d
3.	d	10.	b	17.	c	24.	a
4.	b	11.	b	18.	a	25.	d
5.	a	12.	d	19.	c	26.	c
6.	b	13.	c	20.	b	27.	b
7.	c	14.	a	21.	a	28.	b

CHAPTER 19

Test your understanding.

1. stadholder
2. Colbert
3. entered
4. disaster
5. John Churchill
6. Laud

1. d	8. d	15. c	22. c
2. a	9. c	16. c	23. a
3. d	10. b	17. c	24. a
4. d	11. a	18. c	25. c
5. a	12. c	19. b	26. a
6. b	13. c	20. b	27. d
7. a	14. a	21. b	

CHAPTER 20

Test your understanding.

1. Peter the Great
2. Johann Sebastian Bach
3. increased
4. Suleiman the Magnificent
5. maintained
6. Frederick II (Great)
7. (1) 4   (2) 1   (3) 3   (4) 2   (5) 5   (6) 6
8. weaker

Multiple-choice questions.

1. d	8. b	15. a	22. b
2. c	9. c	16. b	23. d
3. a	10. b	17. a	24. a
4. c	11. b	18. d	25. c
5. d	12. c	19. d	26. a
6. b	13. c	20. d	27. d
7. a	14. b	21. b	28. c

CHAPTER 21

Test your understanding.

1. water, earth
2. did not
3. motion
4. universal gravitation
5. philosophy
6. Portugal
7. was not
8. did not
9. skeptic
10. Newton
11. failed

Multiple-choice questions.

1. a	8. b	15. c	22. b
2. c	9. a	16. c	23. d
3. d	10. a	17. d	24. a
4. d	11. a	18. a	25. c
5. c	12. b	19. d	26. d
6. b	13. a	20. d	27. a
7. a	14. b	21. c	28. a

CHAPTER 22

Test your understanding.

1. limited	4. potato	7. the common people
2. was not	5. longer	8. Wesley
3. did	6. cowpox	

Multiple-choice questions.

1. b	8. d	15. b	22. d
2. d	9. a	16. b	23. b
3. b	10. d	17. a	24. c
4. c	11. b	18. b	25. c
5. b	12. c	19. d	26. d
6. a	13. a	20. a	27. a
7. b	14. d	21. a	28. b

CHAPTER 23

Test your understanding.

1. Brazil	3. Muslim holy war	5. Taj Mahal
2. England	4. janissaries	

Multiple-choice questions.

1. b	8. c	15. c	22. d
2. b	9. d	16. b	23. b
3. b	10. b	17. a	24. d
4. c	11. a	18. c	25. a
5. b	12. a	19. c	26. c
6. c	13. b	20. a	27. a
7. b	14. d	21. a	28. b

CHAPTER 24

Test your understanding.

1. Hung Wu
2. increased, more
3. was
4. was
5. growth

Multiple-choice questions.

1. d	8. a	15. b	22. b
2. b	9. a	16. c	23. a
3. c	10. b	17. b	24. b
4. c	11. b	18. a	25. c
5. a	12. a	19. b	26. c
6. b	13. b	20. d	27. b
7. a	14. d	21. a	28. c

CHAPTER 25

Test your understanding.

1. Trafalgar
2. an important
3. Thomas Paine
4. Montesquieu
5. were not
6. Louis XVI
7. opposed
8. Mountain
9. decrease
10. victory
11. military ruler

Multiple-choice questions.

1. c	8. d	15. b	22. d
2. d	9. d	16. d	23. d
3. d	10. d	17. d	24. a
4. a	11. b	18. c	25. b
5. d	12. a	19. b	26. c
6. c	13. a	20. d	27. c
7. a	14. b	21. c	28. b